TOURISM INFORMATION TECHNOLOGY

2nd Edition

Pierre J. Benckendorff

The University of Queensland, Australia

Pauline J. Sheldon

University of Hawaii, USA

Daniel R. Fesenmaier

University of Florida, USA

www.cabi.org

CABI is a trading name of CAB International

CABI
Nosworthy Way
Wallingford
Oxfordshire OX10 8DE
UK

CABI
38 Chauncy Street
Suite 1002
Boston, MA 02111
USA

Tel: +44 (0)1491 832111
Fax: +44 (0)1491 833508
E-mail: info@cabi.org
Website: www.cabi.org

Tel: +1 800 552 3083 (toll free)
Tel: +1 (0)617 395 4051
E-mail: cabi-nao@cabi.org

A catalogue record for this book is available from the British Library, London, UK.

Library of Congress Cataloging-in-Publication Data

Benckendorff, Pierre.
  Tourism information technology / Pierre J. Benckendorff, The University of Queensland, Australia; Pauline J. Sheldon, University of Hawaii, USA; Daniel R. Fesenmaier, University of Florida, USA. -- 2nd Edition.
       pages cm.
  Revised edition of: Tourism information technology / Pauline J. Sheldon.
  Includes bibliographical references and index.
  ISBN 978-1-78064-185-0 (alk. paper)
1. Tourism--Information technology. 2. Tourism--Information services. I. Sheldon, Pauline J.
II. Fesenmaier, Daniel R. III. Title.

  G155.A1S485 2014
  910.285--dc23

                    2014006673

ISBN-13: 978 1 78064 185 0

Commissioning editor: Claire Parfitt
Editorial assistant: Alexandra Lainsbury
Production editor: Claire Sissen

Typeset by SPi, Pondicherry, India.
Printed and bound by Gutenberg Press, Malta.

TOURISM INFORMATION TECHNOLOGY

CABI TOURISM TEXTS are an essential resource for students of academic tourism, leisure studies, hospitality, entertainment and events management. The series reflects the growth of tourism-related studies at an academic level and responds to the changes and developments in these rapidly evolving industries, providing up-to-date practical guidance, discussion of the latest theories and concepts, and analysis by world experts. The series is intended to guide students through their academic programmes and remain an essential reference throughout their careers in the tourism sector.

Readers will find the books within the CABI TOURISM TEXTS series to have a uniquely wide scope, covering important elements in leisure and tourism, including management-led topics, practical subject matter and development of conceptual themes and debates. Useful textbook features such as case studies, bullet point summaries and helpful diagrams are employed throughout the series to aid study and encourage understanding of the subject.

Students at all levels of study, workers within tourism and leisure industries, researchers, academics, policy makers and others interested in the field of academic and practical tourism will find these books an invaluable and authoritative resource, useful for academic reference and real world tourism applications.

Titles available

Ecotourism: Principles and Practices
Ralf Buckley

Contemporary Tourist Behaviour: Yourself and Others as Tourists
David Bowen and Jackie Clarke

The Entertainment Industry: an Introduction
Edited by Stuart Moss

Practical Tourism Research
Stephen L.J. Smith

Leisure, Sport and Tourism, Politics, Policy and Planning, 3rd Edition
A.J. Veal

Events Management
Edited by Peter Robinson, Debra Wale and Geoff Dickson

Food and Wine Tourism: Integrating Food, Travel and Territory
Erica Croce and Giovanni Perri

Strategic Management in Tourism, 2nd Edition
Edited by L. Moutinho

Research Methods for Leisure, Recreation and Tourism
Edited by Ercan Sirakaya-Turk, Muzaffer Usyal, William E. Hammitt, and Jerry J. Vaske

Facilities Management and Development for Tourism, Hospitality and Events
Edited by Ahmed Hassanien and Crispin Dale

Events as a Strategic Marketing Tool
Dorothé Gerritsen and Ronald van Olderen

Entertainment Management: Towards Best Practice
Edited By Stuart Moss and Ben Walmsley

Introduction to Tourism Transport
Sven Gross and Louisa Klemmer

Tourism Information Technology, 2nd Edition
Pierre Benckendorff, Pauline Sheldon and Daniel R. Fesenmaier

Dedications

For Kym, Joel and Amy, you are the wind beneath my wings. Thanks for all the love, laughs and moral support.
Pierre Benckendorff

To my husband, friend and mentor Bill Remus for his never-ending support, encouragement and love.
Pauline Sheldon

I would like to dedicate this book to my wife Julie for all her unending support.
Daniel Fesenmaier

Contents

PART III TRAVELING

Contents

PART V   ISSUES AND TRENDS

List of Figures

List of Tables

Foreword

Tourism is a major source of employment, revenue, international awareness, and opportunity for many regions of the world. Traditionally, tourism has been and largely remains an economic sector that attracts people with interests and talents in humanistic rather than technical areas. People working in tourism are usually fascinated by behavioral aspects of traveling, communication, cultural experiences, and languages. Skills in computer science or information technology have always been perceived as "less important" or something that should be "outsourced and handled by others". As a consequence many tourism schools developed technology-averse curricula that only met the expectations of their applicants, but not the needs of the industry. Schools worldwide have now adjusted their programs, but many are still struggling with the long-term consequences of this former misjudgment of developments in technology and its impact on tourism.

Since the mid-1990s, information technologies have influenced nearly all parts of tourism and, as a consequence, the requirements for people working in the industry have changed dramatically. When Pauline Sheldon published her book *Tourism Information Technology* in 1997, it was one of the first comprehensive publications that raised awareness of an area that was to fundamentally change the travel and tourism industry. It was the first comprehensive source to examine the impact of information technologies on all major sectors of travel and tourism. It provided many examples for the potential of technology in marketing, distribution, and management of typical travel and tourism services. Pauline Sheldon anticipated many of the changes in the travel distribution systems that later became standard applications and it is therefore not surprising that her book became an essential source for many tourism professionals, students, and scholars.

Pauline Sheldon, together with her co-authors Pierre Benckendorff and Daniel Fesenmaier, must be congratulated on their decision to publish this new edition. It is a comprehensively revised and extended book, a long overdue development, considering the many changes that have occurred since 1997: the travel distribution process moved to the Internet; new travel intermediaries entered the market; social media applications completely changed all major communication, search, evaluation, and decision processes of travelers and tourists; and new technological devices created new opportunities for visitors and suppliers of tourism services. As competition among destinations for visitors, as well as for public and private financial support, has grown, the planning and implementation of information technology investments have become the crucial success factors for many tourism organizations.

Although the book's content has undergone a significant revision, the structure of the text, which proved so successful in the past, remains the same. Many chapters conclude with a case study demonstrating how information technology is being innovatively used in the industry and the challenges encountered by firms as they utilize information technology. Each chapter concludes with important key terms and discussion questions, making the book particularly valuable for lecturers and students. Significantly more emphasis is given to current findings of researchers in the interdisciplinary area of tourism and information technology than in the previous edition.

The book is appropriate reading for both students of tourism in colleges and universities, as well as students taking courses covering information technology applications to service management in business schools. Travel industry managers and information professionals developing applications for the tourism industry will also find the book of great value as a reference and a guide for their own implementation of information systems.

Karl Wöber
MODUL University, Vienna

Preface

Tourism and information technology (IT) are two of the largest and most dynamic industries in the world. Separately and together they are changing the way society operates. The intersection of these two fascinating industries is the focus of this book, which is designed for students of tourism and hospitality and for industry professionals. We have tried to accomplish two goals with this book. The first goal is to ground the reader in the concepts and theories at the foundation of IT and tourism developments. The second goal is to provide industry relevance with the liberal use of real-world examples and case studies.

When we started to write the second edition of this book we realized very quickly that the content needed to be completely rewritten. Since the first edition of this book was published in 1997 the world has changed dramatically. Very few sectors have experienced the profound and rapid changes we have seen in computing and information technologies. The global connectivity provided by the Internet, mobile technologies such as smartphones and tablets, wireless and broadband communications, faster, smaller and more powerful hardware, and more intelligent and ubiquitous systems were barely in existence in 1997. Today they drive so much economic activity and influence tourism, society and the environment so deeply that a new edition of the book was long overdue. Tourism itself has also changed in ways we never would have imagined. The type of trips tourists take, how they find and book them, how they transport themselves from place to place, and the type of experiences they have when traveling are all hugely different to the world in 1997.

This second edition also differs in that it has greatly expanded content and three authors rather than one. Each of us brings different and complementary perspectives and knowledge to the field of tourism information technology. Together, we have covered new areas of knowledge and expanded, restructured and revised the book so that it barely resembles its forerunner. This change in content is also due to the vast increase in published literature in the field, which we have condensed and integrated into the text as much as possible. New chapters have been added: Chapter 2 on the Digital Tourism Landscape, Chapter 5 on Social Media and Tourism, Chapter 6 on Mobilities and IT, Chapter 10 on Tourist Experiences and IT, and Chapter 12 on Sustainable Tourism and IT. The remaining chapters have similar titles to the first edition; however, the content is not only greatly updated but has a more conceptual approach reflecting the depth of literature in the field that has emerged since the first edition.

More attention has also been given to the pedagogical resources. We have added Research Insights, Industry Insights, a Case Study with questions, and discussion questions for most of the chapters. We have also included QR codes to videos, websites and other multimedia resources for readers to explore on their own. Discussion questions and useful websites are included in each chapter to help students contemplate the material. Each chapter also includes a list of keywords, which are highlighted in the text to assist students when reviewing key concepts. We have also developed a set of PowerPoint slides for instructors. This book has a strategic focus that will give the reader some background to support them in their future management and leadership careers in the tourism industry.

Writing about IT using an antiquated medium like paper is always risky. Rapid changes and innovations will continue to change the travel experience and the tourism industry. We have provided many conceptual frameworks and examples to help you understand how travelers, tourism organizations and destinations use technology. By the time you read this book, however, some of the links, QR codes, examples and applications will already be irrelevant. We ask for your understanding on this, and hope that you will enjoy reading and using the book. It is without question that in the years to come, the rate of change of both IT and tourism will accelerate, meaning that constant updating of your knowledge and understanding of tourism and IT are essential.

The names of the authors on the front cover of a book do not tell the whole story. In reality it takes many people to make a book happen. The second edition of this book has been a 2-year project involving many people. We would like to thank Claire Parfitt, Alexandra Lainsbury and the crew at CABI who have been very supportive and patient as we completed this project. We would also like to thank colleagues who have reviewed various chapters, in particular Rob Law at Hong Kong Polytechnic University, Marianna Sigala at the University of the Aegean, Ulrike Gretzel at the University of Wollongong, Mengya (Lavender) Shu at The University of Queensland, and Paul Lawler, Ivan Wen and Torsha Battacharya from the School of Travel Industry Management at the University of Hawai'i, USA. We would also like to thank James Whyte, whose generous contribution made face-to-face collaboration between the authors possible.

Pierre J. Benckendorff
The University of Queensland, Australia

Pauline J. Sheldon
University of Hawai'i, USA

Daniel R. Fesenmaier
University of Florida, USA

chapter 1

Introduction to Tourism and Information Technology

LEARNING OBJECTIVES

After studying this chapter you should be able to:

- define key terms and concepts in information technology;
- describe the evolution of information technology;
- recognize the types of information technologies relevant to tourism;
- explain the synergies between the travel industry and information technology; and
- evaluate the strategic applications of information technology in tourism organizations and destinations.

INTRODUCTION

The world is experiencing some of the most dramatic social changes in its history. Borders are dissolving and countries, societies, people and organizations are connecting more and in different ways than they ever have in the past. Increases in international trade agreements, global business activity, telecommunication networks and personal and educational travel are linking the planet together like never before. These linkages are being forged and supported essentially by two of the largest and fastest growing industries in the world today – tourism and information technology (IT).

Tourism connects people today in ways that would never have been possible decades ago. It also contributes significantly to many national and regional economies. In 2012, with 1.035 billion international tourists generating US$1.2 trillion it was responsible for over 235 million jobs worldwide. Tourism was responsible for 5% of the global GDP and 30% of the world's export in services in 2011 (United Nations World Tourism Organization, 2013). Tourism is also a powerful force in arenas other than economics.

Its transformative power on cultures and societies, on environments and ecosystems, its contribution to and effects from climate changes are important issues that must be addressed. The increased connectivity that tourism creates between and within societies is one of the most important phenomena affecting society. This is enhanced greatly by information technologies.

The IT industry is equally if not more significant and powerful. We live in a digital world of laptop computers, smartphones, digital cameras, tablets and many more devices. **Information technology** can be defined as "the application of computers and telecommunications equipment to store, retrieve, transmit and manipulate data" (Daintith, 2012). In a business context, information technologies are often referred to as **information systems**. "Information systems are combinations of hardware, software and telecommunications networks that people build and use to collect, create, and distribute useful data, typically in organizational settings" (Valacich and Schneider, 2014, p. 19).

Worldwide IT spending for 2011 was estimated to be US$3.67 trillion – three times the size of the tourism industry (QFinance, 2013). The rapid pace of development in IT is creating millions of electronic connections around the globe, connecting people, the business community, industries, regional and international communities in new ways and is substantially changing the way that enterprises, customers and governments operate. It is expected that by 2015 there will be 15 billion connected devices in the world – far exceeding the global population. The travel and tourism industry is a heavy user of IT and some of the largest telecommunication networks spanning the globe carry travel information. IT, therefore, provides the information backbone that facilitates tourism (Dutta and Bilbao-Osorio, 2012).

This book is about these two industries and the synergies between them. It describes how the different sectors of the tourism industry are being affected by IT and how they apply IT to their operations. It also explores in depth the tourist's use of IT at all stages of the travel experience. This chapter sets a foundation by examining the nature of the IT industry, concepts used, its history and evolution and the factors affecting IT adoption and innovation in tourism. It also presents characteristics of tourism that cause it to be so information intensive. Various typologies of tourism information are also discussed. Its synergy with information technology is explained, and ways in which the two industries interlock and support each other are discussed. Issues relating to the strategic management of information and IT within an organization are also discussed.

TOURISM: AN INFORMATION-INTENSIVE INDUSTRY

The tourism industry thrives on information. The size of the industry alone suggests that it generates large volumes of information to be processed and communicated. For each person embarking on a trip, scores of messages and pieces of information must be exchanged: itineraries, schedules, payment information, destination and product information and passenger information. But the tourism industry exhibits many other unique characteristics, which give rise to an intense need on the part of travelers, organizations and tourism agencies for information and IT to process it. This section will first present a model of tourism information flows and then discuss the characteristics that make tourism so information intensive.

Characteristics of tourism

While the term **product** is frequently used in the industry to refer to accommodation, transport attractions and even destinations, tourism can also be described as a type of **service**. Sometimes the tourism product is also referred to as an **experience**. Pine and Gilmore (1999) argue that products are *manufactured*, services are *delivered* and experiences are *staged*. Furthermore, experiences are usually co-created by the interaction of travelers, tourism organizations and settings (Prahalad and Ramaswamy, 2004). Typically most governments consider tourism to be part of the service sector rather than the manufacturing sector. In this book we use these terms interchangeably, but it is important to understand some of the characteristics of services and experiences and how they differ from manufactured goods.

One of the greatest challenges facing managers is how to increase the productivity of service and knowledge workers (Drucker, 1990). In the past there has often been resistance to automation in service industries due to a misconception that the quality of the customer's experience would decline. But in the 1990s with the change in lifestyle and priorities, time became an important commodity. This led to service expectations of a different nature, where speed and customization are increasingly important. In fact, information has been identified as one of the most important quality parameters for efficient service (Schertler, 1994). IT applications are necessary to more rapidly serve tourists, whether it

be to check a guest out of a hotel or to change their flight reservation. Because of these consumer expectations, time has become an important focus for competitive activities in tourism demanding the application of IT.

Some of the characteristics that differentiate tourism from other products, services and experiences and which make it so information intensive are its heterogeneity, its intangibility, its perishability and its inseparability. The global scope of the industry and the fact that tourism is a service industry also contribute to its information intensity (Table 1.1). Each of these characteristics will be discussed below.

Table 1.1. Characteristics of tourism services and experiences.

Characteristic	Description
Heterogeneity	Travel products and services cannot be standardized and vary enormously
Intangibility	Services cannot be experienced, touched, felt or sampled before purchase
Perishability	Unsold hotel rooms, aircraft seats and tours cannot be stored for later sale
Inseparability	Production occurs alongside consumption. The product or service is being "consumed" as it is delivered
Global	Tourism includes the international movement of people on a mass scale

A typical trip is complex and consists of many component parts, and therefore by nature is **heterogeneous**. The US Standard Industrial Classification System has identified at least 35 industrial components that serve the traveler (Gee *et al.*, 1994). To research and plan a trip, travelers must interact with many private sector organizations and public sector agencies. Coordination and cooperation between each of these organizations, agencies and the consumer is necessary to create the heterogeneous experience called a trip. This requires efficient, accurate and timely information flows to piece together the multifaceted trip. Information and IT provide crucial links between the different industry sectors to make the traveler's planning and experience seamless. If the links break down or are too slow, information is not transmitted in a timely manner and the industry does not function maximally. The more complex and international the trip, the more information is required.

Intangibility is the second characteristic that makes tourism so information intensive. Potential consumers are often unable to see, touch or feel a vacation or a business trip and its components before they purchase it. Instead, they need detailed information about the destination or experience to substitute for the lack of tangibility. This information can be presented via many different media. Travel and destination information that was traditionally distributed in the form of brochures, is increasingly in electronic form. Digital content such as websites, pictures and videos give a more vibrant "sample" of the trip. Virtual reality tours can even be used to provide the consumer with a substitute experience of the product before making a purchase. The intangible nature of tourism has brought the IT

and tourism industries together to creatively market the product and make it more tangible. Information also serves to reduce the risk associated with some travel and therefore is valued by most consumers. Some travelers, however, prefer and feel challenged by trips they know little about before departing.

The third factor that makes tourism information intensive is its **perishability**. If an airline seat is not sold on a given flight, that particular seat can never be sold again. It, or rather the revenue from it, has perished. This is true for almost all products in the tourism industry (accommodation, attractions, transportation), and is due to the time-sensitive nature of tourism products. This characteristic has implications for the application of IT. IT can assist with monitoring inventories and dynamically adjusting prices to maximize load factors, occupancy and attendance rates. Many computer reservation systems (CRSs) in tourism use yield management systems to assist with the challenges created by product perishability. The use of high-speed data communication networks can also assist organizations in the distribution of last minute information about available products to sell them before they "perish".

Tourism consumption is **inseparable** from the production of the experience. Unlike goods, which can be purchased and taken home, there is an interaction between service providers and travelers because the production of the experience happens simultaneously. For example, a hotel guest "consumes" a hotel room that has been made available by the provider for the night. Information technologies play an increasingly important role in ensuring that the simultaneous production and consumption of tourism experiences is efficient and of a high quality.

By its very nature the tourism industry is one of the most **global** industries in the world. This characteristic is central to the industry and contributes further to its information intensity. International travel generates large volumes of information not found in domestic industries. International travelers must have access to information on border controls such as visa and passport regulations, customs regulations, arrival or departure taxes, currency controls and health regulations such as immunization requirements. In addition, they require information on such diverse topics as cultural practices, driving regulations and language translations. For example, travelers from France visiting Peru have higher information needs than travelers from New York to San Francisco. Both leisure and business travelers are expanding their horizons and traveling more globally requiring access to this kind of information. This geographic dispersion requires data communication networks around the globe to link countries, tourism organizations and travelers together. Without IT, the tourism industry would not function as efficiently at the international level.

In summary, the tourism industry is highly information intensive and information is its lifeblood. The application of IT to its operations therefore is critical to its growth and success. In the next section we briefly summarize some of the major applications of IT in tourism.

Applications of information technologies in tourism

The entire tourism industry has been changed by the use of IT. Research shows that IT is influencing the way travel organizations in all sectors communicate with customers, the way they compete, plan their strategies, add value to their products, cost-save and streamline their operations to mention a few (Buhalis and Law, 2008). Different sectors of the tourism industry have adopted IT at different rates.

The **aviation** sector has been the most innovative and heavy user of IT and started early in the 1950s with the implementation of computer reservation systems. These evolved and became known as Global Distribution Systems (GDSs) as they integrated all types of travel reservations in addition to flights. They became the main tool of travel intermediaries when booking trips. They are still very important today but have needed to adapt to new technologies, software environments and mobile applications. These will be discussed in detail in Chapter 3. The airline sector has also been a leader in the use of yield management systems to strategically price airlines' seats to maximize revenue. IT has facilitated the development of frequent flyer programs that require sophisticated database technology and very large amounts of data. With the travel industry alliances in place (such as One World or Star Alliance) connectivity and interoperability between the various systems used by different organizations is essential. As airlines seek to reduce labor costs and speed passengers through airports, self check-in terminals in airports have been introduced. Automated call centers attempt to further reduce labor costs. Use of the Internet for booking flights, and IT applications that allow travelers to use their smartphones for boarding passes, updates on flight status and other functions are becoming popular, reducing paper. Chapters 7 and 8 fully explore how airlines, airports and other transportation carriers are using IT.

Travel intermediaries such as travel agents and tour operators have been significantly affected by technology to the degree that their existence is at stake. In fact many such intermediaries have left the market as Internet and other technologies have replaced them. They have had to adapt to the "disintermediation" caused by the Internet giving consumers access to the same information and more. Many have done this by specializing in certain destinations or travel products (e.g. cruises) or by obtaining cheaper rates through their bulk buying power. New types of intermediaries have emerged in the digital world that will be explained in detail in Chapter 3.

The **hospitality** sector has in general been more reticent to adopt technology, but now has many specialized systems for their operations. Hotel operations are run by property management systems, which process all activity relative to guests, rooms, accounting, housekeeping and customer records. Hotel reservation systems are crucial links to customers, and they may be property specific or for all hotels in a chain or a marketing consortium. Electronic locking systems, in-room technology, energy management systems and self check-in terminals are also becoming common particularly in business hotels. Restaurants main use of IT is in the forms of point-of-sale systems, menu management systems and restaurant management systems. These will be discussed in Chapter 9.

Other sectors of the travel industry including **attractions**, **entertainment**, **casinos** and **conventions** all have specialized IT systems. We will discuss these in Chapter 10. In all of these types of travel organizations, the Internet has made significant changes. IT has particularly helped small and medium enterprises (SMEs), which constitute a large portion of this part of the travel industry worldwide. Since the Internet, these smaller organizations have gained market power as they now are able to access distant international markets in the same way as large multinationals. However, SMEs continue to face considerable challenges in the implementation of these systems, as we will explore in Chapter 12.

Entire **destinations** have found much value to incorporating IT into their marketing and management strategies. IT links together different sectors of the destination, different stakeholders and can connect with travelers in new and different ways with Internet, social media and mobile technologies such as Global Positioning Systems (GPS) and Geographic Information Systems (GIS). IT also has a leveling impact on the power of the different suppliers in destinations, meaning that large monopolistic organizations cannot dominate a destination as they might have in the past. These issues are discussed in Chapter 11.

The **travelers** themselves are gaining much benefit from IT developments. In particular, social media and mobile technologies give them ubiquitous access to information about destinations, travel organizations and experiences. These will be discussed in Chapters 5, 6 and 10.

Typologies of information

Organizations that have benefited the most from the use of IT are ones who recognize that information truly is an important asset that must be carefully managed alongside other economic resources of land, labor and capital. With the recognition of information as a fourth resource, organizations must carefully combine information with the other three to maximize profitability and provide the best levels of service to travelers.

Information, however, differs in numerous ways from the other three resources (Cleveland, 1985). First, information is neither scarce nor depletable. Instead, it expands as it is used. As one traveler gives information to another about a favorite hotel, museum or beach, that information is duplicated and not lost by the giver. This information expansion can create opportunities or threats depending on the nature of the information and the receiver. The expansion of factual information serves to enhance an organization's or a destination's position as its level of awareness is increased. The spreading of subjective information can create positive or negative impacts depending on the perception of the information giver. Negative perceptions can of course damage, and positive ones can further enhance an organization's position.

Second, information and information technology can actually be used by management to substitute for the other three resources of land, labor and capital. When these three are in short supply or are expensive, the creative application of IT can be used instead. Telecommuting is an example of using IT to substitute for land since organizations whose employees telecommute need no longer rent or purchase so much high priced land in expensive districts. IT can also be used to substitute for labor in many ways. In repetitive, lower level tasks in travel organizations IT can reduce the number of employees needed to perform the task. At higher levels of operations, IT can augment human resources with decision support systems, expert systems, and other applications of artificial intelligence.

A third characteristic differentiating information from the other three resources is its tendency to "leak". This can cause security problems and requires management to create particular policies to prevent untoward situations. Information is a highly prized resource and so care must be taken to ensure its security. The careful use of passwords and policies must be used to ensure that traveler information is protected. For example, hotels will not give guest room numbers to casual requests, nor will airlines release information of passengers on a specific flight. The travel industry generates much personal information that must be carefully secured to avoid misuse.

These are just three of the ways in which information differs from the other resources. There are numerous others discussed in Cleveland (1985), but all point to the fact that companies must carefully examine information and treat it as an important resource. Maximizing its use for their competitive advantage is an important challenge to managers operating in this information-intensive industry. Appropriate applications of IT at the strategic level have served to increase the success of many travel organizations, as will be demonstrated in this book.

Tourism information, in addition to being very voluminous, is very diverse in nature. To use a theater analogy, information is produced by different actors to meet the needs of a wide range of audiences. These audiences and their information needs include:

- **Travelers**: information about destinations, transport, activities, facilities, availabilities, prices, border controls, geography and climate;
- **Intermediaries**: information about consumer trends in the market; about

destinations, transport, activities, facilities, availabilities, prices, border controls, geography and climate; and about other branches, suppliers and competitors;

- **Suppliers**: information about the company, consumer behavior, intermediaries and competitors; and
- **Destinations**: information about trends in the industry, the size and nature of tourism flows, marketing, impacts, policies, planning and development.

Some information is static and some dynamic, some is used by travelers prior to their trip, some during their trip and some is shared after the trip. Some is produced by private sector organizations and some by public sector agencies. These different types of travel information require different information technologies to process and distribute them, and are discussed below.

Static and dynamic information

Some tourism information does not change very frequently and therefore is relatively static. Other information changes frequently and is intensely dynamic. Examples of **static** tourism information that may change in the long run but not in the short run are: product descriptions, transportation routes, maps, signage and location information. Static information lends itself to distribution and access on hardcopy, video, DVD, or other offline media. A large volume of tourism information, however, is **dynamic**, and needs electronic media for frequent updates and rapid distribution from suppliers to travelers. Examples are product availability, schedules, fares and rates, and environmental conditions such as weather, snowfalls on ski-slopes or surfing conditions. Some

dynamic information changes daily, some weekly, some monthly and some seasonally. Information systems to process this type of information must be online, real-time systems with the ability to easily capture the changes. These systems are more difficult to implement and more costly to operate. Adequate resources and personnel to ensure that information is continuously and accurately updated must be part of any dynamic information system.

Trip stages

Travelers need information at different times and different places. Pre-trip information in the planning phase of a trip is required in the traveler's home or the prior destination. The type of information (pre-trip versus in-trip) required at different times depends on the type of tourist. For example, adventurous travelers or impulsive travelers will need little or no pre-trip information, whereas risk-averse travelers and those with long planning times will need pre-trip information to be both static and dynamic. In general, travelers are leaving more of their decisions until they are at the destination. This need for more in-trip information is spawning new applications in mobile technologies. After the tourist returns home, both static and dynamic information are used. Dynamic post-trip uses of tourism information are growing as social media and other photo- and video-sharing platforms proliferate. Table 1.2 shows these various dynamic and static information media for different trip stages.

Public and private providers

Some tourism information is provided by the public sector and is more general to the

Table 1.2. Types of tourism information channels.

Trip stage	Static	Dynamic
Pre-trip	Brochures, guidebooks, fax, photos, videos, some information on websites	Phone, email, websites, social media, Internet booking engines, Global Distribution Systems
In-trip	Brochures, guidebooks, signs, maps, kiosks, TV channels in hotels, some mobile apps	Phone, fax, email, websites, social media, mobile apps
Post-trip	Brochures, guidebooks, photos, video	Blogs, social networks, media sharing, reviews

destination, and some by the private sector, which is more specific to a given product or brand. The public sector, however, may provide specific product information, as when a public tourism office distributes information on specific attractions or accommodation in response to general requests. Also some private sector organizations may provide more general information on the destination. They may do this in their advertising to entice consumers to purchase their product. Other examples are tour operators and hotel concierge desks, which can enhance their customers' experience by providing general destination information.

Sources of public sector information are government tourist offices at the regional, national or state level. They tend to provide more objective, unbiased information on both public and private tourist facilities. Information contained in third party websites or guidebooks can also be objective and unbiased if the author has no affiliations with the product. Information provided by private companies tends to be more promotional, and more specific to their individual products.

THE EVOLUTION OF INFORMATION TECHNOLOGIES

The evolution of information technology has been extremely rapid compared to other industries. In fact Intel noted that if the airline industry had developed as rapidly as the computer industry in relation to price and performance, a flight from New York to Paris would today cost about a penny and take less than 1 second (Jordan, 2012). The speed and cost of the Internet, smartphones, GPSs, laptops and digital cameras are far removed from the slow, expensive, room-sized computers of 60 years ago. Many innovations over the decades have led to the explosion of applications in IT. Many of these developments will be discussed in more detail throughout this book.

Computers

The first commercially available computer (UNIVAC I) was unveiled in 1951. IBM soon followed with the world's first mass-produced computer, the IBM650. These large computers used magnetic tape, magnetic drums, and vacuum tubes and punched cards for input, and were mostly used for scientific purposes. The aviation industry was a pioneer in the commercial use of these large machines, which played an important role in the development of the first airline reservation systems.

The invention of the **transistor** by Bell Laboratories eventually led to the development of a second generation of computers, which were smaller, faster and more powerful. In 1958 two engineers working independently invented the **integrated circuit** (or the computer chip). This led to the next generation of computers in 1965, creating even smaller and faster machines that were more viable for business. Many travel businesses such as hotels, travel agencies and other tourism enterprises used these third-generation computers for their operations.

In 1970 Intel Corporation invented the **microprocessor** for use in **microcomputers**. Major commercial microcomputers included the Apple II and the IBM PC. Greater affordability coupled with new storage media, operating systems (such as MS-DOS) and input devices such as the mouse made computing both accessible and user-friendly for average users with no knowledge of programing. In the early 1980s both Apple and Microsoft introduced windows-based "point and click" Graphical User Interfaces (GUIs) to further simplify user interactions with computers. Word processing, spreadsheets, desktop publishing and database management software were developed in the late 1970s and early 1980s and have become common applications in travel industry organizations.

Innovations have continued to result in computers that are smaller and more powerful. In 1965, Intel co-founder Gordon Moore observed that the number of transistors and integrated circuits in computers doubled roughly every 2 years. This prediction, known as **Moore's Law**, has proved to be accurate for over 40 years and can be applied to processing speed, memory, sensors and the number and size of pixels in digital cameras. While many major innovations occurred throughout the 1970s and 1980s, advances since 1985 have involved incremental changes in hardware consistent with Moore's Law. Similar incremental changes have occurred in the development of new versions of software. However, major advances have been made in networking and mobile technologies as we discuss in the following sections and subsequent chapters.

Networking and the Internet

The next wave of information technologies overlaps with some of the developments in electronic computing. While IBM, Apple and Microsoft were laying the foundations for the Digital Revolution, some organizations were already thinking about the potential of linking computers together using networks. In 1970, the science fiction writer Arthur C. Clarke made the following prediction in the magazine *Popular Science*:

> Imagine a console in your office, combining the features of a Touch-Tone (pushbutton) telephone, a television set, a Xerox machine, and a small electronic computer. Tuned in to a system of synchronous satellites, this console will bring the accumulated knowledge of the world to your fingertips. By punching a few digits, you can verify a check, get the data on some historical event, or hear an illustrated lecture on any subject you wish. Or you can hold an electronic

conference with any group of people scattered all over the world, seeing each other as you talk.

Arthur C. Clarke's prediction became a reality 12 years later when networks at the Advanced Research Projects Agency (ARPA) and several universities were connected to create the **Internet** – a network of networks. The Internet expanded rapidly to Europe and Australia in the mid-1980s and to Asia in the late 1980s and early 1990s. The Internet enabled a range of networked services, including email and the World Wide Web (WWW). The early WWW has subsequently been referred to as **Web 1.0**. Unlike today's WWW, early websites provided limited interaction. Websites were updated by **webmasters** and users could view the content but could not contribute to it. **Web 2.0** supported open communication with an emphasis on web-based communities of users sharing data, information, knowledge, resources and files. This was made possible by the development of wikis, blogs, social network sites, Rich Site Summary (RSS), media-sharing sites and virtual worlds. The travel industry also embraced Web 2.0, with sites such as Wikitravel, TripAdvisor, Yelp and Urbanspoon having a major impact on travel behavior. The history and role of the Internet and social media in tourism is explored in more detail in Chapters 4 and 5.

Ubiquitous technologies

The most recent IT wave relevant to travel and tourism is the rise of mobile and **ubiquitous computing**. Many of the technological developments in this field occurred at the same time as the development of the Internet. As a result, many IT innovations have taken advantage of advances in both areas. The history of mobile devices includes developments in a number of parallel technologies that have converged to create the devices used today. These include **mobile phones**, **Personal Digital Assistants (PDAs)**, portable computers, digital cameras and portable music players. In the early 1990s the miniaturization of electronics and batteries made pocket-sized portable devices possible, triggering the new product category of PDAs. These were essentially small handheld computers, which allowed users to read text, send email, schedule appointments and store documents and contacts.

The developments in mobile phones and PDAs are significant because the convergence of these two technologies in 1994 resulted in the first **smartphone**, the IBM Simon. This was followed by a period of intense competition between mobile phone manufacturers, computer makers and electronics companies. The proliferation of mobile devices and apps has created many new benefits for both the travel industry and for travelers. Location-aware mobile devices have had an impact on visitor information, marketing, orientation and interpretation. New innovations in ubiquitous (or wearable) devices have continued to find applications in the travel industry. We will review the evolution and role of mobile technologies in more detail in Chapter 6.

Implications for travel and tourism

The major trends evident in this historical account of information technologies include the **convergence** of information technologies and the increasing **interoperability** of various platforms. The miniaturization and ubiquity of computer technology together with the connectivity of the Internet has created a new level of functionality and the travel industry has benefitted from this. Microprocessors are now found all around us in devices such as ovens, cars and refrigerators, resulting in **ambient intelligence**. **Artificial intelligence** and **expert systems** are now used to support tasks and decision-making that were previously carried out by people. Social media (Facebook, Twitter, etc.) has connected travelers and organizations in new and different ways and has transformed how society operates.

The consequences of this hyper-connectivity coupled with the globalization of business and travel are profound. Technological innovations have caused the **collapse of space and time**, in that time and space no longer restrict us from connecting and working. Work can be done at any time and in any place. IT and the Internet connect us to whomever we want whenever we want. A traveler sitting in Heathrow Airport on their smartphone can make a booking for a Honolulu hotel, for example, and within microseconds receive a confirmation. Meetings with others for business (sales meetings and conferences) or pleasure (family reunions) in different parts of the globe with videoconferencing from a smartphone, tablet or laptop are now commonplace. Person-to-person meetings are likely to be less frequent and yet perhaps more valued. Travel is also likely to be reduced by the implementation of videoconferencing meaning that the travel industry must be alert and innovative to adapt to this trend. For example, Rosenbluth Travel (sold to American Express in 2003), a business travel agency in the US, has added teleconferencing to its product offering so that clients can compare and choose between a face-to-face conference and a teleconference.

If a teleconference is chosen, Rosenbluth organizes it and sells it as part of their product line.

STRATEGIC THINKING AND INFORMATION TECHNOLOGY

Thinking about IT applications in a strategic manner is critical in today's competitive world. There are many ways that IT can be used to support the strategic direction of the organization and support innovation. Some IT applications affect the production of goods and services and others have more impact on the marketing process. Cash *et al.* (1992) provide a model to show how different industries can use IT to improve both their production and marketing. The model uses a two-by-two matrix in which the horizontal axis represents the impact of IT on marketing activities and the vertical axis represents its impact on the production of goods and services. The authors of the model place certain industries on the matrix as shown in Fig. 1.1.

The model suggests that industries further along on the horizontal scale will tend to be ones where product choice is complex, quick customer decisions with confirmations are essential, and where customer tastes and pricing are volatile. Industries will tend to be high on the vertical scale if high technology is embedded in the product, if production requires a long design process, and if time and cost savings are possible through automation. Defense hardware is placed high on production impact and low on marketing impact since the product tends to be highly technical and needs little marketing. High fashion, however, is placed high on

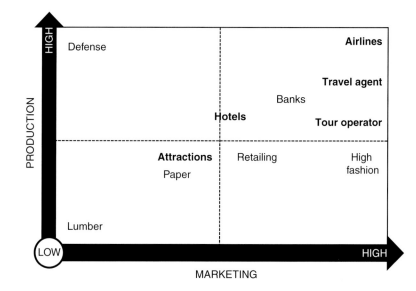

Fig. 1.1. Impact of IT on the production and marketing of different industries.

the marketing impact scale, with moderate impacts on production.

An analysis of various travel industry sectors and their use of IT in marketing and production can position them on the matrix relative to other industries. The travel industry sectors placed on the matrix are airlines, travel agents, tour operators, hotels and attractions (in bold). Most sectors are placed on the right side of the matrix since IT has a strong impact on marketing all tourism products. Travel sectors are positioned from high to low on the production axis since its impact here is not so clear. Insights into these positions are discussed below.

The airline sector is the highest on both dimensions and was placed there in the original matrix of Cash *et al.* (1992). Global Distribution Systems, frequent flyer databases and yield management programs have been heavily used by the airlines to distribute and market their product. IT has also effectively been used in production activities, for example in the design, operation and maintenance of aircraft, and in luggage handling. Other

transportation sectors such as trains and car rentals are not quite so high on the marketing axis, but are equally high on the production axis since new technologies are always being implemented to provide better transportation.

Travel agents, tour operators and other travel intermediaries are perhaps the most information intensive of all travel sectors. They deal almost exclusively with information and have no tangible product of their own. Product choice is complex, quick decisions and confirmations are often necessary and customer tastes and prices are volatile, placing them high on the marketing axis. There is also a high impact on production activities since their product or service is the provision of information.

The accommodation sector is high on both scales, but not as high as the airlines. Computer reservation systems including guest history systems assist in the marketing of hotels. IT's impact on production, however, is lower. Hotels traditionally have not embraced technology as readily as the airlines, but this is changing. More and more accommodation units are installing property management systems, electronic locking systems, energy management systems and guest room technology to make their operations more efficient. The hotel industry therefore has, over time, moved higher and further to the right of the matrix. See the case at the end of this chapter about the Intercontinental Hotels Group (IHG) use of IT for strategic purposes.

The attractions sector is difficult to position since some attractions use technology intensely in their production (e.g. theme parks) whereas others use it hardly at all in production (e.g. natural attractions). Therefore it is placed in the middle of the production axis. It is also positioned in the middle of the marketing axis.

The strategic management of IT is a necessary part of the competitive profile of a tourism organization. It will not bring the organization maximum benefits if simply applied to operational problems without a systematic approach (Poon, 1993). First and foremost, there must be a commitment from top management to support the implementation of IT, by giving it adequate resources, and creating a corporate structure to maximize its implementation. Chief Information Officer (CIO) or Information Technology (IT) Director are increasingly common positions in organizations that prioritize the information function rather than placing a Data Processing Manager on the organizational chart at a lower level. When IT is given this level of visibility and resources, its power can truly be realized. Adequate training of employees to operate the systems is also critical to reap the full benefits. The constant evaluation of new technologies to determine their appropriateness to the organization's strategic direction is also necessary. This should involve input from all employees in the organization, who can be invited to provide feedback on current systems. Funding IT purchases and keeping systems updated even when cash flow is tight is recommended to prevent an organization from falling behind.

There are many ways that enterprises can use IT strategically. Some of the strategic applications of IT that will be explored further in subsequent chapters include:

1. **Managing Value Chains:** value chains are activities or a series of activities that create and build value for destinations, intermediaries or suppliers. This can be done through the design of products and services or through supply chain management. IT applications can affect value chains by changing information and distribution channels, and making them more accessible and transparent, thereby generating more profit. For example, new IT developments have had a substantial impact on the tourism distribution system over the last 20 years.

2. **Managing Knowledge and Information:** the skillful management of information and knowledge as an important resource is essential for success. **Knowledge management** systems in tourism involve the sophisticated use of computers to generate information that can be used in decision-making. Computer technology offers huge potential in this area. Database management systems can store and process millions of customer records, accounts, product reviews etc. to generate knowledge that will guide strategic decision-making. The term **big data** is relevant here. These are huge datasets that an organization can mine for information with special software systems. They can be tapped to answer many questions to assist the organization in its strategic thrust such as "Who are our high value

customers?" or "Who are our most engaged customers?"

3. Marketing and Competitive Advantage: the application of IT provides a strong competitive advantage in the areas of sales and marketing. The use of electronic distribution channels, social media platforms and other innovations connect the supplier with new and different markets. In other operational areas, organizations can be early adopters of technology for competitive advantage. Examples are hotels installing self check-in terminals, airlines offering mobile boarding passes, or destinations using GPS systems to guide the tourists to the key sites.

4. Service Delivery and Customer Relationship Management: because of the unique characteristics of the tourism experience, knowledge about tourist needs, wants and expectations is an important part of effective service delivery. Customer relationship management (CRM) is a business philosophy that focuses on the consumer and attempts to create a meaningful relationship with them. This is most effectively done through a large organization-wide database (containing data on customers, their buying habits and needs) that helps tourism suppliers to build a relationship with the customer by understanding their needs and providing superior customer service.

5. Strategic Listening: part of an organization's success is based on strategic listening. Listening to employees, customers, suppliers and competitors provides deeper understanding of how the organization can strategically change and move forward. It can provide more shared meaning and direction. IT is an excellent tool to assist in that listening process. As face-to-face meetings are not always possible listening can be done by teleconference, by smartphone or tablet or in many other ways. Social media provides new ways to access market intelligence by monitoring blogs and other online media to understand more about customers and competitors.

BOOK OUTLINE

In order to give the reader a clear map of the book content, this book is organized into five main sections as shown in Fig. 1.2. The first section entitled *Understanding Tourism IT* includes the first two chapters. They lay the foundation for the rest of the book by introducing the reader to basic IT concepts and to the uniqueness of tourism information systems. In Chapter 2, entitled *The Digital Tourism Landscape*, the scope of digital technology and how it is influencing tourism is presented. A model of electronic consumer access to travel information is also described in this chapter.

The second main section of the book relates to *The Trip* and constitutes the main part of the text. It is here that we examine how technology is used and impacts upon the pre-consumption, consumption and post-consumption stages of the travel experience (Gretzel *et al.*, 2006). Part II is entitled *Looking and Booking* and examines how tourists search for information and book their trips. It includes three chapters: Chapter 3 covers the travel distribution process and the various travel intermediaries that exist today and how they have been influenced by IT. Chapter 4 discusses the Internet and the ways that tourists can use it to enhance their trip. It also covers different types of travel organizations that have a presence on the Internet. Chapter 5 is devoted to social media and its use by the different tourism stakeholders, in particular with a focus on assisting tourists in their information search and their options to make reservations.

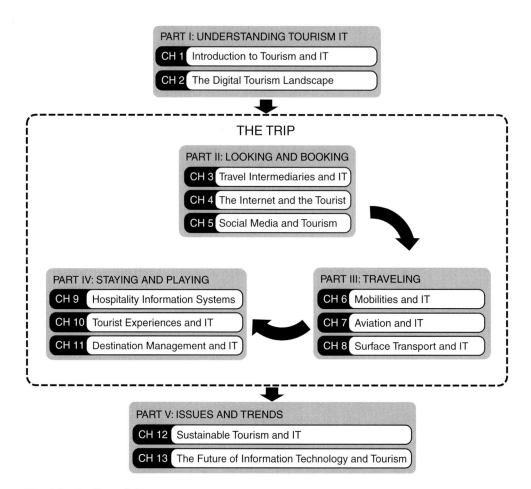

Fig. 1.2. Outline of chapters.

Part III of the book picks up the next part of a typical trip, and that is the travel from the home region to the destination region. The first chapter in this part will address the very important topic of mobile technologies in the context of tourism. The second chapter is devoted to IT and the aviation industry. IT is used aggressively by most airlines in many parts of their operations. The final chapter in this part will cover the use of IT by other transportation modes, such as rail, road and water transportation carriers.

Part IV of the book, the last one in the section entitled *The Trip*, details how IT influences the Staying and Playing at the destination. In particular the influence of IT on the hospitality sector is discussed in Chapter 9. This includes accommodation in all its varieties as well as foodservice operations. Chapter 10 covers the ways that IT affects the tourist experience, such as leisure experiences, entertainment and attractions. Chapter 11, the last in this section, is devoted to the use of IT by destinations including destination management systems.

The final part of the book, Part V entitled "Issues and Trends", analyzes the most important issues and trends that are influencing the application of IT to tourism. The first chapter in this section, Chapter 12, picks up on the increasingly important but less researched theme of sustainability and tourism IT. The last chapter (Chapter 13) examines other emerging trends of the future of IT and tourism. These include societal, economic and technological trends.

Most chapters in the book have case studies of tourism applications with questions for learners to consider. There will also be special insights based on the work of researchers in the particular area of tourism IT. In some cases chapters will also include special insights of industry applications. Each chapter will conclude with important key terms and discussion questions. Much information is available from the WWW on each topic, and so a list of important websites related to the chapter topic is included.

SUMMARY

This chapter has introduced the reader to the basic background of information technology, its development and evolution over the centuries and its status today. Aspects of computer hardware and software have been described, giving the reader an understanding of the scope of this important phenomenon. The chapter has described various models of how technology is adopted by organizations in general. It goes on to explain the uniqueness of the tourism industry, its characteristics and size that make it such a heavy user of information technology. The ways in which technology can be used strategically in tourism is also discussed. The chapter ends with a schematic diagram explaining the layout of the book.

KEY TERMS

ambient intelligence, artificial intelligence, big data, convergence, destination, dynamic information, experience, expert system, heterogeneity, information systems, information technology (IT), inseparability, intangibility, integrated circuit, intermediary, Internet, interoperability, knowledge management, microcomputer, microprocessor, mobile phones, Moore's Law, perishability, personal digital assistant (PDA), product, service, smartphone, space-time collapse, static information, strategic listening, supplier, transistor, traveler, ubiquitous computing, Web 1.0, Web 2.0, World Wide Web (WWW).

DISCUSSION QUESTIONS

1. In your opinion, what are the three most important inventions that have led to the information technologies we have available today? Provide examples to justify your answer.
2. Why is tourism such an information-intensive industry? Explain and give some examples.
3. What is the difference between static and dynamic tourism information? Give examples of each.
4. A hotel manager asks you why she should incorporate more technology into her hotel. How would you respond to this question so that the hotel is inspired to invest?
5. Identify one travel organization in your area that you think has used technology in a particularly creative way. Which of the strategic applications discussed at the end of the chapter would it fit into?
6. Which part of the textbook (based on the diagram of the chapters) are you most looking forward to studying? Why?

USEFUL WEBSITES

QR Code	Website	Description
	Eye for Travel http://www.eyefortravel.com/	Industry information about IT and travel. Includes sections on mobile technologies, social media and marketing, revenue and data management and distribution strategies.
	International Federation for Tourism and Technology http://www.ifitt.org/	Website of the only international association on tourism technology. This association also hosts the annual ENTER conference.
	International Hospitality Information Technology Association http://hita.camp7.org/	iHITA is a global association of educators and practitioners seeking to advance the use of IT in the hospitality industry through education and research.
	Tnooz http://www.tnooz.com/	News and updates about IT and travel.
	Travel Technology Initiative http://www.tti.org/	TTI coordinates technology and business projects and works to establish technology standards within the travel industry.

Case Study: Intercontinental Hotels Group

Hotels are often criticized for not using IT as strategically as other industries. There are exceptions to this and one of the world's largest hotel chains, Intercontinental Hotels Group (IHG), has invested heavily in its strategic use of IT. IHG owns seven large international hotel chains including Crowne Plaza, Holiday Inn and InterContinental Hotels. It has a total of 4503 hotels and 656,661 rooms, and is strongly committed to the strategic use of IT for its competitive edge.

IHG has appointed a Chief Information Officer (CIO) and spends about US$200 million annually on IT innovations, or about 1.2% of its revenue. The organization is always looking to IT for new ways to innovate. They are passionate about making hotel guests "the center of our universe" and this is the focus of all the company's strategic innovations. The company has designated one of its properties as the test bed for new technologies that can help achieve this aim: The Atlanta Crowne Plaza Hotel in Atlanta, Georgia USA has a huge customer database holding 200 million guest profiles. When integrated with other systems in the hotel, the system can analyze customer activity, trends and preferences. The technology is more advanced than most hotels and will process requests more rapidly because IHG has developed its own search technology called BOSS, which will soon be integrated with Google, providing GPS support and voice search. In the lobby of the hotel guests can access airline flight boards and touchscreen PCs to check flights and search for local amenities.

IHG is also strategically innovating in the area of mobile technologies. It is experiencing a 400% increase in the number of hotel rooms booked with mobile phones, and has therefore created apps for both iPhone and Android. With these apps guests can check availability, make a reservation, check themselves in and even unlock their rooms with their smartphone.

Another strategic initiative involves the concierge staff, which now uses iPads to access information for their guests. This unleashes them from their desks so that they can engage more dynamically with hotel guests in different parts of the hotel. An application currently being developed by IHG is the ability for the concierge to create a sightseeing itinerary of the area where the hotel is located and to transmit this to a guest's mobile device.

IHG is also innovating strategically with its commitment to **cloud computing** for many of its operations. It is building a private cloud environment called Camelot to move its core customer relationship management (CRM) systems off its mainframes and on to industry-standard equipment. IHG's loyalty program, its analysis of current guest activity information and historical records, and its system for sending promotional material to individual guests run on Camelot. IHG is working on also using Camelot for its revenue management and room yield system that determines room rates. It is using public cloud infrastructure for application development and testing, and also to host web content accessible by to customers worldwide. It is also evaluating moving key proprietary systems, such as room reservation software, into the cloud.

(Continued)

Case Study. Continued.

Adapted from Babcock, C. (2011) Four Companies getting Real Results from Cloud Computing. *Information Week*, 15 January.

Study Questions

1. Evaluate why the volume of reservations from smartphones has increased so rapidly. What future opportunities do smartphones offer for hotels?

2. Download the IHG app on to your smartphone and evaluate its features. Choose another app from a competing hotel chain and compare the features with IHG's. Are there any features you would add?

3. Explain how the Cloud will help IHG with its operations. What are the benefits of cloud computing compared with having all systems stored on local computer hardware?

4. Visit the IHG website and read about their strategies. Evaluate how IT supports their strategic vision. How else can IHG innovate with technology to support their strategies? Compare the IT strategies of two other major hotel chains. Which do you think is most innovative and why?

REFERENCES

Babcock, C. (2011) Four companies getting real results from cloud computing. *Information Week* 15 January.

Buhalis, D. and Law, R. (2008) Progress in information technology and tourism management: 20 years on and 10 years after the Internet – the state of eTourism research. *Tourism Management* 29(4), 609–623.

Cash, J.I., McFarlan, F.W., McKenney, J.L. and Applegate, L.M. (1992) *Corporate Information Systems Management: Text and Cases*. Irwin, Boston, Massachusetts.

Cleveland, H. (1985) *The Knowledge Executive: Leadership in an Information Society*, 1st edn. Truman Talley Books, New York, 263 pp.

Daintith, J. (2012) *A Dictionary of Physics*. Oxford University Press, Oxford, UK.

Drucker, P. (1990) *Managing the Non-Profit Organization*, 1st edn. Harper Collins, New York.

Dutta, S. and Bilbao-Osorio, B. (eds) (2012) *The Global Information Technology Report 2012: Living in a Hyperconnected World*. World Economic Forum and INSEAD, Geneva.

Gee, C.Y., Makens, J.C. and Choy, D.J.L. (1994) *The Travel Industry*, 2nd edn. Van Nostrand Reinhold, New York.

Gretzel, U., Fesenmaier, D.R. and O'Leary, J.T. (2006) The Transformation of Consumer Behaviour. In: Buhalis, D. and Costa, C. (eds) *Tourism Business Frontiers*. Elsevier, Burlington, Massachusetts, pp. 9–18.

Jordan, J.M. (2012) *Information, Technology and Innovation: Resources for Growth in a Connected World*. John Wiley and Sons, New York.

Pine, B.J. and Gilmore, J.H. (1999) *The Experience Economy: Work is Theatre and Every Business a Stage*. Harvard Business School Press, Boston, Massachusetts.

Poon, A. (1993) *Tourism, Technology and Competitive Strategies*. CAB International, Wallingford, UK.

Prahalad, C.K. and Ramaswamy, V. (2004) Co-creation experiences: the next practice in value creation. *Journal of Interactive Marketing* 18(3), 5–14.

QFinance (2013) Information Technology Industry. Available at: http://www.qfinance.com/sector-profiles/information-technology/ (accessed 15 November 2013).

Schertler, W. (1994) Tourism 2000: an information business. Paper presented at the Proceedings of the International Conference on Information and Communication Technologies in Tourism, Vienna.

United Nations World Tourism Organization (2013) Why Tourism? Available at: http://www2.unwto.org/en/content/why-tourism/ (accessed 15 November 2013).

Valacich, J.S. and Schneider, C. (2014) *Information Systems Today*, 6th edn. Prentice Hall, Englewood Cliffs, New Jersey.

chapter 2

The Digital Tourism Landscape

LEARNING OBJECTIVES

After studying this chapter you should be able to:

- analyze the drivers of innovation and technological change in the digital landscape;
- explain and evaluate the components of information technology in tourism using a digital tourism ecosystem perspective;
- apply concepts of tourist behavior to explain how digital travelers use and respond to information technologies in tourism settings;
- evaluate the factors that determine whether travelers will use a particular technology;
- explain the role of information technology in tourists' decision-making processes; and
- compare and contrast traditional and electronic tourism distribution systems.

INTRODUCTION

The first chapter provided a foundation for understanding the evolution and links between tourism and information technology (IT) and presented a framework based on the tourism experience. Much of the literature and research on tourism and technologies focuses on business applications and strategic uses of IT (Pearce, 2011). However, the purpose of this chapter is to examine the digital landscape from four disciplinary perspectives to provide a foundation for our discussions in later chapters. We start by adopting an ecological perspective to analyze the role of various entities and technologies by introducing the digital tourism ecosystem.

In the second section we examine models from economics and sociology to explain technological change and innovation in tourism. These models help us understand the factors influencing the spread of IT innovations and their power to revolutionize economies and industries. We also explore how organizations respond strategically to cycles of innovation. We then turn to psychology and consumer behavior to understand the relationship between travelers and IT. This approach helps us understand why some travelers are enthusiastic adopters of new technology, and others avoid technology when traveling. We also consider how technology impacts traveler decision-making, information sharing and the co-creation of experiences. The models in these two sections examine technological change at different levels of analysis. The concepts from economics and sociology describe the **macro-environment**, or large-scale changes across economies or industries. They also provide an understanding of the **meso-environment** and how organizations respond to changes in the digital landscape. The concepts in the second section help us understand the **micro-environment** and how individual characteristics, responses and behaviors drive the adoption of innovations.

Finally, we examine the use of IT in tourism from a management perspective by analyzing the supply chains, or distribution channels, that connect travelers with travel suppliers. We discuss the traditional structure of these distribution channels and track the increasingly complex development of electronic channels. A key benefit of examining these approaches is that each contributes to our understanding of a dynamic digital landscape that is continuously changing.

THE DIGITAL TOURISM ECOSYSTEM

We can draw inspiration from biological ecosystems to understand the role of IT in tourism. This might seem surprising when discussing technology, but the concept of an ecosystem provides a useful analogy to understand different aspects of IT in tourism. An **ecosystem** is a network of interactions among living organisms and between these organisms and their environment (Tansley, 1935). A key feature of ecosystems is that organisms change and adapt in response to each other and the physical environment, resulting in the process of evolution.

According to the World Economic Forum (2007), a **digital ecosystem** consists of users, companies and governments who converge in the space of IT, telecommunications, and media and entertainment industries. The concept describes the technology-mediated interaction between key entities and the technologies that support these interactions. We can apply this concept to tourism. A **digital tourism ecosystem** is composed of the interactions between living entities such as travelers, suppliers, intermediaries, governments and communities, and the nonliving technological environment of devices, connections, content and touch points. A digital tourism ecosystem can apply to a particular sector of the travel industry, to a specific destination or to the global travel phenomenon. Figure 2.1 provides an overview of the major entities and technologies in the digital tourism ecosystem. Their functions are discussed in the next section.

Digital ecosystem functions

Travelers' needs are at the core of the digital tourism ecosystem. The functions required by travelers during the travel lifecycle are:

1. Inspiration: the digital ecosystem delivers the information, pictures and videos that inform and inspire travelers. Important considerations include providing high-quality information, rich media and personalization to support traveler decision-making and trip planning.

		Ecosystem functions			
		Inspiration	Transaction	Experience	Reflection
Entities	Suppliers	■	■	■	□
	Intermediaries	■	■	□	□
	Other travelers	■	■	□	□
	Governments & DMOs	■	■	□	□
Communities	Social networks	■	□	■	■
	Blogs and micro-blogs	■		□	■
	Reviews	■	■	□	■
	Forums	■	■	□	□
	Wikis	■	■	□	□
	Local experts	■		□	
	Photo and video sharing	□		□	■
Devices	Desktop computer	■			■
	Smart TVs	■		□	
	Mobile devices	■	■	■	■
	Digital kiosks			■	
Connections	Wired broadband	■			■
	Mobile broadband and WiFi	■	■	■	■
	Near field communication		□	■	
	Global Positioning System (GPS)			■	
	Broadcasting	■	■	■	
	Protocols / standards	■	■	□	□
Content	Rich media (text, image, video)	■	■	□	□
	Maps and navigation	■		■	
	Transactions		■		
	Dynamic content	■	■		
	User-generated content	■			■
Touch points	Websites	■	■	□	□
	Search engines	■	■	□	□
	Mobile apps	□	□	■	■
	Email	■	■	□	□
	Telephone	■	■	■	□
	Face to face	■	■	■	□

■ Strong influence   □ Weak influence

Fig. 2.1. The digital tourism ecosystem.

2. Transaction: travel intermediaries, global distribution systems (GDSs), booking engines and payment gateways support travel transactions. Security, privacy and real-time availability are important in the delivery of this function.

3. Experience: various entities use technologies to create experiences during the trip (see Chapter 10). Location-based services, mobile apps and on-site technologies provided by destinations, suppliers and intermediaries play a major role in information and experience delivery.

4. Reflection: IT advances have allowed visitors to reflect on and share travel experiences with family and friends or with large audiences of followers using platforms such as blogs, review websites and social networks. This reflection in turn influences the inspiration phase of subsequent trips.

These functions are provided by an integrated and constantly changing network of entities and technologies. The influence of different entities and technologies varies across these different functions as shown in Fig. 2.2. To deliver these functions a digital ecosystem must be healthy. The health of an ecosystem can be measured in terms of productivity, resilience and diversity (Iansiti and Levien, 2004):

- **Productivity** relates to the ecosystem's ability to provide innovations that improve the efficiency of ecosystem functions. The efficiency of a digital tourism ecosystem can be measured using click-through and conversion rates, the number of users, the number of transactions, the value of transactions, the timeliness of delivery and the satisfaction of travelers.
- **Resilience** refers to the ecosystem's ability to withstand external shocks. The survival rate of entities within the ecosystem is a good indicator of resilience.
- **Diversity** is the ecosystem's capacity to create new entities or niches. An ecosystem with a diverse range of entities occupying various niches is more sustainable than one dominated by a few large entities because diversity drives both productivity and resilience.

While our analysis of travel distribution systems later in this chapter will demonstrate an increasingly complex web of channels, the ecosystems perspective suggests that the system may be more productive and resilient because of the greater diversity of entities and technologies.

Digital entities and communities

We have already discussed the role of intermediaries and suppliers in the distribution chain. According to Arina (2009), the entities that constitute the living aspects of a digital ecosystem can adopt a number of roles:

1. Catalyzers increase the survival chances of entities by supporting the evolution of a living, functioning ecosystem. Governments and Destination Management Organizations (DMOs) play this role by using research, patents, regulation and licensing to encourage competition and innovation. Catalyzers who push for interoperability, open systems and common standards enable new entities to design products that increase the diversity of the system.

2. Dictators aim to own or control a large portion of the ecosystem. The strategy adopted by some of the GDSs is an example of this role.

3. Milkers extract more value from the ecosystem than they contribute. The insidious discounting of hotel room rates by some online travel agents (OTAs) is an example.

4. Niche players offer specialized services and niche skills distinguishing them from others in the ecosystem. TripAdvisor is an example but there are other innovative IT services and features provided by entities in the digital tourism ecosystem (see Case Study).

Drawing further on the ecosystems analogy, we can argue that as the technological environment changes, some entities move into niches previously occupied by other entities. Good examples of this are Google Flights and Google Hotel Finder, which provide a service already offered by specialized travel meta-search engines. Existing entities may also evolve to fill new niches created by technological advances or new entities may be created to fill these niches, as in the case of new travel apps for smartphones. Some entities also co-exist in a symbiotic relationship, where both entities depend on each other for survival.

Without travelers no digital ecosystem would be needed, but travelers also play an important role in creating content for other travelers through a range of **digital communities**. A digital community connects online to communicate, share knowledge or exchange content (World Economic Forum,

2007). Many communities establish their own unique culture and individuals contribute time for no economic gain. Communities include travelers and local experts in the destination who volunteer their time to offer local advice. Local experts provide advice on fora such as TripAdvisor and LonelyPlanet. Other examples include Google City Experts and local recommendation platforms such as Localeur. These communities will be examined in Chapter 5.

Digital technological environment

The technological environment allows entities to access **content** using **connections** and **touch points** provided by digital **devices**. The following observations can be made about each of these four elements:

1. Devices: there is a trend toward the convergence of digital devices. We are witnessing the convergence of communications, media and entertainment technologies – consumers can listen to the radio or watch videos on a laptop or tablet but can also surf the web using a Smart TV. The smartphone also represents a similar convergence of technologies. All of these devices provide travelers with access to travel information.

2. Connections: information moves between devices using various connections. Digital broadcasting, broadband and wireless connections are most common but there is growing interest in mobile technologies such as Near Field Communication (NFC) and Bluetooth to facilitate contactless transactions and information exchange. Some destinations provide free WiFi in city centers and tourist sites to facilitate the sharing of travel experiences through social media. The network of satellites of the Global Position-ing System (GPS) provides connections for navigation and location-based applications. Protocols and standards, which allow various travel distribution systems to communicate, are also an important part of connectivity.

3. Content: different media deliver information about travel experiences, from high quality documentaries and travel shows to User Generated Content (UGC) on social media websites. The marketing of travel experiences relies on rich content such as text, colorful pictures and videos to communicate the attributes of a destination or holiday. Important considerations for travel suppliers and intermediaries include the quality, trustworthiness and persuasiveness of the information. There is a shift towards personalizing information delivery by collecting user information and tailoring content to individual preferences. Trip planning tools, recommender systems and intelligent agents all help to support trip planning and decision making. Content and information not only serve utilitarian needs in the digital ecosystem, they also serve hedonistic needs by contributing to enjoyment, entertainment and learning.

4. Touch points: touch points provide interfaces for entities to engage with each other and with technological systems. Traditional touch points include face-to-face and telephone communication. The Internet has delivered a suite of new touch points, including websites, search engines and email. Innovations in smartphones have created a range of travel apps used to interface with intermediaries, suppliers and other travelers. Travel organizations must manage all of these touch points to ensure consistency and quality in communications and marketing. Recent advances in voice recognition allow users to search for information by speaking to a smartphone or computer. Examples include Apple's Siri and Google's Voice Search. Advances in context-aware semantic searches create new ways for entities to interact with touch points.

INNOVATION AND CHANGE IN THE DIGITAL LANDSCAPE

Successful technologies often arrive at just the right time to exploit windows of opportunity. Some innovations are radical causing a quantum leap in how an organization or industry does business. For example, when the Internet substantially reduced the need for travel agencies as consumers started booking their own travel online, and the travel intermediary business had to re-engineer itself in response to this radical innovation. Other innovations are smaller and more incremental, for example small advances in the online booking of air travel following the innovations of low-cost carriers.

Some innovations fall into the **bandwagon** phenomenon in which new technologies are adopted because competitors are using them, without carefully analyzing their strategic relevance (Hashim *et al.*, 2014). This type of "mindless" innovation is rarely successful. Careful analysis of how the new technology gives strategic competitive advantage is essential, as we discussed in Chapter 1.

Some innovations fail because they are created before their time, or before they can gain social acceptance. For example, the widespread use of smartphones and tablets suggests that the Apple Newton (launched in 1993) should have been hugely successful. But batteries were less reliable and technologies such as handwriting recognition and wireless communication were still in development.

As a result it was discontinued after 5 years. In contrast, the iPod touch, iPhone and iPad became huge success stories for Apple just 10 years later because they took advantage of converging technologies. Technological change then depends on a combination of political, economic, social and technological factors in the macro-environment.

Technological change

To understand how technologies change the travel industry it is necessary to understand changes in user practices, markets, culture, supplier networks, producer capabilities, policy and regulation, and infrastructure. Together these create the **socio-technical regime** (Geels, 2002). By using a **multi-level perspective (MLP)** as shown in Fig. 2.2 we can analyze this socio-technical regime at three levels:

1. Landscape developments: technological changes occur against the backdrop of wider political, cultural and economic factors that facilitate or constrain innovation.

2. Socio-technical regime: stability is maintained in social systems through practices, rules and technologies that are part of a dominant paradigm. Change occurs incrementally at the regime level when something disrupts the status quo to create a window of opportunity.

3. Niche innovations: fledgling technologies develop in safe havens protected from pressures at the regime level. In the IT field, these safe havens have included venture capitalists, universities and research organizations such as CERN and ARPA. California's Silicon Valley provided an incubator for many new information technologies to emerge.

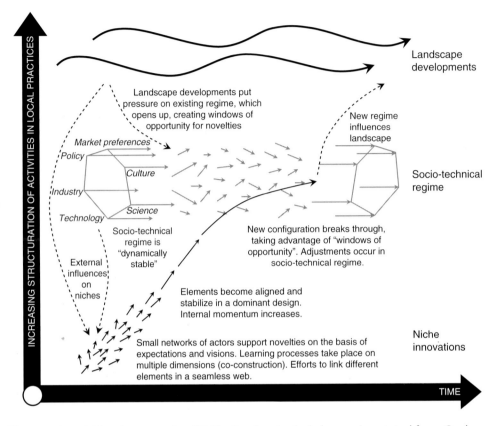

Fig. 2.2. A multi-level perspective (MLP) of technological change (reprinted from Geels (2002) with permission from Elsevier).

Change occurs due to the interplay between the three levels, resulting in a regime shift. The interaction of various actors, practices and rules stabilizes the socio-technological regime, locking in particular technologies and preventing change. However, pressures from landscape developments may open windows of opportunity that allow niche innovations to break through and change the regime. Windows of opportunity might include changes to dominant attitudes and values or major disruptive events. If an innovation is not mature enough when a window of opportunity opens, the technology may not be able to take advantage of the opportunity. The

shift from traditional travel agents to OTAs provides an example of a disruptive technology that exploited a window of opportunity. Once niche innovations become part of a new regime they may in turn influence the broader landscape, as we will see later in this chapter when we discuss the impact of technology on travel distribution.

The Internet provides a good example of an innovation that has followed this trajectory. It has changed rules and practices at the regime level and in turn this has influenced the broader landscape in unexpected ways. It is not difficult to find examples of this process at work in the travel industry. TripAdvisor is an example of a niche innovation that has disrupted the dominant practices of accommodation providers at the regime level. But how do these technologies emerge from niche innovations into the mainstream? How are new technologies adopted?

Innovation and technology adoption

There are several macro-level theories that help us understand the social adoption of new technological innovations in an economy. Three useful models include the Diffusion of Innovations Theory, Technological Innovation Theory and the Garter Hype Cycle.

The **Diffusion of Innovations Theory** argues that individuals adopt a new innovation at different rates (Rogers, 1962). The theory builds on the **Technology Adoption Lifecycle**, which describes the social adoption of a new innovation based on five successive groups of adopters:

1. **Innovators:** the first to adopt a new innovation. They are eager to try new ideas and prepared to take risks such as adopting technologies that may fail.
2. **Early adopters:** opinion leaders who embrace change but are not as obsessive as innovators.
3. **Early majority:** not leaders but tend to adopt new innovations before the average person. They tend to take fewer risks, and will thoroughly research a new innovation before deciding to adopt.
4. **Late majority:** will only adopt an innovation after the majority have tried it. Their adoption may be the result of economic necessity or social pressure.
5. **Laggards:** traditionalists and are the last to adopt an innovation because they are skeptical of change.

The number of adopters in each category is presented using a bell-shaped curve, while the rate of adoption over time follows an S-curve as shown in Fig. 2.3. This cycle consists of an initial innovation stage followed by rapid growth and maturity (Perez, 2002). In a tourism and IT context, the Diffusion of Innovations model can be applied to the adoption of technology by travel organizations as well as travelers.

We can also examine waves of IT innovation in a longer-term historical perspective by using elements of the Diffusion of Innovations Theory. Technological innovations have occurred throughout history as old technologies are supplanted by innovations. The famous Austrian economist Joseph Schumpeter argued that innovation, entrepreneurship and technological change are at the heart of economic growth. Innovations not only improve products, services and processes, they can disrupt an enterprise or even an entire economy, giving rise to new opportunities and challenges. Schumpeter (1934) observed that economies follow distinct waves or cycles based on technological innovation consisting of alternating periods of high growth and relatively slow growth. Following this observation, the **Technological Innovation Theory** suggests that basic innovations launch technological revolutions that in turn create leading industrial or commercial sectors (or waves). In the context of IT, these cycles can be visualized as six waves as shown in Fig. 2.4.

Each wave follows the S-curve lifecycle described by the Diffusion of Innovations Theory (Perez, 2002). Each successive wave is higher and shorter, indicating that with each wave adoption rates are more rapid, the peaks are closer together and performance

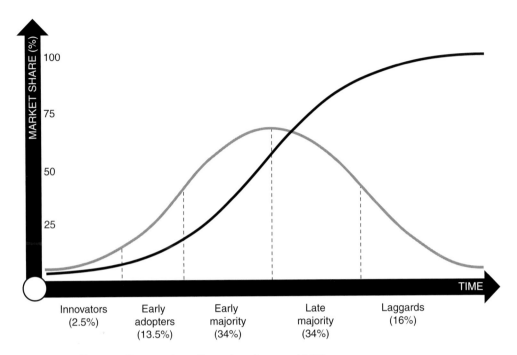

Fig. 2.3. Diffusion of innovations (based on Rogers, 1962).

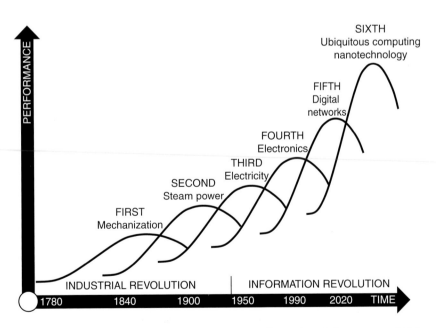

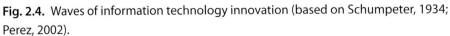

Fig. 2.4. Waves of information technology innovation (based on Schumpeter, 1934; Perez, 2002).

gains more pronounced. For example, the adoption of smartphones and mobile apps has been much more rapid than earlier adoptions of technologies such as the Internet, television, electricity and steam-powered transport. This creates a perception that technological change is speeding up and becoming more pronounced.

The **Gartner Hype Cycle** provides another model for understanding the cycle of technological innovation at the macro-level. The hype cycle was developed by Gartner Inc. in 1995 to provide a visual representation of the evolution (lifecycle) and social adoption rates of various technologies. A version of the hype cycle is presented in Fig. 2.5. According to this model, many technologies go through a cycle of initial development, followed by inflated expectations (hype), disillusionment, enlightenment and productivity. New innovations tend to have a certain amount of "hype" attached to them and this engenders high expectations of their benefits. Disillusionment and a decline in usage follow because applications may have not been strategically driven or live up to expectations. If the technology survives this phase, there can be a period of increased usage called enlightened growth as people adjust to more realistic expectations. Mainstream adoption commences in the last phase of this cycle. The first three groups of adopters from the Diffusion of Innovations model can be seen on the hype cycle.

The cycle is updated annually by Gartner by mapping individual technologies on the curve (visit http://www.gartner.com/ for the latest examples). While the model has intuitive appeal it can be criticized because it is deterministic and lacks objectivity and scientific rigor. The success or failure of an innovation may depend on the technology itself and a

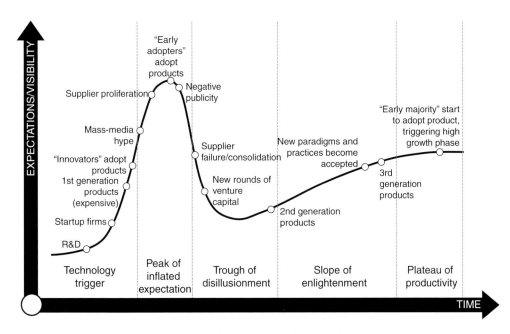

Fig. 2.5. Gartner Hype Cycle (adapted from Tarkovskiy, 2013).

wide range of other contextual factors. Nevertheless, the model is useful as a frame of reference for positioning various technologies.

Strategic responses to technological innovation

The models we have discussed assess whether emerging technologies will continue to evolve and whether they will take hold. An understanding of the macro-environmental trends and cycles can help inform changes and responses in the meso-environment. For travel organizations, an understanding of the position of a technology in the cycle may influence strategic decisions about the timing of adoption. Wheeler (2002) suggests a process

that allows organizations to strategically evaluate technology-based innovation cycles (see Fig. 2.6). The process involves first scanning the environment to identify emerging or enabling technologies relevant to the firm, then matching those technologies to opportunities such as serving customers better, reducing costs or enhancing data management. The third step is executing the innovation for firm growth – choosing the right system and ensuring the realization of benefits. Finally, the new technology is assessed by all users to check its effectiveness.

This section has provided frameworks for understanding how technological innovations emerge and evolve. We have also examined the adoption of IT. These models are useful

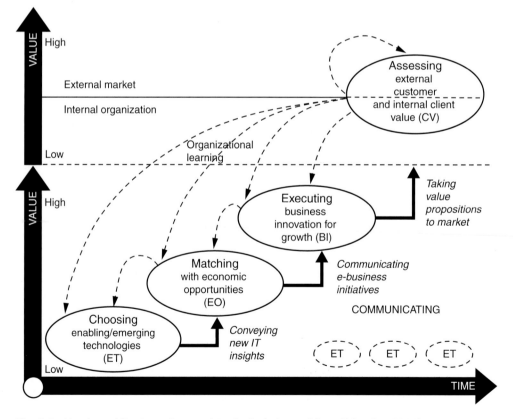

Fig. 2.6. Net-based Business Innovation Cycle (adapted from Wheeler, 2002).

for travel enterprises and destinations because they provide a broader framework for operational and strategic decision-making about the adoption of technologies. We have seen from a few examples how timing and broader socio-technical factors are critical when investing in technological innovations. In the next section, we explore the use of technology at the micro-, or individual level.

UNDERSTANDING THE DIGITAL TOURIST

At a micro-level it is useful to consider how travelers interact with IT. The study, planning and design of interactions between people and computers is called **Human–Computer Interaction (HCI)**. As we have seen above, the success of technological innovations often depends on the socio-technical regime. The market and the consumers in various market segments are an important part of this regime. New technologies fail if their entry into the marketplace is poorly timed or if they do not meet the perceived needs of consumers. On the other hand, emerging markets or changes in behavior can create opportunities for technological innovations. So there is a two-way relationship between consumers and technology: technology can change consumers' behavior but consumers can also influence the development and use of new technologies.

Learning about the interactions between travelers and IT can help us understand the following aspects of behavior:

- **Technology use and acceptance:** affective and cognitive responses toward technology use in travel settings vary according to personal characteristics such as demographics, trip characteristics, attitudes, perceptions, motives and experience;

- **Decision-making:** the impact of IT on information search behavior, decision-making and trip planning;

- **Information sharing:** it is useful to understand the "who, what and why" of sharing content online and how this content influence readers; and

- **Co-creation of experiences:** the role of technology in the co-creation of visitor experiences. Travelers may use their own devices or on-site technologies to complement or supplement their experience. An example is the use of audio guides or podcasts at European heritage attractions.

We explore each of these points in more detail in the following sections, before concluding with a brief overview of methods for understanding the behavior of digital tourists.

Technology use and acceptance

Technology acceptance is a traveler's willingness to use a technology. Travelers' attitudes, perceptions and responses to technology vary based on demographic, psychographic and trip characteristics. **Demographics** include attributes such as gender, age, income and education level. Gender differences in technology use occur because males and females process information differently. Females are more exhaustive in their information search and consult a wider variety of media and information channels when making travel decisions (Kim *et al.*, 2007). Females also are more active users of social networks and mobile devices when searching for travel information (Okazaki and Hirose, 2009).

Age is also an important variable, but a more sophisticated approach studies generational cohorts (Bonn *et al.*, 2000; Beldona, 2005). Generational cohorts are "groups of individuals who are born during the same time period and who experienced similar external events during their formative or coming-of-age years (i.e., late adolescent and early adulthood years)" (Noble and Schewe, 2003, p. 979). These similar experiences influence the behaviors and values of individuals throughout their lifespan. Each generation has a different worldview because of these shared experiences (Mannheim, 1952). Each successive cohort appears more at ease with communications, media and entertainment technologies. For example, members of Generation Y have been described as early adopters of new technologies (Benckendorff *et al.*, 2010). Another demographic model related to age is the Family Life Cycle (FLC) (Lansing and Kish, 1957). Travelers can be divided into singles, couples, families without children, families with children, retired and solitary survivors. These distinctions are important because family lifecycle impacts length of stay, travel expenditure and activities. As a consequence, the technologies used to support these differences are likely to vary (Brown and Venkatesh, 2005).

Trip characteristics influence technology use. The purpose of the trip impacts the choice of technologies and information, and leisure and business travelers have different IT needs (Lo *et al.*, 2002). Whether the trip is domestic or international may influence technology use as it often costs more for international travelers to access communications networks. Journey length may also impact technology use as communication needs and trip planning tools increase with the length of stay. Finally, the composition of the travel party can influence traveler use of the Internet and mobile apps (Luo *et al.*, 2004).

Psychographics may be more accurate in predicting behavior than demographics. Psychographic traits such as attitudes and perceptions are important in determining how individuals respond to technology. Research shows that some people experience anxiety when using a computer in work or education settings (Hackbarth *et al.*, 2003; Wilfong, 2006). **Computer anxiety** is a psychological construct measuring the extent to which individuals are "uneasy, apprehensive, or fearful about the current or future use of computers" (Igbaria and Parasuraman, 1989, p. 375). Computer anxiety is strongly linked with attitudes towards computers and to behavioral intentions and performance (Fagan *et al.*, 2003; Vician and Davis, 2003; Wilfong, 2006). Computer anxiety is also related to concepts like **computer phobia** and **technophobia**. As a result of these anxieties, travelers may avoid technology-oriented tools even though they are superior to conventional options. Technophobic travelers might seek out visitor centers, guidebooks and brochures, rather than using mobile apps to plan their activities, and choose travel experiences not dependent on technology.

Naisbitt (1982) coined the phrase "high tech/high touch" after observing people reacting differently to technology in different settings. Some people enjoy the novelty of new technologies and appreciate **high-tech** travel experiences including technology to create experiences. Conversely, some travelers seek out **high-touch** experiences with more personalized human interactions. While high-tech may enable high-touch experiences, the need to "unplug" from technology creates a thirst for more personal interactions.

While the high-tech/high-touch distinction has intuitive appeal it is overly simplistic. Benckendorff *et al.* (2005) developed and tested a segmentation model based on tourist preferences for technology in tourist experiences and in everyday life. This model identifies four segments of travelers as shown in Table 2.1.

Spillovers use technology both at work and home and also seek out technology-mediated experiences when traveling. The *compensators* are regular users of technology in everyday life but compensate for the lack of high-touch experiences by avoiding technology when traveling. The *opportunity seekers* are not heavy users of technology but seek out high-tech experiences when they travel – perhaps because they are novel. The *luddites* avoid technology in their daily lives as well as when holidaying. The term "Luddite" comes from a group of 19th-century textile workers in the UK who protested against the introduction of new machinery. Inspired by a worker called Ned Ludd, the group carried out several riots during which they destroyed knitting frames and other machines.

Travel organizations must provide the right balance of high-tech innovation and high-touch interactions. If they rely heavily on technology to create front-stage experiences this may alienate luddites and compensators. Travel companies serving high-touch customers should not ignore technology, but use it to enhance the delivery of experiences (Benckendorff *et al.*, 2005). Examples include customer databases, guest history systems, financial systems and security systems. In fact, some tourism suppliers may actively target luddites and compensators by providing technology-free zones to escape the "always connected" stresses of the modern world (Pearce and Gretzel, 2012).

Scholars have adapted theories from psychology, such as Fishbein and Ajzen's (1975) Theory of Reasoned Action (TRA) and Ajzen's (1991) Theory of Planned Behavior (TPB) to explain how beliefs and attitudes impact a person's intention to use technology. One of the most widely used theories is the **Technology Acceptance Model (TAM)**. The TAM proposes that "perceived usefulness" and "perceived ease of use" influence whether a person will use a technology. In a travel context, **perceived usefulness** is the degree to which a traveler believes a technology will enhance their experience. **Perceived ease of use** is the extent to which a traveler believes that using a technology will be effortless (Davis, 1989). Often these perceptions are influenced by social factors, technology anxiety, playfulness and confidence. The original TAM has been extended to study travelers' acceptance of websites, booking systems, online communities, social networks, smartphones and mobile apps (Luo *et al.*,

Table 2.1. Segmentation of high-tech and high-touch travelers.

		Everyday life	
		High tech	High touch
Travel	High tech	Spillovers	Opportunity seekers
	High touch	Compensators	Luddites

2007; Kim *et al.*, 2008; Bader *et al.*, 2012). Despite its intuitive appeal the model has been criticized for being too simple and deterministic and omitting essential determinants of decisions and actions (Bagozzi, 2007).

In 2003, several researchers compared the various technology acceptance models (including TAM) and constructed a new model called the **Unified Theory of Acceptance and Use of Technology (UTAUT)**, which was subsequently extended and refined for consumer settings (UTAUT II) (Venkatesh *et al.*, 2003, 2012). According to UTAUT II, six constructs (performance expectancy, effort expectancy, social influence, hedonic motivation, price value and habit) influence a consumer's intention to use a technology. The actual use of a technology is

in turn influenced by a number of facilitating factors (resources, knowledge, compatibility and support) and the intention to use the technology. Gender, age and experience mediate the impact of these key constructs on usage intention and behavior. An illustration of all these concepts is shown in Fig. 2.7.

Venkatesh *et al.* (2012) define the key components of the UTAUT II model as follows:

1. Performance expectancy: the degree to which a technology provides benefits to consumers in performing activities. For example, a mobile app in a heritage attraction may help tourists learn more about the site.

2. Effort expectancy: the degree of ease associated with consumers' use of technology. For example, tourists are more likely to

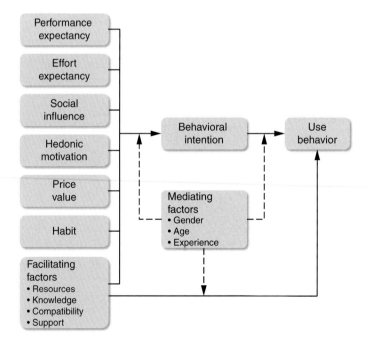

Fig. 2.7. Unified Theory of Acceptance and Use of Technology II (UTAUT II; adapted from Venkatesh *et al.*, 2012).

use a mobile app if it is easy to learn how to use it.

3. Social influence: the extent to which consumers perceive that important others (e.g. family and friends) believe they should use a particular technology. If a mobile app is socially acceptable, and other tourists are using it, then an individual is more likely to do so.

4. Hedonic motivation: the fun or pleasure derived from using a technology. Continuing with our example, if the mobile app is enjoyable to use then tourists are more likely to continue using it.

5. Price value: consumers' tradeoff between the perceived benefits of the applications and the monetary cost. For example, if our mobile app is free and there is a clear benefit then tourists are more likely to use it.

6. Habit: the extent to which consumers perform behaviors automatically. For example, if tourists use mobile apps in other settings they may use a mobile app in a tourist setting. Conversely, if travelers rarely use mobile apps they are less likely to use a mobile app in a travel setting.

The UTAUT II model is a new framework and has not been widely tested in tourism settings but a few studies have applied the original UTAUT model to the study of online bookings and mobile apps (San Martín and Herrero, 2012; Lai, 2014). Lai (2014) uses the UTAUT model to identify antecedents and determinants affecting travelers' acceptance of a mobile tour guide app. The author examined performance expectancy, effort expectancy, social influence and facilitating factors. The author also added two antecedents related to information quality (informativeness and entertainment). The entertainment construct is similar to the hedonic motivation construct used in UTAUT II. The results suggest entertainment and informativeness are important features of travel apps.

A cautionary note is needed as we conclude this section. The TAM and its variations (including the two UTAUT models) are useful frameworks but they represent one of many paradigms for considering technology use. Psychology and social psychology are replete with theories designed to predict human decision-making and behavior based on personality, motives, identity, goal attainment, attitudes beliefs and values. Any one of these models could be applied to the use and acceptance of technology in travel settings. TAM and UTAUT are underpinned by theories related to "reasoned action" and "planned behavior". Consequently they are useful in situations where travelers make conscious decisions to use technologies. However, many tourist decisions are unplanned and spontaneous and often based on heuristics or mental shortcuts. The theories explored in this section and other goal-oriented models proposed by researchers such as Bagozzi (2007) may not be particularly useful in these situations. Instead theories that explore concepts such as sensation seeking, unplanned behavior and impulsiveness may be more useful. Other criticisms of TAM and UTAUT are discussed in the Research Insight below. UTAUT II was designed and tested in a consumer setting and addresses some of these criticisms but these frameworks are a work in progress. Astute travel professionals and managers need to develop a critical eye and strive to keep up to date with the latest developments in these research fields.

Research Insight: Limitations of TAM and UTAUT I

Bagozzi, R.P. (2007) The legacy of the technology acceptance model and a proposal for a paradigm shift. *Journal of The Association for Information Systems* 8(4), 3.

Bagozzi (2007) provides an interesting critique of the TAM and its variants. He points out limitations of the TAM and UTAUT I models and argues that they neglect many important determinants of individual decision-making identified by other theories of psychology. The key limitations include:

- a lack of evidence supporting the link between intended behavior and actual behavior;
- a strong focus on the individual with limited acknowledgement of the group, cultural and social dynamics of technology acceptance;
- limited acknowledgement of the impact of anticipated emotions on technology use; and
- a deterministic approach that disregards human agency and the possibility that a decision maker is capable of choosing to act in a self-regulated way rather than following an impulsive, compulsive, habitual, coerced or bribed response.

Bagozzi proposes a new paradigm for understanding technology acceptance that considers goals, actions and self-regulation. His paper draws on theories regarding attitudes, motives, values and identity. The take-home point from his work is that it is important to continually reassess how advances in psychology and consumer behavior help us understand technology use and acceptance.

Technology and decision making

IT is used by travelers to support both pre-trip and on-site decision-making (Gretzel *et al.*, 2006). According to Hyde (2008), the pre-trip decision-making process can be broken down into three distinct phases:

1. Information search: many researchers have examined the technology-mediated information search behaviors of travelers (Jang, 2004; Luo *et al.*, 2004; Ho and Liu, 2005; Xiang and Gretzel, 2010). An understanding of how digital channels influence destination image and choice can help suppliers and destinations design more engaging content (Jacobsen and Munar, 2012). Online and offline information search processes differ as do the factors that influence travelers' choices

about these information sources (Ho *et al.*, 2012). The online information search process will be explored in more detail Chapter 4.

2. Trip planning: in the trip-planning phase, travelers use media to compare alternatives and combine different elements of the trip. For complex trips this can be time consuming and frustrating, but online tools assist travelers. Social networks help trip planning, but there are other innovative online itinerary planning tools such as Utrip, TouristEye and Mygola (see Case Study). We can understand the dynamics of trip planning by exploring how travelers use the Internet and social media to plan their trips (Pan and Fesenmaier, 2006; Fotis *et al.*, 2012).

3. Purchasing: during the purchasing phase travelers commit to an itinerary and complete the booking process through a diverse range of channels. Some travelers search for information using digital channels but use traditional channels to purchase. Individual characteristics and external factors influencing consumer preferences for digital channels are considered in this phase. We can also examine the influence of quality and presentation of digital information on travelers' purchase intentions.

Once travelers are at the destination secondary decisions need to be made about where to eat, what to see and how to get around. These decisions are supported by traditional information sources such as brochures, maps, guidebooks and hotel concierges, but digital technologies such as mobile devices and apps are playing an increasingly important role in on-site decision making. Location- and context-aware apps and augmented reality will support on-site decision-making more in the future and these aspects are explored in greater detail in Chapters 6 and 10.

Information sharing

Travelers can share information about their travels more easily due to the development of **Web 2.0** websites where they can generate their own content. This **User Generated Content (UGC)** can be found on wikis, blogs, reviews, photo- and video-sharing sites and social networks and is referred to as **electronic word of mouth (eWOM)**. We are interested in understanding how and why digital tourists create online communities and share information, and how the readers of this information are influenced by eWOM. For example, how are travelers influenced by negative reviews on TripAdvisor? Does the reaction depend on the characteristics of the reviewer? Are there particular message characteristics that influence readers? Do the characteristics of the reader matter? How do reviewers and readers react to replies posted by hotel managers? The answers to these questions have implications for the management and marketing of tourism organizations. The far-reaching, dynamic and transient nature of the Internet offers new ways of capturing, analyzing and interpreting the information that users share online (Litvin *et al.*, 2008). We will explore some of these themes in Chapter 5.

Technology and the co-creation of experiences

Technology-mediated experiences are co-created by the interaction of travelers and technology. They can be explained with the ABC approach. ABC stands for Antecedents, Behavior and Consequences: the antecedents that lead to an experience, the behavior that constitutes the experience and the consequences of the experience. Some antecedents of technology-mediated experiences include personal factors, facilitating factors and key constructs from the technology acceptance theories presented earlier in this chapter. Other antecedents include the cognitive and affective state of the traveler, including their motives, mood and fatigue levels.

We can examine travelers' behavior, how they interact with the technologies, the usability of the technology, and whether it satisfies the travelers' motives. Memorable technology-mediated experiences may use sight, sound, touch, smell and taste to arouse the senses. For example, technology is used at the National Wine Centre in Adelaide, Australia to allow visitors to appreciate the colors and smells of different varieties of grapes. Visitors use touchscreens to mix different varieties of grapes to make a blended wine that is then "judged" by a virtual judge. Holograms equipped with interactive dialogue allow visitors to ask questions about the wine-making process.

The consequences of the technology-mediated experience should not be overlooked. In tourist attractions, the aim is to entertain and educate travelers. In hotels, the technology may contribute to meeting the needs of guests. An additional motive for organizations and destinations may be to increase the time and money spent by travelers. The role that technology plays in the co-creation of experiences will be discussed in more detail in Chapter 10.

Methods for understanding the digital tourist

A range of methods can be used to understand the behavior of digital tourists. While a full review of research methodologies is beyond the scope of this book, we will briefly summarize various approaches to understand traveler behavior and technology use. Methods for understanding the digital tourist fall into quantitative and qualitative methods. **Quantitative** approaches quantify behavioral processes and responses by using numbers, statistics and mathematical models. **Qualitative** approaches rely on ideas, concepts and themes to gain an in-depth understanding of behavior. Some of the common data collection techniques used to understand digital tourists are summarized in Table 2.2.

Quantitative methods involve the construction of surveys using numeric or categorical questions and scales. However, IT offers a suite of techniques for organizations to understand travelers. Online surveys are more flexible than traditional surveys because they incorporate rich media and support the conditional display and branching of questions based on how users respond to initial filter questions. Online polls are a quick way to collect simple data about traveler preferences.

As travelers use online environments certain metrics can be collected in the background to monitor behavior using web analytics. **Web analytics** include the number of page views, unique visitors, repeat visits, bounce rate, referring pages and search engines. **Big data** describes the harvesting and analysis of very large datasets. Some web analytics generate very large datasets but this can also be collected through GPS devices or mobile apps. The digital tourist generates hundreds of data points a day and this "big data" can be harnessed to deliver better experiences. Visitor tracking using destination or supplier apps provides information about visitor flows,

Table 2.2. Quantitative and qualitative methods for understanding digital consumers.

Quantitative methods	Qualitative methods
Traditional surveys	Interviews
Online surveys	Focus groups
Polls	Content analysis
Web analytics	Sentiment analysis
Big data	Netnography
Visitor tracking	Observation
Experiments	Prototyping

patterns and time use. Another useful quantitative technique uses experiments to measure how travelers use or respond to technologies or designs. Responses are measured by conventional methods to track user behavior and eye movements (Pan *et al.*, 2011).

Qualitative methods include techniques such as interviews and focus groups, but here too, new technologies provide access to qualitative data for further analysis. Easy access to blogs, reviews and social media allows market researchers to conduct content or sentiment analysis. **Content analysis** identifies concepts and themes. For example, analysis of negative reviews for a hotel on TripAdvisor helps us to discover whether there are systemic problems that management must address. **Sentiment analysis** is useful for tracking consumer attitudes based on comments on social networks and blogs.

Netnography studies online communities. It is derived from ethnography, and involves a researcher infiltrating an online community to learn about its participants. We can also learn a lot from simply observing how travelers interact with IT, either in a controlled environment, where users are given a specific task or in a real tourist setting. If we are interested in testing a new technology, we might develop a **prototype**. This approach is used in combination with a focus group or observation to evaluate strengths and weaknesses of the design. Researchers might also engage users in a conversation as they use the technology.

TRAVEL DISTRIBUTION SYSTEMS

We now turn our attention to supply chain models that explain how the travel distribution system connects suppliers with travelers.

A **system** is a group of components that are interrelated, interdependent and interacting with each other (Anderson and Johnson, 1997). These can be both tangible objects and entities or intangible notions, like processes, information flows, interactions or relationships. The **travel distribution system** consists of **intermediaries**, or middlemen, that facilitate the sale and delivery of tourism services from suppliers to travelers (Buhalis and Laws, 2001).

There are two ways for travelers to source and book travel experiences in the travel distribution system:

1. Direct: travelers can access information and make bookings directly with suppliers through advertising, brochures, call centers, supplier websites, social media or in person at the point of sale (POS).

2. Indirect: travelers can access information and bookings through third party intermediaries such as traditional travel retailers, Travel Management Companies (TMCs), Online Travel Agents (OTAs), tour operators and wholesalers.

Advances in IT have delivered a bewildering array of options for travelers to book a trip. But it was not always this way. Before the commercialization of the Internet, travelers could do so through face-to-face, telephone or fax communications with a travel agent or directly with travel suppliers. As travelers accessed the Internet, the range of channels and tools available for booking travel expanded dramatically. This has created a confusing travel distribution landscape for travelers and travel suppliers. In this section we explore how technology has changed the ways travelers interact with tourism suppliers.

The traditional travel distribution system

The traditional travel distribution system was structured with clear roles attached to different entities in the chain. The traditional travel distribution channels shown in Fig. 2.8 used phone, fax and travel agents as the major booking sources between travelers and suppliers.

Figure 2.8 shows that a collection of players occupy three different layers. The top layer consists of travel suppliers such as airlines, hotels, car rentals, cruises, rail and tours. The connections layer provides links between suppliers and touch points where travelers can book travel experiences. Large suppliers maintain their own **Computer Reservation Systems (CRSs)**, which store rates and availability for products (e.g. seats, rooms, tours, cars). For individual airlines, these are called **Airline Reservation Systems (ARS)**. The **Global Distribution Systems (GDSs)** were developed to provide connectivity between airlines and travel agents. GDSs can be distinguished from ARSs and CRSs because they provide travel intermediaries with access to different suppliers. A GDS aggregates travel inventory from many CRSs into one system where it can be displayed in a standardized format. A more detailed discussion of GDSs is provided in Chapter 3.

Connections between hotel CRSs and GDSs were not widespread until the 1990s and travel agents and travelers made reservations in person or by contacting the hotel's reservations department. Hotel chains maintained centralized call centers for this purpose. The first **switch** company (THISCO) was created in 1988 by a consortium of 16 hotels to overcome the inefficiencies of this system. A switch acts as a bridge between the GDSs and hotel CRSs. By using a switch, a hotel can distribute inventory to all GDSs. This is discussed further in Chapter 9.

In the bookings layer, travelers can find and book travel experiences at the POS or by contacting the supplier by phone. A traveler also books travel through an intermediary such as a travel agent or tour operator. **Retail travel agents**, or travel retailers, were

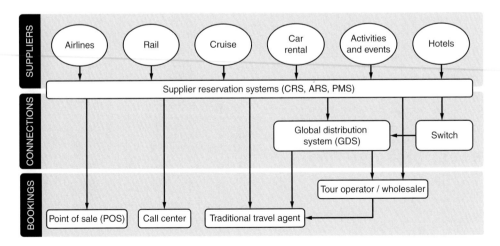

Fig. 2.8. The traditional travel distribution system.

traditionally the contact for travelers seeking advice about flight, accommodation and tour options. Travel consultants booked travel products either directly with the supplier or by accessing travel inventory through a GDS. Travel retailers adopted one of the major GDSs, which included the hardware and software required for product searches and ticketing. **Tour operators** combine accommodation, tours, transport and meals together to create packaged tours. They specialize in developing programs and itineraries for direct distribution to travelers or through travel retailers and wholesalers. **Travel wholesalers** on the other hand buy travel products in bulk at discounted prices and then sell these through retail travel agents. Both tour operators and wholesalers source products directly from suppliers and through GDSs.

Although this traditional system looks simple and the role of each entity seems clear, in reality the lack of electronic content and poor connectivity between systems meant that complex itineraries took a long time to organize.

The digital travel distribution system

The tourism distribution system changed dramatically throughout the 1990s as a result of improved access to personal computers, the commercialization and widespread use of the Internet, and the vertical and horizontal integration of travel intermediaries. **Vertical integration** occurs when a travel company acquires another company above or below them in the distribution chain, as when a travel agent acquires a tour operator or wholesaler. Conversely, **horizontal integration** takes place when a company acquires another

company with the same function in the distribution chain, as when a travel agency acquires another travel agent. By the 2000s the travel distribution system was dominated by large intermediaries managing several brands. But the entry of new online intermediaries created more choice, with cross-over in the roles and functions of players in the distribution system. Figure 2.9 represents this new digital tourism distribution system.

In the digital distribution system travelers have more choice and flexibility when sourcing and booking travel. Suppliers access a mix of distribution partners to reach their target consumers. The connections layer has become much more crowded. The GDSs and switch companies have been joined by other players. **Channel managers** specialize in helping suppliers manage the bewildering array of distribution channels. Some technology companies specialize in providing **Internet Booking Engines (IBEs)** for suppliers to connect directly with travelers through their own websites, social media and mobile apps. Typically they are linked with **payment gateways** that process transactions securely. **GDS New Entrants (GNEs)** provide similar services to GDSs but use new technologies and open architecture to provide connectivity without investment in costly legacy systems. The development of GNEs is discussed in Chapter 3. The connections layer includes **Destination Management Systems (DMSs)**, which consolidate and distribute travel products and services for a particular destination. A detailed discussion of the role of DMSs is provided in Chapter 11.

At the booking layer, travelers now have a wide range of choices for purchasing travel experiences. **Travel Management Companies (TMCs)** are a specialist type of travel retailer focused on the corporate travel market.

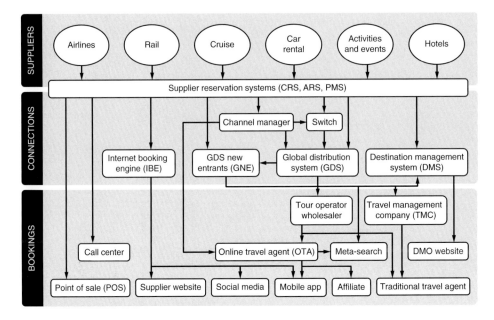

Fig. 2.9. The digital travel distribution system.

The Internet has supported the creation of local and global **Online Travel Agencies (OTAs)** who sell travel products online and through mobile apps. Like traditional travel retailers, OTAs source travel inventory from the GDSs and GNEs as well as directly from tour operators and suppliers. Some of the first OTAs were founded by the airlines and GDSs. OTAs also allow **affiliates** to sell their products on third party websites. The proliferation of OTAs means price-sensitive travelers must search multiple sites to find the best deals. Not surprisingly, several new companies have emerged to solve this problem. **Meta-search Engines** allow travelers to search and compare prices from multiple sources, including OTAs, tour operators, GDSs, GNEs and DMSs. These metasearch engines do not manage bookings or transactions; they refer travelers to OTAs and supplier websites to complete the booking process. They include technology companies such as Google, which introduced Google Flights and Google Hotel Finder (Kracht and Wang, 2010). Researchers suggest that market power has shifted to this new category of intermediaries. Wholesalers and travel agents have also moved into online ventures in addition to offering their services from a retail shop.

Our discussion of the evolution and characteristics of the digital tourism distribution system provides a useful framework for understanding information flows between travelers, intermediaries and suppliers – as shown by the arrows in Fig. 2.9. This information is the "lifeblood" of the travel industry and generally falls into four categories:

- **Descriptive information:** descriptions of product features, pricing, availability, legal information, terms and conditions that support the travel process. For example, supplier, intermediary and DMO websites contain text, images and videos

---

Research Insights: Evolution of Travel Distribution

Kracht, J. and Wang, Y. (2010) Examining the tourism distribution channel: evolution and transformation. *International Journal of Contemporary Hospitality Management* 22(5), 736–757.

John Kracht and Youcheng Wang from the University of Central Florida provide a detailed analysis of the evolution and transformation of tourism distribution channels using a series of graphical representations over time. Their analysis and discussion reveals the evolving complexity of the tourism distribution system by focusing on intermediary categories and the pioneers within these categories. Their findings indicate that IT advances have not simplified the travel distribution system, but rather have increased its complexity. They observe that advances in IT have impacted the distribution system by:

- adding new layers of intermediaries;
- bypassing (or "disintermediating") some traditional intermediaries; and
- supporting the "reintermediation" of some players who have adapted to the changing market environment by embracing new technology to provide value-added services.

This has led to many types of intermediaries forming a complex web-like distribution structure with many layers. They suggest that the pressure to survive in this environment will result in more competition, cooperation, merging and forming of partnerships.

---

to help prospective travelers understand various features of a travel experience.

- **User information:** metrics are harvested through background processes such as "cookies" and other tracking tools. These data sometimes inform intelligent agents and recommender systems to personalize the search process.

- **Analytical information:** trends, patterns and comparisons that assist decision-making for players in the distribution chain. For example, metasearch engines allow travelers to compare options or monitor trends in airfares and room rates. Reports and metrics also provide vital information for suppliers and intermediaries.

- **Transactional information:** information generated from product acquisition and payment systems. For example, traveler details, electronic funds transfers,

invoices and receipts and booking confirmations.

It is clear from Fig. 2.9 that the Internet has become a central hub for travel distribution, creating a link between travelers and a plethora of travel experiences. Through these channels, consumers can now access almost everything that a traditional travel agent can, and they continue to use a variety of channels. As we have seen, their channel preferences are likely to be influenced by a range of factors, including traveler type and characteristics as well as trip and destination characteristics. For example, traditional channels such as brochures, guidebooks and the telephone continue to be important for suppliers in peripheral or developing tourism destinations. The shifting structure of the digital tourism distribution system affects not only the traveler, but also the business models and marketing strategies adopted by players in the distribution system (Pearce *et al.*, 2004). Pearce and Schott (2005) suggest that suppliers must consider the nature of their own product or service, markets and broader destination characteristics to develop a strategic approach to distribution. Chapter 3 discusses these developments and the implications for travelers, suppliers and intermediaries.

SUMMARY

In summary, we have examined the digital landscape from different disciplinary perspectives. First, we adopted the analogy of an ecosystem to explore the broader role that IT plays to fulfill the functions of inspiration, acquisition, experience and reflection. Second, we explained that socio-technical factors influences technological change. We have also demonstrated how an understanding of economic or industry innovation cycles can help travel organizations make strategic decisions about their technology adoptions. Third, we used ideas from psychology and consumer behavior to understand how and why travelers use IT. Finally, we discussed how travelers connect with suppliers through various channels using a distribution systems perspective. Our analysis moved between the macro (economies and industries), the meso (organizations) and the micro (individuals). Together, these perspectives provide theoretical foundations for understanding concepts in later chapters.

KEY TERMS

affiliate, airline reservation system (ARS), bandwagon, big data, channel manager, computer anxiety, computer phobia, computer reservation system (CRS), connections, content analysis, demographics, destination management system (DMS), Devices, diffusion of innovations theory, digital community, digital tourism ecosystem, ecosystem, ecosystem niche, electronic word-of-mouth (eWOM), GDS new entrant (GNE), global distribution system (GDS), high tech, high touch, horizontal integration, human-computer interaction (HCI), hype cycle, intermediary, Internet booking engine (IBE), macro-environment, meso-environment, metasearch engine, micro-environment, multi-level perspective, netnography, online travel agent (OTA), payment gateway, perceived ease of use, perceived usefulness, prototyping, psychographics, qualitative, quantitative, retail travel agent, sentiment analysis, socio-technical regime, switch, system, technological innovation theory, technology acceptance model (TAM), technology adoption lifecycle, technophobia, touch points, tour operator, tour wholesaler, travel distribution system, travel management company (TMC), unified theory of acceptance and use of technology (UTAUT), user-generated content (UGC), vertical integration, Web 2.0, web analytics

DISCUSSION QUESTIONS

1. In 2007 the World Economic Forum released three scenarios of digital ecosystems, which are summarized in the following YouTube video: http://youtu.be/jnrAtXt3uu4/. Considering IT developments since 2007, which one has been the most accurate? Justify your answer and discuss the implications for IT and tourism.

http://youtu.be/jnrAtXt3uu4/

2. Which of the innovation models presented in this chapter are most relevant to the tourism industry? Explain why.

3. Conduct your own research about the major generational cohorts alive today (Baby Boomers, Gen X, Gen Y and Gen Z). Do they differ in how they use technologies? Are older consumers as likely to use IT for travel purposes as younger consumers?

4. Provide examples of how the use of technology can deliver both high-tech and high-touch outcomes.

5. What are the key elements of the Unified Theory of Acceptance and Use of Technology II (UTAUT II)? Provide your own tourism and technology example to illustrate the various components of this model.

6. What challenges do small and medium tourism enterprises (SMTEs) face in travel distribution? How might SMTEs respond to the increasingly complex structure of the digital tourism distribution system?

USEFUL WEBSITES

QR code	Website	Description
	American Society of Travel Agents (ASTA) http://www.asta.org/	ASTA is the leading global advocate for travel agents, the travel industry and the traveling public. Their website provides useful updates about travel distribution.
	Mygola http://www.mygola.com/	Mygola is an online trip-planning tool (see Case Study) and provides an innovative example of how a new startup can fill a niche in the digital tourism ecosystem.
	World Economic Forum Digital Ecosystems http://www.weforum.org/reports/digital-ecosystem-convergence-between-it-telecoms-media-and-entertainment-scenarios-2015/	The WEF Digital Ecosystems page provides scenarios and a video to explain the concept of a digital ecosystem.

Case Study: Mygola

Mygola (http://www.mygola.com/) is an online trip-planning tool that aims to answer three of the most common questions travelers ask: What should I see? How do I get there? What should I look out for? According to Mygola co-founder and CEO Anshuman Bapna, "travel planning is a long, leaky funnel" that crushes the joy of anticipation and makes planning a holiday hard work. The company claims that it can compress 6 weeks of itinerary planning into 15 minutes. Bapna claims that:

"Travel suffers from the blind-men-and-the-elephant problem. JetBlue knows when you're landing, AirBnB knows where you are staying and Viator knows which tour you are taking. If we can combine these elements into an itinerary that the traveler takes on their trip, we could become the gateway through which all online travel will get delivered. This could be the way to crack open the last bastion in online travel."

The company has created over 5000 curated itineraries sourced from sites like the *New York Times* and *Fodors* using custom text-mining software that parses travel articles, extracts the structure of a trip and guesses the path taken by the traveler. Bapna gives the following insight into how this software works:

"A traveler might say that she had 'sausages for breakfast in my camper van' and ended up 'in Wellington for a hearty meal'. Our algorithms would interpret that to mean that they reached Wellington for lunch, probably by driving, and then backtrack to figure out what place they might have been 5–6 hours ago at breakfast."

Travelers can use the default itineraries and travel circuits or they can "mix and match" to create a customized itinerary featuring information, reviews and tips using a "drag and drop" scheduling interface (see Fig. 2.10).

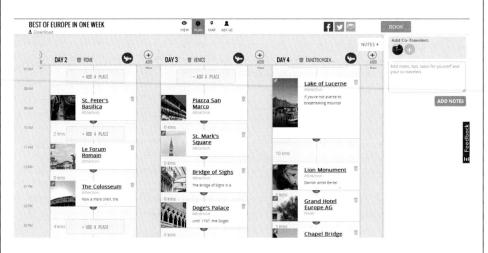

Fig. 2.10. An example of the Mygola itinerary planning tool.

(Continued)

Case Study. Continued.

Using a combination of data mining, algorithms and freelance curators, Mygola recommends feasible itineraries, commonly traveled circuits and scenic highlights. Once users have built their own customized trip the site uses crawling, indexing and ranking algorithms to source visually stunning creative-commons images and videos to match the itinerary. It also mines useful metadata about locations such as attraction opening hours, travel distances and tips from travelers to ensure the itinerary is feasible. Once the itinerary is finalized, Mygola provides a facility to book components of the trip in one place. For an overview, take a look at the following YouTube video: http://youtu.be/AlCnjNpmHhg/.

http://youtu.be/aicnjnpmhhg

The company collects user feedback through short popup polls to fine-tune the use of images and itinerary features. Users can also customize their itineraries by selecting interests (e.g. architecture, heritage, nature), which are fed back into the company's database, creating a rich "big data" source for refining the predictive power of the platform.

The approach adopted by Mygola illustrates concepts in this chapter. The site addresses an important stage in the decision-making process. Their efforts to understand trip planning behavior by observing, listening to and learning from travelers has resulted in an intuitive and user-friendly "drag and drop" interface. The company uses deep algorithms that mine unstructured data combined with thousands of human freelancers curating the data. From a technology acceptance perspective the tool requires very little effort and clearly provides a performance benefit by making the trip planning process more efficient. The stunning media-rich interface also appeals to the hedonic motivations of travelers. Mygola represents a new channel for planning and booking travel and occupies a new niche in the digital ecosystem.

Sources: Grant, 2013; Prabu, 2013; Mygola, 2014.

Study Questions

1. Visit the Mygola website at http://www.mygola.com/ and build an itinerary for a 3-day trip to New York. What features of the site do you like? Are there features you don't like? Use the UTAUT model to evaluate the site's features.
2. What niche does Mygola fill in the digital tourism ecosystem? Do you think there is a need for websites like Mygola?
3. What methods does Mygola use to understand the behavior of digital tourists?

REFERENCES

Ajzen, I. (1991) The theory of planned behavior. *Organizational Behavior and Human Decision Processes* 50(2), 179–211.
Anderson, V. and Johnson, L. (1997) *Systems Thinking Basics*. Pegasus Communications, Waltham, Massachusetts.

Arina, T. (2009) Digital Ecosystems. Available at: http://tarina.blogging.fi/concepts/digital-ecosystem/ (accessed 20 October 2014).

Bader, A., Baldauf, M., Leinert, S., Fleck, M. and Liebrich, A. (2012) *Mobile Tourism Services and Technology Acceptance in a Mature Domestic Tourism Market: the Case of Switzerland*. Springer-Verlag, Vienna.

Bagozzi, R.P. (2007) The legacy of the technology acceptance model and a proposal for a paradigm shift. *Journal of the Association for Information Systems* 8(4), 3.

Beldona, S. (2005) Cohort analysis of online travel information search behavior: 1995–2000. *Journal of Travel Research* 44(2), 135–142. doi: 10.1177/0047287505278995

Benckendorff, P., Moscardo, G. and Murphy, L. (2005) High tech versus high touch: visitor responses to the use of technology in tourist attractions. *Tourism Recreation Research* 30(3), 37–47.

Benckendorff, P., Moscardo, G. and Pendergast, D. (eds) (2010) *Tourism and Generation Y*. CAB International, Wallingford, UK.

Bonn, M.A., Furr, H.L. and Hausman, A. (2000) Employing Internet technology to investigate and purchase travel services: a comparison of X'ers, boomers, and mature market segments. *Tourism Analysis* 5(2/4), 137–143.

Brown, S.A. and Venkatesh, V. (2005) Model of adoption of technology in households: a baseline model test and extension incorporating household life cycle. *MIS Quarterly* 29(3), 399–426.

Buhalis, D. and Laws, E. (2001) *Tourism Distribution Channels: Practices, Issues and Transformations*. Continuum International Publishing Group, London.

Davis, F.D. (1989) Perceived usefulness, perceived ease of use, and user acceptance of information technology. *MIS Quarterly* 13(3), 319–340.

Fagan, M.H., Neill, S. and Wooldridge, B.R. (2003) An empirical investigation into the relationship between computer self-efficacy, anxiety, experience, support and usage. *Journal of Computer Information Systems* 44(2), 95.

Fishbein, M. and Ajzen, I. (1975) *Belief, Attitude, Intention, and Behavior: An Introduction to Theory and Research*. Addison-Wesley, Reading, Massachusetts.

Fotis, J., Buhalis, D. and Rossides, N. (2012) Social media use and impact during the holiday travel planning process. In: Fuchs, M., Ricci, F. and Cantoni, L. (eds) *Information and Communication Technologies in Tourism 2012*. Springer-Verlag, Vienna, pp. 13–24.

Geels, F.W. (2002) Technological transitions as evolutionary reconfiguration processes: a multi-level perspective and a case-study. *Research Policy* 31(8), 1257–1274.

Grant, R. (2013) Mygola could (at last) be the startup to make your travel planning dreams come true. *VentureBeat*. Available at: http://venturebeat.com/2013/10/17/mygola-could-at-last-be-the-startup-to-make-your-travel-planning-dreams-come-true/(accessed 20 October 2014).

Gretzel, U., Fesenmaier, D.R. and O'Leary, J.T. (2006) The transformation of consumer behaviour. In: Buhalis, D. and Costa, C. (eds) *Tourism Business Frontiers*. Elsevier, Burlington, Massachusetts, pp. 9–18.

Hackbarth, G., Grover, V. and Yi, M.Y. (2003) Computer playfulness and anxiety: positive and negative mediators of the system experience effect on perceived ease of use. *Information and Management* 40(3), 221–232.

Hashim, N.H., Murphy, J., Doina, O. and O'Connor, P. (2014) Bandwagon and leapfrog effects in Internet implementation. *International Journal of Hospitality Management* 37, 91–98.

Ho, C. and Liu, Y. (2005) An exploratory investigation of web-based tourist information search behavior. *Asia Pacific Journal of Tourism Research* 10(4), 351–360. doi: 10.1080/10941660500363645

Ho, C.I., Lin, M.H. and Chen, H.M. (2012) Web users' behavioural patterns of tourism information search: from online to offline. *Tourism Management* 33(6), 1468–1482. doi: http://dx.doi.org/10.1016/j.tourman.2012.01.016

Hyde, K.F. (2008) Information processing and touring planning theory. *Annals of Tourism Research* 35(3), 712–731. doi: http://dx.doi.org/10.1016/j.annals.2008.05.001

Iansiti, M. and Levien, R. (2004) Strategy as ecology. *Harvard Business Review* 82(3), 68–81.

Igbaria, M. and Parasuraman, S. (1989) A path analytic study of individual characteristics, computer anxiety and attitudes toward microcomputers. *Journal of Management* 15(3), 373–388.

Jacobsen, J.K.S. and Munar, A.M. (2012) Tourist information search and destination choice in a digital age. *Tourism Management Perspectives* 1(0), 39–47. doi: http://dx.doi.org/10.1016/j.tmp.2011.12.005

Jang, S.C. (2004) The past, present and future research of online information search. *Journal of Travel and Tourism Marketing* 17(2/3), 41–47. doi: 10.1300/J073v17n02_04

Kim, D.Y., Lehto, X.Y. and Morrison, A.M. (2007) Gender differences in online travel information search: Implications for marketing communications on the internet. *Tourism Management* 28(2), 423–433. doi: http://dx.doi.org/10.1016/j.tourman.2006.04.001

Kim, D.Y., Park, J. and Morrison, A.M. (2008) A model of traveller acceptance of mobile technology. *International Journal of Tourism Research* 10(5), 393–407.

Kracht, J. and Wang, Y.C. (2010) Examining the tourism distribution channel: evolution and transformation. *International Journal of Contemporary Hospitality Management* 22(5), 736–757. doi: 10.1108/09596111011053837

Lai, I.K. (2014) Traveler acceptance of an app-based mobile tour guide. *Journal of Hospitality and Tourism Research* Forthcoming.

Lansing, J.B. and Kish, L. (1957) Family life cycle as an independent variable. *American Sociological Review* 22(5), 512–519.

Litvin, S.W., Goldsmith, R.E. and Pan, B. (2008) Electronic word-of-mouth in hospitality and tourism management. *Tourism Management* 29(3), 458–468.

Lo, A., Cheung, C. and Law, R. (2002) Information search behavior of Hong Kong's inbound travelers - a comparison of business and leisure travelers. *Journal of Travel and Tourism Marketing* 13(3), 61–81. doi: 10.1300/J073v13n03_04

Luo, M., Feng, R.M. and Cai, L.A. (2004) Information search behavior and tourist characteristics: the internet vis-a-vis other information sources. *Journal of Travel and Tourism Marketing* 17(2/3), 15–25. doi: 10.1300/J073v17n02_02

Luo, M.M., Remus, W. and Sheldon, P.J. (2007) Technology acceptance of the Lonely Planet website: an exploratory study. *Information Technology and Tourism* 9(2), 67–78. doi: 10.3727/109830507781367429

Mannheim, K. (1952) The problem of generations. In: Mannheim, K. (ed.) *Essays on the Sociology of Knowledge*. Routledge and Kegal Paul, London, pp. 276–322.

Mygola (2014) Mygola. Available at: http://www.mygola.com/ (accessed 1 January 2014).

Naisbitt, J. (1982) *Megatrends: Ten New Directions Transforming Our Lives*. Warner, New York.

Noble, S.M. and Schewe, C.D. (2003) Cohort segmentation: an exploration of its validity. *Journal of Business Research* 56(12), 979–987.

Okazaki, S. and Hirose, M. (2009) Does gender affect media choice in travel information search? On the use of mobile Internet. *Tourism Management* 30(6), 794–804. doi: 10.1016/j.tourman.2008.12.012

Pan, B. and Fesenmaier, D.R. (2006) Online information search: vacation planning process. *Annals of Tourism Research* 33(3), 809–832. doi: 10.1016/j.annals.2006.03.006

Pan, B., Zhang, L.X. and Smith, K. (2011) A mixed-method study of user behavior and usability on an online travel agency. *Information Technology and Tourism* 13(4), 353–364. doi: 10.3727/1098305 12x13364362859975

Pearce, D.G. and Schott, C. (2005) Tourism distribution channels: the visitors' perspective. *Journal of Travel Research* 44(1), 50–63.

Pearce, D.G., Tan, R. and Schott, C. (2004) Tourism distribution channels in Wellington, New Zealand. *International Journal of Tourism Research* 6(6), 397–410.

Pearce, P.L. (2011) *Tourist Behaviour and the Contemporary World*, Vol. 51. Channel View Publications, Bristol, UK.

Pearce, P.L. and Gretzel, U. (2012) Tourism in technology dead zones: documenting experiential dimensions. *International Journal of Tourism Sciences* 12(2), 1–20.

Perez, C. (2002) *Technological Revolutions and Financial Capital: the Dynamics of Bubbles and Golden Ages*. Elgar, Cheltenham, UK.

Prabu, K. (2013) MyGola raises $1.5 million in bid to become top travel planning site. *Tnooz*. Available at: http://www.tnooz.com/article/mygola-raises-series-a-funding/ (accessed 26 December 2013).

Rogers, E.M. (1962) *Diffusion of Innovations*. Free Press of Glencoe, New York.

San Martín, H. and Herrero, Á. (2012) Influence of the user's psychological factors on the online purchase intention in rural tourism: integrating innovativeness to the UTAUT framework. *Tourism Management* 33(2), 341–350.

Schumpeter, J.A. (1934) *The Theory of Economic Development: An Inquiry into Profits, Capital, Credit, Interest, and the Business Cycle.* Harvard University Press, Cambridge, Massachusetts.

Tansley, A.G. (1935) The use and abuse of vegetational concepts and terms. *Ecology* 16(3), 284–307.

Tarkovskiy, O. (2013) General Gartner Research's Hype Cycle Diagram. Available at: http://en.wikipedia.org/wiki/File:Hype-Cycle-General.png (accessed 5 January 2014).

Venkatesh, V., Morris, M.G., Davis, G.B. and Davis, F.D. (2003) User acceptance of information technology: toward a unified view. *MIS Quarterly*, 425–478.

Venkatesh, V., Thong, J. and Xu, X. (2012) Consumer acceptance and use of information technology: extending the unified theory of acceptance and use of technology. *MIS Quarterly* 36(1), 157–178.

Vician, C. and Davis, L. (2003) Investigating computer anxiety and communication apprehension as performance antecedents in a computing-intensive learning environment. *Journal of Computer Information Systems* 43(2), 51–57.

Wheeler, B.C. (2002) NEBIC: a dynamic capabilities theory for assessing net-enablement. *Information Systems Research* 13(2), 125–146.

Wilfong, J.D. (2006) Computer anxiety and anger: the impact of computer use, computer experience, and self-efficacy beliefs. *Computers in Human Behavior* 22(6), 1001–1011.

World Economic Forum (Producer) (2007) Digital Ecosystem Convergence between IT, Telecoms, Media and Entertainment: Scenarios to 2015. Available at: http://www.weforum.org/reports/digital-ecosystem-convergence-between-it-telecoms-media-and-entertainment-scenarios-2015/ (accessed 17 October 2013).

Xiang, Z. and Gretzel, U. (2010) Role of social media in online travel information search. *Tourism Management* 31(2), 179–188. doi: 10.1016/j.tourman.2009.02.016

chapter 3

Travel Intermediaries and Information Technology

LEARNING OBJECTIVES

After studying this chapter you should be able to:

- explain the evolution, role and features of Global Distribution Systems (GDSs) as travel intermediaries;
- analyze the challenges faced by a GDS as a result of technological change and innovation;
- explain how traditional travel retailers use IT;
- explain how IT has led to disintermediation and evaluate how this has impacted travel intermediaries;
- describe and critically evaluate the different types of online travel intermediaries that have developed as a result of IT; and
- explain how tour operators can use IT to improve productivity and competitiveness.

INTRODUCTION

This chapter examines the application of IT to travel intermediaries. Travel intermediaries are firms who connect travel suppliers with customers. There are many different types of travel intermediaries in the travel distribution chain. In this chapter we will look in more detail at how IT has impacted GDSs, tour operators and wholesalers, traditional travel retailers, travel management companies, online intermediaries and channel managers. Chapter 2 explained all these types of intermediaries.

Travel intermediaries of all types use information intensely and IT plays an important role in managing this information. Real-time information on travel products, destinations, schedules, fares, rates and availabilities is critical to the services offered by intermediaries. Access to electronic information allows travel retailers to provide timely, accurate and efficient service. While some travel intermediaries have maintained a "bricks and mortar" presence, many have moved into online services and bookings. As a result, the tourism industry is a prime example of how IT can change an industry's structure. New technology-based intermediaries have altered the power of traditional intermediaries (Berne *et al.*, 2012). IT will continue to play a critical role in increasing the efficiency, productivity and market reach of travel intermediaries. This chapter discusses all of these IT applications, the hardware and software configurations, and their benefits and impacts.

GLOBAL DISTRIBUTION SYSTEMS

Global Distribution Systems (GDSs) play a crucial role as electronic intermediaries in the travel distribution system. GDSs enable suppliers to obtain bookings from markets they could not reach without GDS. They also assist travel retailers by aggregating and homogenizing supplier information and inventory and by providing a booking capability. It is useful to understand the history and evolution of these systems in order to appreciate the issues and challenges faced by GDSs. It is also important for travel professionals to understand the features of GDSs as well as the future developments likely to emerge.

Evolution of reservation systems

The reservation systems used by travel agents had their genesis in early **computer reservation systems (CRSs)** developed by airlines. Prior to the development of CRSs, airlines used manual methods to keep track of flight schedules, seat inventories and passenger information. These approaches required intermediaries to call an airline's booking center to confirm availability. The information was stored at a central booking center using wall charts, filing cabinets or a rotating system of index cards that could be visually inspected by a small team of operators to see whether flights were full (see Fig. 3.1).

By the early 1950s the aviation industry faced serious challenges in handling airline reservations. In 1953 Trans-Canada Airlines (TCA) designed a computer-based system called ReserVec. At the same time, American Airlines (AA) and International Business Machines (IBM) began a partnership to develop a computer system to handle airline reservations, ticketing, schedules, seat inventories and **passenger name records (PNRs)**. By 1964 the system, known as Semi-Automated Business Research Environment (SABRE), was rolled out to all AA ticketing offices (see Case Study). Other US airlines subsequently developed similar online reservation systems throughout the 1960s and early 1970s (see Fig. 3.2).

These new systems were used primarily by airline ticketing offices. Travel agents had to contact several airlines by phone for availability and price information, which was passed to the customer for confirmation. The agent then contacted the airline again to make a booking. This process took several days and seats were often sold out.

By the 1970s travel intermediaries requested access to CRS, but with each airline having its own reservation system, having a terminal for each was not practical. In 1975 the idea to create a single industry reservation system giving travel agents access to all major airlines' information was forwarded. This effort called the Joint Industry

Fig. 3.1. American Airlines advertisement *c*.1940s (Reproduced by permission of the copyright owner, American Airlines).

Computer Reservation System brought together the major carriers but the effort failed (Copeland and McKenney, 1998). Travicom, the world's first multi-airline distribution system, was created in 1976. In the same year Sabre and Apollo added other airlines to their systems and leased these to travel agents to book reservations directly. At this point a distinction appeared between **Computer Reservation Systems (CRSs)** and GDSs. CRSs were used by the airlines, while GDSs were used by travel intermediaries to access the inventory of multiple airlines.

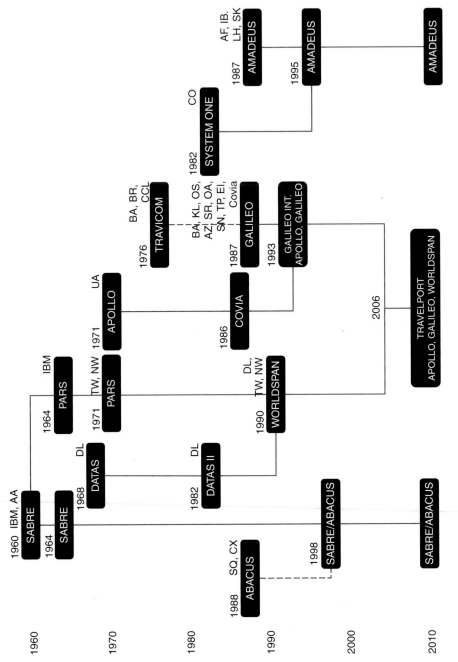

Fig. 3.2. The evolution of major global distribution systems.

By the 1980s US travel agents had a choice of five systems to automate their bookings. In 1987 a second European consortium of airlines established Amadeus and Galileo replaced Travicom. In Asia, Singapore Airlines and Cathay Pacific launched the Abacus system in 1988. By now, airlines included their inventory in multiple GDSs but the parent airlines displayed their own flights before others. For example, travel agents using the Sabre GDS would see AA flights on the first screen, even if more convenient or affordable flights were available from competitors. Legislation limited **screen bias** or **preferential display**. These developments resulted in airlines distancing themselves from the GDSs that they originally founded. The GDSs were restructured into separate companies or sold to other parties.

The 1990s saw the consolidation of GDSs. DATAS and PARS were merged in 1990 to create Worldspan. In 2006 and 2007 Galileo and Worldspan were acquired by a new company called Travelport. Today the three major GDSs (Galileo, Amadeus and Travelport) compete globally, while Abacus has a strong presence in Asia-Pacific (see Table 3.1) and the state-owned TravelSky (founded in 2000) is a major channel in China. It should be noted that a number of smaller technology companies have also designed reservation systems that are used by some airlines, including low-cost carriers. Some airlines do not participate in the major GDSs and instead operate their own proprietary systems. Costs are involved for each supplier to be listed on the GDS. Therefore, even though most travel sectors can be booked through the GDS the smaller, lower-priced travel products tend to be under-represented, whereas the larger suppliers are well represented.

More comprehensive destination information systems are being developed by tourism offices to fill that gap by representing all the destination's facilities. These will be discussed in Chapter 11.

The development of the Internet in the mid-1990s also created opportunities for GDSs to partner with other technology providers to create **online travel agents (OTAs)**, which in some cases completely bypassed traditional travel intermediaries. It did not take long for some entrepreneurs to develop **meta-search engines** that consolidated the search results of major GDSs and OTAs. The major GDSs have also created their own online end-user brands, which sell travel inventory direct to travelers.

Most airlines and hotels have adopted a strategy of **direct selling** to their customers by investing in their own reservations and distribution systems and reducing their dependency on GDSs. Many airlines that originally founded the major GDSs are now in conflict with GDS vendors. This conflict has come about because the direct booking systems set up by airlines on their own websites make them less reliant on GDSs to sell airline seats. The GDSs make their revenue from charging the airlines fees (typically US$5–12) for each booking, but a transaction through an airline's own website can cost the carrier as little as US$1 (Perkins, 2012). In addition, when bookings are made through an airline website the airline has "control" of the customer, allowing it to build a relationship or sell additional services and bundles more easily.

Legacy GDSs are also facing increasing competition from new entrants into the travel distribution space. **GDS New Entrants (GNEs)** such as Farelogix have taken advantage of new technologies and open systems

Table 3.1. Characteristics of major GDSs (Source: Abacus, 2014; Amadeus, 2014; Sabre Holdings, 2014; Travelport, 2014).

GDS	Founded	Founders	Market share	Locations
Sabre	1960	American Airlines	30%	56,000 travel agency locations. Global presence, strong in US and Asia Pacific
Amadeus	1987	Air France, Lufthansa, Iberia and SAS	39%	104,000 travel agency locations. Mainly Western Europe, Middle East and Asia Pacific
Abacus	1988	Singapore Airlines and Cathay Pacific	5%	20,000 travel agency locations. Mainly Asia-Pacific
Travelport	2006	Merger of Galileo and Worldspan	26%	67,000 travel agency locations. Global presence, strong in US and Western Europe
Worldspan	1990	United Airlines		
Galileo	1987	Nine major European airlines		
Apollo	1971	Delta, TWA and NW Airlines		

architecture to aggregate content and data from multiple GDSs. The International Air Transport Association (IATA) has also led a project called the **New Distribution Capability (NDC)**, which aims to provide new standards and protocols for airline reservations. Most recently, major technology companies such as Google have moved into the travel distribution space with products such as Google Flights and Hotel Search. Social networks such as Facebook have also provided tools to inspire and sell travel products to potential travelers. As a result, modern technology advancement and changes in business models have substantially weakened the power of traditional GDSs in the travel distribution system.

Global distribution system functions

GDS vendors offer a broad suite of products and services aimed at all stakeholders in the travel distribution chain. The following section discusses those used by travel intermediaries and describes how GDSs have diversified to other travel providers.

Core GDS functions

The main purpose of a GDS is to provide travel intermediaries with a central hub for accessing schedules, fares, availability and bookings. These core functions include:

- **Availability**: a GDS aggregates available inventory from many CRSs and displays available options in a standard format for searching and comparison. Hotels show different room types, features and maximum occupancy. Airlines provide information about the availability and pricing of seats in different classes.
- **Booking requests**: the GDS infrastructure supports an enormous volume of requests and transactions 24 hours a day, 7 days a week. Once the availability of a product is confirmed, the consultant makes a booking request. The request is transmitted to the GDS and is either processed directly by the GDS servers, or forwarded to the server of the appropriate supplier's CRS. Seat maps can be displayed on screen to assist with seat selection.
- **Passenger information**: each reservation has passenger information attached to it in the form of a **Passenger Name Record (PNR)**. This contains the passenger's name, address, phone number, payment details, ticketing deadlines, frequent flyer number (if appropriate) and seat preferences (e.g. aisle or window). Other requests such as special meals (e.g. vegetarian, kosher, diabetic), wheelchair requests, and assistance for unaccompanied minors are stored with the PNR. The communication history is part of the PNR, including agent's special remarks. The PNR connects with the airline's frequent flyer database.

- **Rates and conditions**: ARS contain large databases of fares and rules for each class of service. Reservation and payment deadlines, deposits, cancellation policies and blackout dates are stored for each rate. Rates and fares are determined by revenue management systems that run on separate computers outside the GDS environment.
- **E-ticketing and itinerary management**: in the past, travel consultants were required to issue paper tickets to travelers, but e-ticketing has removed this requirement. However, traditional travel retailers and travel management companies (TMCs) will produce a summary of all of the traveler's bookings.

GDSs also facilitate the sale of **interline tickets**, which allow passengers to travel on multiple carriers within the same itinerary (e.g. a multi-sector flight first on Singapore Airlines and then on Lufthansa). Passengers' ability to check baggage on the whole itinerary depends on airline alliances. Interline tickets are simpler if the carriers are part of an alliance such as Oneworld, Skyteam or Star Alliance or if there is a bilateral partnership between two carriers. The GDSs keep track of these alliances and support multi-carrier itineraries and fares.

Secondary functions

GDSs have added more IT tools to streamline the workflow of travel consultants by managing the complexities of multiple suppliers, many time zones and many currencies. GDS vendors offer a suite of solutions, including some or all of the following:

- **Booking ancillary services**: the GDSs allow travelers to book ancillary services such as car rentals, transfers, rail, cruises, tour packages, entertainment and foreign currency in addition to flights.

- **Passenger document requirements**: provides information on visas and passports, health, customs, currency controls and departure taxes.
- **Integrated travel management**: back-office systems that integrate with the GDS to reduce redundant data entry and automate manual tasks.
- **Decision support systems**: tools that integrate information to generate financial and operational reports and analyses to support decision-making.
- **Financial management**: solutions that support commission management, general ledger, currency conversion, invoicing, accounts payable and accounts receivable.
- **E-commerce tools**: tools that provide retailers with the ability to access, market and sell content across all channels. They improve workflow, profitability and customer service.
- **Corporate travel management**: tools to manage corporate client activities such as travel policies or entitlements, personal preferences and risk.
- **Communication and scheduling**: communication and scheduling tools such as calendars, email, fax, SMS and social media. Some integrate with search tools so that travel consultants can email trip options to clients.

GDSs realize that they cannot rely on only providing services to travel retailers. They have developed revenue streams by offering IT solutions to travel suppliers also as shown in Table 3.2.

Airline seats still represent the majority of bookings through a GDS. Other products such as cruises and tour packages tend to be booked less through a GDS because of their complexity, the need for more detailed information, and because agents are not so confident to electronically book them.

Information technology infrastructure

GDSs are supported by some of the largest **data centers** in the world and are the central hub for processing the billions of transactions each day, operating 24/7. Any interruption can bring the travel industry to its knees. Systems and processes exist to manage risk, avoid system failure and protect customer data. GDS data centers are protected by perimeter fencing, CCTV cameras, high-tech intrusion detection and 24-hour manned security patrols. In some cases they are in secure underground facilities. The centers are powered by primary and secondary (backup) electricity feeds. Large quantities of diesel are stored on site to power generators in the event of power failure. For example, the Worldspan Data Center in Denver, Colorado stores enough fuel for 6 days, and others have independent backup diesel generators housed in separate buildings. Battery rooms provide power to bridge the gap between a power failure and activating diesel generators.

Inside the data center, servers are in separate rooms so that data processing continues in the event of damage to one room (see Amadeus Industry Insight). Rooms are equipped with surveillance and entry authentication, CCTV monitoring of all entrances, cooling systems and sophisticated fire suppression systems. The computer hardware systems are designed with double redundancy, meaning that all of the systems are replicated so that a backup system is available in the event of failure. Some centers operate a triple redundancy model.

Table 3.2. GDS-owned IT solutions.

Service	Sabre	Amadeus	Travelport
GDS interface	Sabre Red Workspace	Amadeus Selling Platform	Smartpoint, Universal Desktop
Back-office solutions	Sabre Red Suite	–	–
TMC solutions	Sabre Red Suite	Amadeus One Travel Portal	Smartpoint, Universal Desktop
Portable devices	TripCase	Amadeus Mobile Solutions	Mobile Agent; ViewTrip Mobile
Online corporate sites	GetThere Travelocity Business	Amadeus e-Travel Management	Traversa Orbitz for Business
Online consumer sites	Travelocity, World Choice Travel, lastminute, Zuji	Opodo	Orbitz, eBookers, HotelClub, RatesToGo, CheapTickets
Itinerary management	VirtuallyThere TripCase	CheckMyTrip	ViewTrip
Aviation	Sabre AirCommerce	Altéa Suite	Interchange Suite
Car rental	Sabre Cars	Amadeus Cars	CarMaster
Hotels	SynXis CRS	LinkHotel	Galileo RoomMaster; Worldspan Hotel Select
Cruises	Sabre Cruises	Amadeus Cruise Data Cache, e-Cruise	Travelport Cruise and Tour
Rail	Sabre Rail	Reservation Track	Travelport Rail Distribution
Travel insurance	Travel Protection	Amadeus Insurance	–
Tour packages	Sabre Vacations	Amadeus Travel Packaging	Travelport Cruise and Tour

Industry Insights: Amadeus Data Centre

The Amadeus Data Centre (Fig. 3.3) is located at Erding, near Munich in Germany and is the largest privately owned data processing center in Europe. The center houses petabytes of storage and processes over 1 billion transactions per day with a response time of less than 3 milliseconds.

The data center itself is an impressive building with 1 meter thick reinforced external walls that contain 30,000 cubic meters of concrete and 3500 tonnes of steel. External doors are 50 centimeters thick and made of solid steel. Amadeus has a duplicate disaster recovery center in Munich in case anything happens to the main site. Both centers cost €500 million to build.

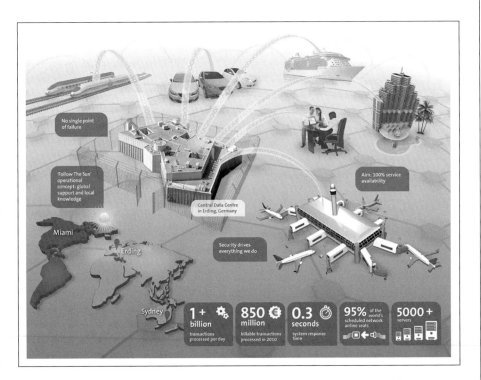

Fig. 3.3. Amadeus Data Centre at Erding (Reproduced by permission of the copyright owner, Amadeus IT Group, S.A. and further reproduction or publication without the express permission of Amadeus is prohibited).

Inside the center there are three "fire cell" rooms and six server rooms with nine diesel power generators in four separate locations. The six secure rooms containing the servers are separated from the outside world by five secure zones. The center is powered by four

(Continued)

Continued.

uninterrupted electricity supply systems. Supplying power to the building costs Amadeus over €4 million per year.

Smaller data centers in Miami and Sydney serve local markets. The company operates a "follow the sun" concept to maintain 24/7 operability; at the end of each day control of the center is handed over to staff in Miami, who in turn hand over responsibility to staff in Sydney to run the center remotely.

http://youtu.be/xOeRdvOB vy

These remarkable statistics illustrate just how far GDSs have evolved from the days of wall charts and punched card systems and highlight the significant investment in infrastructure and hardware. For more information see: http://youtu.be/xOeRdvOBvyg/.

Connections and interfaces

Travel consultants interact with a GDS using a **Graphical User Interface (GUI)**. GDS user interfaces were traditionally command-driven using formats and codes to request information (see Fig. 3.4). Command-driven "green screen" or "cryptic entry" systems are faster for trained users and so are still used. However, "point and click" GUIs require less training and increase productivity by reducing the number of keystrokes and time required for transactions (see Fig. 3.5 for an example). Modern windows-based operating systems also allow consultants to move between applications, PNRs or functions more easily, and are generally more user friendly for multi-tasking.

As information moves from the GDS to other systems, an **Application Programming Interface (API)** specifies how software components of different systems interact (see Fig. 3.6). An API includes specifications for routines, data structures, object classes and variables and is needed due to a lack of standardized protocols between different travel systems. A language-neutral message format such as **Extensible Markup Language (XML)** is needed as a bridge for the message exchange. The New Distribution Capability (NDC) being developed by IATA provides a set of XML specifications for the exchange of travel information.

The future of global distribution systems

New companies emerged in the late 1990s and early 2000s as alternatives to the GDSs. These **GDS New Entrants (GNEs)** include Farelogix, ITA Software, Triton and G2 Switchworks. GNEs took advantage of the opportunity to lower prices when GDSs renegotiated contracts with suppliers and retailers. GNEs exploit innovative technologies and open architecture to connect systems. Farelogix enables travel retailers to aggregate and manage content from multiple sources, including GDSs, the Internet and direct connections to suppliers' CRSs. It is a bridging solution for retailers to source inventory from multiple channels, and also offers direct

```
112MAYLCAATH«
12MAY TUE LCA/Z‡2 ATH/‡0
1CY 322 J7 C7 D7 I7 Z4 Y7*LCAATH 0700 0845 319 S 0 123 DCA /E
        B7 N7 S7 M7 T7 W7 L7 X7
2A3 903 C4 D4 Z0 A0 I0 J0*LCAATH 0830 1010 321 B 0 DC /E
        Y4 B4 M4 K4 W4 S4 H4 L4
```

Fig. 3.4. Traditional GDS "Green Screen" command line display.

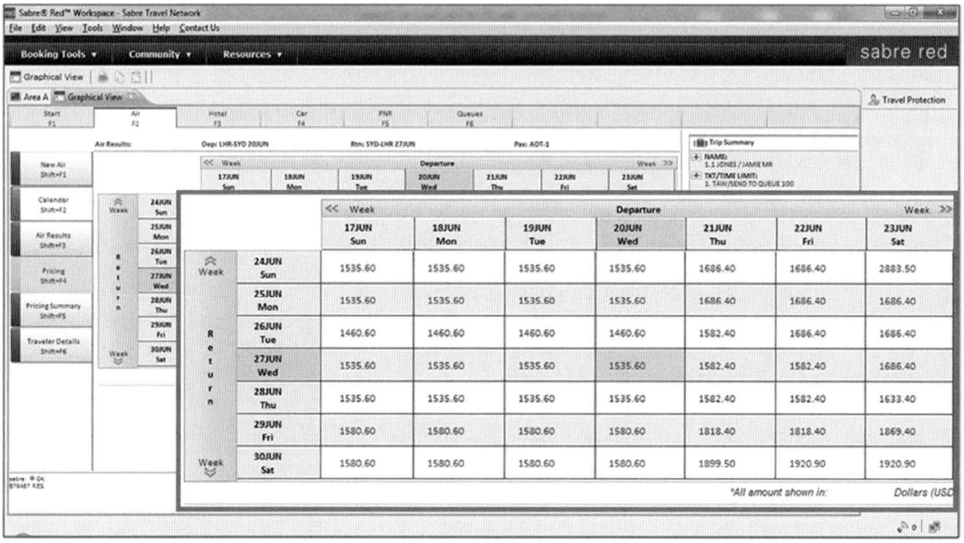

Fig. 3.5. Sabre Red Graphical Workspace (Reproduced by permission of the copyright owner, Sabre Holdings).

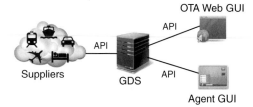

Fig. 3.6. GDS interfaces.

connectivity to some airlines, making it an alternative to GDSs (Sismanidou *et al.*, 2009).

Some GNEs have been acquired by other intermediaries including established GDSs. Travelport purchased some technology patents developed by G2 Switchworks, while ITA Software was purchased by Google to power Flight Search but provides distribution solutions for airlines and retailers. Some GDSs have responded to the threat of GNEs by buying these startup companies to acquire their technology. More than a decade after GNEs first emerged most travel retailers still rely on at least one GDS. The discussion thus far has highlighted characteristics and issues associated with GDSs. Table 3.3 provides a

SWOT analysis allowing us to draw conclusions about the future directions of GDSs.

The SWOT analysis highlights how GDSs might best position themselves to be successful (Alford, 2006). Future developments may result in GDSs acquiring GNEs and other intermediaries to protect their market dominance. GDSs will also continue to diversify into back-office systems and marketing and service companies for a broader range of travel industry sectors (Carroll and Siguaw, 2003). Travelport has developed a *Universal Desktop* that allows travel agents to book products across multiple channels

Table 3.3. A SWOT analysis of GDSs.

	Positive	**Negative**
Internal	Strengths	Weaknesses
	Market power. GDSs have greater buying power and allow suppliers to reach a much larger market. **Homogenized content**. Intermediaries can compare multiple suppliers in a standard format. **Interline bookings**. GDSs have the best market reach and coverage to enable interline bookings. **Back-office integration**. A range of ancillary and back-office tools. **Client loyalty**. Travel retailers are reluctant to change to another GDS.	**Legacy-based systems**. Old technology designed to sell standard airline seats rather than the range of products and ancillary services available today. **Connectivity**. While connectivity continues to improve, the lack of standard protocols hampers efforts to include some products in the GDSs. **Pricing innovation**. More flexible pricing and contract options for a wider range of suppliers.
External	Opportunities	Threats
	New suppliers. New connectivity with other sectors such as rail. **New clients**. IT solutions for new industry users such as airports, hotels, OTAs. **Dynamic packaging**. More sophisticated approaches to dynamic packaging, such as those used by OTAs. **Interoperability**. Collaboration between GDSs to improve connectivity between systems.	**GDS new entrants (GNEs)**. Use of new platforms such as XML and standard APIs may offer better connectivity and more innovative features. **Open systems**. IATAs NDC will reduce barriers to new entrants and may pose a threat if GDSs are unable or unwilling to work with new standards. **Direct bookings**. Suppliers who bypass the GDSs altogether.

using a single interface. Some GDSs have created B2B platforms similar to the Apple iTunes App Store where travel retailers can download proprietary and third-party apps to extend core GDS functionality. Examples include the Travelport Marketplace, Amadeus Partner Network and Sabre's Red App Center.

These developments signal six major trends in travel distribution:

1. Diversifying IT solutions: rather than just aggregating inventory from a range of suppliers, GDSs are viewing these suppliers as clients. The GDSs are developing IT solutions for travel retailers, airlines, rail, airports, hotels and other travel industry suppliers. Back-office integration is an incentive for retailers to remain with a GDS.

2. Consolidation: GDSs will continue to acquire smaller travel technology startups to protect their market share, resulting in a portfolio of brands and channels targeted at particular markets. This will continue the horizontal and vertical integration of travel distribution and will provide a variety of end-to-end distribution pathways between suppliers and travelers, creating opportunities to integrate data and systems.

3. Connectivity and interoperability: systems are increasingly integrated and interconnected. Metasearch engines, GNEs, the NDC and the Travelport Universal Desktop indicate the potential of connecting channels, databases and reservation systems to simplify the booking process. Uniform technical standards and open architecture will create streamlined communication between suppliers and distributors. Despite privacy concerns, traveler data will be harnessed to understand booking behavior and prefer-

ences thereby providing improved service to travelers.

4. Transparency: travel products are increasingly complex, and often include ancillary options, taxes and fees. GDSs are developing systems to display pricing information more transparently.

5. Personalization: direct bookings, the NDC and booking engines embedded in social networks and travel review sites provide opportunities to personalize the booking process. Both traditional and online travel agents will offer more flexible options to travelers and will provide support for travelers at the destination.

6. Social, Local and Mobile (SoLoMo): OTAs and GDSs are delivering booking capabilities across a range of platforms, including mobile devices. Apps have been developed for smartphones, tablets and a range of wearable technologies allowing travel retailers to sell products to travelers on location. Access to advice from "local experts" and friends who have previously visited a destination add to these capabilities.

These developments will continue to reshape the distribution of travel products. As long as GDSs provide value to suppliers and distributors they will continue to play a central role in the distribution system.

TOUR OPERATORS

Tour operators both design and package tours, which they then sell through the travel distribution system, making them both suppliers and intermediaries. Because they make bulk reservations they are sometimes regarded as wholesalers. They require access to GDSs to book tour components, but they use IT to perform other functions. Third party and GDS vendors offer tour operator software packages, which include package creation software, systems to help in the distribution of packages, and systems to handle reservations and customer management. Some operators also use spreadsheets, relational databases and financial packages to perform some of these added functions.

Package creation

The creation of a tour package involves the identification of travel products and their combination into a tour. IT can assist by facilitating negotiations with destination suppliers to reduce rates based on volume. Email, file transfers or videoconferencing make the negotiation process smoother and less costly, but must be combined with site visits for familiarity with the destination and its facilities.

Software vendors provide solutions to create and distribute customized tour itineraries and packages. The most sophisticated IT solutions include end-to-end tour management including itinerary creation, pricing, distribution, booking, supplier and customer documentation and profit and loss reports. Such software must cost the tour components and the entire tour, and do sensitivity analysis. It must also handle the tour inventory, each tour itinerary, and group tour quotes for special groups.

Tour package distribution

Tour packages are marketed using brochures or online media such as PDF documents or videos. Desktop publishing software can create hardcopy and electronic brochures. Software tools such as Microsoft Publisher are easy to use, and desktop publishing software such as Adobe Photoshop and Adobe Illustrator are favored by graphic designers. Printed bro-chures are costly and so electronic documents and web content are more common.

Many tour operators place their inventory on a GDS to facilitate bookings from wholesalers and travel retailers, or on the World Wide Web to distribute product information. More sophisticated websites include booking engines for travelers to book directly with the tour operator. Some operators have a social media presence and use this to promote new packages and build a more personal relationship with travelers. The creation of sites such as YouTube and video editing software for novice users means tour operators can produce and share their own video content.

Reservations and customer management

Tour operators need computers to handle reservations and payments at two levels: (i) to handle the outgoing reservations for tour components; and (ii) to handle incoming reservations from travelers for their own tour packages. To make block reservations and payments with the component suppliers, a GDS terminal may be used, particularly for air reservations. Some GDSs provide **Reverse Access**, which allows the tour operator to retrieve flight information and availability and create PNRs and advance seat reservations (Weber, 1995).

Reservations for their tour packages require an internal CRS, which can either be designed in-house or purchased from a third-party vendor. This database contains information on tour availability, descriptions of tour itineraries and components, payment and booking deadlines, costs, travel agent commissions, credit card processing and customer profiles. The system should also contain a yield management function and a multilingual and multi-currency support module. Some tour operator software permits the reservationists to switch between the GDS and their own reservation system, or in a windows environment, to view both.

Many tour operators offer independent tours with modular components allowing customers to construct their own tour from an array of accommodation, event and flight options. This requires a more flexible reservation system; instead of an inventory of tours, an inventory of tour components is needed for selection and combination into packages. The reservation software must allow the easy building of a tour and the ability to modify independent selections when necessary (Weber, 1995). Tour operator CRS should also interface with the GDS so that travel agents can transmit bookings to their in-house reservation systems.

TRADITIONAL TRAVEL RETAILERS

In this section, we will explore how traditional travel retailers use IT and how they have responded to changes in the IT landscape by discussing retailer use of GDSs, back-office systems and the impact of new technologies on the structure of the industry.

Front-office systems

Front-office systems support direct interaction with customers. Most front-office IT applications reside in the reservation system or GDS, although the World Wide Web and email systems might also be considered front-office IT tools (see Chapter 4). GDS systems are no longer just channels for accessing travel inventory; they also provide travel agents with IT solutions and services. A travel retailer's choice of GDS should consider many factors. Although GDSs share common features, there are variations in the product and in the contract. The goal of most agencies is to access the widest range of inventory and channels, the most flexible contract at the lowest cost, and support for service and training.

Travel consultants need access to comprehensive and unbiased information in order to customize itineraries. Screen bias has been addressed through legislative changes, but there are still differences in the amount of detail consultants can access for suppliers, creating a "halo effect", which increases bookings to some carriers and reduces bookings to others. Some supplier websites and GNEs allow consultants to personalize the journey by purchasing extra legroom, in-flight meals and baggage allowance but legacy systems tend not to. This is important because travel retailers compete directly with supplier websites. If travelers can customize their booking at a cheaper price than a travel consultant, this creates competitive pressure for travel retailers. This in turn pressures the GDSs to provide travel agencies with greater comparison capabilities and price transparency. In a nutshell, travel consultants want a system with all the information and features in one application so they can deliver quicker and more relevant customer service. The NDC is addressing this and the extent GDSs adopt the NDC standards will affect travel agent selection in the future.

Another factor influencing system choice is the level of connectivity the GDS has with other travel computer systems. Travel agents prefer a GDS to provide connectivity to as many suppliers as possible. Direct access links between reservation systems create quicker communication, faster confirmations and access to last seat/room availability with non-vendor airlines and hotels. Travel consultants can look and book directly with a wider range of suppliers, giving them more complete information. This is important for accessing independent or boutique hotels and low-cost carriers, which are often not represented in the GDSs.

The next consideration in choosing a system is the contract the retailer must sign with the GDS vendor. GDS contracts were originally very restrictive on travel retailers and were referred to as the "golden hand-cuff". The term refers to the very tight clauses and penalties which left travel agents feeling "handcuffed" to the vendor while "golden" refers to the benefits gained by signing these contracts. Since most GDSs no longer provide hardware, it is easier for retailers to switch to another system by simply changing their software. As a result, the GDSs now provide flex-ible 3–5 year contracts and financial rewards based on the volume of business generated. For example, Sabre offers a 3-year contract with no fees or a month-by-month option with monthly fees. Rather than locking retailers into their system with contracts, GDSs provide added benefits to entice retailers. Back-office systems are discussed in the next section.

The level of training and support pro-vided by the GDS vendor is also important. Support for software and hardware problems is provided by toll-free help desks that assist with troubleshooting. Most GDSs also offer online FAQs and support sites. Travelport's Galileo and Worldspan are supported by a national service company designated by the GDS vendor to service travel agents world-wide. Training is provided online or centrally or locally. The training included in the con-tract is important, however new GUI applica-tions require little training.

Another issue for multinational travel agencies is whether the GDS vendor per-mits their international branches to access and/or change PNRs created by a branch in another country. As travel agency merg-ers cross international borders, this is an important consideration. Fortunately the consolidation of GDS vendors and legisla-tive changes around privacy laws in North America, Europe and Australia has vastly improved global access to GDSs.

Back-office systems

Back-office Systems (BOS) automate back-office functions and relieve employees from tedious accounting and reporting functions, and release staff time to service clients. These functions include:

1. Accounting systems: enable travel retailers to store transaction information for reports such as financial statements, sales reports, customer receipts and invoices, taxation, payment settlement, accounts pay-able, accounts receivable and general ledger. Examples include TravCom and Trams Back Office.

2. Human resource systems: systems auto-mate the tracking of employee data such as personal histories, skills, capabilities, train-ing, performance, scheduling, leave and payroll.

3. Customer relationship management (CRM): a relational database, which captures client information and manages marketing efforts and frequent traveler programs.

4. Communication: software applications such as email and word processors communicate with suppliers, customers and other partners.

5. Commission tracking: to track and analyze commissions on bookings and to report commissions due to each agent.

6. Transaction settlement: the settlement of ticket transactions between suppliers, travel agencies and travel management companies is managed by IATAs Billing Settlement Plan (BSP) or by the Airline Reporting Corporation (ARC) in the US.

BOS are available from both GDS and third-party vendors. GDSs provide a queuing function that queues messages to an agent's GDS workstation. These queues identify tasks to be worked on by the agent. Another useful GDS feature is custom scripts, which store a sequence of commands so that often-used research and booking functions can be performed more quickly.

Back-office functions can be integrated into cross-functional systems known as **Enterprise Resource Planning (ERP)** systems. These systems give large travel retailers an integrated real-time view of core business operations by tracking financial and human resources. Popular systems include the Sabre Red Suite, Abacus Powersuite, CentralCommand, Trabacus and Travel IntraNet Application (TINA). ERP systems create benefits as follows:

- **Productivity**: automating workflow and reducing data entry between systems diminishes the need for manual data entry, which in turn reduces errors;
- **Reporting**: reporting tools help a travel retailer to develop targeted marketing programs based on historical data and to identify unpaid commissions and fees;

- **Customer satisfaction**: an integrated system supports rapid, detailed and accurate reporting to support customer expectations;
- **Supplier relationships**: tracking of supplier contacts, commissions, products, prices and contracts; and
- **Forecasting**: trend analysis allows a travel retailer to forecast trends based on real-time data.

Information required for back-office functions must interface with the PNRs stored in the host GDSs. To accomplish this, the PNRs must be formatted and transferred to the back-office system of third-party ERP vendors and their own. GDS vendors install most back-office systems, and a travel agency is likely to install the back-office system from their GDS vendor (Godwin, 1987).

Hardware and networking

The hardware configuration appropriate for a travel retailer depends on the size and strategic focus of the business. However, the hardware configuration for traditional retailers includes a **local area network (LAN)** of workstations that communicate with the wider Internet (see Fig. 3.7).

The hardware components include workstations linked to a server, modem, router and hub or switch as shown in Fig. 3.7. Multifunction devices with printing, copying, scanning and fax capabilities are also connected to the LAN. A router is needed if there are multiple wired and wireless devices in the network. This consolidates the messages from each workstation so they can all be transmitted through the modem. A hub or switch is used to connect wired workstations, servers and printers so that they can communicate with each other and the Internet.

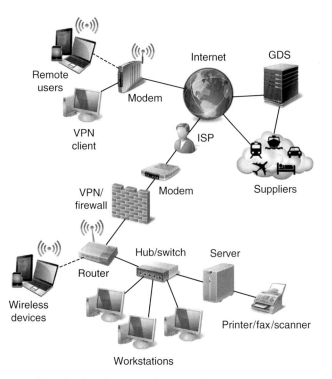

Fig. 3.7. Simple travel retailer hardware and network.

Many travel retailers operate as part of a franchise or a larger chain. The hardware therefore needs to allow communication between outlets of the same brand. A company **intranet**, which is protected from unauthorized access by a **firewall**, allows retailers to share documents and data across multiple outlets. Similarly, retailers access **extranets** when working with travel producers, suppliers and partners to generate packages, itineraries and financial reports. Remote users (i.e. suppliers, partners or employees) who access intranet or extranet resources authenticate through the firewall with a **virtual private network (VPN)**.

The future of traditional travel retailers

The continued viability of traditional travel retailers has been questioned, given the technological developments and structural changes in the industry. The rapid growth of OTAs and direct Internet booking engines has had a profound impact on travel distribution. This process of **disintermediation** has threatened traditional travel agents.

At the same time, starting in the US, airlines started **decommissioning**. Travel agent commissions were first capped, but as technology evolved airlines no longer needed travel agents. Led by the low-cost carriers, airlines reduced or abolished commissions and instead invested in their websites. This was a major problem for travel retailers because commissions represented their main revenue source. Hotel chains soon followed and by early 2000 the death of traditional travel retailers was predicted.

But there still are many successful travel retailers 20 years after the first OTAs. Like

Lazarus rising from the dead, they reinvented themselves to compete in the new online travel world. To understand why they survived let us consider the strategic advantages and disadvantages of traditional travel agents. Table 3.4 provides a SWOT analysis of traditional travel retailers.

The SWOT analysis indicates that traditional travel agents have advantages. For complex trips the online searching and booking process is time consuming and costly, so using a travel consultant can save time and money (Anckar and Walden, 2001). Consumers researching trips on the Internet still may use a travel agent to verify the information and

Table 3.4. A SWOT analysis of traditional travel intermediaries.

	Positive	Negative
Internal	Strengths	Weaknesses
	Time. Agents save customers time and effort. **Cost**. Some agents have special agreements with travel suppliers and can access products at discounted or wholesale rates. **Expertise**. Travel consultants provide local knowledge and advice and are knowledgeable about terms and conditions for bookings. **Security**. There is someone to contact if something goes wrong. **Packaging**. Travel agents can negotiate better deals for complex itineraries. **Value adding**. Agents can access ancillary products such as insurance, ground transfers and VIP offers. **Personalization**. Agents provide a personal touch by learning about your preferences and customizing an itinerary to suit your needs. **Special needs**. An agent can make arrangements for infants, children, elderly and disabled travelers.	**Cost**. With fewer commissions, agents may charge service or booking fees and cancellation fees. **Bias**. Agreements between agents and suppliers mean that they may not be impartial. **Errors**. Agents make mistakes – if you book your own trip and make an error you have only yourself to blame. **Less choice**. For reasons of bias and customization, agents may present travelers with less choice than online alternatives. **Less transparency**. Pricing information and comparisons can be less transparent than online. **Less control**. Travelers have less control over product features when agents make selections. **High fixed costs**. Increasing costs in real estate, personnel and overheads. **Limited opening hours**. Agents are normally open during normal business hours.

(Continued)

Table 3.4. Continued.

	Positive	Negative
External	Opportunities	Threats
	Emerging markets. Changes in the marketplace result in new products, destinations and niche markets in which agents can specialize (e.g. corporate travel, developing countries). **Hybrid models**. "Clicks and mortar" retail models, which blend online services with a high street presence are emerging. **Consolidation**. Horizontal and vertical integration reduces competition and creates new efficiencies and opportunities.	**Decommissioning**. Ongoing pressure from suppliers to reduce commissions and drive bookings through their own direct channels. **Digital competitors**. Online competitors and mobile apps continue to threaten agents. **Public perceptions**. Negative public perceptions of traditional travel agents. **Failure to attract talent**. Other sectors have been more successful at attracting good talent. **Lack of investment**. Investors have focused on Internet startups rather than traditional agents.

book. Through special agreements and access to wholesale products, travel consultants can provide cheaper travel options than those booked through the Internet. Travel consultants are also more knowledgeable about the travel industry and destinations (Dolnicar and Laesser, 2007).

Successful travel retailers have built on these strengths, while addressing the weaknesses. Some are exploiting opportunities and limiting the risks associated with threats. For example, some traditional travel retailers offer services to consumers on the Internet, significantly increasing their geographic reach. In some cases traditional retailers have acquired online businesses and other intermediaries to expand their portfolio of services (see Industry Insight).

Agents want to know what information their clients are accessing themselves, and are training staff to use the Internet as a research tool. Some have also refocused their efforts on business travelers who are less likely to book their own travel. Another approach specializes in products that are risky for travelers to book alone, such as high-cost trips and travel to less developed destinations. Other retailers become destination specialists. The Internet has empowered a special category of travel retailers known as home-based travel agents. IT connects these agents to host agencies and customers (Bowden, 2007). In summary, traditional travel intermediaries must continuously redefine themselves as OTAs develop innovative solutions for travelers booking online.

Industry Insights: Flight Centre

The Flight Centre Travel Group is Australia's largest travel company. Founded in 1981 by Graham "Skroo" Turner, the company has over 2500 stores in more than 11 countries. The company grew rapidly when other travel retailers were collapsing as a result of online travel agents and direct bookings. Flight Centre avoided the same fate by establishing or acquiring the following brands in the travel distribution chain:

- **Leisure Travel:** Flight Centre, Liberty Travel, Escape Travel, Travel Associates, Round the World Experts;
- **Corporate Travel:** Corporate Traveller, FCm Travel Solutions, cievents, Stage and Screen, Campus Travel, Travel Club Getaways;
- **Youth Travel:** Student Flights, gapyear.com, Overseas Working Holidays, My Adventure Store;
- **Cruises:** Cruiseabout, Discount Cruises;
- **Tour Operations:** Back Roads Touring;
- **Online Travel Agents:** quickbeds.com, flightcentre.com;
- **Wholesale:** Infinity Holidays, Explore Holidays, Gogo Vacations;
- **Foreign Exchange:** Travel Money Oz;
- **Travel Education:** Flight Centre Business School, Flight Centre Travel Academy.

This horizontal and vertical diversification has shielded the company from the impacts of a downturn in any one sector. The company has invested heavily in IT solutions such as a universal desktop to book low-cost carrier airfares not available via the GDSs. More recently the company has developed a Blended Travel model that combines the best features of online travel agencies with the strengths of physical shop fronts. The Blended model provides travelers with 24/7 access and support through a blend of web offerings, extended shop hours, call centers, smartphone services and after-hours sales team. Travelers can switch seamlessly between these channels.

http://www.flightcentrelimited.com

For example, travelers might start their booking in store and complete the transaction online. Travel consultants are also allocated to online customers to provide support and advice. This innovative model addresses many of the strengths, weaknesses, opportunities and threats identified in this chapter.

Source: Flight Centre Limited (2014)

TRAVEL MANAGEMENT COMPANIES

Travel Management Companies (TMCs) provide services that meet the travel needs of businesses and organizations. Depending on corporate travel policies, employee travel requests may be handled by the TMC or by online self-booking tools provided by the TMC. A TMC must manage a company's travel policies, business-to-business (B2B) negotiations and contracts with preferred suppliers, traveler safety and security, corporate credit cards and travel expense reporting and benchmarking.

According to Quinby and Hoffman (2009), the business travel market can be distinguished from leisure and personal travel based on the following characteristics:

- **Contracts and preferred suppliers**: businesses negotiate volume-based discounts with preferred travel suppliers, including upgrades, VIP privileges and airport lounge access. These additional benefits must be incorporated into the reservation process so employees can access the entitlements negotiated by their employer;
- **Travel policy compliance**: corporate travel programs develop policies with a TMC and configure them in the reservation system. For example, corporate policies may permit a higher class of service for international trips or higher-level executives. IT systems can support these policies by considering scheduling, preferred suppliers, fare class policies and pricing. They also manage compliance based on traveler or trip characteristics;
- **Employee productivity**: business travelers are more concerned with productivity and schedules than the cost of travel. The lowest logical fare may not be the cheapest, but one that balances employee productivity and schedules with costs;
- **Risk management**: the management of risk and employee safety is important in corporate travel programs. TMCs use IT to track the locations of their employees and to know of international travel advisories. Apps for smartphones also support employees when they are traveling;

- **Travel expense management**: TMCs provide corporate clients with periodic reports and benchmarking of travel expenses. IT systems provide data feeds into corporate expense management and accounting systems. IT also handles expense management by capturing spending details and integrating these into corporate purchasing, accounting and reporting systems.

TMCs are less prone to competitive threats from OTAs because business travelers are less price sensitive and do not book their own travel. Business travel is also a high yield market segment and trips are often booked at short notice, generating lucrative profit margins. Despite these strengths, TMCs are also facing challenges. The decommissioning and disintermediation described earlier also impact TMCs. Innovative online TMCs such as Engencia (owned by Expedia) are providing direct discount booking portals for corporate clients.

ONLINE INTERMEDIARIES

In 1996, when commercial use of the Internet was beginning, Microsoft set up a small online travel booking website known as Expedia. In the same year, Sabre established Travelocity to allow travelers to access schedule and fare information and to purchase travel without the help of a traditional travel retailer. These new **Online Travel Agencies (OTA)** quickly claimed a large market share from traditional retailers. Their popularity also posed a threat to travel suppliers, and airlines responded by forming consortia to establish sites such as Orbitz, Opodo and Zuji. In 2012 a consortium of leading international hotel chains founded Room Key to counter the increasing market dominance of OTAs.

Types of online intermediaries

The Internet and IT developments have supported different types of intermediaries with different business models. These intermediaries fall into one of the following categories.

1. OTAs: the first successful online travel intermediaries. OTAs follow a similar revenue model to traditional travel agents but sell inventory from GDSs and suppliers to travelers using websites or mobile apps. While OTAs earn revenue from commissions, many also charge a booking fee or buy bulk inventory at a discount and sell at a markup. Expedia and Travelocity are popular in Western countries, but eLong and Qunar have a strong presence in China. Some OTAs, such as lastminute.com and wotif.com, specialize in distressed inventory by offering last minute deals.

2. Metasearch engines: also known as comparison shopping sites, metasearch engines consolidate information from OTAs and compare products side by side. Travelers save time because they do not have to visit multiple OTAs to find the best deal. Metasearch engines do not take bookings, they simply refer users to an OTA. This business model relies on fees paid by the OTAs when a booking is made from a metasearch engine. This is known as a "cost-per-acquisition" (CPA) business model. Examples include Kayak, Qunar, Trivago, Skyscanner, Hipmunk, Room77 and Mobissimo. Google Flights and Google Hotel Finder are also examples of metasearch engines.

3. Aggregators: these companies aggregate travel inventory from multiple GDSs. Some GNEs can also be considered aggregators.

A good example is ITA Software (now owned by Google), which created a tool called QPX for searching fares, schedules and availability across multiple distribution platforms.

4. Trip planning sites: provide tools to build customized itineraries for specific destinations based on user preferences. In some cases the sites also allow the user to book trip components. Examples include Mygola, Tripeye, Utrip, Plnnr and TripIt.

5. Affiliates: market OTA travel products on their own websites, and earn a fee for driving bookings to the OTA's platform. Some affiliate programs use a "cost-per-click" (CPC) model to reward affiliates. While many affiliates are online intermediaries they also include travel suppliers wishing to bundle other travel products with their own. OTAs may provide a **"white label"** booking service that is rebranded by the airline keeping the OTA brand invisible.

6. Group buying sites: offer "deal of the day" specials at significantly reduced prices if a minimum number of buyers make the purchase. These deals are negotiated with individual suppliers and travelers receive a voucher from the supplier. Examples include Groupon and LivingSocial.

7. Opaque sites: a special category of OTAs that sell "distressed" travel inventory at a discounted price. The supplier is hidden until the purchase is completed. Some sites, such as lastminute.com, offer mystery hotels with a fixed price, while others such as Priceline involve a bidding process like an online auction. These sites avoid heavily discounted travel inventory from cannibalizing full-price offers on other sites.

8. Product review sites: product review sites have become online travel intermediaries by combining travel reviewer data with the features of a metasearch engine.

Online intermediaries have leveraged IT to build successful new business models. While many sell directly to the price-sensitive leisure market, some have diversified into business travel. Several OTAs have created portals providing traditional travel intermediaries with incentives to bypass GDS channels by booking online. A good example is the Orbitz for Agents website. The popularity of online intermediaries is derived from IT innovations allowing travelers to compare products, schedules and pricing across a large number of suppliers. Online intermediaries have also pioneered other innovations that will be discussed next.

Information technology innovations

According to Quinby and Hoffman (2009), some of the most important IT innovations developed by online travel intermediaries have included:

- **The Matrix Display**: developed by ITA Software and first used by Orbitz, the matrix display allows travelers to click on any cell within the matrix to sort search results according to criteria such as price, airline, duration and number of stops. Hipmunk has built on this concept by providing an "agony" ranking of flights and an "ecstasy" ranking for hotels based on criteria such as price, duration/distance and guest ratings;
- **Search filters**: many OTAs and meta-search engines allow travelers to narrow their search by applying filters based on price range, brand, review ratings, star ratings, location, distance from a specified location and product features;
- **Opaque pricing**: intermediaries such as Priceline have pioneered opaque pricing for flights and hotels;

- **Dynamic packaging**: allows travelers to bundle several products into a package that can be booked at a lower price than purchasing each component separately. Expedia is well known for developing this feature with its "Flight + Hotel" options. The approach is also used by airlines, which combine their flights with hotel inventory drawn from an OTA using an affiliate model. Dynamic packaging allows hotels to conceal their discounted rates within packages to avoid alienating high yield customers. Tanford *et al.* (2012) provide a detailed account of pricing transparency and dynamic packaging;
- **Flexible date search**: travelers can compare flights across multiple departure and return dates to locate the lowest possible fare;
- **Alternative airport search**: travelers can search across multiple departure and arrival airports within a defined area to find the lowest possible fare or most convenient schedule;
- **Low-fare notifications**: travelers can register for an alert when parameters – such as an airfare below a specified amount – are met;
- **Mapping**: OTAs have contributed to the display of search results on maps. Google Flights use Google Maps, and other OTAs display hotel searches on a map to make it easier for travelers to identify options. Hipmunk provides a heat map overlay showing proximity to shopping, food and nightlife;
- **Semantic search**: travelers can search for products using natural language queries instead of forms, drop-down menus and calendars. For example, a traveler might type in "New York to London next week" and the search engine will analyze this

request before presenting the results. Examples include Adioso and Cheapair.com's Easy Search. Smartphones and wearable devices extend this capability with voice-driven searches.

Finding ways to display complex search results for hundreds of suppliers is one of the biggest challenges for online intermediaries. The features illustrate how IT can manage information overload to improve the search experience for travelers.

The future of online intermediaries

While online intermediaries have experienced tremendous growth and innovation over the last decade, some have attracted negative publicity. The bargaining power of large OTAs has had a detrimental impact on hotel chains, which have lost control of their pricing. Table 3.5 provides a detailed summary of the strengths, weaknesses, opportunities and threats confronting online travel intermediaries.

The SWOT analysis indicates that the creative use of IT has sustained many online travel intermediaries, while creating new opportunities for startup companies. Search innovations by large IT companies such Google are likely to impact online intermediaries. Google has indicated on many occasions that it does not intend to be a supplier or OTA. The company sees itself as an information broker and aggregator and has invested in tools that improve the search experience. These developments are likely to impact metasearch engines because Google's search tools provide some of the same functionality.

CHANNEL MANAGERS

While the developments above have made sourcing and booking travel easier for travelers, they have resulted in an increasingly complex distribution system for suppliers (see Chapter 2). Not surprisingly, a new type of intermediary has emerged to help suppliers deal with this complexity. **Channel Managers** provide suppliers with the tools to manage availability and rates across the many online channels. Examples include SiteMinder, RateTiger and Ezyield.

Channel managers provide suppliers with a single website on which they can add and remove channels and manage availability and price parity across channels. This provides an excellent example of the application of technology to eliminate the duplication of tasks. Staff can update availability and pricing across multiple sites by making a single change through their channel manager account. This reduces the potential for errors and ensures rate parity across different channels. Channel managers also adjust inventory across multiple channels when a booking occurs on one channel, preventing overbooking. Channel managers are providing integration with major hotel reservation systems and property management systems.

SUMMARY

To exist and thrive in an information-intensive industry, travel intermediaries must learn about and embrace all aspects of IT. Travel intermediaries now rely on computerized reservation terminals, and must now

Table 3.5. A SWOT analysis of online travel intermediaries.

	Positive	Negative
Internal	Strengths	Weaknesses
	Low entry costs. An OTA can establish a large footprint more easily than a traditional travel retailer.	**Lack of transparency**. Some OTAs levy taxes and fees not included in the initial "display price".
	Price. Discounts perceived to be better online and price comparisons are easy.	**Cancellation and changes**. Special fares and rates are often non-refundable and non-transferable.
	Convenience. 24/7 access from home.	**Security**. Most transactions use secure connections but there are risks with OTAs in countries without robust consumer protection laws.
	Customization. User-friendly websites with filters to support specific searches.	**Time consuming**. Finding and comparing travel options can be time-consuming and confusing.
	Choice and control. A wide range of options and user control over the selection of features.	**Limited advice**. Often limited advice about other travel arrangements such as visas and insurance.
	Instantaneous. Instant confirmation of availability and bookings.	**Special needs**. Not always possible to confirm special requests when booking.
	Comparison. Easier to compare options based on rates, features, star ratings and descriptions.	**Support**. It can be difficult to get live support when problems occur.
	Flexibility. Digital content can be updated quickly.	**Lack of expertise**. OTAs rarely provide the level of expert knowledge offered by traditional retailers.
	Multimedia. Use of pictures, video and maps.	
	Investment. Venture capitalists willing to fund OTA startups.	

(Continued)

Table 3.5. Continued.

	Positive	**Negative**
External	Opportunities	Threats
	Social. Integration of social media (e.g. user ratings, reviews and photos) reduces risk of a poor decision. **Mobile**. On-site traveler support provided using mobile apps and itinerary managers. **Integration**. Vertical and horizontal integration with other intermediaries creates new opportunities for connectivity and service provision. **Innovation**. Technology innovation made possible by new connections and developments such as ubiquitous computing and the semantic web.	**Competition**. New startups and established technology companies such as Apple, Google, Microsoft and Facebook moving into the travel distribution space. **Direct bookings**. Suppliers offering better deals and incentives that entice travelers to book direct.

Research Insight: Internet Versus Travel Agencies

Del Chiappa, G. (2013) Internet versus travel agencies. The perception of different groups of Italian online buyers. *Journal of Vacation Marketing* 19(1), 55–66.

In this chapter we have examined the strengths and weaknesses of both traditional travel intermediaries and OTAs. Del Chiappa (2013) has taken a different approach by surveying 1448 Italian tourists and comparing occasional, moderate and frequent on-line buyers. He finds that differences exist in buying behavior based on gender, age, cultural background, education level and income. The study also finds that the Internet is more likely to be used for booking shorter trips but that traditional agents should create a presence in the online market to remain competitive.

---

learn other hardware and software applications. This requires careful analysis of when and how IT can offer value-added services to their clients. The development and marketing of those services will redefine the role of the travel intermediary in the future. In particular, the major challenge is to use emerging Internet and mobile technologies to their advantage. IT, when used appropriately, will assist in developing new strengths and

---

Research Insights: Hotels and Intermediaries

Carroll, B. and Siguaw, J. (2003) The evolution of electronic distribution: effects on hotels and intermediaries. *The Cornell Hotel and Restaurant Administration Quarterly* 44(4), 38–50.

IT has been one of the most important drivers contributing to structural change in the travel distribution chain. These structural changes highlight some of the relationships and tensions between intermediaries and suppliers such as hotels. OTAs have challenges for hotels which no longer control the pricing and distribution of rooms. Carroll and Siguaw (2003) review the key players and developments in electronic hotel distribution and discuss factors driving change. They provide an excellent review of the OTS and hotel strategies to control electronic distribution channels. They predict the following:

- Hotels will challenge OTAs and establish their own direct online channels.
- OTA markups and profit margins will decrease.
- Hotel commission payments to intermediaries will give way to pay-for-performance programs.

---

managing weaknesses. As we have seen, IT can also turn threats into opportunities.

KEY TERMS

affiliate, aggregator, ancillary service, application programing interface (API), back-office system, blended travel, channel manager, computer reservation system (CRS), data center, decision support system (DSS), decommissioning, direct selling, disintermediation, dynamic packaging, e-ticket, enterprise resource planning (ERP), extensible markup language (XML), extranet, firewall, GDS new entrant (GNE), Global distribution system (GDS), graphical user interface (GUI), group buying site, interline ticket, intranet, itinerary, local area network (LAN), metasearch engine, new distribution capability (NDC), online travel agent (OTA), opaque site, passenger name record (PNR), preferential display, product review site, reverse access, screen bias, tour operator, traditional travel retailer, travel management company (TMC), travel wholesaler, trip planning site, virtual private network (VPN), white label

DISCUSSION QUESTIONS

1. What is the difference between a GDS and a GNE? Visit the GDS and GNE websites to help you answer this question. Do you think GNEs are a threat to the GDSs? Justify your answer.

2. You have started your own small travel retail business. Which GDS would you choose and why?

3. What is the role of traditional intermediaries in the travel distribution system and are they still needed? How might traditional intermediaries use IT to compete against the innovative features offered by OTAs?

Case Study. Continued.

C.R. Smith, president of American Airlines, and Blair Smith, a senior sales representative for IBM, met on an American Airlines flight. A conversation about the challenges of automating airlines led to a system making real-time airline reservations data available electronically to travel agents. The project required over US$40 million of initial investment in research and development before the experimental system went online in 1960. The system, known as Semi-Automated Business Research Environment (SABRE), was the first private real-time online transaction system and is often regarded as an early pioneer of electronic commerce. By 1964 the system was in all American Airline ticketing offices and by 1976 access had been expanded to travel agents.

In 1986 Sabre was restructured and became part of AMR, the parent company for American Airlines. Ownership changed again in 2000, when Sabre Holdings was spun off from AMR as a publically traded company. The company passed to private ownership in 2007 when Sabre was wholly acquired by Silver Lake Partners and Texas Pacific Group. These changes distanced Sabre from the airline that initially founded the company and subsequent relations between American Airlines and Sabre Holdings have been tense.

Today Sabre Holdings is a privately held company with over 9000 employees in 59 countries. While the company's major asset is the Sabre GDS, Sabre Holdings regards itself as a travel technology company and has developed or acquired a range of IT solutions used by airlines, airports, hotels, car rental providers, rail providers and tour operators. The company is organized around four business units:

1. Sabre Travel Network: a range of IT solutions built around the Sabre GDS to sell airline trips, hotel stays, car rentals, cruises and tour packages through travel agencies and OTAs. The network connects over 350,000 travel professionals with more than 400 airlines, 93,000 hotels, 25 car rental brands, 50 rail providers, 13 cruise lines and other global travel suppliers. This business unit includes the Sabre Red Suite of software solutions for travel retailers.

2. Sabre Airline Solutions: a suite of IT solutions for the aviation industry, including an airline reservations system, marketing, planning, customer sales, service and operations software used by more than 380 airlines and over 100 airports around the world.

3. Sabre Hospitality Solutions: a suite of IT solutions for the hospitality industry, including a computer reservations system (SynXis), a property management system (Sabre PMS), a customer relationship system (CRS), marketing and distribution software, GDS connectivity and Internet marketing, e-business and mobile solutions used by more than 12,000 hotel properties around the world.

4. Travelocity: an OTA created in 1996 to provide consumer-direct travel services. Travelocity.com was the first website to provide travelers with the ability to book airline seats, hotel rooms, rental cars, cruises and packaged vacations from the Sabre GDS without the help of a travel agent or broker. Travelocity also launched a full service online TMC called Travelocity

(Continued)

Case Study. Continued.

Business, which was acquired by BCD Travel in 2013. Other brands include lastminute.com, Zuji and World Choice Travel. Travelocity also operates a travel affiliate program.

Strategically, the company's diversified portfolio of brands has positioned it well for challenges confronting travel intermediaries. It spans the entire travel distribution value chain with a GDS, an OTA with several niche brands, and reservations systems and other IT solutions for suppliers. The company also maintains the Sabre Red App Center, offering proprietary and third-party applications to extend the capabilities of the Sabre Red Workspace.

Recent efforts have focused on developing innovative new mobile technology solutions for travelers, intermediaries and suppliers. For example, in 2013 Sabre launched the Sabre Red Mobile Workspace for intermediaries. The company also owns Tripcase, a consumer-oriented itinerary management tool accessed using the web or a mobile device. Tripcase monitors travel details and provides flight alerts, itinerary messages and pre-trip notifications,

http://youtu.be/zdi4-OsyEus

weather delay updates, security notices and other travel information and offers a convenient channel for connecting travelers with intermediaries and suppliers. The tool also suggests alternate flights and options if the planned itinerary is no longer viable. For a preview of how Sabre sees the future of travel technology, check out the following YouTube video: http://youtu.be/zdi4-OsyEus/.

This case illustrates how GDSs are repositioning themselves. Sabre's GDS and the Travelocity OTA make it an important intermediary, while also providing tools and systems for other intermediaries and suppliers. Sabre then is capitalizing on the strengths we reviewed in this chapter and protects the company against some of the threats.

Study Questions

1. Visit the Sabre Holdings website and explore their range of services and technology solutions. Use the model of the digital tourism distribution system in Chapter 2 to map out the different places where Sabre's products might be used. Are there any gaps in their portfolio of products?

2. Visit the Amadeus or Travelport website and compare their products and services with Sabre's. What are the differences and similarities?

3. Why would a GDS like Sabre be interested in operating an OTA such as Travelocity?

4. Visit the Travelocity website and carry out a search for an international flight of your choice. What website features of this OTA do you like? Do you prefer these tools to booking with a traditional travel agent? Visit a newer OTA such as Hipmunk and repeat your search using the same parameters (cities, dates). Are the results different? Which OTA do you prefer? Why?

5. View the YouTube video embedded in the case study. What future innovations do you think travelers will expect from companies like Sabre? How do these high-tech solutions support high-touch interactions?

REFERENCES

Abacus (2014) Abacus International. Available at: http://www.abacus.com.sg/ (accessed 13 November 2013).

Alford, P. (2006) Global distribution systems. *Travel and Tourism Analyst* 7, 1–46.

Amadeus (2014) Amadeus. Your Technology Partner. Available at: http://www.amadeus.com/ (accessed 13 November 2013).

Anckar, B. and Walden, P. (2001) Self-booking of high- and low-complexity travel products: exploratory findings. *Information Technology and Tourism* 4(3/4), 151–165.

Berne, C., Garcia-Gonzalez, M. and Mugica, J. (2012) How ICT shifts the power balance of tourism distribution channels. *Tourism Management* 33(1), 205–214. doi: 10.1016/j.tourman.2011.02.004

Bowden, J.L. (2007) The rise of the ICT-dependent home-based travel agents: mass tourism to mass travel entrepreneurship. *Information Technology and Tourism* 9(2), 79–97. doi: 10.3727/109830507781367375

Carroll, B. and Siguaw, J. (2003) The evolution of electronic distribution: effects on hotels and intermediaries. *Cornell Hotel and Restaurant Administration Quarterly* 44(4), 38–50. doi: 10.1016/s0010-8804(03)90257-6

Copeland, D. and McKenney, J.L. (1988) Airline reservation systems: lessons from history. *MIS Quarterly*, September, 353–370.

Del Chiappa, G. (2013) Internet versus travel agencies. The perception of different groups of Italian online buyers. *Journal of Vacation Marketing* 19(1), 55–66.

Dolnicar, S. and Laesser, C. (2007) Travel agency marketing strategy: insights from Switzerland. *Journal of Travel Research* 46(2), 133–146.

Flight Centre Limited (2014) Flight Centre Travel Group. Available at: http://www.flightcentrelimited.com/ (accessed 13 November 2013).

Godwin, N. (1987) *Complete Guide to Travel Agency Automation*, 2nd edn. Delmar Publishing, New York.

Perkins, E. (2012) Airlines fight with distribution systems. *Chicago Tribune*. Available at: http://articles.chicagotribune.com/2012-10-10/travel/sns-travel-ed-perkins-airlines-fight-with-distribution-systems-20121010_1_gds-first-airline-fare-packages/ (accessed 13 November 2013).

Quinby, D. and Hoffman, C. (ed.) (2009) *The Role and Value of the Global Distribution Systems in Travel Distribution*. PhoCusWright, Sherman, Connecticut.

Sabre Holdings (2014) Sabre - Technology that makes travel better. Available at: http://www.sabre.com/ (accessed 13 November 2013).

Sismanidou, A., Palacios, M. and Tafur, J. (2009) Progress in airline distribution systems: the threat of new entrants to incumbent players. *Journal of Industrial Engineering and Management* 2(1), 251–272.

Tanford, S., Baloglu, S. and Erdem, M. (2012) Travel packaging on the Internet: the impact of pricing information and perceived value on consumer choice. *Journal of Travel Research* 51(1), 68–80. doi: 10.1177/0047287510394194

Travelport (2014) Travelport Home. Available at: http://www.travelport.com/ (accessed 12 November 2013).

Weber, M. (1995) Changes in the leisure travel market result in new requirements for tour operator systems. In: Schertler, W., Schmidt, S., Tjoa, A.M. and Werthner, H. (eds) *Information and Communication Technologies in Tourism*. Springer-Verlag, Innsbruck Austria, pp. 95–102.

chapter 4

The Internet and the Tourist

LEARNING OBJECTIVES

After studying this chapter you should be able to:

- understand the historical evolution and key terms related to the Internet;
- explain how the Internet can be used by travelers and travel organizations and categorize different types of travel sites found on the Internet;
- explain the online information search process and analyze the factors that influence search rankings and online search behavior; and
- apply an understanding of communications, marketing and user experience design to the development of successful tourism websites.

INTRODUCTION

The Internet has featured prominently as a key technological innovation in the previous two chapters. Its rapid growth over the last two decades has changed the structure of the tourism industry and has altered strategic and operational practices. The Internet's ability to provide low cost global communications has had a fundamental and far-reaching impact on the way travel experiences and destinations are marketed, distributed and delivered. The Internet and travel are perfect companions – information is the lifeblood of the tourism industry and the Internet has become a critical tool for providing visually rich content to inspire and support all stages of the travel lifecycle.

In this chapter we examine the Internet in more detail to understand its origins and functionality, and the technologies and terminologies associated with its ubiquitous use. Intranets and extranets, which are special applications of the Internet used by tourism enterprises to enhance their communications, are also discussed. We will take a detailed look at the World Wide Web, which is one of the most powerful uses of the Internet. We will then build on the previous two chapters by examining how travelers search for information and how search engines work. Finally, we will apply concepts from communications, marketing and user experience design to examine the elements of successful travel websites.

HISTORY AND EVOLUTION OF THE INTERNET

The **Internet** is a global network comprised of many worldwide networks that use a common protocol to communicate with each other. Its name is derived from the idea of "inter-networking", which implies the connection of many host computers and their networks together to create a network of networks. It began in the 1960s when a network called ARPANet was used to send the first data messages between a computer science professor's laboratory at the University of California Los Angeles (UCLA) to another at Stanford Research Institute (SRI) (see Table 4.1). Other similar packet-switched networks followed that used different protocols (communication standards). In 1982, a protocol called TCP/IP was standardized and introduced for the Internet. This was the birth of the Internet as we know it today. However, it was not until 1995 when the networks linking research and educational institutions (ARPANet and NSFNET) were decommissioned that the Internet became commercial. Commercial **Internet service providers (ISPs)** who provided Internet services to organizations and individuals soon emerged, giving individuals and organizations access to the Internet.

No one "owns" the Internet; in a sense it is the ultimate democratizer. However, various bodies oversee its development. Two of the most important are the UN Working Group on Internet Governance, which deals with policy governance issues, and the Internet Engineering Task Force, which deals

with technical issues. The Internet expanded rapidly to Europe and Australia in the mid-1980s and to Asia in the late 1980s and early 1990s. The exponential growth of the Internet created a need for search tools to find files stored on various hosts, resulting in the first Internet search engine known as Archie.

The Internet has reached around the globe with users in almost all countries. Figure 4.1 shows the usage and penetration in different parts of the world in 2012. It is interesting to note the high number of users in Asia, an area where tourism is growing dramatically. The penetration in the population is the highest in North America and Europe (particularly Northern Europe) with the lowest penetration in Africa. Figure 4.1 shows how quickly Internet adoption is occurring in the developing world.

Users prefer websites in their native language. English is the major language of Internet users with 26.8% of all users, with Chinese speaking users second, followed by Spanish users (European Travel Commission, 2013). Multi-lingual websites are important for tourists who access sites from all over the world, however they are not commonly found. In fact the issue of cross-lingual information retrieval has surprisingly been given little attention by tourism websites and researchers (Li and Law, 2007). O'Connor (2011) agrees with this assessment but also argues that tourism websites do not consider cultural and social differences in various markets, making them less effective than they could be. German tourists, one of the largest international markets, find that travel sites do not accommodate their language, making it difficult for them to book online (Arlt, 2006). As an example of cultural differences, India (one of the fastest growing countries in Internet usage) has a population that values service, trust and security on

Table 4.1. Development of Internet technologies.

When	What	Who	Details
1969	ARPAnet	ARPA	One of the world's first operational packet switching networks, precursor of the Internet
1969	SITA	SITA	The first packet switch network used in the travel industry
1971	Email	Ray Tomlinson	The first system able to send mail between users on different hosts connected to ARPAnet
1973	Ethernet	Robert Metcalfe	Networking technologies for local area networks (LANs)
1982	Internet	ARPA	A worldwide network of interconnected computers based on the TCP/IP protocol
1985	Domain name	Symbolics Inc.	First .com domain registered
1989	ISP	The World	The first commercial Internet Service Provider in the US
1991	World Wide Web	Tim Berners-Lee (CERN)	A service supporting hyperlinked pages of text using the HyperText Transfer Protocol (HTTP)
1993	Mosaic	Marc Andreessen	First popular WWW browser with a graphic interface, precursor to Netscape, Mozilla and Firefox
1994	WebCrawler	Brian Pinkerton	First crawler-based text search engines
1996	Hotmail	Microsoft	First free web-based email
1996	Cable Modem	Rogers Communication	First broadband services
1997	Six Degrees	Andrew Weinreich	Early precursor of modern social networks
1997	Google Search	Larry Page, Sergey Brin	Development of the most used search engine in the world
1998	PayPal	Elon Musk	Internet payment service

(Continued)

Table 4.1. Continued.

When	What	Who	Details
2003	LinkedIn	Reid Hoffman	A social networking site for professionals
2004	Facebook	Mark Zuckerberg	Launch of the most popular social media site
2004	Skype	Heinla, Kasesalu, Tallinn, Friis, Zennström	Launch of the most popular voice-over-IP (VoIP) service and instant messaging client
2005	YouTube	Chad Hurley, Steve Chen, Jawed Karim	Popular video-sharing website
2006	Twitter	Jack Dorsey	Release of the popular online social networking and micro-blogging service
2010	Pinterest	Ben Silbermann, Paul Sciarra, Evan Sharp	A pinboard-style photo-sharing website that allows users to create and manage theme-based collections
2011	Google+	Google Inc.	Google's social networking and identity service

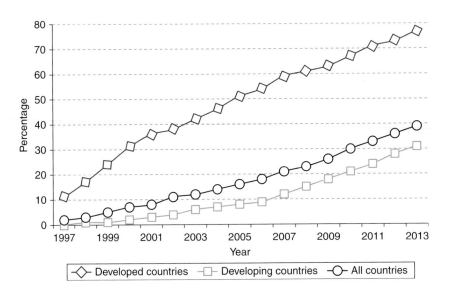

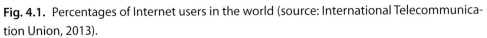

Fig. 4.1. Percentages of Internet users in the world (source: International Telecommunication Union, 2013).

websites more than other nations when booking travel (Arpita and Anshuman, 2011).

INTRANETS AND EXTRANETS

The Internet can also serve as the backbone for private communications within organizations and also between an organization and its related external stakeholders. This communication occurs through an intranet and extranet, as shown in Fig. 4.2.

An **intranet** uses the same TCP/IP protocol to share proprietary information that is relevant to that organization, and to share its computing services. It is not open to the general public. This takes the form of one or more websites hosted on a **server**, but all of its pages are behind a secure **firewall** allowing only authorized users to access the information. Intranets can be used for tasks such as employee training, collaboration on projects, corporate information, or human resource issues. Each employee in the organization will have her/his own portal to the intranet that allows access to areas that are needed for their work.

Similarly, an **extranet** uses Internet protocols and is not accessible to the general public, however it connects together one or more organizations, customers, suppliers and other approved stakeholders. Users must log in to a secure website with a password to gain access. These can be useful in the tourism context where different groups in a destination need to

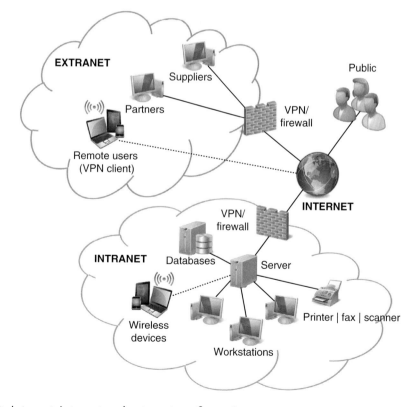

Fig. 4.2. Internet, intranet and extranet configuration.

collaborate. Marcussen and Skjoldgager (1998) describe how national tourism organizations benefitted from extranets as more players became involved in the destination's issues.

THE WORLD WIDE WEB

The **World Wide Web (WWW)**, or simply "the web", is perhaps one of the most popular and powerful uses of the Internet. We all use it every day to access all kinds of information and perform all kinds of transactions. Contrary to popular belief, the Internet and the WWW are not the same. Like email, the WWW is a service supported by the Internet. Tim Berners-Lee laid the foundations for the WWW in 1991 while working at the European Organization for Nuclear Research (CERN). Berners-Lee combined the concept of hypertext with the Internet to create a system of interlinked documents. While the WWW was initially designed as a communication system for CERN, its application as a worldwide system was quickly recognized and in 1993 CERN announced that the WWW would be free to everyone.

Public use of the WWW was greatly enhanced by the development of the Mosaic **browser**, which provided a graphical user interface (GUI) for navigating the web. A number of browsers have subsequently been developed, including Netscape, Mozilla, Firefox, Microsoft Internet Explorer and more recently Safari and Google Chrome. Like the Internet, the proliferation of webpages soon created a need for a **search engine** and the development of the W3Catalog in 1993 was followed a year later by WebCrawler, which searched for text on websites. This was followed by many search engines, including the relatively late entrant Google in 1997. Many

popular search engines in the late 1990s disappeared as Google established itself with superior search results using the PageRank algorithm developed by founder Larry Page and Sergey Brin. Google developed a successful revenue model, which not only funded the ongoing refinement of Google Search, but has also financed the development of other new technologies discussed in this book.

The next chapter in the Internet's history was largely influenced by the increase in **bandwidth** delivered by **broadband** connections. The first commercial cable modem was marketed in 1996 but not until 2000 did broadband services become more affordable. Before this, users had to connect to the Internet using a dialup modem, which was limited in speed and connectivity. This limited the use of images and video. Faster Internet speeds have supported new photo- and video-sharing sites such as Instagram and YouTube. For the tourism industry, higher bandwidth meant that rich multimedia such as images and video could be incorporated into online marketing.

The ongoing evolution of the WWW led to **Web 2.0**, which increased interaction and collaboration on the Internet. Whereas **Web 1.0** consisted of one-way communication with static content created by those with the technical knowledge of web authoring, Web 2.0 allowed open communication with an emphasis on web-based communities of users sharing data, information, knowledge, resources and files. This was possible by the development of wikis, blogs, social networks, Rich Site Summary (RSS) and the media-sharing sites. Popular services that developed as part of Web 2.0 include Wikipedia, YouTube, Facebook, Twitter, Google+, LinkedIn, Instagram and Pinterest. Many of these services were censored or banned in China, where homegrown versions such as Weibo and Renren emerged. The travel industry also embraced Web 2.0, with sites such as Wikitravel, TripAdvisor, Yelp and Urbanspoon having a major impact on travel behavior. The role of the social media in the travel industry is explored in more detail in Chapter 5.

DOMAINS, PROTOCOLS AND LANGUAGES

For the Internet and the WWW to evolve as they have, oversight by computer scientists and policy makers has been necessary. They have created standards and protocols enabling smooth and increasingly sophisticated worldwide communication. There are three key technologies that underpin the WWW. They are **domains**, **protocols** and **languages**.

Domains

The Internet Corporation for Assigned Names and Numbers (ICANN) coordinates and oversees the two main name spaces in the Internet, the Internet Protocol address space and the Domain Name System. Each webpage has an identifier called the Universal Record Locator (URL) made up of three parts. For example the United Nations World Tourism Organization has as its URL "www.unwto.org". The **host** name is "www", the **domain name** is "unwto" and the **top-level domain** is ".org", signifying that it is an organization. There are many top-level domains that specify different types of organizations as shown in Table 4.2.

Protocols

The primary protocol on the Internet is **TCP/IP** (transmission control protocol/Internet

Table 4.2. Top-level domain names on the Internet.

Domain	Description
.edu	Educational institutions
.com	Commercial institutions
.org	Organizations
.net	Networked organizations
.gov	Governmental organizations
.mil	Military organizations
.travel	Travel organizations
.au	Country domains, in this case Australia (hundreds of other countries have their own two-letter code for a top-level domain e.g. .fr France, .cn China)

protocol), which relays information around the Internet between networks. Another protocol is **SMTP** (simple mail transfer protocol), which is responsible for transferring emails. There are two other standards that are in common use on the Internet for the transmission of documents. **Electronic Data Interchange (EDI)** is a standard for document exchange used by companies when transmitting and tracking large volumes of documents (e.g. orders or checks). To transfer files across the Internet another protocol called **File Transfer Protocol (FTP)** is used. An important protocol for the web is the **hypertext transfer protocol (HTTP)** used for data communication on the web. Similarly, the **hypertext transfer protocol secure (HTTPS)** is used for secure communication and payments over the Internet.

government. Similarly governments connect to businesses in **G2B** eCommerce, such as when a restaurant needs approval to build. And finally government departments often need to perform transactions with other government departments either in the same country or other countries and this is referred to as **G2G** eCommerce. An example is when the Ministry for Tourism for a country needs to liaise online with the Customs and Immigrations Department. Table 4.4 shows these different eCommerce models with additional examples.

Helping us to understand further the types of tourism Internet sites, Pan and Fesenmaier (2000) distinguish between **travel websites** (focusing on the needs of travelers, including communication with travel professionals) and **tourism websites** (focusing on communication between tourism professionals or tourism researchers). This gives rise to a typology of websites that can be analyzed in terms of the information flows as explained in Table 4.5.

Some websites are designed so that the tourist can interact with the site in multiple different ways (e.g. to make a reservation, to send a request, to chat), whereas others do not have interactive capabilities. Another dimension is vividness, which relates to how dynamic or static the site is and whether it is animated or contains videos. Higher bandwidths and higher levels of security are needed for the more interactive and more vivid websites (Pan and Fesenmaier, 2000). Increasingly tourists expect interactive, vivid sites as they research and book their travel options.

Table 4.4. Different types of e-commerce in tourism.

Term	Description	Example
B2C	Business to consumer	A traveler purchases a flight on Lufthansa's website
B2B	Business to business	A tour operator purchases a block of rooms from a hotel using the Internet
C2B	Consumer to business	A tourist offers her/his services as an attorney to a hotel where she/he is staying
C2C	Consumer to consumer	A tourist sells souvenirs to another tourist on eBay
G2C	Government to consumer	A tourist applies for a passport online
G2B	Government to business	A museum applies for a building permit to a government agency online
G2G	Government to government	Two governments negotiate a bilateral air service agreement using the Internet

Table 4.5. A typology of tourism websites by information flows (adapted from Pan and Fesenmaier, 2000, p. 162).

Description	Term	Explanation	Website examples
Travel Websites			
Travelers–travelers	C2C	Facilitate information exchange between travelers	Online traveler communities: http://www.lonelyplanet.com/
Professionals–travelers	B2C	Facilitate information exchange between travelers and difference tourism professionals	Online visitor information: http://www.enjoyillinois.com/
Tourism Websites			
Professional–professional	B2B	Business-to-business communication websites of tourism professional associations or tourism administrations	Destination Marketing Association international: http://www.destinationmarketing.org/
Researchers–professionals	R2B	Websites to enhance communication between professionals and researchers	National Laboratory for Tourism and eCommerce: http://sthm.temple.edu/nltec/
Researchers–researchers	R2R	Communication between researchers	TRINET: http://www.trinet.org/

A typology of travel websites

Many types of travel providers have a presence on the Internet and the web. Most of them perform some or all of the functions discussed above. To better understand the ways tourism uses the Internet we can organize travel websites into several categories. These categories and examples are presented in Table 4.6.

Different chapters in this book cover the way these travel providers use the Internet and the web. The Research Insight later in this chapter discusses issues faced by destinations and DMOs as search engines crawl through the web to find information.

ONLINE INFORMATION SEARCH

Search engines are an important tool for locating travel information and products. Search engines can be thought of as the "Hubble Telescope of the Internet", as they provide

Table 4.6. A typology of travel websites.

Category	Description	Examples
Travel intermediaries	Agents (OTAs), metasearch engines, aggregators and other intermediaries that allow travelers to compare and book a range travel experiences. For more details see Chapter 3.	expedia.com kayak.com
Travel suppliers	Corporate and consumer websites for airlines, transport, hotels, attractions, restaurants and other suppliers usually providing information about the organization's products. Some of these sites also have direct booking capabilities. For more details see Chapters 7, 8, 9 and 10.	ihg.com singaporeair.com
Social media	Websites that support the creation of user-generated content such as reviews, blogs, wikis and forums. For more details see Chapter 5.	tripadvisor.com travelpod.com wikitravel.org
Online travel portals	Combine a range of services, including booking tools, social media, feature articles and other content to offer travelers a compelling mix of trip planning tools.	virtualtourist.com
Online travel guides	The sites have often evolved from hardcopy travel guides to provide a mix of information, commentary and tools about a range of destinations.	lonelyplanet.com frommers.com
Trip planning	These sites provide tools to build customized travel itineraries for a range of destinations.	utrip.com mygola.com
Destinations	Official visitor information sites for national, state and local destinations. These are usually maintained by DMOs or CVBs. Some DMOs maintain separate corporate and consumer portals. For more details see Chapter 11.	australia.com tourism.australia.com visit-queensland.com visitbrisbane.com.au

(Continued)

Table 4.6. Continued.

Category	Description	Examples
Government	Most government tourism ministries maintain websites featuring information about visas and passports, travel advisories, statistics and reports. Many embassies also maintain websites for travelers.	tourism.gov.in smartraveller.gov.au usa.embassy.gov.au
Education	Many universities and colleges offer education projects and conduct research in the travel area and their websites often include research reports and statistics.	tim.hawaii.edu
Non-government organizations (NGOs)	NGOs also maintain websites that provide statistics, information and reports about various aspects of tourism.	unwto.org tourismconcern.org.uk ecotourism.org

access to the huge amount of information on the Internet by crawling, indexing, retrieving and representing relevant information for users based upon unique algorithms (Xiang *et al.*, 2008, 2009). This section provides an overview of how they work and how travelers search for travel.

Search engines

Search engines take user queries, retrieve related documents found in the searchable indexes, produce snippets with web address, a short description, similar pages and cache, and display them in a ranked order on the **search engine reply page (SERP)** (see Fig. 4.3). The major part of the search engine interface displays results based on the internal ranking (i.e. organic listing) and major search engines such as

Google display paid advertisements on the top and right side of major result pages These are ranked by businesses' bidding price on clicks and the quality of pages, which is termed a **paid listing**.

A **search engine algorithm** used to rank webpages in **organic listings** determines which webpages to display and in what order. The ranking of a webpage is mainly determined by:

1. Whether or not the keywords are in the **Uniform Resource Locator (URL)** of that page.
2. The **frequency** and **size** of the keywords on a webpage.
3. The **keywords** in the link anchor text (those pieces of text which contain a link).
4. Alternative text for images.
5. **Metatags**, keywords in **titles** and **descriptions** embedded on a given webpage.

Fig. 4.3. Google search engine results page for "New York".

Some search engines further incorporate the link structure of the web to determine the importance of webpages (Brin and Page, 1998). A webpage with many inbound links is considered "more valuable" and thus has a higher importance than ones with fewer inbound links. In addition, search engines use an iterative process to determine the quality of links (Brin and Page, 1998; Levene, 2006). Other criteria affecting page ranking include the age of the site and the frequency of updating, page loading time and the popularity of the page. While the most popular search engine, Google, claims to index more than 1 trillion webpages, the entire information space on the Internet can only be covered in small parts by a single search engine. "Deep web" pages such as those buried in databases and dynamically generated pages are not indexed by general search engines

and therefore are not accessible to users who query a search engine (Bergman, 2001).

Google has recently introduced additional features to their SERPs. You will notice that the New York example also includes a section called Knowledge Graph. **Knowledge Graph** is a display that supplements search results by providing semantic-search information gathered from a wide variety of sources, such as Wikipedia, Freebase and the CIA World Factbook. In the case of places, the information is also mapped using Google Maps and is contextualized with information such as the local time and weather. This has obvious applications for travel and tourism. Information such as upcoming events and points of interest are also shown. Knowledge Graph uses a **link graph** to model relationships between different people, places and things, to help determine which are popular and relevant for particular searches. Knowledge Graph appears only when necessary, but the database contains more than 500 million objects, as well as more than 3.5 billion facts about and relationships between these different objects (Singhal, 2012). For more information, watch: http://youtu.be/mmQl6VGvX-c/.

http://youtu.be/mmQl6VGvX-c

When a similar search is conducted for "New York Hotels" a different SERP format is shown (see Fig. 4.4). The search still includes paid listings along the top, but now also has paid advertisements along the right hand side. The search engine recognizes that we are searching for hotels and includes a panel from Google HotelFinder. Clicking this panel takes the user directly to Google's metasearch engine for hotels. The information shows real-time ratings and room rates. The SERP also includes organic location-based listings from Google Maps on the main search page as well as a mini-map on the right hand side. This highlights Google's attempt to contextualize its search results with location, pricing and user-generated reviews. Finally, the organic search results are shown below all of this content. In this example, the bottom line for New York hotels is that unless they have a paid listing or have managed their property through Google Places they will not appear in the top half of the first page of results.

Online information search behavior

A general framework of search engine use is illustrated in Fig. 4.5. There are three general stages of search engine use related to the travel planning process:

1. The **pre-search** conditions, which is a form of knowledge representation reflecting the integration of the trip planning search process and the perceived usefulness of travel planning tools on the Internet.

2. The **search** process, which includes the task frames as well as the behavioral aspects influenced by these frames.

3. The **evaluation** of the overall search process, which culminates in attitude formation toward search engines and online travel planning.

The first stage sets the foundation for the search strategy used by travelers and is based upon their perceptions of the task as well as the functions of the tools to support this task directly. They affect the extent and nature of use of search engines. The second stage describes the basic strategies travelers use to navigate through the Internet to find information so that travel decisions (i.e. destinations, accommodations, attractions, routing) can be made. As such, these strategies act as "frames" within which the information accessed through search engines is evaluated. The third stage focuses on the overall evaluation of search engines within the travel planning process. Importantly, this stage of search engine use not only results in overall evaluation (i.e. satisfied versus not satisfied), but also forms attitudes toward search engine use for travel planning (Pan and Fesenmaier, 2006). This

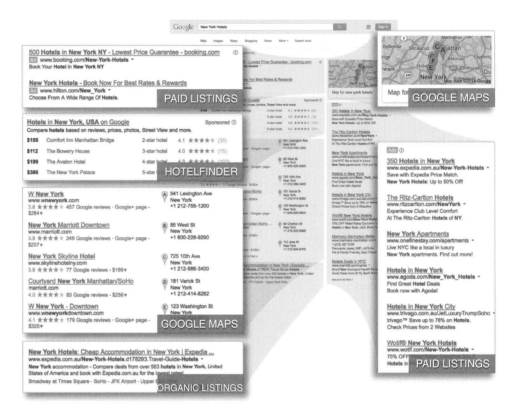

Fig. 4.4. Google search engine results page for "New York Hotels".

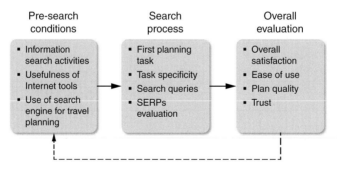

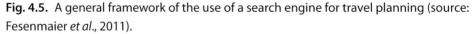

Fig. 4.5. A general framework of the use of a search engine for travel planning (source: Fesenmaier *et al.*, 2011).

third stage also sets the stage for future use of the search engine for trip planning, and therefore is linked to the first stage in the overall process.

A number of factors influence online information search and decision making within the context of travel planning and are discussed in detail by Gretzel *et al.* (2012). The most important factors include attitudes, cognitive style, decision frames, involvement, situation, context, socio-demographic characteristics, and finally, trust; each are discussed briefly.

Attitudes are defined as a positive or negative evaluation and contain cognitive, affective and behavioral components. As such, attitudes can be a good predictor of whether or not a destination is chosen. Interestingly, cognitive styles refer to the ways in which individuals process information. This affects information gathering, evaluation and selection processes used in vacation trip planning (Grabler and Zins, 2001). Travel-related decisions are framed depending on personal preferences for decision- making strategies and the needs from the specific trip-planning situation. For instance, trips may be defined around a specific activity such as golfing, which will strongly influence the choice of destination. Activities associated with golfing will be preferred and beach access at the destination might be desired, but not perceived as important.

Travel information search and processing also depend on individuals' level of involvement. Highly involved travelers are likely to use more criteria, search for more information, use more information sources, process information in detail, make more inferences, and form attitudes that are less likely to change (Fesenmaier and Johnson, 1989). In a complex choice situation, commitment is needed to accomplish the task; this contrasts to simple and routine decisions, which require low consumer involvement (Reid and Crompton, 1993). Knowledge, often obtained through direct experience or online search, can be represented either as travel knowledge in general and/or as knowledge of alternative destination(s); in either case, knowledge influences the range of alternatives considered (Snepenger, 1987). Further, research shows important differences in the choice of destinations/attractions between first-time visitors

and repeat visitors; first-time visitors tend to choose destinations that are easily accessible (McKercher, 1998).

Destination-related decisions are highly sensitive to the situation in which they occur; for example, trip characteristics such as travel purpose, length of travel, distance between origin and destination, travel group composition and travel mobility are important determinants of travel behavior in destination choice and visitor expenditures. Socio-demographic characteristics including age, education, income and marital status can be surrogates for traveler resources and constraints. For example, older travelers rely more on family and past experience as information sources and are more interested in satisfying hedonic, aesthetic and sign needs in the information search process; and, women are more likely to consider functional aspects in their information search than men and are more likely to respond to subtle cues than males. Finally, trust is essential for the success of any online business and refers to the willingness to be vulnerable in uncertainty and plays a critical role in online travel planning by enabling travelers to manage the complexity of online travel planning. Recent studies indicate that travelers (and tourism businesses) have learned the cues reassuring them that the website is trustworthy. This includes the last date the site was updated, the use of protection protocols, and the degree to which the website addresses the traveler's needs.

Intelligent assistants and online recommender systems

Intelligent agents and **online recommender systems** embedded within websites such as Tripadvisor.com, Yelp.com and the many smartphone apps have changed the nature of search and the travel planning process. As described in Fesenmaier *et al.* (2006), recommender systems match user preferences with alternative products using different approaches. In their book, they describe the theories, methods and applications used for developing online recommender systems. Further, research by (Gretzel, 2011) demonstrates that recommender systems do not simply inform about alternative choices, but they persuade users by posing questions. This is because travelers read a lot into the questions the system asks even if it is not directly related to the travel product category to be recommended. Additionally, recent developments in smartphone apps support new creative ways to support decision-making. For example, travelers do not have to commit to a "complete" travel plan before they embark on the trip. Instead, knowing that the information is always available enables travelers to postpone many of their decisions to a later stage resulting in more dynamic en route decisions.

Research Insights: Destinations and Search Engines

Tourists increasingly use search engines to access information on destinations. The results of such searches are voluminous and generate hundreds of websites for the tourist to sift through. The tourist is often left wondering which is the official destination site? This also causes destination marketing organizations (DMOs) to consider how they can best list their site so that is predominant on most search engines. This study assesses the visibility of DMO websites in Google Web Search. A set of 18 cities in the US were selected to be used as case studies. The study examined the visibility of their websites in relation to travel queries identified using Google Adwords Keyword Tool.

The research questions that drove this study were:

1. To what extent are DMOs visible in Google?
2. How do DMOs compare to each other in terms of search engine visibility?
3. To what extent are DMOs visible in relation to travelers' search queries?

The results of the study show that tourists start their searches with general terms (e.g. destination name) and then move to the more specific attributes. The results also indicate that there are substantial differences in the relative positions of destination websites on Google. Some destinations are more visible to online travelers than others, and the volume of search within those online domains also varied. The research results suggest that DMOs must improve their understanding of their destination's visibility in search engines to be competitive. The study offers a number of implications for research and practice of search engine marketing for tourism destinations.

Source: Xiang *et al.* (2010)

DIGITAL MARKETING COMMUNICATIONS

We can use models from the communications field to better understand how the Internet has changed marketing communications. The interactive nature of the Internet provides a much better means of communicating with the customer than conventional media because the effort required by the customer to respond is much lower. Unlike television or radio, the Internet allows users to control the delivery of information by selecting only that data which is valuable to them. The Internet makes it possible to cost-effectively market to as many or as few people as appropriate. Hoffman and Novak (1996) explain how the Internet has transformed communications between organizations and customers by contrasting the traditional marketing communications model with a model for computer-mediated environments.

Traditional marketing communications

Traditional communications channels allow organizations to reach current and potential consumers through marketing efforts with only limited forms of feedback from the customer. Figure 4.6 demonstrates how traditional marketing media follow a passive one-to-many communication model in which the organization (O) transmits content through a medium to consumers (C). The model does not indicate any interaction between individual consumers and organizations.

Digital marketing communications

The Internet has revolutionized marketing communications by establishing new models replacing the simple linear process where marketing messages were sent to a passive audience. The model for marketing in **computer-mediated environments** shown in Fig. 4.7 presents a many-to-many communications model. In this model, consumers actively choose whether to approach organizations through digital touch-points and exercise unprecedented control over the content. The model demonstrates how two-way interactive communication takes place between customers and organizations (i.e. B2C), customers and customers (i.e. C2C) and organizations and organizations (i.e. B2B). As a result, the flow of the communication becomes more like a web of conversations spinning around the

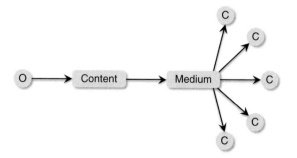

Fig. 4.6. Traditional one-to-many marketing communications model (adapted from Hoffman and Novak, 1996).

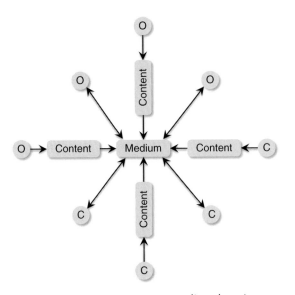

Fig. 4.7. Marketing communications in computer-mediated environments (adapted from Hoffman and Novak, 1996).

organization. The role of the organization in this model is to facilitate these conversations through strategic listening and active participation.

The Hoffman and Novak (1996) model was developed when social media was in its infancy, but the framework accurately captures the idea that Web 2.0 allows customers to not only interact with organizations, but also to create their own content.

DESIGNING AND MAINTAINING TOURISM WEBSITES

A website is a virtual extension of an organization's physical presence. As a consequence, the time and effort spent on this virtual presence should complement offline activities. The website should be viewed as a touch point for travelers before, during and after their journey. Travel organizations should focus on the entire travel lifecycle and how a website can provide information at each stage of the journey. The growth in mobile technologies means this point is even more important than in the past. Tourism websites are not just a tool for marketing, they are also a means for delivering support and customer service and enhancing the visitor experience. Therefore, the online experience is just as important as the offline experience (Garrett, 2011). In this section we draw on aspects from the field of **User Experience Design (UXD)** to discuss how tourism organizations and destinations can design successful websites.

Benckendorff and Black (2000) published one of the first comprehensive studies of website design in tourism. Their 1998 analysis of Australian DMOs combined information from academic and practitioner literature with a survey of 45 DMOs and a content analysis of 16 DMO websites. They identified 12 elements of successful website development and grouped these into four categories: planning, design, content and management. Since the late 1990s many other scholars have developed web design or website evaluation frameworks for the tourism and hospitality industries (Park and Gretzel, 2007; Law *et al.*, 2010). Table 4.7 presents 14 elements of successful tourism websites by synthesizing these studies to develop an updated version of Benckendorff and Black's (2000) framework. We will explore each of these elements in more detail below.

Planning

Kotler and Armstrong (2012) argue that an essential step in developing a framework for any marketing effort involves the definition of goals and strategies in a marketing plan. In fact, the entire structure and content of the website will depend on the Internet marketing objectives. This is because an organization's website is one tool in the toolkit of marketing channels, albeit an increasingly important one. From an **Integrated Marketing Communications (IMC)** perspective it is critical that all of these channels are integrated to present the desired brand image of the organization or destination (Belch *et al.*, 2003). For example, all offline marketing collateral should contain links to the organization's website. Conversely, the website should include links to offline materials such as media releases, brochures, maps and reports. Some travel organizations like EasyJet also display their web address prominently on their buildings, cars, buses or aircraft. Other businesses display signs to guide travelers to their social media pages.

Design

Navigation

One of the most important issues facing users is the problem of being "lost" in the virtual space provided by a website. To combat this problem webpages should be arranged in a logical structure or hierarchy so that the user can develop a mental model of the site and its contents. This **information architecture** must be supported by a menu system for the user to navigate from one page to another (Baloglu and Pekcan, 2006). Ensuring that page titles or breadcrumbs at the top of each page reflect the titles presented in menus can further reinforce a sense of place. **Breadcrumbs** typically appear horizontally across the top of a webpage and provide links back to parent pages (e.g. Home > About Us > Investor Information).

For complex sites a site map or site index can present the site in full detail. A good index page presents every page on the site in a hierarchical structure. The site map or index should also be fully interactive so that the user can move to any desired location on the index. Complex sites, such as destination websites, can also benefit from search engines that scan the site for keywords entered by the user. Many large websites are generated dynamically from content stored in databases. This content provides the building blocks for building pages "on demand", ensuring that content is always current and contextualized to the user's needs. In these cases navigation systems require careful attention to ensure that users can locate the resources they need.

Interaction

Site design should make use of the unique attributes of the Internet to provide an

Table 4.7. Elements of successful tourism websites (adapted from: Benckendorff and Black, 2000; Baloglu and Pekcan, 2006; Beldona and Cai, 2006; Chan and Law, 2006; Park and Gretzel, 2007; Bevanda *et al.*, 2008; Schmidt *et al.*, 2008; Stepchenkova *et al.*, 2010).

Dimension	Elements
Planning	Formulate and formalize electronic marketing strategies and goals in a marketing or business plan.
	Integrate online efforts with other marketing communications channels to ensure a consistent brand image.
Design	Design clear navigation paths and include navigation aids that allow users to find information (e.g. menus, icons, site maps, search tools).
	Facilitate interaction between the user, the organization and other users (e.g. email, hyperlinks, social media, live chat, virtual tours).
	Balance aesthetics and functionality to inspire travelers (e.g. multimedia, language support, currency conversion, weather, itinerary planning, recommender systems, ancillary products and services, FAQs).
	Ensure functionality across different platforms (i.e. different browsers, operating systems and devices).
Delivery	Ensure that information is optimized for online readability and is credible, trustworthy and accurate (i.e. up-to-date pricing, no broken links, "About Us", privacy policy, testimonials and awards, physical location, contact details).
	Personalize information for targeted market segments (e.g. itinerary planning, advice for business travelers, families, accessibility information, social media).
	Incorporate all elements of the marketing mix (e.g. product, pricing, promotion, people, point-of-sale, planning, packaging, programing and partnerships).
Management	Schedule regular maintenance to add, revise or remove content.
	Provide appropriate financial, human and physical resources to support a positive online experience (e.g. customer support, staff training, suitable IT systems).
	Drive traffic to the site (e.g. Search Engine Optimization, affiliate marketing, viral marketing, permission-based marketing).
	Leverage social media and CRM to encourage repeat visitation (e.g. user accounts, loyalty programs, social media integration, newsletters).
Evaluation	Monitor usability and utility (i.e. site metrics, analytics, user satisfaction, competitors).

informative, interactive experience. According to Ellsworth and Ellsworth (1995), interactivity and responsiveness to user feedback are common characteristic of successful websites. As we have already discussed, "many-to-many" interactivity makes the web different from other marketing media. Examples of features that add interactivity include email, live chat, virtual tours and contests. Hyperlinks invite users to interact with the content. The development of Web 2.0 provides new opportunities for organizations to create virtual spaces where travelers can also share content with each other. Embedding user reviews, blogs, forums and social networking pages into a website will increase interactivity enormously (see Chapter 5).

Aesthetics and functionality

There are at least two ideologically opposed schools of thought about web design (O'Connor, 2004). The first is the **aesthetic school** and supporters are usually designers who emphasize new and different ideas and argue that the latest multimedia elements should be used to enhance the visitor experience (Siegel, 1996). These websites are visually stunning and might even be called works of art. The second is known as the **functionalist school** and supporters usually include marketers and IT experts who argue for less emphasis on visual design and more focus on content and usability (Nielsen, 2000).

The distinction between these approaches was important in the early 2000s, when people accessed the Internet using dialup modems and the rule of thumb was that pages should take less than 10 seconds to load! Today webpages load almost instantaneously and the growth in Internet bandwidth has reduced some of the tradeoffs previously necessary when designing websites. Travel marketing depends on visual stimulation and current broadband speeds allow designers to strike a balance between aesthetics and functionality. Examples of aesthetics include balancing text with visual images and whitespace to ensure the site (and particularly the homepage) is not cluttered. Functionality means including features that add value and usability to the site, such as language support, currency conversion, weather, itinerary planning, recommender systems, links with ancillary products and services and Frequently Asked Questions (FAQs).

Cross-platform compatibility

Despite all of our technological wizardry, it is still difficult to design a webpage that is rendered the same way across all platforms. Cross-platform compatibility means the website should render correctly and continue to function in different web browsers (e.g. Internet Explorer, Chrome, Firefox, Safari), across different operating systems (e.g. Windows, Linux, OSX, iOS, Android), across different form factors (e.g. desktops, laptops, tablets, smartphones) and on different screens (i.e. different sizes and resolutions). Some travel organizations have designed mobile versions of their websites, which are automatically loaded when the site detects a mobile browser. The best way to ensure cross-platform compatibility is to test the website across the most common configurations used by customers before the site is launched.

Delivery

Readability and credibility

Trust is a major issue for Internet users and credible content is one of the most important traits of a well-designed site.

Using high-quality graphics and proper written expressions can increase credibility. Ensuring that content is free from spelling and grammatical errors is a basic element of professionalism in business. Yet it is surprising how many organizations neglect this simple rule, either on their own website or on social media communications. Sloppily written expressions send mixed signals about the organization's reliability. There are other readability considerations. Web users tend to scan webpages rather than read them. To accommodate this webpages should use: highlighted keywords (hyperlinks or typeface variations), meaningful sub-headings, bulleted lists, simple paragraphs containing one idea, an inverted pyramid style (i.e. starting with the conclusion) and at least half the word count of conventional writing (Nielsen, 1997). It is also important for organizations to ensure that information is accurate and up to date. This is particularly important in the travel industry where pricing, dates, times and other information change frequently.

There is more to credibility than ensuring that content is accurate and up to date. Two common elements of credibility are trustworthiness and expertise (Fogg *et al.*, 2001). There are a few easy ways to improve these elements, such as including an "About Us" link and privacy policy on the website. These have become standard links on most websites and consumers will often look for these to establish the credibility of the organization. The "About Us" page should present information such as the history of the organization, its mission and vision, information for investors, testimonials and awards. A physical address and location map send a clear message that the business is legitimate and not a "fly by night" operation.

Personalization

As with traditional advertising, an effective site must be designed around the needs and motivations of the target market. This suggests that target markets must be identified in the planning stages because the information provided by the website must be tailored to the users' needs. Travel websites provide many opportunities to personalize the experience. Information and tips can be provided for specific market segments but CRM databases can also personalize dynamically generated online content. The tracking of online behavior using cookies enables organizations to adjust the products that are recommended to travelers. The integration of social media is an effective personalization strategy because these tools draw on the user's own personal network. For destination websites, tools such as trip planners and customizable itineraries can assist with personalizing the experience. Personalization also means paying attention to the needs of the traveler with disability or accessibility challenges (Han and Mills, 2007).

The digital marketing mix

As we have noted in Chapter 1, the intangibility, perishability, inseparability and heterogeneity of tourism experiences makes the industry very different. As a result, online marketing efforts have to emphasize the value of experiences and make it easy for travelers to acquire the products and services being promoted. The eight Ps of tourism marketing (also known as the tourism marketing mix) provide a comprehensive framework for considering the delivery of online travel services (Morrison, 2010). Table 4.8 describes how we can use these eight Ps when creating travel websites.

Table 4.8. Application of the eight Ps to website design.

Element	Application
Product	Clearly present the features and benefits of core product(s) and services, including ancillary features (e.g. upgrades, breakfasts, WiFi). A comparison feature or a search function with different filters is useful for organizations with many products (e.g. OTAs, DMSs, metasearch engines). Real-time product availability should be clearly indicated.
Price	Pricing should be up to date and be transparent for all products and ancillary features.
Promotion	Promotional content should be integrated with other marketing efforts and should be tailored to the organization's key market segments. The Internet offers multiple distribution channels and promotional efforts need to be coordinated across all of these channels.
Point-of-sale	Sometimes called "place", this element facilitates product distribution and fulfillment. Organizations should provide the facility for travelers to book or reserve products and services online. Particular attention needs to be paid to streamlining the online ordering and payment process and ensuring all transactions are conducted securely.
People	Since travel experiences are made up of a collection of products and services, the people who provide the services are a key to the success of the transaction. Websites should showcase the organization and its people. Online customer service is just as important as offline service.
Programing	Exclusive programing adds value to the core product and distinguishes it from competitors. Websites provide many opportunities to offer ancillary features and to personalize and customize the product to individual needs. Special events can also address such preferences and draw in additional customers.
Packaging	Websites provide many opportunities to packaging different elements of the travel experience together. Features such as dynamic packaging and affiliate programs allow complementary products to be sold together online.
Partnerships	The digital tourism distribution system involves many partners and stakeholders who need to be coordinated to ensure online efforts are consistent. There are many opportunities to partner with a range of organizations in the travel and IT sectors to deliver a better online experience for customers. One example is the partnership between TripAdvisor and hotels.

Management

Managerial issues are a necessary part of the Internet marketing effort. Changes in user demographics, social media and computer technology mean that a website requires constant monitoring, maintenance and promotion. Site maintenance is essential for a site to be accurate, competent and professional. The maintenance involves removing outdated information and links (linkrot) and the addition of new information. Content concerning prices, products and events must be revised regularly. This process is automated in some larger organizations by using content management systems. The maintenance of a website needs appropriate financial, human and physical resources. Organizations should evaluate what resources are realistically available as this is critical for ensuring the quality of online customer service. It is important to ensure that individuals in the organization receive appropriate training to develop skills and knowledge in dealing with the Internet.

One of the most difficult aspects of website management involves attracting visitors once the site has been built. Unlike traditional media the WWW is a "pull" technology, requiring the organization to develop strategies to attract visitors to its site. Promotion of the site through links on other sites and online directories requires a never-ending commitment. Organizations can also drive traffic to their websites by using directory listings, paid listings, metatags, sponsored links and search engine optimization. As we discussed earlier, search engines provide an easy, convenient method to find sites on the Internet. Many tourism organizations perform poorly in SERPs (Wöber, 2006). The process of improving search engine rankings is known as **search engine optimization (SEO)**. SEO involves a combination of strategies, including optimizing the use of titles, keywords and metatags embedded in webpages, managing cross links and external links to the site, updating content regularly, and maintaining a social media presence (Fesenmaier *et al.*, 2011; Xiang and Pan, 2011). Ensuring that the organization is included in a range of search engines (e.g. Google Maps, Google Images) is also important and the first step to achieving this is to create a Google Places account. Once the site has been submitted to a search engine the listing should be monitored.

Organizations should also strive to attract repeat visitors to the website. We have noted earlier that there are opportunities for organizations to encourage pre-trip, on-site and post-trip use of their sites. Many websites offer users the opportunity to create a personal account so that details can be stored for future purchases. Often travelers will sign up for these accounts to receive special offers and newsletters from the organization. Such accounts are linked to the organization's CRM or loyalty program. The login for personal accounts can be integrated with social media such as Google+ and Facebook, creating other opportunities to engage with travelers. A simpler alternative to individual user accounts is to encourage visitors to "like" and "share" the organization's social network pages. These features can be easily incorporated on websites by embedding html code provided by social media sites.

Another strategy used by many travel websites is **permission marketing**, whereby users give the organization explicit permission to send promotional messages such as email newsletters, special offers and push notifications to mobile devices (Marinova *et al.*, 2002). Permission is usually provided through an online opt-in form or when a traveler creates an account to make a purchase. Permission marketing is a more efficient use of resources because promotions are sent only to travelers interested in the organization. These communications can also be personalized and more targeted based on the characteristics of travelers (Brey *et al.*, 2007).

Evaluation

A website is a dynamic and organic medium and needs to be continuously monitored to maintain its usability. This should be done using both internal and external benchmarking. Internal benchmarking involves monitoring site metrics and analytics to identify performance issues and user trends. Website **metrics** provide quantitative data about user behavior including log files, landing pages, the number of visits to individual pages, the time spent on individual pages, referring websites, broken links, conversion rates, click rates, heat maps and other tools. Google Analytics is the most commonly used web analytics service but many ISPs and other vendors provide analytics tools with various features. **Web analytics** includes the measurement, collection, analysis and reporting of metrics and other data to assess and improve the effectiveness of a website (Plaza, 2011). External benchmarking can include comparing the usability and features of a website with those provided by competitors. These methods should be supplemented by other business intelligence tools, including monitoring social media actively asking users for their feedback.

SUMMARY

This chapter has explored some of the key concepts required to understand the Internet and its application to the travel industry. We have examined the historical evolution of the Internet. Although its widespread commercial use has only been since the 1990s, it is clear from this chapter and others that this channel has had a profound effect on the structure of the tourism industry. Travel was an early adopter of this new technology and has continued to lead many other industries, but the Internet is still in its infancy. There are also many tourism organizations that have not leveraged the power of the Internet. As the number of devices that can connect the Internet continues to grow it will become critical for organizations to develop strategies, processes and digital resources to support their virtual presence.

KEY TERMS

aesthetic school, B2B, B2C, bandwidth, breadcrumbs, broadband, browser, C2B, C2C, computer-mediated environment, digital marketing mix, domain, domain name, eCommerce, EDI, extranet, firewall, Flash, FTP, functionalist school, G2B, G2C, G2G, host, HTML, HTTP, HTTPS, information architecture, Integrated Marketing Communications (IMC), intelligent assistants, Internet, Internet Service Provider (ISP), intranet, Java, knowledge graph, language, link graph, metatag, metrics, MP3, organic listing, paid listing, permission marketing, protocol, recommender system, search engine, search engine optimization (SEO), Search Engine Reply Page (SERP), server, SMIL, SMTP, TCP/IP, tourism websites, travel websites, top-level domain, Uniform Resource Locator (URL), user experience design (UXD), Web 1.0, Web 2.0, web analytics, web analytics, web design, World Wide Web (WWW), XML

DISCUSSION QUESTIONS

1. Identify a travel enterprise that uses an Intranet. What features does it provide? Can you suggest other ways that the enterprise could use the Intranet?

2. Find one specific example each of a G2G, G2B and G2C network in the tourism industry. Explain in detail.

3. In this chapter we present a typology of travel websites. Conduct a search to find your own examples of sites for each category. Were there any sites that do not fit into this typology?

4. Identify two search engines (e.g. Bing and Google) and compare and contrast

how they deal with travel requests. Do this by choosing a specific trip you would like to go on.

5. We have presented a number of elements that make tourism websites successful. Visit the travel website for your local region and conduct your own assessment of the quality of this website based on the elements we have presented. Prepare a set of recommendations to improve this website.

USEFUL WEBSITES

QR code	Website	Description
	The Search Engine List http: //www. thesearchenginelist.com/	A comprehensive list of search engines.
	Search Engine Land http: //searchengineland. com/	A useful resource for news, feature articles, blogs and commentaries on search engine developments.
	E-Tourism Frontiers http: //www. e-tourismfrontiers.com/	A source of ecommerce information for the tourism industry in Africa.
	Nielsen Norman Group http://www.nngroup.com/ articles/	Many practical web design articles from web design guru Jakob Nielsen.

QR code	Website	Description
	The Internet Society http: //www. internetsociety.org/	A global cause-driven organization dedicated to ensuring that the Internet remains open and transparent.
	Internet Corporation for Assigned Names and Numbers (ICANN) http://www.icann.org/	ICANN is responsible for the stable and secure operation of the global Internet's systems of unique identifiers.
	World Wide Web Consortium (W3C) http: //www.w3.org/	Founded and currently led by Tim Berners-Lee, W3C is the main international standards organization for the WWW.
	Google http: //www.google.com/	Global technology company specializing in the Internet and related services.

Case Study: AirBnB

The amount of tourist-to-tourist (C2C) communication on the web is increasing dramatically. One of the successful ventures that links consumers to consumers is AirBnB (http://www.airbnb.com/). This is a community marketplace where people can list, discover and book unique accommodations around the world online or from a mobile phone, and was launched in 2007. Most importantly, the accommodations are not commercial in the sense that hotels are, but are typically spaces in residents' homes. This allows people to make money from extra rooms in their home, although listings also include castles, boats and other unusual accommodations. At the time of writing there are over 500,000 accommodations listed in 192 countries.

Trust is an issue when booking accommodation on AirBnB. Potential tourists want to know they are staying in a clean and safe place with a person they trust, and hosts need to

Case Study. Continued.

know that their guests are reputable. To address this issue, the website takes a number of measures. First, it suggests that hosts and guests verify each other on their social networks. Second, a part of the website has reviews and profiles of hosts and their properties and also on guests, which are visible to everyone. The validity of the review is ensured by allowing only those that have completed their reservation and their stay to post reviews. Third, for quality control, a list of hospitality standards that each host must abide by (e.g. cleanliness, amenities, accuracy of information) is provided on the site. Fourth, there is a private feedback mechanism for the host and guest to communicate in private. Possible guests can also ask questions of potential hosts by using a messaging feature on the site.

Guests search for accommodation on location, dates, room type and other filters. The AirBnB search engine lists the accommodations that are most relevant to the search criteria. Quality of reviews and responsiveness of the host are also considered in the order of the listing. Photographs and maps of the location are included in each accommodation listing, as is advice for the host on how to best describe their accommodation, determine their pricing, or make special offers. Financial transactions can be completed in numerous ways: PayPal, credit card, wire or check. The website provides many more details for hosts and guests to ensure satisfaction.

This venture has created a worldwide community of travelers that prefer to stay in local accommodations and meet residents directly. It would not have been possible without the Internet platform.

Study Questions

1. Visit the http://www.airbnb/ site as a potential host. Learn as much as you can about hosting guests in this way. Write a report giving advice to someone wanting to sign up their space.

2. Find other tourist-to-tourist sites on the web and analyze their functionality.

3. To what degree do you think that C2C sites like AirBnB are threatening the traditional travel industry? Explain. How should traditional hotels respond to the threat of AirBnB?

REFERENCES

Arlt, W.G. (2006) Not very Willkommen: the internet as a marketing tool for attracting German-speaking tourists to non-European destinations. *Information Technology and Tourism* 8(3/4), 227–238. doi: 10.3727/109830506778690803

Arpita, K. and Anshuman, K. (2011) Blending information technology in Indian travel and tourism sector. *Services Marketing Quarterly* 32(4), 302–317. doi: 10.1080/15332969.2011.606761

Baloglu, S. and Pekcan, Y.A. (2006) The website design and Internet site marketing practices of upscale and luxury hotels in Turkey. *Tourism Management* 27(1), 171–176. doi: 10.1016/j.tourman.2004.07.003

Belch, G.E., Belch, M.A., Kerr, G.F. and Powell, I. (2003) *Advertising and Promotion: An Integrated Marketing Communications Perspective*, 6th edn. McGraw-Hill, Boston.

Beldona, S. and Cai, L.A. (2006) An exploratory evaluation of rural tourism websites. *Journal of Convention and Event Tourism* 8(1), 69–80.

Benckendorff, P. and Black, N.L. (2000) Destination marketing on the Internet: a case study of Australian Regional Tourism Authorities. *Journal of Tourism Studies* 11(1), 11–21.

Bergman, M.K. (2001) The deep web: surfacing hidden value. *Journal of Electronic Publishing* 7(1), 1–7.

Bevanda, V., Grzinic, J. and Cervar, E. (2008) Analysing the users' perception of web design quality by data mining tools. *Tourism and Hospitality Management* 14(2), 251–262.

Brey, E.T., So, S.I., Kim, D.Y. and Morrison, A.M. (2007) Web-based permission marketing: segmentation for the lodging industry. *Tourism Management* 28(6), 1408–1416. doi: 10.1016/j.tourman.2007.01.002

Brin, S. and Page, L. (1998) The anatomy of a large-scale hypertextual Web search engine. Paper presented at the 7th International Conference on World Wide Web.

Chan, S. and Law, R. (2006) Automatic website evaluations: the case of hotels in Hong Kong. *Information Technology and Tourism* 8(3/4), 255–269. doi: 10.3727/109830506778690858

Ellsworth, J.H. and Ellsworth, M.V. (1995) *Marketing on the Internet: multimedia strategies for the World Wide Web*. John Wiley and Sons, New York.

European Travel Commission (2013) Digital Portal. Available at: http://etc-digital.org (accessed 19 November 2013).

EyeforTravel (2012) Travel Consumer Report 2012–2013. 177 pp.

Fesenmaier, D. and Johnson, B. (1989) Involvement-based segmentation: implication for travel marketing in Texas. *Tourism Management* 10(4), 293–300.

Fesenmaier, D., Wöber, K. and Werthner, H. (2006) *Destination Recommendation Systems: Behavioral Foundations and Applications*. CAB International, Wallingford, UK.

Fesenmaier, D.R., Xiang, Z., Pan, B. and Law, R. (2011) A framework of search engine use for travel planning. *Journal of Travel Research* 50(6), 587–601. doi: 10.1177/0047287510385466

Fogg, B.J., Marshall, J., Laraki, O., Osipovich, A., Varma, C., Fang, N. *et al.* (2001) What makes Web sites credible?: a report on a large quantitative study. Paper presented at the Proceedings of the SIGCHI conference on Human factors in computing systems.

Garrett, J.J. (2011) *The Elements of User Experience: User-Centered Design for the Web and Beyond*. Pearson Education, Berkeley, California.

Grabler, K. and Zins, A.H. (2001) Analysis of Available Cases Report, Diagnosing 200 Travel Counselling Dialogues. *DIETORECS, IST-200-29474*. Trento-Wien.

Gretzel, U. (2011) Intelligent systems in tourism: a social science perspective. *Annals of Tourism Research* 38(3), 757–779. doi: http://dx.doi.org/10.1016/j.annals.2011.04.014

Gretzel, U., Hwang, Y.H. and Fesenmaier, D. (2012) Informing destination recommender systems design and evaluation through quantitatve research. *International Journal of Culture, Tourism and Hospitality Research* 6(4), 297–315.

Han, J.H. and Mills, J.E. (2007) Are travel websites meeting the needs of the visually impaired? *Information Technology and Tourism* 9(2), 99–113. doi: 10.3727/109830507781367401

Hoffman, D.L. and Novak, T.P. (1996) Marketing in hypermedia computer-mediated environments: conceptual foundations. *Journal of Marketing* 60(July), 50–68.

International Telecommunication Union (2013) The World in 2013: ICT Facts and Figures. Available at: http://www.itu.int/en/ITU-D/Statistics/Pages/facts/default.aspx/ (accessed 2 January 2014).

Kotler, P.J. and Armstrong, G.M. (2012) *Principles of Marketing*, 15th edn. Prentice Hall, New Jersey.

Law, R., Qi, S. and Buhalis, D. (2010) Progress in tourism management: a review of website evalua-tion in tourism research. *Tourism Management* 31(3), 297–313. doi: http://dx.doi.org/10.1016/j.tourman.2009.11.007

Levene, M. (2006) *An Introduction to Search Engines and Web Navigation*. Addison-Wesley, New York.

Li, K.W. and Law, R. (2007) A novel English/Chinese information retrieval approach in hotel website searching. *Tourism Management* 28(3), 777–787. doi: 10.1016/j.tourman.2006.05.017

Marcussen, C.H. and Skjoldgager, D. (1998) *Extranets of National Tourist Organizations*. Paper presented at the Information and Communication Technologies in Tourism, Istanbul, Turkey.

Marinova, A., Murphy, J. and Massey, B.L. (2002) Permission e-mail marketing as a means of targeted promotion. *Cornell Hotel and Restaurant Administration Quarterly* 43(1), 61–69. doi: 10.1016/s0010-8804(02)80009-x

McKercher, B. (1998) The effect of market access on destination choice. *Journal of Travel Research* 37, 39–47.

Morrison, A.M. (2010) *Hospitality and Travel Marketing*. Delmar Cengage Learning, Clifton Park, New York.

Nielsen, J. (1997) How Users Read on the Web. Available at: http://www.nngroup.com/articles/how-users-read-on-the-web/ (accessed 4 January 2014).

Nielsen, J. (2000) *Designing Web Usability: The Practice of Simplicity*. New Riders Publishing, Indianapolis.

O'Connor, P. (2004) Conflicting viewpoints on web design. *Journal of Travel and Tourism Marketing* 17(2/3), 225–230. doi: 10.1300/J073v17n02_17

O'Connor, P. (2011) Assessing the global e-readiness of hotel chain websites. *Information Technology and Tourism* 13(4), 365–376. doi: 10.3727/109830512x13364362859984

Pan, B. and Fesenmaier, D. (2000) A typology of tourism-related web sites: its theoretical background and implications. *Information Technology and Tourism* 3(3/4), 155–166.

Pan, B. and Fesenmaier, D.R. (2006) Online information search: vacation planning process. *Annals of Tourism Research* 33(3), 809–832. doi: 10.1016/j.annals.2006.03.006

Park, Y.A. and Gretzel, U. (2007) Success factors for destination marketing web sites: a qualitative meta-analysis. *Journal of Travel Research* 46(1), 46–63. doi: 10.1177/0047287507302381

Plaza, B. (2011) Google Analytics for measuring website performance. *Tourism Management* 32(3), 477–481.

Reid, L.J. and Crompton, S. (1993) Communicating tourism supplier services: building repeat visitor relationship. *Journal of Travel and Tourism Marketing* 2(2–3).

Schmidt, S., Serra Cantallops, A. and Santos, C.P. dos (2008) The characteristics of hotel websites and their implications for website effectiveness. *International Journal of Hospitality Management* 27(4), 504–516. doi: 10.1016/j.ijhm.2007.08.002

Siegel, D.S. (1996) *Creating Killer Websites: The Art of Third-Generation Site Design*. Hayden Books, Indianapolis.

Singhal, A. (2012) Introducing the Knowledge Graph: things, not strings. Available at: http://google-blog.blogspot.com.au/2012/05/introducing-knowledge-graph-things-not.html/ (accessed 3 January 2014).

Snepenger, D.J. (1987) Segmenting the vacation market by novelty-seeking role. *Journal of Travel Research* 26(2), 8–14.

Stepchenkova, S., Tang, L.A., Jang, S.C., Kirilenko, A.P. and Morrison, A.M. (2010) Benchmarking CVB website performance: spatial and structural patterns. *Tourism Management* 31(5), 611–620.

Valacich, J. and Schneider, C. (2014) *Information Systems Today: Managing in a Digital World*. Pearson Education, New Jersey.

Wöber, K.W. (2006) Domain specific search engines. In: Fesenmaier, D.R., Wöber, K. and Werthner, H. (eds) *Destination Recommendation Systems: Behavioural Foundations and Applications*. CAB International, Wallingford, UK.

Xiang, Z. and Pan, B. (2011) Travel queries on cities in the United States: implications for search engine marketing for tourist destinations. *Tourism Management* 32(1), 88–97. doi: http://dx.doi.org/10.1016/j.tourman.2009.12.004

Xiang, Z., Wöber, K. and Fesenmaier, D.R. (2008) Representation of the online tourism domain in search engines. *Journal of Travel Research* 47(2), 137–150.

Xiang, Z., Gretzel, U. and Fesenmaier, D.R. (2009) Semantic representation of tourism on the internet. *Journal of Travel Research* 47(4), 440–453.

Xiang, Z., Pan, B., Law, R. and Fesenmaier, D.R. (2010) Assessing the visibility of destination marketing organizations in Google: a case study of convention and visitor bureau websites in the United States. *Journal of Travel and Tourism Marketing* 27(7), 694–707. doi: 10.1080/10548408.2010.519672

chapter 5

Social Media and Tourism

LEARNING OBJECTIVES

After studying this chapter you should be able to:

- understand the types and functions of social media;
- explain why electronic word of mouth is important to travel organizations;
- analyze the advantages and disadvantages of different social media platforms;
- discuss how different social media platforms can be used to engage with travelers; and
- adopt a strategic approach to using social media for a range of applications in travel organizations.

INTRODUCTION

In this chapter we will examine social media and their impact on travelers, tourism intermediaries, suppliers and destinations. Social media relies on web and mobile technologies to provide interactive platforms through which individuals and communities can share, collaborate, discuss and modify user generated content. This cross-platform accessibility means that travelers use social media across all stages of the travel lifecycle to share and document their experiences. This capability shifts the control of information from marketers and public relations departments to travelers – creating a number of challenges and opportunities for the travel industry.

This chapter will start by providing some foundations, then shift to the different social media platforms and how travelers and travel organizations can use them. The chapter concludes by considering the need for a strategic approach to the use of social media by travel organizations. We will also examine the mobile and localization aspects of social media in Chapter 6.

UNDERSTANDING SOCIAL MEDIA

The phrase **social media** has two components. "Media" is the plural of medium and refers to the communication channels through which information, news and entertainment are delivered. The "social" part of the phrase suggests that these media are interactive. Social media can be defined as "a group of Internet-based applications that build on the ideological and technological foundations of Web 2.0, and that allow the creation and exchange of user-generated content" (Kaplan and Haenlein, 2010, p. 61). This **user-generated content (UGC)** distinguishes **Web 2.0** and social media from the largely static, marketing generated content found on websites.

Social media consists of virtual communities in which different users access, discuss, share, collaborate and update web content (Lange-Faria and Elliot, 2012). This "collective intelligence" challenges the hegemony of marketers and public relations managers who have produced most of the information traditionally used by travelers to plan their trips (Xiang and Gretzel, 2010). In this section we will explore these developments by examining the social media landscape, discussing its functional building blocks concluding with

the concept of social media as a digital platform for word-of-mouth communication.

The social media landscape

Social media include many diverse platforms and technologies, including social networks, blogs, wikis, forums, social bookmarking, media sharing and virtual social worlds. An organizing framework is useful for making sense of all of these. Kaplan and Haenlein (2010) identify six different types of social media, which are arranged in a two-dimensional framework as shown in Fig. 5.1. Along the horizontal dimension social media sites vary based on media richness and social presence. **Social presence** is related to the level of acoustic, visual and physical contact between individuals (Kaplan and Haenlein, 2010). In a media environment, richness is often closely linked with social presence. A rich medium provides more cues on which to base social responses. Blogs and wikis are largely text-based and as a

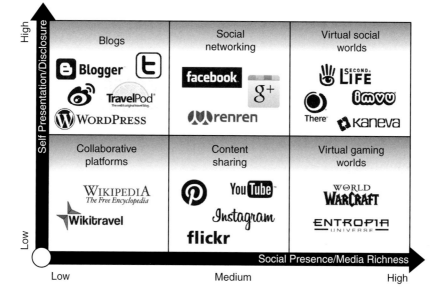

Fig. 5.1. Classification of social media (Reprinted from Kaplan and Haenlein (2010) with permission from Elsevier).

result their richness and social presence tends to be lower. Social networks and content-sharing sites provide greater visual richness, and images and video offer more cues for social interaction. Virtual worlds are rich simulated environments with real-time animated avatars that allow people to interact in a digital space.

The second dimension is related to the amount of self-presentation or **self-disclosure** facilitated by the platform. The content on collaborative platforms and content-sharing sites is often subject-centric rather than author-centric. Similarly, in virtual gaming worlds the fantasy environment obscures the disclosure of real personal details. In contrast, blogs and social networks are author-centric and often encourage the sharing of personal details, images and video. This classification is useful because it highlights the unique traits of each platform and allows consideration of how a travel company might establish a presence across social media types. However, the boundaries between the different types have become increasingly blurred and new social media platforms have emerged since the development of this model.

A more recent framework for understanding the social media landscape is provided by Cavazza (2012), who updates his blog annually with a new depiction of social media. His 2012 framework, shown in Fig. 5.2, divides social media into six categories.

1. Publishing: sites that allow content creators and curators to develop new content, create "mashups" of existing content or to post questions and answers (e.g. Blogger, Wikipedia, Quora).
2. Sharing: sites that allow users to share text, links, images, slides, documents and videos (e.g. Pinterest, YouTube, Slideshare).
3. Playing: sites that support online multi-player games (e.g. Zynga, Playdom).

4. Networking: social networking sites that allow users to share updates and information for personal or professional contexts (e.g. Facebook, Qzone, LinkedIn).
5. Buying: social commerce sites that provide customer intelligence, reviews and recommendations (e.g. Tripadvisor, Urbanspoon, Bazaarvoice).
6. Localization: mobile apps and websites that provide information and opportunities for social interaction based on the location of users (e.g. Foursquare, Tinder, Yelp).

The major players (Google, Facebook and Twitter) are included at the center of the model because they have developed entire social media ecosystems where functions and tools and are connected. For example, Facebook Graph Search provides users with access to a social semantic search tool, while Google Maps provides location-based recommendations, pictures and reviews. The framework identifies that some media are more about conversations while others are about

Social Media Landscape 2012

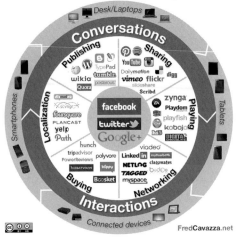

Fig. 5.2. The social media landscape (Cavazza, 2012).

creating interactions. Different technologies also dominate particular types of social media, as shown by the outside ring of Fig. 5.2, but these distinctions are also becoming increasingly blurred. Although some of the tools listed in the figure are already defunct and new players have emerged, it provides a useful framework to understand social media sites.

There are a number of regional differences in the use of social media. For example, a social network site (SNS) called orkut has been popular in Brazil and India, Xing is well known in Germany, and Russia has a number of homegrown social networks. China has one of the largest and most unusual social media landscapes. The Chinese Government restricted access to most Western social media platforms in 2009. As a result a number of similar social networks have emerged in China to fill the same niches as those in the rest of the world. Table 5.1 provides some examples of these networks, although it is important to note that some Chinese social media have evolved rather differently to Western social media. Cultural differences also impact on the behavior of Chinese social media users. For example, Sina Weibo does

provide a microblog, but the company also provides a range of other social media features. Mobile messaging is also much more popular in China than other parts of the world. Companies such as WeChat have expanded well beyond text-based messaging by offering a number of social networking features such as friending, group chat, video chat, file sharing and photo feeds. An awareness of these parallel social media platforms will be important for travel organizations as the number of outbound Chinese travelers continues to grow.

Social media functions

Having considered the types of social media sites, we now turn our attention to the building blocks and dynamics of social media. Here we are concerned with the features and functions that characterize social media sites. Kietzmann *et al.* (2011) propose a honeycomb framework of social media is made up of seven functional building blocks (see Fig. 5.3).

Kietzmann *et al.* (2011) highlight overlaps between the functional blocks and note that they are not always present in every social media context. But the model is useful

Table 5.1. Popular Western and Chinese social media platforms.

Platform	Western examples	Chinese examples
Blogs	Blogger, Wordpress	Blogbus
Microblogs	Twitter	Sina Weibo, Tencent Weibo
Wikis	Wikipedia	Baidu Baike
Social Networks	Facebook	Qzone, Renren, Pengyou
Video Sharing	YouTube	Youku, Tudou
Location-based	Foursquare	Jiepang
Review Sites	TripAdvisor	DaoDao

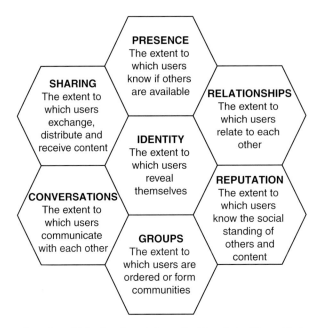

Fig. 5.3. The seven functional blocks of social media (Reprinted from Kietzmann *et al.* (2011) with permission from Elsevier).

because each building block provides insights into a specific aspect of the user experience and the implications for travel organizations. The following observations can be made for each building block:

- **Identity** is the extent to which users reveal their identities in a social media setting. Users share information, thoughts, feelings, likes and dislikes to reinforce who they are or how they would like others to see them. This can include disclosing personal information such as name, age, gender, location and other information that forms part of their identity. For travel organizations, there are issues around striking the right balance between sharing information and privacy, data mining and surveillance;

- **Conversations** refer to the extent to which users communicate with other users in a social media setting. Many sites facilitate conversations among individuals and groups. The management of negative sentiment and encouragement of positive sentiment are important challenges for travel organizations;

- **Sharing** is the extent to which users exchange, distribute and receive content. The "social" part of social media implies that the exchange of "objects" between people is crucial. These shared objects can include text, links, images, videos, sounds and locations. It is important to understand how, what and why objects are shared and how travel organizations might facilitate the sharing of objects (such as evocative destination images) for strategic purposes;

- **Presence** is the extent to which users can know where others are and whether they are available. Location and context-aware applications offer great potential for travel organizations (see Chapter 6), but the availability of real-time online support is also important in some travel contexts;

- **Relationships** is the extent to which users converse, share objects, meet up, or list each other as friends. For organizations, the relationship between social media users often determines what and how information is exchanged. The position of a user in a network is important. Opinion leaders often have large, dense networks of followers and identifying these opinion leaders can be important for platforms such as forums, blogs and microblogs;

- **Reputation** is the extent to which users can identify the standing of others, including themselves, in a social media setting. Monitoring an organization's reputation in terms of strength, sentiment and reach across multiple social media channels is important;

- **Groups** refer to the extent to which users can form communities and sub-communities. In a travel context, the challenge is how organizations build virtual communities around their brands.

Different social media platforms have strengths in different functions of the framework. For example, LinkedIn is particularly successful at the identity and relationship functions, while YouTube excels as a channel for sharing. As we will see later in this chapter, travel organizations need to be aware of the various strengths in order to engage with social media platforms in a way that is consistent with the organization's strategic objectives.

Electronic word of mouth

The influence of **word of mouth (WOM)** has been acknowledged in the consumer behavior literature for many decades (Dichter, 1966; Richins, 1983). WOM has been defined as "all informal communications directed at other consumers about the ownership, usage, or characteristics of particular goods and services or their sellers" (Westbrook, 1987, p. 261). The honeycomb model identifies conversations and sharing as two of the key communication functions of social media. These two functions are perhaps the most interesting for tourism organizations because they facilitate a special type of WOM that has been called **electronic Word of Mouth (eWOM)** (Litvin *et al.*, 2008). eWOM can be defined as: "any positive or negative statement made by potential, actual, or former customers about a product or company, which is made available to a multitude of people and institutions via the Internet" (Hennig-Thurau *et al.*, 2004, p. 39). Research suggests that travelers consider eWOM to be more trustworthy than other information sources (Xiang and Gretzel, 2010).

eWOM differs from traditional WOM in a number of ways.

1. **Scale**: eWOM can influence travelers on an unprecedented scale because it is available in a digital format that can be searched, linked and shared (Dellarocas, 2003; Litvin *et al.*, 2008).
2. **Relationships**: the strength of the relationship between communicators and recipients is often weaker in a social media setting. The recipient of an eWOM communication may not even know the original communicator.
3. **Anonymity**: the anonymity of many social media platforms calls into question the legitimacy of some eWOM communications.
4. **Durability**: eWOM messages are more durable – once a message is in the public domain it continues to influence consumers over time.

5. Variety: eWOM can take many forms, including blogs, product reviews, social network status updates, tweets and YouTube videos.

In 2008 United Airlines broke Canadian musician Dave Carroll's guitar. While it was not the first time an airline had damaged luggage, we may never have heard about Carroll's difficulties in seeking compensation from the airline had it not been for social media. Carroll wrote and recorded three music videos about the experience and posted these on YouTube. The first video in the series went viral and received over 1 million views in the first 4 days. By 2014 the video had been viewed more than 13 million times. See the video at: http://youtu.be/5YGc4zOqozo/.

http://youtu.be/5YGc4zOqozo

The video was widely reported by the press, generating very negative publicity for United Airlines. Twitter has also become a popular platform for customer complaints. Each year millions of luggage items are "displaced" by airlines. In 2013 Hasan Syed paid for a promoted tweet that simply read: "Don't fly @BritishAirways. Their customer service is horrendous." He followed this up with a series of messages criticizing the airline and threatened to continue paying for Twitter ads until British Airways resolved an issue with his father's lost luggage. British Airways responded swiftly and issued a public apology. These examples illustrate

the power of eWOM and the challenges for travel organizations, particularly when opinion leaders with many followers report negative experiences.

We can understand eWOM using a two-dimensional model in which various eWOM channels are organized according to communication scope and level of interactivity (Litvin *et al.*, 2008). **Communication scope** refers to whether the channel involves one-to-one communication, one-to-many communication or many-to-many communication (see also Chapter 4). **Level of interactivity** can be organized on a spectrum ranging from asynchronous to synchronous. **Asynchronous** communication takes place between individuals who respond at different times while **synchronous** communication involves real-time or "live" responses. Figure 5.4 shows how different online channels (including social media) can be organized using this framework.

We can also understand the dynamics of eWOM from a communications perspective. In Chapter 4 we saw how the Internet transformed one-to-many **Sender-Message-Receiver (SMR)** communication into many-to-many communication. If we break these communications down into the basic SMR components we can investigate some of the variables that impact eWOM (see Fig. 5.5).

The first important element in the SMR model is the **sender**. The features of an individual who initiates an eWOM communication can impact how the message is perceived and used. Researchers have identified a number of important sender characteristics:

- **Motives** attempt to explain why a sender might share their experiences online.

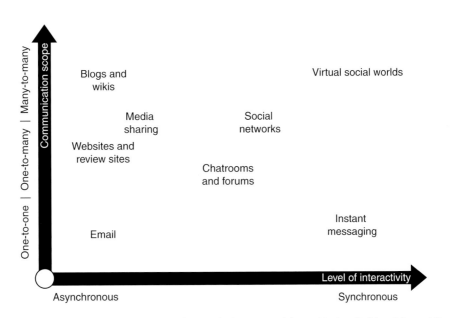

Fig. 5.4. Typology of various eWOM channels (Reprinted from Litvin, Goldsmith and Pan (2008) with permission from Elsevier).

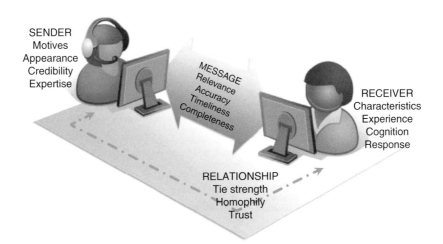

Fig. 5.5. Communication factors influencing eWOM.

Research suggests that senders are motivated by a desire for social interaction, economic incentives, altruism toward other consumers and the opportunity to enhance their own self-worth (Hennig-Thurau *et al.*, 2004; Yoo and Gretzel, 2008);

- **Appearance** can be difficult to establish unless the social media platform uses profile photos. Research in traditional communication contexts has found that communicators with more positive attributes (e.g. physical attractiveness) are more persuasive than ones with less positive attributes (Nabi and Hendriks, 2003);

- **Source credibility** is how believable, competent and trustworthy the sender is believed to be (Cheung *et al.*, 2009). Senders perceived to be more credible often possess **expertise** or product knowledge and express this knowledge in a trustworthy manner. Senders on product review sites and forums often earn badges or points based on their contributions, which can be used to indicate expertise or trustworthiness. The challenge for travel organizations is determining who the opinion leaders are and how to encourage them to spread positive eWOM.

The second key element of the SMR model is the quality of the information contained in the **message** (Sussman and Siegal, 2003). Four dimensions contribute to information quality: relevance, accuracy, timeliness and completeness. If recipients perceive a message to be important and **relevant** they are more likely to read it carefully (Petty and Cacioppo, 1986; Bhattacherjee and Sanford, 2006). The perceived usefulness of the information depends on its **accuracy**, whether it is correct and reliable. Related to this is the issue of **timeliness**, whether the information is current and up-to-date. **Completeness** refers to the comprehensiveness of the message. It is important for travel organizations to develop a better understanding of how the information quality of a message can impact travelers. A recent study of hotel reviews confirmed that information accuracy, relevance and timeliness were strong predictors of travelers' adoption of information in a social media context (Filieri and McLeay, 2014).

The characteristics of the **receiver** can also influence how the message is received and how the recipient responds. Their age, gender, cultural background and experience can influence whether they pay attention to the message and how it is interpreted. **Experience** may include familiarity with the social media platform, past interactions with the sender or involvement with the product or product class (e.g. hotels). The **cognitive** processes of the recipient will determine what meaning the recipient attaches to the message. The receiver can **respond** to the message by ignoring it, reading and then discarding it, committing it to memory or choosing to share it with others. Understanding how receivers perceive and share these messages is critical for travel organizations. Although an organization may not always be able to control senders or messages, it can respond to the messages.

The final element in Fig. 5.5 is the **relationship** between the sender and receiver. As we have seen in the honeycomb model, relationships are a key function of social media. Scholars have used network analysis to examine how relationships impact the flow of information. From a communications perspective we are interested in the intensity of the social relationship (**tie strength**), the similarity between the sender and the receiver (**homophily**) and the level of **trust** between these two individuals. The tie strength can range from strong primary ties (such as family and friends) in the individual's personal network to weak secondary ties (acquaintances, friends of friends, strangers). Strong ties usually provide emotional or substantive support while weak ties tend to propagate information sharing on more diverse topics (Mittal *et al.*, 2008). In some cases, such as product review sites, forums and media-sharing sites, there may be no relationship at all between the sender and receiver. Homophily refers to the similarity between the sender and receiver in gender, age, education and lifestyle. Individuals with a higher level of perceived homophily are more likely to interact with each other and to engage in eWOM communication because they share similar traits (Steffes and Burgee, 2009; Thelwall, 2009).

SOCIAL MEDIA PLATFORMS IN TRAVEL

Now that we have a better understanding of the social media landscape, core functions and eWOM, we can consider how travelers, intermediaries, suppliers and destinations use different social media platforms. The following section explores the implications of social network sites, wikis, blogs, product review sites, forums, media sharing, crowdsourcing and virtual worlds for travelers and travel organizations.

Social network sites

According to boyd and Ellison (2007, p. 211), social network sites (SNSs) are defined as "web-based services that allow individuals to: (i) construct a public or semi-public profile within a bounded system; (ii) articulate a list of other users with whom they share a connection; and (iii) view and traverse their connections and those made by others within the system." SNSs such as Facebook, LinkedIn and Google+ allow individuals and organizations to find new connections or establish and maintain relationships with people they may know offline. The core of modern

SNSs consists of visible profiles and mechanisms that allow "followers" or "friends" to leave public messages on these profiles. Using the honeycomb model, we can suggest that the key strengths of SNSs are built on conversations, sharing and identity. However, many SNSs also provide additional services, including image and video sharing, instant messaging, blogging, status updates and online apps.

Most SNSs fall into one of four categories:

1. Universal SNSs: general networks with global appeal open to anyone above a minimum age with an email address. Examples include Facebook, Bebo and Google+.

2. Professional SNSs: services that allow professionals to interact and build business networks. Examples include LinkedIn and Yammer. While LinkedIn is an open platform Yammer provides tools that allow organizations to create internal social networks of employees.

3. Regional SNSs: these include sites that are used in particular regions of the world, such as orkut in Brazil and India, Vkontakte in Russia, Biip.no in Norway, and Qzone and Renren in China.

4. Niche SNSs: sites that cater for groups based on shared interests or activities. Examples include school reunion networks (e.g. classmates.com, FriendsReunited), art and design (e.g. deviantART), music (e.g. Buzznet, Last.fm), movies (e.g. Flixter), academic research networks (e.g. academia.edu and ResearchGate), African-Americans (Blackplanet), teens (e.g. Habbo), languages (e.g. Busuu) and travel (e.g. WAYN, travbuddy). SNS tools such as Ning provide platforms for people to create their own micro-SNS.

For travel organizations, SNSs offer four major opportunities. First, organizations can create pages for travelers to join or "like". This connection generates regular updates and newsfeeds to travelers who are highly involved with a product or destination. Some destinations were early adopters of social media and have built large communities of followers (see Industry Insight) through innovative campaigns and contests. Second, this allows organizations to use SNSs as online touch points to deliver customer service (to be discussed later in this chapter). Third, while there are privacy and ethical concerns related to the use of personal data, many sites harvest this "big data" to develop detailed profiles of consumers. By using profile data and monitoring online behavior such as the amount of time users spend online, what they click on and what they share, social network companies can develop accurate dossiers on the interests, activities and opinions of each user. This information is then used to target SNS users with more relevant advertising messages. Advertising on SNS sites is a cost-effective marketing tool for travel companies because the ability to accurately target users based on their interests and online behavior increases the click through rate of online advertising. Finally, many travel industry professionals use professional SNSs such as LinkedIn for networking, strategic listening and recruitment.

From a traveler perspective, SNSs are playing an increasingly important role in the travel lifecycle. While sites such as WAYN

Industry Insight: Australia.com on Facebook

Australia has been described as the most popular tourism destination on Facebook, Google+ and Instagram (O'Neill, 2013). Australia's Facebook page is maintained by Tourism Australia, whose fan base grew from 1.2 million to 4.1 million in 2012 after a series of social media campaigns. By the end of 2013 the page had over 5.1 million "likes". This popularity is the result of a number of strategic decisions and careful planning.

In 2010 the Managing Director of Australia, Andrew McEvoy, decided that Tourism Australia should prioritize social media to market the destination. Jesse Desjardins, its first social media and advocacy manager, created a series of viral marketing campaigns to boost Australia's social media presence. Tourism Australia invited locals and fans to submit their favorite destination photos to a "Friday Fan Photos" album on Facebook. The idea quickly spread and users shared some of the more inspirational images on their own walls. In 2011 the agency shifted its focus to locals, and enlisted Australians as brand advocates. Locals were encouraged to submit and share images of Australia's "hidden secrets" in the "There's Nothing Like Australia" contest. Australians uploaded over 60,000 stories and photos illustrating the theme. The agency also allowed locals and fans to post content to its timeline, creating a rich visual storyline of Australian travel stretching back 150 years.

Many of Tourism Australia's social media campaigns leverage off breaking news and trending online conversations. For example, when the rest of the world was concerned about the end of the Mayan calendar in 2012, Tourism Australia used Australia's time zone advantage to create a social media campaign around the following tagline:

(Continued)

Continued.

"Don't worry about the world coming to an end today, it's already tomorrow in Australia". This campaign was picked up by news broadcasts around the world and generated over 180,000 likes and 7000 comments. Tourism Australia also launched a Facebook app that allowed travelers to tap into their own network of friends for inspiration and ideas to plan their holiday in Australia. Today, 95% of Tourism Australia's social media content is user generated. The agency has expanded its social media staff and uses other sites such as Instagram, Twitter, Sina Weibo and Tudou.

and Travbuddy provide examples of travel-focused SNSs that connect travelers, the mainstream SNSs like Facebook and Google have developed tools that support different functions in the digital tourism ecosystem (see Chapter 2). In the inspiration stage, comments, photos and videos shared by travelers can motivate others to plan a holiday. Apps have been developed to allow travelers to book travel products from SNS pages, supporting the acquisition phase of the lifecycle. During the experience, the accessibility of SNSs through mobile apps supports the sharing of stories, photos, videos and status updates that in turn inspire other travelers (see Chapter 6). Travel organizations can support this behavior by providing free WiFi to make it easy for travelers to share positive experiences. SNSs provide a range of tools to allow travelers to document their journeys, including linking GPS enabled digital images to maps. In the reflection stage, SNSs allow the convenient cataloging of travel experiences in a useful timeline format.

Recent SNS developments include improved connectivity and the development of tools that harness the massive amounts of user-generated content. Facebook's Graph Search is a good example. It is a **semantic search engine** that provides users with answers to natural language search queries.

It combines user-generated big data from within a user's network of friends with other information to provide user-centric results. For example, a user might ask for: "Friends who have been to New York". Graph Search will then return results that combine friends' content with external data from the web. This tool provides a powerful search function for eWOM and meshes this content with other information sources to create results that are unique to the user's social context. The connectivity between various Google tools offers similar functionality and social elements from Google+ are incorporated into its web search, maps and other tools. Travel organizations can take advantage of these developments by encouraging travelers to share positive content about their experiences to reach their social network.

External travel companies have also developed innovative apps for SNSs. For example, OTA eDreams has developed a Facebook app called Domingo, which allows users to share their travel experiences and be inspired by seeing where their friends have been. Another example is the integration between Facebook and TripAdvisor. Users who log in to TripAdvisor using their Facebook username will see reviews from friends or "friends of friends" before reviews from strangers. These examples illustrate that the search for travel information is becoming increasingly personalized and social as a result of harnessing the "big data" available to SNSs.

Wikis, blogs and product reviews

Wikis, blogs and product review sites provide asynchronous platforms for sharing digital content. A **wiki** is a real-time editable website that helps users create content through cooperative development and ownership (Bean and Hott, 2005). The term **blog** is a contraction of the phrase "web log" and refers to a personal website or webpage that allows an individual to present content and opinions. The key difference between a wiki and a blog is that one author controls the content on a blog, whereas a wiki supports multiple authors. A **product review site** is a website devoted to providing subjective consumer feedback on products and services.

Wikis

Ward Cunningham, the founder of Wikipedia, created the first wiki in 1995. The word was derived from the Hawaiian *wiki-wiki*, which means quick. Today there are two types of wikis. The first category includes wikis in the public domain, which allow anyone to contribute content. The second type includes private wikis where access is limited to users collaborating together on a project. Unlike SNSs, individual contributions to wikis are often anonymous. The world's largest wiki project, Wikipedia, contains many entries about places that travelers may use as an authoritative information source. The Internet also offers several specialist travel wikis. A travel wiki is a crowdsourced travel guide offering information about travel products and destinations authored by an online travel community. WikiTravel attracts more than 350,000 readers per day and is a good example of a travel wiki. The key strength of a travel wiki is that the content is dynamic and constantly updated by travelers. Consequently, the information is more timely, complete and personalized than that provided in commercial guidebooks (Schwabe and Prestipino, 2005).

Savvy tourism organizations can contribute to wiki pages to present travel products and destinations in a favorable light. However, care needs to be taken that the information is factual, written objectively and supported by reputable sources. Blatant attempts at marketing prose are likely to be quickly edited or corrected by other members of the wiki community. Collaborative editing is the defining feature of wikis. An individual can edit any content and changes are logged using a history feature so that users can see and restore previous versions of a wiki page. Travel organizations can use private wikis for collaborating on strategic plans, marketing materials, reports, manuals, project management and software (Majchrzak *et al.*, 2006). These features are particularly useful when collaborators are in different locations.

Blogs and microblogs

Blogs have evolved separately to wikis. The first blogs emerged in the late 1990s as online diaries allowing authors to record regular entries. Technological developments led to web-based applications for authors to post entries without learning HTML coding. A number of different types of blogs have emerged, including the following.

1. Traditional blogs: personal entries or opinion pieces in text format and organized in reverse chronological order. Popular mainstream online platforms include Blogger, Wordpress and Blogbus. Some sites, such as Travelpod, provide a platform for travelers to document their travel stories in a blog format.

2. Microblogs: sometimes called "social blogs", microblogs allow users to broadcast short status updates (140–200 characters) to followers. Microblogs can be public or distributed to private followers. They offer higher levels of immediacy and portability because posts can be quickly created using different devices. Typically posts are tagged so that multiple posts related to particular topics, events, places or people can be easily retrieved. Examples include Twitter and Sina Weibo, but many mainstream SNSs also include microblogging tools.

3. Multi-author blogs: some blogging platforms support blogs with multiple authors (e.g. Wordpress). This allows blog owners to increase the content and reach of the blog but also requires management of multiple authors. A good travel example is National Geographic's Intelligent Travel blog.

4. Video blogs: video blogs use tools like YouTube, YouKu and Vimeo to allow bloggers to share their opinions and content in video format. Video bloggers typically set up a channel used to provide regular "broadcasts" based on their topic of expertise.

5. Curated blogs: curated blogs involve discovering, gathering and presenting digital content on a specific topic from a variety of sources. This amalgamation is called a "mashup" and can include text, articles, links, images, video and maps. For travel professionals and companies, content curation assists with search engine rankings because linking multiple pieces of content about a specific topic increases its exposure when that topic is searched.

Schmallegger and Carson (2008) propose that blogs have a number of travel-related applications, including communication, promotion, product distribution, management and research. While the first three suggestions are clear, the management and research elements of blogs are often overlooked. Travel organizations can use blogs as internal management tools to communicate with employees, intermediaries, partners and VIP customers. Many travel organizations have adopted a pro-active approach by embedding blogs on their own websites. For example, the Marriott Rewards Insiders site includes hotel reviews, forums and a blog for members of its loyalty program. There is also scope to mine traveler blogs for market intelligence. Bosangit *et al.* (2012) suggest that the representations of places found in blogs provide rich insights into how travelers perceive destinations. Destination marketers could use these insights to inform marketing strategies and destination branding efforts.

Twitter is perhaps the most ubiquitous of all the blogging platforms. Travel organizations are increasingly establishing twitter accounts to engage with travelers. Like SNSs, microblogs provide another channel for public relations, marketing and customer service. However, in the travel industry there is also a focus on engaging prominent bloggers who are opinion leaders. These blogs blur the lines between travel features found in the traditional press and the diary format already discussed. As a result they are becoming increasingly influential in traveler decision-making. As travel companies offer free familiarization trips to travel writers and travel intermediaries, the best travel bloggers are now invited to experience the best a destination has to offer. Many well-known travel bloggers are nomads who move from one destination to another, often gathering and writing about their experiences courtesy of the travel organizations who sponsor them. Tourism destinations also routinely recruit and reward their own "ambassadors" to write favorable blogs about their experiences.

The "Best Job in the World" competition is an example of how elaborate some campaigns have become (see Case Study). In 2009 Tourism Queensland invited people worldwide to apply for the best job in the world – caretaker of a tropical island on the Great Barrier Reef. The position was primarily a public relations role that required the winner to blog regularly about their adventures. The competition was won by 34-year-old Ben Southall. People could follow Ben's adventures by visiting "Ben's Blog", which acted as a central digital portal for media interviews, videos, stories and photo diaries based on his experiences. This format has subsequently been copied by a number of other destinations using increasingly sophisticated blogs, microblogs and other social media.

Product review sites

Product review sites offer another UGC platform for travelers to record their travel experiences. Unlike blogs and wikis, product review sites aggregate short reviews from many travelers in a searchable database. TripAdvisor is perhaps the best-known example in the travel industry. Other examples include Urbanspoon for restaurants, Yelp for localized reviews and Skytrax for airlines. Some product review sites also specialize in particular

market segments, for example Minitime, which has planning tools for families with children.

TripAdvisor, originally focused on accommodations, has expanded to provide reviews on attractions, tours and restaurants. It has also developed innovative links with SNSs and rewards reviewers by awarding badges. The site has grown significantly in the number of images submitted by reviewers, indicating that a more connected and media-rich format is developing. Recently the site has become a travel metasearch engine by facilitating bookings through links with suppliers and intermediaries. This provides a seamless service for people to read reviews and book a product on one website.

The growth of product review sites has encouraged eWOM and has taken the control of information out of the hands of marketers and handed it to consumers. While they help to identify dubious operators and give more market power to reputable ones, product review sites have created challenges for travel organizations. Some provide organizations with an opportunity to respond to traveler reviews. The challenge for managers is to determine whether a response is required and how it should be worded (O'Connor, 2010). In the case of negative reviews, a standard response under each review might have little impact, whereas a personalized response following well established service recovery steps could restore the trust of readers.

Malicious use of review sites by competitors who post positive reviews of their own product and negative reviews of rival offerings is another problem (Yoo and Gretzel, 2009). While most mainstream product review sites employ sophisticated software and human intervention to detect suspicious reviews, some fake reviews do slip through. Once online, it is difficult to remove them, damaging the reputation of the business in the interim. However, product review sites can also be harnessed for positive outcomes. Many suppliers actively encourage travelers to post reviews and some embed live feeds of the most recent reviews on their websites.

Forums

Forums represent one of the oldest examples of social media. An Internet forum, or discussion board, is a website where members can post comments and respond to posts from others. These comments are typically organized into threads or topics to keep particular conversations together. Forums usually require membership before they can post comments. Members are typically identified by a **handle**, or nickname and an **avatar**, but some forums also display real names and photos. During the registration process members are asked to agree to forum rules relating to online etiquette, such as respecting other members and refraining for the use of inappropriate language. Members can usually edit their own posts, start new topics and reply to posts written by other members. Many forums are moderated by senior members to restrict content posted by trolls and spammers.

Two common uses of forums can be found in the travel industry. The first application involves the use of forums to discuss particular destinations or to seek travel advice. For example, TripAdvisor is not only a product review site but also a forum where travelers can pose questions about destinations, which are answered by local volunteers or other travelers. Other well-known examples include VirtualTourist and LonelyPlanet's Thorn Tree. In the airline sector, FlyerTalk provides a forum for aviation buffs and the frequent flyer community. The second application is by intermediaries, suppliers and destinations for customer service purposes. For example, the Department of Tourism in Kerala, India, maintains a traveler forum where users can post questions that are answered by members of the local tourism industry.

Media sharing

Many travelers share photos and videos of their journey using media-sharing sites like Flickr, YouTube and YouKu. Greater bandwidth and cheaper electronic devices to capture images and video has caused media sharing sites to grow rapidly. For example, by 2013 more than 1 billion unique users visited YouTube each month and more than 100 hours of content was added each minute. These sites not only facilitate the easy upload of visual content, but also allow followers to share, rate and leave comments about images and videos. It is this interactive aspect that makes media-sharing sites special.

Photo-sharing sites like Flickr have obvious applications for the tourism industry, which often relies on evocative images to sell holidays. The sharing of photos on SNSs is powerful to build virtual communities around a brand. But the images and associated metadata, such as tags, geotags and temporal information can also be useful information about the sites travelers visit. Most digital cameras and smartphones embed GPS geotags and timestamps into image data, which provides useful market intelligence about the duration of visits to sites and visitation patterns in a region (Popescu and Grefenstette, 2009). The comments left by viewers can also provide market intelligence.

Video-sharing sites offer tools for travellers to share their journey with family and friends. Aside from documenting their trips, travelers are also using YouTube to share their reviews of hotel rooms, tours and attractions. Hotel room walkthroughs with commentary are now common and provide viewers with content that cuts through professional photography and marketing hype found on hotel websites. Travel organizations can also contribute content to video-sharing sites but promotional videos produced for traditional media are not suitable for video-sharing sites (Reino and Hay, 2011). Travelers use sites like YouTube to search for information, watch reviews, and seek advice about a product or destination. As a result, consumer-generated videos are more pervasive than marketer-generated videos (Lim *et al.*, 2012). The use of authentic travelers, ambassadors or locals with genuine insights into the product or destination is more successful in this medium. As with other social media platforms, video-sharing sites also provide a visual platform for viral marketing campaigns. Embedding videos on other social media platforms facilitates the sharing of video content. However, like many other platforms disgruntled guests and employees can upload content that could cast a product or destination in an unfavorable light.

Another application of media-sharing sites is the use of document-sharing services such as Slideshare and Scribd. These sites allow organizations to share documents such as reports, infographics and presentations with internal and external stakeholders.

Document-sharing sites also allow readers to rate, comment on and share uploaded content. These sites are useful for communicating with stakeholders such as investors and the media and therefore serve an important public relations function. Most document-sharing services also allow travel organizations to easily share digital versions of traditional marketing collateral such as brochures and other printed material.

Crowdsourcing

Crowdsourcing involves using the Internet to "find people to perform tasks that computers are generally lousy at" (Howe, 2006, p. 5). These tasks require very little time from each individual, and consequently they offer little, if any, compensation. In Chapter 2 we explained how Mygola allows travelers to construct custom itineraries. The content for these itineraries is sourced automatically using a number of crawlers and algorithms but the site also relies on crowdsourcing to fine-tune itineraries. It does this by drawing on the expertise of thousands of travel experts who curate the itineraries on the site as well as everyday users who perform small tasks such as completing quick online polls.

Crowdsourcing also offers a number of opportunities for destinations. The Tourism Australia campaigns that were discussed earlier in this chapter are a good example of how crowdsourcing can rapidly develop a library of thousands of travel images. Tourism Australia is fond of saying that its social media team does not consist of three employees but thousands of users who contribute content. In 2012, the Philippines government decided to crowdsource its next tourism campaign by asking Facebook and Twitter followers to combine the "It's More Fun in the Philippines" tagline with their own images and ideas. This resulted in hundreds of images that were shared across social media platforms. Other destinations, such as Colorado, have used a similar approach by inviting visitors and locals to answer the question "What makes Colorado, Colorado?"

An emerging application of crowdsourcing involves the use of local experts to provide information, tips and advice to travelers. Google's City Experts was created to provide visitors and locals with a source of expert advice about the best places to eat, shop and play. City experts write reviews and upload photos, which are displayed on Google maps. The experts are rewarded with invites to exclusive local events, gifts and online recognition. This initiative has enormous potential for travelers when coupled with location-aware devices such as smartphones and Google Glass. Location-based review site Yelp operates on a similar crowdsourcing principle, while Localeur offers a service aimed specifically at young travelers (see Chapter 6).

Virtual worlds

Virtual worlds are three-dimensional, computer-based simulated environments through which users can interact using avatars. Virtual worlds are generally divided into virtual social worlds (e.g. SecondLife) and virtual gaming worlds (e.g. World of Warcraft). Virtual social worlds offer opportunities for users to participate in virtual representations of tourist experiences. These representations may be copies of real-world sites, such as hotels, theme parks, heritage sites and even

entire destinations, or they may be completely artificial fantasy environments. The advantage for travelers is that they can experience places that they may be unable to visit in reality because of budget or time limitations, poor mobility or restricted access. Virtual worlds can also offer substitute experiences for sites that may be too sensitive to visit (see Chapter 12).

Many travel organizations and destinations have established headquarters and sites in virtual worlds such as SecondLife. This virtual presence provides another touch point for interacting with potential travelers and offers many marketing opportunities, including browsing virtual brochures, viewing videos, linking to external websites and visiting virtual representations of tourist sites. A number of travel companies have also used SecondLife to generate and test new product ideas. For example, Starwood Hotels used SecondLife to test designs and hotel room features for its Aloft brand before the first real property opened in 2008 (Sigala, 2007). Residents of SecondLife have set up tours, opened travel agencies and written guidebooks to help visitors navigate around the complex virtual environment. Virtual worlds also provide a virtual meeting place for travel employees in different locations.

STRATEGIC APPLICATIONS OF SOCIAL MEDIA

Social media offers a number of opportunities for travel organizations, as our review of various platforms has revealed. However, social media is not the panacea of marketing – it is merely a new tool in the toolbox of media and information channels available to travelers and organizations. Travel organizations need to consider their target markets and their expectations because not all market segments expect engagement through social media. In addition, some markets will expect engagement through specific social media channels, suggesting that organizations need to spend time to understand their key markets. Organizations need to ensure that traditional tools are not ignored and that social media efforts are well planned and integrated into the firm's overall strategy.

A strategic approach means that organizations need to plan their engagement with social media (see Fig. 5.6). This involves **learning** what social media can do by using it, studying case studies, hearing from practitioners and exploring the latest trends. A strategic approach also requires the organization to prioritize its social media **objectives**. We will look at some of the key strategic applications of social media below, but these objectives may include marketing, customer

engagement, public relations and recruitment. There are risks attached to the use of social media and it is important to establish a **governance framework** to identify opportunities, manage risk and establish policies. Once this framework is in place the organization should project manage its social media efforts by defining key **activities** and stages. The capacity of employees and managers should also be considered and if necessary the organization should invest in developing the **capabilities** of social media champions. A strategic approach requires that efforts are **measured** and refined by establishing key performance indicators and reporting mechanisms. Finally, the nature of social media means that the organization needs to prepare to **engage in conversation** regularly and to **listen** by monitoring markets, communities and key influencers.

The framework displayed in Fig. 5.6 demonstrates the need for a strategic approach. In the following sections we will summarize

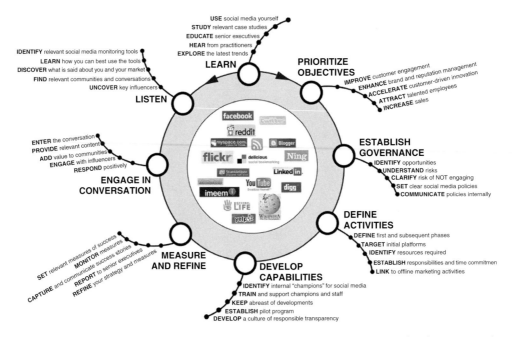

Fig. 5.6. Strategic social media framework (source: Advanced Human Technologies, 2013).

some of the key strategic applications of social media and illustrate how they can contribute to the objectives of travel organizations.

Marketing and sales

From a strategic perspective, social media may be particularly effective for building virtual communities around a brand. This is done through viral marketing campaigns and contests that attract "likes" and encourage people to engage with the organization – whether it be a social network page, media-sharing website or blog. Increasingly, social media can also play a role in the sales and distribution of tourism experiences.

The two key lessons from organizations successfully using social media are that marketing campaigns need to be consumer driven and integrated across several channels, meaning that **integrated marketing communications (IMC)** should drive marketing efforts. IMC is a strategic marketing approach that requires the coordination of both traditional and digital channels to ensure that they reinforce each other and are centered on the consumer. IMC leverages the strengths of each channel to accomplish an outcome better than that achieved by each individual channel. This means that organizations need to understand the limitations of each channel and how different target markets respond to these channels. For example, when Tourism Queensland launched the "Best Job in the World" campaign (see Case Study) it initially made use of traditional media to advertise the contest. However, the focus quickly moved to leveraging several social media channels as contestants submitted their videos and news of the competition went viral.

The Tourism Queensland example illustrates the power of leveraging the strengths of each platform. Each channel offers a unique formula for engagement, creating a deeper, more enriching experience. Table 5.2 indicates how blogs and media-sharing sites can be used to generate **exposure**. SNSs provide the perfect platform to **engage** and **influence** followers while seamless links to booking platforms can support product **acquisition**. Another application of social media in the travel industry is the idea of social booking and seating. A good example is SeatID, which specializes in providing ticketing and booking websites and apps with social elements that allow travelers to log in with their social media profile. Information from their profile is then used to determine whether any of their social contacts have flown with the same airline, stayed in the same hotel or visited the same attractions or events. Travelers are even able to choose a flight and a seatmate based on their social network profiles.

Market intelligence

As we have seen throughout this chapter, social media can play an important role in strategic listening. The social interactions between and among organizations and customers generate a vast amount of "big data" that can be mined for market intelligence. This includes information about market trends, customer sentiment and the impact of competitors. Organizations can monitor social media channels or outsource this to media monitoring companies specializing in tracking conversations in the social media space. Social media also allow companies to listen directly to customers by encouraging questions, feedback and suggestions. Questions from travelers can generate more accurate FAQs, and inform marketing campaigns and product design.

Case Study. Continued.

http://youtu.be/74p9qSoKSzA

Study Questions

1. Which of the key concepts discussed in this chapter are evident in the "Best Job in the World" campaign?

2. Use the Internet to find examples of social media campaigns orchestrated by other destinations. What are the key features of these campaigns?

3. The "Best Job in the World" campaign occurred in 2009 when many social media platforms were still evolving. Use the Strategic Social Media Framework presented in this chapter to explain how you would design your own campaign for a destination of your choice using the social media tools available today.

REFERENCES

Advanced Human Technologies (2013) Strategic Social Media Framework. Available at: http://ahtgroup.com/services/social-media-strategies (accessed 28 October 2013).

Bean, L.A. and Hott, D.D. (2005) Wiki: a speedy new tool to manage projects. *Journal of Corporate Accounting and Finance* 16(5), 3–8.

Bhattacherjee, A. and Sanford, C. (2006) Influence processes for information technology acceptance: an elaboration likelihood model. *MIS Quarterly* 805–825.

Bosangit, C., Dulnuan, J. and Mena, M. (2012) Using travel blogs to examine the postconsumption behavior of tourists. *Journal of Vacation Marketing* 18(3), 207–219. doi: 10.1177/1356766712449367

boyd, D.M. and Ellison, N.B. (2007) Social network sites: definition, history, and scholarship. *Journal of Computer-Mediated Communication* 13(1), 210–230. doi: 10.1111/j.1083-6101.2007.00393.x

Cavazza, F. (2012) Social Media Landscape 2012. Available at: http://www.fredcavazza.net/2012/02/22/social-media-landscape-2012/ (accessed 23 October 2013).

Cheung, M.Y., Luo, C., Sia, C.L. and Chen, H. (2009) Credibility of electronic word-of-mouth: informational and normative determinants of on-line consumer recommendations. *International Journal of Electronic Commerce* 13(4), 9–38.

Dellarocas, C. (2003) The digitization of word of mouth: promise and challenges of online feedback mechanisms. *Management Science* 49(10), 1407–1424.

Dichter, E. (1966) How word-of-mouth advertising works. *Harvard Business Review* 44(6), 147–160.

Filieri, R. and McLeay, F. (2014) E-WOM and accommodation: an analysis of the factors that influence travelers' adoption of information from online reviews. *Journal of Travel Research* 53(1), 44–57. doi: 10.1177/0047287513481274

Hennig-Thurau, T., Gwinner, K.P., Walsh, G. and Gremler, D.D. (2004) Electronic word-of-mouth via consumer-opinion platforms: what motivates consumers to articulate themselves on the internet? *Journal of Interactive Marketing* 18(1), 38–52.

Howe, J. (2006) The rise of crowdsourcing. *Wired Magazine* 14(6), 1–4.

Kaplan, A.M. and Haenlein, M. (2010) Users of the world, unite! The challenges and opportunities of Social Media. *Business Horizons* 53(1), 59–68.

Kietzmann, J.H., Hermkens, K., McCarthy, I.P. and Silvestre, B.S. (2011) Social media? Get serious! Understanding the functional building blocks of social media. *Business Horizons* 54(3), 241–251.

Lange-Faria, W. and Elliot, S. (2012) Understanding the role of social media in destination marketing. *Tourismos. An International Multidisciplinary Journal of Tourism* 7(1), 193–211.

Lim, Y., Chung, Y. and Weaver, P.A. (2012) The impact of social media on destination branding: consumer-generated videos versus destination marketer-generated videos. *Journal of Vacation Marketing* 18(3), 197–206. doi: 10.1177/1356766712449366

Litvin, S.W., Goldsmith, R.E. and Pan, B. (2008) Electronic word-of-mouth in hospitality and tourism management. *Tourism Management* 29(3), 458–468. doi: 10.1016/j.tourman.2007.05.011

Majchrzak, A., Wagner, C. and Yates, D. (2006) Corporate wiki users: results of a survey. Paper presented at the Proceedings of the 2006 International Symposium on Wikis.

Mittal, V., Huppertz, J.W. and Khare, A. (2008) Customer complaining: the role of tie strength and information control. *Journal of Retailing* 84(2), 195–204.

Nabi, R.L. and Hendriks, A. (2003) The persuasive effect of host and audience reaction shots in television talk shows. *Journal of Communication* 53(3), 527–543.

O'Connor, P. (2010) Managing a hotel's image on TripAdvisor. *Journal of Hospitality Marketing and Management* 19(7), 754–772.

O'Neill, S. (2013) In a QandA, Tourism Australia reveals the secrets of its Facebook dominance. *Tnooz.* Available at: http://www.tnooz.com/article/in-a-qa-tourism-australia-reveals-the-secrets-of-its-facebook-dominance/ (accessed 27 October 2013).

Petty, R.E. and Cacioppo, J.T. (1986) The elaboration likelihood model of persuasion. In: *Communication and Persuasion*. Springer, New York, pp. 1–24.

Popescu, A. and Grefenstette, G. (2009) Deducing trip related information from Flickr. Paper presented at the Proceedings of the 18th International Conference on World Wide Web.

Reino, S. and Hay, B. (2011) The Use of YouTube as a Tourism Marketing Tool. Paper presented at the Proceedings of the 42nd Annual Travel and Tourism Research Association Conference, London, Ontario, Canada.

Richins, M.L. (1983) Negative word-of-mouth by dissatisfied consumers: a pilot study. *The Journal of Marketing* 47(1), 68–78.

Schmallegger, D. and Carson, D. (2008) Blogs in tourism: changing approaches to information exchange. *Journal of Vacation Marketing* 14(2), 99–110.

Schwabe, G. and Prestipino, M. (2005) How tourism communities can change travel information quality. Paper presented at the 13th European Conference on Information Systems (ECIS) 2005, Regensburg, Germany.

Sigala, M. (2007) Web 2.0 in the tourism industry: a new tourism generation and new e-business models Available at: http://www.traveldailynews.com/columns/article/20554/web-2-0-in-the-tourism (accessed 2 January 2014).

Steffes, E.M. and Burgee, L.E. (2009) Social ties and online word of mouth. *Internet Research* 19(1), 42–59.

Thelwall, M. (2009) Homophily in myspace. *Journal of the American Society for Information Science and Technology* 60(2), 219–231.

Watts Sussman, S. and Schneier Siegal, W. (2003) Informational influence in organizations: an integrated approach to knowledge adoption. *Information Systems Research* 14(1), 47–65.

Westbrook, R.A. (1987) Product/consumption-based affective responses and postpurchase processes. *Journal of Marketing Research* 24(3), 258–270.

Xiang, Z. and Gretzel, U. (2010) Role of social media in online travel information search. *Tourism Management* 31(2), 179–188. doi: 10.1016/j.tourman.2009.02.016

Yoo, K.H. and Gretzel, U. (2008) What motivates consumers to write online travel reviews? *Information Technology and Tourism* 10(4), 283–295. doi: 10.3727/109830508788403114

Yoo, K.H. and Gretzel, U. (2009) Comparison of deceptive and truthful travel reviews. In: *Information and Communication Technologies in Tourism 2009*. Springer, pp. 37–47.

chapter 6

Mobilities and Information Technology

LEARNING OBJECTIVES

After studying this chapter you should be able to:

- apply the mobilities paradigm to the understanding of mobile technologies and travel;
- explain the key elements of mobile devices using the mobile technologies ecosystem;
- know what a context-aware tourism system is and how it can facilitate the tourist experience;
- explain how the various mobile functions described in this chapter can be used to enhance travel experiences; and
- appreciate some of the opportunities and challenges in implementing mobile technologies.

INTRODUCTION

Over the last decade mobile devices such as smartphones and tablets have become such an essential part of our lives that many of us experience anxiety when we are separated from

them for even short periods of time. This chapter is concerned with how travelers use mobile technologies during the travel experience. In the digital tourism ecosystem (Chapter 2), mobile technologies have the capacity to address not only the inspiration and transaction stages of the journey, but also the on-site experience and reflection on past experiences. Arguably mobile technologies have the greatest impact when visitors are on the move because they help travelers to deal with risk and uncertainty (Hwang, 2010). They play a critical role in unplanned behavior and support the creation of a range of personalized, location and time specific, value-added experiences that were not previously possible (Sharma and Nugent, 2006; Wang *et al.*, 2012). Instead of acting as a substitute for travel, they are playing a complementary role in fueling travel demand, thereby changing the very nature of the travel experience (Line *et al.*, 2011; Aguiléra *et al.*, 2012).

The remarkable uptake of mobile technologies over the last decade has disrupted traditional paradigms and ideas about travel. This disruption has generated renewed interest in mobilities from scholars working in the fields of transport, economics, anthropology, sociology and geography (Sheller and Urry, 2006). The **mobilities** paradigm explores the movement of people, ideas and things, as well as the broader social implications of those movements (Sheller, 2011). Mobilities is a useful paradigm for understanding the impact of IT because travel is enabled by increasingly complex socio-technical systems composed of interconnected infrastructures, services and modes of transportation and communication (Pellegrino, 2009; Molz, 2012). The use of mobile devices means that there is no longer a clear separation between everyday life and the liminal nature of travel experiences. There is a **spillover** of habits and behaviors from everyday life as travelers use mobile devices during all stages of the travel experience (MacKay and Vogt, 2012). On the other hand, some travelers seek experiences where they can escape from these technologies as we discussed in Chapter 2.

Mobile technologies are enabling the **fluidity** and **liquidity** of experiences by providing connectivity and softening the links between activities, space and time (Green, 2002; Uriely, 2005). They break down the boundaries between tourist experiences and everyday life, arguably removing some of the magic and sense of escape created by travel (Jansson, 2007; Pearce, 2011). They can transform how travelers engage with places by transporting them to virtual social settings (Dickinson *et al.*, 2012). As a result, travelers can experience a site physically but may be socially engaged by interactions with family and friends located in other places. Urry (2002) suggests that this use of technology creates occasional co-presence, imagined co-presence and virtual

co-presence, which results in travelers enjoying an experience not just for themselves but also for the benefit of others. Pearce (2011) uses the phrase **digital elasticity** to describe how travelers remain electronically linked with everyday life as they explore other places. Mobile technologies also blur the distinctions between activity time and travel time by supporting **micro-coordination** and making travel time more productive (Aguiléra *et al.*, 2012).

Pellegrino (2009) suggests that the technologies of mobility are characterized by the following phenomena:

- **Convergence**: the miniaturization and portability of electronics has resulted in the amalgamation of multiple technologies into one device. Nowhere is this more evident than the smartphone, which combines a camera, mobile phone, portable music player, GPS, personal digital assistant (PDA) and microcomputer into one small device;

- **Saturation**: mobile devices saturate the environment increasing expectations of continuous availability. In the travel context, this feature reduces the importance of pre-trip planning and coordination. Mobile technologies are transparent, invisible and difficult to grasp, but we become aware of their importance when technology fails;

- **Hybridization**: as technologies converge and saturate our environments they blur the distinction between the human and non-human – our interactions increasingly involve a hybrid of the natural and the artificial. Similarly we increasingly find ourselves in hybrid spaces that merge social connections, digital information and physical space (de Souza e Silva, 2006);

- **Ubiquity**: mobile technologies are omnipresent and are embedded into our surroundings. These devices communicate with users, each other and the surrounding environment using a range of signals and sensors.

Mobile technologies also empower travelers to create new engaging, interactive experiences that increase creative capital by enabling personal development and identity creation (Richards and Wilson, 2006). These conceptual foundations are important to understand as we explore the practical applications of mobile technologies. In the following pages we present a model of the mobile IT ecosystem and explore its various components. We conclude by considering the many applications of mobile technologies for both travelers and organizations.

THE MOBILE TECHNOLOGIES ECOSYSTEM

As we have done in previous chapters, we can adopt an ecosystem perspective to better understand the potential applications and impacts of mobile devices. Figure 6.1 presents a schema of the mobile technologies ecosystem in a travel context. The mobile technologies ecosystem consists of six major components:

1. Mobile device: the key components of most devices include an operating system (OS), apps, signaling technologies and sensing technologies. The components allow the device to detect inputs and to perform a range of functions.

2. Context: sensing and signaling technologies work together to collect contextual information about space, time and other objects in the user's environment.

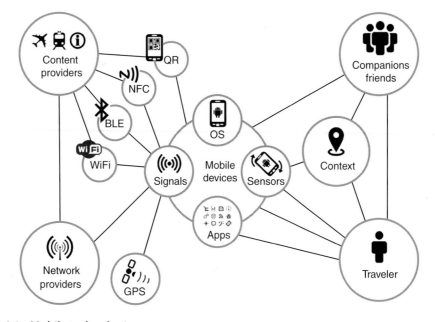

Fig. 6.1. Mobile technologies ecosystem.

3. Content providers: these can include travel suppliers, intermediaries, advertisers, websites, social media, search engines and third-party information (e.g. weather forecasts, currency conversion).

4. Network providers: users must subscribe to a network provider or carrier to access a cellular network.

5. Travelers: users who interact with mobile devices in a travel context by using OS and app interfaces. Devices also use sensors to gather contextual information from travelers (e.g. eye tracking, movement).

6. Companions and friends: travelers use mobile devices to interact with travel companions as well as friends and relatives located in other places. It is this element that brings the social aspects of everyday life into the travel experience.

Mobile devices collect and combine data from a range of inputs and then use apps to perform particular functions. The most innovative applications in travel rely on sensing and signaling technologies as well as intelligent apps to anticipate travelers' needs. In this chapter we will explore how various devices, inputs and applications are used in travel.

MOBILE DEVICES

Mobile devices are characterized by enormous hardware diversity. Devices vary in terms of: screen parameters (e.g. size, resolution, color depth, orientation, aspect ratio); memory size and processing power; input modes (e.g. keyboard, touchscreen, voice recognition); sensing technologies (e.g. camera, accelerometer, gyroscope, compass); and signaling technologies (e.g. NFC, BLE, WiFi, GPS) (Gruber, 2011).

These differences exist because particular devices are designed for specific tasks and markets. For example, a digital camera has different capabilities to a smartphone. Smartphones may combine features found in other mobile devices but they do not always provide all of the functionality found in purpose-built devices such as cameras and navigation devices. The most common mobile devices carried by travelers are GPS navigation devices, digital cameras, smartphones and tablets. We will review the key features of each below and will conclude with an overview of the latest developments in ubiquitous mobile technologies.

Global positioning system navigation devices

A GPS navigation device receives signals from the **Global Positioning System (GPS)** to determine a user's location (latitude and longitude) on Earth. Their key capabilities include a digital map, an indicator to show the location of the user, turn-by-turn directions (by text or voice), traffic congestion updates, speed limits, warnings for fixed speed and red light cameras and nearby points of interest (POI) such as attractions, restaurants and fuel stations. Newer devices also can link to smartphones and other devices using Bluetooth to share information such as POIs. In the travel industry these devices are mainly used by motorists, cyclists and pedestrians to find attractions and other points of interest. They are included as an option by rental car companies, which charge a rental fee for the device.

Mass transport operators also use navigation devices as a key component of **geographic information systems (GIS)**. A GIS stores, analyzes and displays geographically referenced information provided by the GPS

(US Government, 2013). GISs are used by rail, bus and other services to improve on-time performance, monitor vehicle locations and advise passengers of precise arrival times (see Chapter 8). Navigation devices are important in outdoor recreation by guiding hikers, sailors, mountain bikers, cross-country skiers and other outdoor adventures. Newer navigation devices have the ability to download and share waypoints with other adventurers. A good example is the travel-bygps.com website, which allows travelers to download hundreds of GPS maps, tour guides and POI.

Delays from getting lost or stuck in congestion on highways can impact the enjoyment of travel and may result in property damage, personal injuries, increased air pollution and excess fuel consumption (US Government, 2013). GPS navigation devices have reduced inefficiencies and improved safety by greatly reducing the likelihood of travelers getting lost. They have improved road safety by advising motorists of speed limits, reducing distractions such as reading maps while driving and providing directions. However, the use of navigation devices can also impact the travel experience negatively. Unfortunately the fastest route identified by navigation systems is not always the safest, or perhaps the most scenic. These observations highlight the need for additional contextual information to provide travelers with better route recommendations.

Digital cameras

Affordable photography has been available to travelers since the 1930s. Since this time devices have changed from bulky box cameras to color cameras, instant cameras and finally filmless digital cameras. Modern "point-and-shoot" digital cameras produce vastly superior color images to the 35 mm color film cameras from 20 years ago. This is due to advances in electronic image sensors, digital memory, image stabilization, improvements in lens technology, and post-processing to enhance images. Most modern digital cameras can capture both still images and video. The latest digital cameras also include a GPS receiver and WiFi connectivity. A GPS receiver allows images to be **geotagged** with contextual data that can later be combined with mapping tools such as Google Maps. Geotagged images can also be used by destinations and other content providers as inputs for GIS applications and tourist recommender systems (Cao *et al.*, 2010). WiFi connectivity allows users to easily transfer images from the camera to other digital devices or to social media accounts.

Despite the rapid growth in smartphone ownership, compact digital cameras are still the most common mobile devices carried by travelers (Pearce *et al.*, 2009), perhaps because they can be easily slipped into a pocket. Unlike film cameras, there is no cost associated with taking multiple images of the same scene and users can easily delete unwanted images. Their advanced digital zooming capabilities also allow travelers to capture scenes that are not easily accessible (Pearce, 2011). This has fundamentally changed the experience of travel photography as travelers can now capture higher quality images with little effort and planning (Lee, 2010). Digital cameras have also made it easier for images to be displayed, printed, stored, manipulated, transmitted and archived. This capability is particularly important for travel operators because it means that images of a bad meal, dirty hotel room or strange travel companions can be instantly transmitted and shared on social media and photo-sharing sites. On the other hand, suppliers can easily capture and share special moments using their own websites and social media channels.

Smartphones and tablets

As we have seen, **smartphones** are a hybrid of many other technologies including the laptop, PDA, mobile phone, wristwatch, portable music device, camera and GPS navigation device. The smartphone puts a relatively inexpensive supercomputer in the hands of users. This computer has the sensing and signaling capability to communicate with other devices, people and objects around the user, providing contextual information to deliver more relevant digital content. The capabilities of smartphones support millions of mobile apps that extend their functionality. We will explore some of the technologies and travel applications behind these capabilities later in this chapter.

Tablets are the big cousins of smartphones. They typically have larger screens, making them more suitable for reading, gaming and Internet browsing. Unlike other portable computers such a laptops, tablets generally do not use external input devices such as a keyboard or mouse. Most are equipped with the same sensing and signaling technologies as smartphones, although cellular access is often an optional additional feature.

Ongoing advances in surface materials (e.g. **graphene** and bendable glass) and electronics (e.g. more efficient batteries and **organic light-emitting diodes (OLEDs)**) are resulting in thinner, lighter and more durable devices that allow digital content to be updated and manipulated through a variety of inputs.

Ubiquitous devices

Ubiquitous technologies involve the use of **smart devices** and objects connected to each other and to networks using technologies such as Bluetooth, NFC and WiFi. They are a key element of **ambient intelligence** and are sometimes referred to as the **Internet of things**. Users interact with ubiquitous technologies in natural ways, using eye movements, voice commands, gestures or touch. Wearable technologies are one example of the many devices that make up the ecosystem of ubiquitous technologies.

Wearable technologies such as the wristwatch and portable music players have played an important role in travel for many decades (Pearce, 2011). However, these technologies are not "smart" devices. **Wearable smart devices** are miniature electronic devices worn by the user. A number of wearable smart devices have been used for industrial, medical and military applications, but the commercialization of these technologies has only been realized in the 2010s, with the development of small lightweight smartwatches such as the Samsung Galaxy Gear and Sony Smartwatch and **optical head-mounted displays (OHMD)** such as Google Glass (see Case Study). Many use the same platforms and architecture as smartphones, enabling users to install a variety of third-party apps. As a result, these technologies have the same application as smartphones but the wearable nature of devices like Google Glass creates additional opportunities for the delivery of information and interpretation using augmented reality.

MOBILE SIGNALS AND SENSORS

Mobile devices rely on a range of signaling and sensing technologies to provide inputs and contextual data. **Sensing technologies** are able to detect sensory data such as movement, touch, images and sound. **Signaling technologies** receive or read data from mobile phone towers, transmitters and beacons. Together, these technologies allow smart devices to see, hear and feel, imbuing them with the capacity for ambient intelligence (Manes, 2003). Each offers different capabilities and it is important to understand these before considering how travelers and tourism organizations might use them.

Sensing technologies

Most mobile devices include a range of contextual sensors that provide the device with inputs about users and their surroundings. Sensors are what make smartphones "smart". Modern smartphones typically contain the following sensing technologies:

- **Touchscreens**: interactive screens that respond to touch from fingers or a stylus are part of most handheld mobile devices. Haptic feedback is also becoming common, allowing two-way exchange of tactile sensations. Some touchscreens also can collect biometric information, such as fingerprints for security applications.
- **Gyroscopes, magnetometers and accelerometers**: these technologies allow the device to detect the direction and magnitude of movements. Sensing the tilt, rotation and orientation of a device supports applications such as navigation, photography, gamification and augmented reality.

- **Digital cameras**: digital cameras are used as the "eyes" of many mobile devices. Their application extends far beyond their common use in capturing photos and video. In many cases the camera also detects gestures and eye movements. This is used for automatically scrolling text when reading, pausing a video when a user looks away and touch-free navigational gestures. Cameras are also used to capture **Quick Response (QR) codes** that can then be interpreted with suitable apps.
- **Ambient light sensors**: many digital devices can adjust displays based on the amount of ambient light. This reduces power consumption and increases battery life. Some sensors can also detect the user's presence and proximity.
- **Temperature, humidity and pressure sensors**: weather is important to travelers and the integration of ambient temperature, humidity and pressure sensors has many applications when combined with other sensory inputs and data sources.
- **Microphones**: these are the "ears" of mobile devices and, like cameras, they can do more than capture sound, such as speech recognition and commands. They can also analyze voice patterns and adjust digital content and access to features based on the user's identity.

Signaling technologies

Signaling technologies allow mobile devices to receive or read data transmitted by radio waves, microwaves or light waves. Many mobile devices now incorporate multiple signaling technologies. Smartphones may contain some or all of the following signaling capabilities:

- **Radio-frequency identification (RFID)**: a wireless non-contact use of radio-frequency electromagnetic fields to identify and track items using an information-encoded chip. RFID chips are the size of a rice grain and can be embedded in a range of items, including animals and people. They can be battery-powered or unpowered and activated when they come near an electromagnetic reader. Passive RFID tags are used in travel settings because they are smaller and less costly. Travel applications include smart cards (ID cards, credit cards and integrated public transport cards), luggage tracking, e-toll tags, loyalty cards, mobile payments, inventory tracking, ski passes and e-passports.
- **Near Field Communication (NFC)**: a set of standards supporting two-way communication by allowing mobile devices to act as RFID readers/transponders. NFC allows devices to communicate with each other when they are very close (less than 7 inches). The technology also allows devices to communicate with unpowered NFC chips embedded in objects. A user can wave their smartphone near an NFC tag area and information will be transferred instantly. For example, by reading a NFC tag a device can launch an app or access a website link (Pesonen and Horster, 2012). NFC devices can be used in contactless payment systems, electronic ticketing, exhibits and attractions, information sharing, social networking, electronic identification and virtual frequent flyer cards. A good example is Disney's MagicBand (see Chapter 10 Case Study).

- **Bluetooth**: a wireless technology standard for exchanging data over short distances using short-wavelength microwave transmissions. Bluetooth is similar to NFC, but with much greater range (up to 30 feet). The latest version of Bluetooth is referred to as **Bluetooth Low Energy (BLE)** or Bluetooth Smart. BLE is more cost effective than conventional Bluetooth and is useful for low power applications. In 2013 Apple developed a low-power, low-cost transmitter known as iBeacon based on BLE technology. iBeacon is a pervasive context-aware wireless sensor that can pinpoint the location of mobile users and send out push notifications. In a travel context, the technology can be used as a geofencing tool to provide localized visitor information, interpretation and orientation.
- **WiFi**: a technology that allows mobile devices to exchange data or connect wirelessly to the Internet using radio waves. Connections are established through a wireless hotspot, with a range of around 65 feet in indoor settings and greater in outdoor settings. The technology is used in airports, cafes, hotels and public spaces. Some destinations have rolled out extensive free WiFi networks.
- **LiFi**: visible light communication (VLC) systems using light waves from diodes to provide high-speed connections between mobile devices and network access points. LiFi is a new technology and is expected to be cheaper and faster than WiFi but since light waves cannot penetrate walls, LiFi will be shorter-range for indoor settings.
- **Cellular network**: wireless communication networks distributed over large land

areas. Users buy a **subscriber identification module (SIM) card** and pay a fee to a telecommunications provider to access voice or Internet services. Some carriers offer global roaming services so that international tourists can use their SIM card on overseas networks, but this can be costly. As a result many smartphone users rely on WiFi hotspots or purchase pre-paid SIM cards when they arrive at a destination.

- **Global Positioning System (GPS)**: a space-based satellite system that provides location and time information anywhere on the Earth. We have already discussed the use of GPS navigation devices, but the GPS satellite service supports other mobile device applications, including digital cameras, smartphones and tablets. Its global nature makes it well suited to navigation in outdoor environments. GPS can also be combined with context-aware mobile apps to create geofences that trigger specific activities and notifications.

It is important for tourism organizations to understand the applications and limitations of each of these technologies. One of the most obvious distinctions is their range, which in turn impacts how they can be deployed and used (see Fig. 6.2). A combination of technologies may be needed to create a ubiquitous network that keeps travelers connected. It is important to ensure that the transition between different networks is seamless and transparent (Kaplan, 2012).

MOBILE OPERATING SYSTEMS AND APPS

The hardware on a mobile device (including sensory and signaling technologies) is controlled by a **mobile operating system (OS)**. Most smartphones, tablets or wearable devices use Google Android, Apple iOS or various versions of Microsoft Windows. The downloading of mobile apps is an important feature of mobile devices. **Apps** refer to tailor-made software that

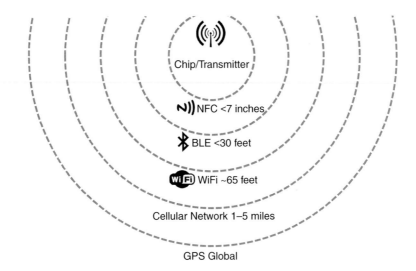

Chip/Transmitter

NFC <7 inches

BLE <30 feet

WiFi ~65 feet

Cellular Network 1–5 miles

GPS Global

Fig. 6.2. Typical range of various mobile signaling technologies.

exploits the hardware found in mobile devices to provide additional functionality. They are provided by mobile device manufacturers and also by third-party developers through online **app stores**. There is now a vast range of apps, including games, productivity tools, media and entertainment, navigation, education, lifestyle and travel apps.

Many third-party travel apps are also available for the three major mobile operating systems. Wang and Xiang (2012) grouped travel apps into 12 categories based on functionality and app store user reviews. They found that travelers use a combination of different apps for different travel purposes. Travelers prefer designs that: reduce decision-making effort; provide instant support/feedback and a sense of control; and are fun, easy to use and interactive. An example of this is Urbanspoon, which randomly selects a restaurant near the user when they shake their device. Travelers dislike apps that are copies of websites or brochures and do not add any value to their decision-making. Dickinson *et al.* (2012) provide a useful overview of travel apps and their capabilities and organize travel apps into five functional categories: information, two-way sharing, context awareness, Internet of things and tagging.

FUNCTIONS OF MOBILE DEVICES IN TOURISM

Mobile devices can be used both by travelers and tourism organizations. While mobile apps enable much of this functionality, interactions between mobile devices and other systems, such as GIS and CRM applications, are also possible. Mobile devices can harness the information collected by sensors and signals and combine this with existing "big data" sources such as social media profiles, online behaviors and individual preferences. In Table 6.1 we present the ten functions of mobile devices in tourism, starting with the most basic (information provision) and progressing to increasingly more sophisticated applications relying on the interaction of a complex ecosystem of sensors, signals, systems and technologies. These functions have been expanded from the original work done by Dickinson *et al.* (2012) and Wang and Xiang (2012).

Informing

The delivery of information is the primary function of most travel apps. Mobile apps can change travelers' behavior and emotional states by addressing a wide variety of functional and hedonic information needs (Wang *et al.*, 2012). The types of information provided by travel apps include: marketing and visitor information about attractions, accommodation and dining; local information such as travel safety advisories, weather and exchange rates; transport information such as timetables and flight status; or interpretive information about people, places and objects (Mirski and Abfalter, 2004; Kang and Gretzel, 2012; Wang and Xiang, 2012). Travelers can also search for tips, recommendations and user-generated content such as reviews, blogs and travel forums. Table 6.2 provides a useful schema to illustrate the different types of tourist information needs addressed by mobile apps.

Table 6.1. Major functions of mobile devices in tourism.

Function	Description	Travel applications
Informing	The ability to source and access information while traveling	Attraction and destination guides Timetables and schedules Currency conversion Interpretation (e.g. virtual guides, QR codes)
Contextualizing	Services based on the smartphone's contextual sensors. Ability to communicate not just with other people but also with the "Internet of Things"	Interactive, real-time location awareness Push notifications relative to location and context Provision of live travel information, flight status, weather, safety, events and offers Real-time public transport and luggage tracking
Personalizing	Combining contextual information with user data to provide personal services	Recommender systems Trip planning and scheduling Facilitating personal interactions
Socializing	Communication capabilities such as telephony, social media and messaging	Mobile telephony and messaging Mobile social media (e.g. SNSs, blogs, reviews, media sharing)
Managing	Collecting data about the user and presenting management interventions to change behavior	Data mining (e.g. visitor behavior, travel flows and patterns, dwell time) Push notifications to manage behavior
Translating	Use of online or offline capabilities to translate image, text and voice inputs	Real-time translation of brochures, signs, speech Multi-lingual apps
Purchasing	Ability to source and book travel products	Suppliers, travel intermediaries, metasearch
Gamifying	Using digital information to incentivize travel experiences	Geocaching Virtual games set in the real world

(Continued)

Table 6.1. Continued.

Function	Description	Travel applications
Augmenting	Overlaying the real world with digital content	Destination and attraction information Interpretation
Reflecting	Capturing travel experiences for future enjoyment	Geotagged photographs and video Personal diaries and messages

Table 6.2. Visitor information needs addressed by mobile app (adapted from Wang *et al.*, 2012).

Type	Description
Functional	Tourists need information to learn, add value to the trip, improve efficiency and reduce uncertainty.
Innovation	Tourists need information to inspire novel, spontaneous and creative experiences.
Hedonic	Tourists need information to be excited, enjoy the destination and experience the local culture and life.
Aesthetic	Tourists need information to imagine destinations and form expectations.
Social	Tourists need information to give advice to others, share their experience and be valuable for their friends.

There are two strategies for delivering information to mobile users:

- **Web-centric information**: content is delivered over the mobile web using a mobile browser and standard web technologies (e.g. HTML/HTML5, JavaScript, CSS). Web-based content can be accessed on devices using different OSs but may not be suitable in some travel settings where a constant network connection is not available; and
- **App-centric information**: purpose-built apps use the hardware capabilities of the device (e.g. cameras, microphones, location, Bluetooth) to deliver travel information needs (Gruber, 2011).

Mobile-based information can be presented in a variety of formats. Hyun *et al.* (2009) provide a typology of mobile information sources based on the concept of **telepresence**. They suggest that mobile communication systems can be organized according to two dimensions:

- **Fidelity**: the sensory intensity or vividness of the presentation based on the depth (text, 2D effect, 3D effect) and breadth (audio, visual) of the content; and

- **Interactivity**: the ability of users to shape the form and content of information based on speed (synchronized, asynchronized), range (changing, rotating, zooming) and mapping (observational self, functional self and intelligent self).

The framework allows us to organize a range of mobile information sources into categories as shown in Fig. 6.3. The typology of mobile-mediated virtual experiences highlights that information can be delivered in a variety of formats, from text-based systems to interactive virtual guides.

It is also important to distinguish between **pull** communication (initiated by the traveler) and **push** communication (initiated by the content provider) (Kaplan, 2012). Apps can deliver both types of content but many replicate existing information sources, such as travel guides or websites. It is important

for apps to provide an effective mechanism to search for this information. Innovative approaches to this challenge include the use of **semantic search** tools recognizing verbal requests presented to **virtual assistants** like Siri or Google Now.

Tourism organizations use QR codes (such as those in this book) to deliver visitor information and interpretation. Hotels are creating in-room guides containing QR codes, Las Vegas casinos are using QR codes to promote shows and events around the city, and historic sites are placing QR codes on buildings and near objects to provide guests with historical, architectural, regional or cultural information (Vela, 2012). An example of an interpretive QR code is shown in Fig. 6.4. BLE and NFC technologies can also be used for pull communications.

Contextualizing

The pervasive availability of information means that users suffer from information

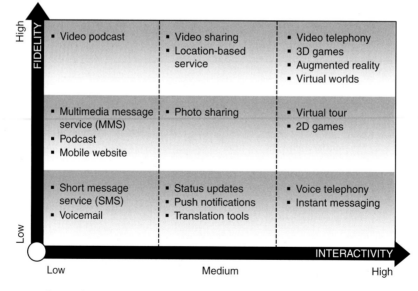

Fig. 6.3. Typology of mobile-mediated virtual experiences (adapted from Hyun *et al.,* 2009).

As a mountain swells from magma pressure, its surface rises. Absolute altitude is constantly measured at numerous spots around the island to determine the rise and fall of ground level.

Additional information about this exhibit can be accessed using a QR (Quick Response) code reader app on your camera-enabled smartphone.

1) *Download a QR reader app*

2) *Take a picture (scan) of this QR code to view the linked information.*

Fig. 6.4. Example of a QR code used for interpretation, Hawai'i Volcanoes National Park.

overload. This is avoidable because mobile apps can filter content to present relevant, context-based information. At the very least, a mobile app should use location information garnered through GPS, WiFi or BLE to filter out information irrelevant to the location. GPS-enabled apps are good examples of **location-based services (LBS)** in travel (Tussyadiah and Zach, 2012). The overlaying of digital maps with various layers, such as restaurants, hotels, attractions and traffic congestion offers a basic level of contextualization. However, context is about more than location. Travelers are not only interested in where something is, they want to know how to find it, how long it will take to get there, whether they will like it, and what the weather will be like.

Tan *et al.* (2009) argue that mobile travel content must be based on a rich understanding of the context. They propose a framework called the **TILES Model** to refer to the five categories of contextual data considered by mobile apps to customize data:

- **Temporal**: content contextualized according to time (e.g. current time and day of the year, current events, seasons, itinerary);
- **Identity**: content contextualized based on the user's identity (e.g. interests, demographics, motives, food and activity preferences, activities already completed, language, budget, trip characteristics);
- **Location**: content contextualized based on the user's movement and location (e.g. current location, nearby attractions, traveling speed and direction, mode of transport);
- **Environment**: content contextualized according to the user's environment (e.g. weather, traffic conditions, congestion and availability, waiting times); and
- **Social**: content contextualized according to the user's social setting (travel companions, group interests, nearby friends and family, recommendations, social media activity).

Context-aware apps therefore consider location, time, people and objects when selecting information to present to users (Paganelli and Giuli, 2008). This provides travelers with local contextual knowledge that would otherwise take time, repeat visitation and extended familiarization to achieve. The combination of everyday objects transmitting data and people carrying sensing devices allows for the co-production and consumption of travel experiences to occur in real-time (Dickinson *et al.*, 2012). Contextual information may have other unanticipated benefits. By revealing distances and journey times on different transport modes, travelers may decide to walk rather than using a car or public transport, thereby reducing CO_2 emissions. This can be enhanced by ensuring that quality navigation information is available not just for drivers but also for pedestrians (Riebeck *et al.*, 2008). Contextual information can also be used to improve traveler convenience and safety. For example, GPS devices embedded in taxis, buses and other types of public transport can help visitors to track these vehicles in real time.

Some of the information necessary for fine-grained context-aware applications can only be provided by locals. Google has created innovative programs to develop this local knowledge. Google+ Local takes advantage of the convergence of social, local and mobile content. The program combines business listings from Google Places with reviews and photos contributed by customers, including reviews aggregated from other review sites. The company also runs the Google City Experts program to further supplement this information with local expertise which is displayed on Google Maps. Another innovative example includes Locish, the crowdsourcing app that matches travelers with locals who have similar interests and profiles.

Another application of context-aware technologies in travel is **geofencing**. A geofence is a virtual perimeter generated for a real-world setting, such as a hotel lobby or a precinct. Travelers using LBSs can trigger push notifications or other activities when entering or exiting a geofence. The user's location is determined from the GPS, NFC, BLE or WiFi capabilities of their device. Google's Field Trip uses this technique to push content (called cards) to mobile devices whenever a user approaches something interesting. This content includes everything from local history to the best places to shop, eat and have fun. It has enormous potential for travel when combined with wearable devices such as Google Glass.

Travel organizations and destinations will need to consider how they are represented in these global apps. Watch the following video to learn more about Field Trip and how it is integrated with Google Glass: http://youtu.be/yyRJG2rrw0E/.

http://youtu.be/yyRJG2rrw0E

Personalizing

We have seen how mobile devices can contextualize information based on various inputs. Now imagine what that information would look like if it were personalized to individual needs. Data from the contextual sensors can be combined with personal information and used to further extend a sense of context and customization. This personal information can be sourced from details stored on the mobile device (e.g. personal records, apps, photos, email and calendar), information from social media profiles and usage data such as search histories and device habits. This is the "identity" component of the TILES model, but is treated separately in this chapter because of its richness for travel industry applications.

Individuals often provide organizations with personal information in exchange for better services or special benefits. Frequent flyer programs and hotel loyalty cards are good examples. In addition, users often agree to the terms and conditions of a new app without reading them and may be unaware that they are sharing information with providers. Travel app providers can aggregate these data to collect business intelligence about app use, purchase behavior and temporal and spatial travel data (Dickinson *et al.*, 2012). This type of business intelligence can enhance visitor experiences in airports (Chapter 7), attractions (Chapter 10) and destinations (Chapter 11).

Google again provides one of the leading examples of personalization with its Google Now service. Google Now interacts with photos, Google Maps, Gmail and Google Calendar to "surface" the information individuals need during the day without summoning it. A good example is the extraction of travel itineraries from emails sent by travel providers. Travel itineraries can fetch other information such as maps and weather forecasts. These details can then be displayed on personalized cards shown on the mobile device.

Personalization is also at the heart of technologies known as **mobile recommender systems**. Mobile recommender systems use spatial, temporal and personal data to filter content to offer context-sensitive recommendations (Ricci, 2010). There is evidence that travelers using mobile recommender systems spend more time at a destination and are able to see more sights (Modsching *et al.*, 2007). The various trip planning apps (e.g. Gogobot, Citybot) now available for mobile devices are a good example of mobile recommender systems. The more these apps learn about you, the more accurate their recommendations become (Rodríguez *et al.*, 2012). Watch the following video to see an example: http://youtu.be/kQZBHko8A5M/. Another example is SmartMuseum (http://www.smartmuseum.eu/), an app that aims to personalize interpretive content about museum exhibits.

http://youtu.be/KQZBHko8A5M/

Mobile technologies can also be used by staff at hotels, attractions, airports and other facilities to personalize the visitor experience. The Disney MagicBand discussed in Chapter 10 is a good example of the innovative use of mobile technologies to personalize guest experiences. Cast members can preview the names of guests and greet them personally.

Socializing

With all of their functions it is easy to forget that mobile devices are still in essence communications devices. Most people own a smartphone so they can talk to others. The socialization function is as much about communication as it is about social media. This is an important point for travel professionals – mobile devices provide a range of telephony features but few organizations use channels such as Skype and FaceTime. These would seem to be obvious applications for a high touch industry like tourism. Similarly, very few travel organizations utilize services such as SMS and instant messaging. Beyond these communication functions, there is a range of social media applications unique to mobile devices.

The integration of social media with mobile devices is called **mobile social media** (Kaplan, 2012) and is differentiated from traditional social media because it incorporates contextual factors. Mobile social media applications can be classified into four categories, depending on whether the message takes account of the user's location (location sensitivity) and whether it is received and processed by the user instantaneously or with a time delay (time sensitivity) (see Table 6.3).

Social media allows individuals to express their identity and self-disclose by sharing their travel experiences if they are consistent with how they would like to be seen by others. Organizations can encourage social mobile behaviors by incentivizing contributions such as reviews, status updates, check-ins and photos. For example, visitors to a theme park may receive a voucher for a free drink if they check in from various locations more than ten times during their visit. Providing NFC touch points or WiFi for visitors to check-in or post content on social media is an important part of this strategy. This social media activity contributes to the virtual presence of the organization and is an important source of business intelligence.

Travelers also use mobile social media while traveling because it reduces the social distance from their social circles. In some cases social media is used for safety and security purposes – by checking in regularly travelers can let their friends and family know they are OK. Travel retailers can use these same features to provide better in-destination service by monitoring mobile social media activity and providing proactive support when travelers share problems online. Another interesting example is Fearsquare, a UK application that compares Foursquare check-ins with official police statistics to inform users of the safety of their current location.

Organizations can integrate their app with social media, making it possible to use mobile social media and LBSs to socialize the experience itself by helping users find "friends of friends" or travelers with similar interests. Social discovery apps that allow travelers to see whether their friends have stayed in the same hotel or whether acquaintances may be on the same flight are a good example. These apps use information from social networking sites such as Facebook and LinkedIn to help travelers identify seatmates or potential travel

Table 6.3. Mobile social media applications (adapted from Kaplan, 2012).

	Location sensitive	**Location agnostic**
Instantaneous	Space-timers: exchange of messages with relevance for one specific location at one specific point in time (e.g. Facebook Places, Foursquare)	Quick-timers: transfer of traditional social media to mobile devices to increase immediacy (e.g. Tweets, Facebook status updates)
Time delay	Space-locators: exchange of messages, with relevance for one specific location, which are tagged to a certain place and read later by others (e.g. Urbanspoon, TripAdvisor)	Slow-timers: transfer of traditional social media to mobile devices (e.g. YouTube, Wikipedia)

companions. Social information can also be used to personalize the information presented by mobile recommender systems. By combining personal data with data from mobile social media, such as check-ins and status updates, apps filter content so that users see the recommendations and reviews of travelers sharing their traits (Spindler *et al.*, 2008).

Real-time information from locals and travelers can be crowdsourced to improve the travel experience. For example, apps can allow travelers to report crowded or congested areas. The Waze app is a good example of combining mobile social media with LBSs to save travelers time and money by sharing real-time traffic and road information.

Some travelers may find the use of social media to monitor their mobile activities intrusive and disturbing. Care is therefore needed to ensure that mobile social relationships are built on trust and reciprocity. Kaplan (2012) advises organizations to follow the "Four I's of mobile social media" when engaging with travelers.

1. Integrate activities into your users' life to avoid being a nuisance.
2. Individualize activities to take account of user preferences and interests.
3. Involve the user through engaging conversations.
4. Initiate the creation of user-generated content.

In short, the socialization function is about combining information, contextualization, personalization and social data to deliver more relevant content and experiences.

Managing

Mobile devices can be used by travel organizations to manage traveler experiences by providing business intelligence and enabling management interventions. The managing function is often dependent on travelers agreeing to share information in exchange for better experiences. Mobile devices can provide time and location data about travelers to use for business intelligence. Once permission is obtained (either implicitly or explicitly) travel organizations can use data mining techniques to aggregate and visualize the "big data" generated by individual mobile devices. Examples include location and personal data to better understand visitor catchments, travel routes, dwell times, activity patterns and frequently visited attractions (Shoval and Isaacson, 2007; Modsching *et al.*, 2008; Dickinson *et al.*, 2012). More innovative applications include the use of geotagged photos to examine activity patterns (Sugimoto, 2011).

Organizations can identify the exact time a traveler arrives at their premises and what content they shared with others in their social circle. Embedded in this information is demographic data about the age and gender of visitors. Organizations may even determine where travelers live, what school they attended, their marital status and other personal information. These data can be linked with information stored in CRM databases.

The use of mobile devices to monitor visitor activities and behavior is only part of the equation. In order to create better experiences organizations need to act on these data. Organizations can turn observation into intervention by using mobile devices to influence traveler decision-making and change behavior. This might be: map updates showing congested routes; push notifications warning travelers about long queues or delays; alerts about carparks, attractions or areas that are underutilized; special offers; or safety and security information.

Translating

Smartphones and tablets can translate both text and speech in real time. There are many international travel contexts where this feature is important. Apps like Google Translate and Word Lens can translate written text when travelers point their mobile camera at a sign or menu. Purpose-built mobile apps also provide travel organizations with the ability to deliver marketing and interpretive content in various languages. Destinations, museums, airports and attractions are no longer constrained by providing signage in only one or two languages. Similarly, hotels and restaurants can use apps to deliver in-room guides and menus in different languages. The ability to translate any language in real time profoundly changes the travel experience for both international travelers and customer service staff working in the tourism industry. Some of these applications will be discussed in more detail in Chapter 10.

Purchasing

Mobile devices are also convenient tools for purchasing travel. This function is particularly relevant to travel intermediaries and travel suppliers seeking to streamline the purchase process for travelers. Many online travel agents (OTAs) and metasearch engines provide mobile apps that allow travelers to find, compare and book airline seats, hotel rooms, rental cars and other travel products. These apps are designed to be used on smaller screens and so serve a different purpose to websites, which are often difficult to navigate on mobile devices.

Apps also allow travelers to book products while they are on the move. This is a particularly important point for travel services that may be booked en route or when travelers are at the destination. We have seen how the contextualization, personalization, socialization and facilitation of information can change travelers' decisions while they are on the move. These changes can only be fully realized if travelers can act on those decisions by booking and reserving various activities. Once a transaction has occurred the mobile device can be used for ticketing, admission, check in, boarding, purchasing and other services required during the journey. Technologies such as NFC could be used at the check-in counter, security screening, boarding gate, car rental counter, the hotel reception and at entrances to attractions and events.

The sensing and signaling technologies we have already discussed support a number of these functions. Mobile payment and ticketing systems such as Apple Passbook and Google Wallet also play an important role. There are also mobile business applications that allow organizations to accept payments by credit card when travelers do not have their own mobile device. A good example is Square (http://www.squareup.com/), a small card reader that connects to a mobile device to turn it into a POS payment system. This technology is useful for settings such as hotels, restaurants and tours where staff require greater mobility or in situations where guests are not carrying cash. PayPal offers a similar service called PayPal Here.

Gamifying

Mobile technologies can also contribute to the gamification of travel experiences. **Gamification** is an informal umbrella term for the use of game design elements in non-game contexts to improve user experience and user engagement (Deterding *et al.*, 2011). Gamification can impact individuals' experience of their surroundings as well as their mobility choices (Frith, 2013). Everyday experiences are increasingly being "gamified" using the contextual and social features of mobile devices. Getting a loyalty card stamped at your local café so that you can be rewarded with a free coffee is a low-tech application of gamification. By earning frequent flyer points travelers are essentially participating in a game with rewards attached to particular behaviors.

In the high-tech world of mobile technologies, travelers can become "mayors" and earn "badges" or real rewards for checking in on Foursquare, posting updates on Facebook or Twitter or reviewing hotels on TripAdvisor. Another approach involves setting travelers challenges and quests, such as a treasure hunt or a local version of *The Amazing Race* (Zichermann and Cunningham, 2011). This gamification is made possible by the convergence of social, local and mobile (SoLoMo) technologies to create a hybrid experience where virtual activities are layered over physical spaces. These types of experiences closely resemble **geocaching**, an activity where participants use a location-based service to hide and seek containers called caches (Schlatter and Hurd, 2005). Geocachers use websites (e.g. http://www.geocaching.com/) or apps (e.g. Geocaching, iGeocacher, CacheSense) to discover the coordinates of caches hidden in various locations.

Gamification can be applied to any sector of the travel industry, but is particularly useful for destinations and larger facilities such as ski resorts, casinos, airports, museums, attractions and events. Rather than taking a tour, visitors wishing to explore a destination can install an app that sends them on a quest to find various clues. Digital breadcrumbs or tags can guide a traveler to particular waypoints (e.g. sites of interest) and LBSs can reveal a new clue once the traveler reaches the waypoint. A competitive

element can be introduced by requiring players to collect digital tokens. The aim is to create an experience characterized by playfulness, challenge, achievement and reward. For destinations, the use of gamification has the potential to not only enhance experiences, but to disperse travelers to less well-known sites. Linking rewards to commercial locations may also support marketing goals and increase length of stay and expenditure. Companies like Wildgoose (http://www.huntthegoose.co.uk/) and Strayboots (http://www.strayboots.com/) specialize in the design of tour apps that incorporate games and quests. Some destinations have partnered with Foursquare to offer travelers special badges for visiting particular sites (Tussyadiah, 2012).

The EpicMix app developed by Vail Resorts in the US is a good example of gamification. The app allows skiers to track the amount of vertical feet skied using RFID tags embedded in ski passes. Skiers can also connect with family and friends using social media, compete with other skiers and earn virtual pins for various challenges. Another example is the Aviation Empire mobile game created by KLM Royal Dutch Airlines. A larger scale application is Ingress, the augmented reality game created by Google startup Niantic Labs (see Industry Insight). These examples illustrate that mobile apps inspire the co-creation of new experiences. Indeed, there is some evidence that mobile apps can create more spontaneous and creative experiences by stimulating surprise, excitement and imagination (Wang *et al.*, 2012).

Augmenting

Like gamification, augmented reality represents another application made possible by the convergence of various mobile technologies. Augmented reality enhances or augments the

Industry Insights: Ingress

Ingress is an augmented reality game created by Google startup Niantic Labs. The game blends virtual events with physical settings in the real world. Ingress is based on the premise that the Earth has been seeded with exotic matter (XM) by an exotic alien phenomenon called the Shapers. Players compete in one of two factions: the Enlightened who believe that XM will benefit humanity; and the Resistance, who believe that XM is part of some kind of ingression by the Shapers. The game is played using a mobile app (the "XM scanner") that requires users to establish "portals" at various real landmarks and public spaces. The app uses GPS data to present a real map of the user's area indicating local sculptures, murals and cultural landmarks with virtual portals that are shown as green, blue or white light. White portals can be claimed by deploying virtual devices called resonators. Rival faction members can attack a portal by destroying the resonators to claim it as their own. Portals can be linked to create triangular control fields over physical geographic areas.

The game's creators cleverly mix events in the real world with the narrative and storyline that drive the game by releasing daily updates and staging various ad hoc events. From a travel perspective it is interesting to consider how this game may increase the mobility of travelers. Travelers are likely to continue playing the game while they travel and there are opportunities to create portals at key tourist sites and locations. Special codes can also be included on products, tickets and brochures to unlock additional items that can be used at specific locations. The development of wearable technologies such as Google Glass has also introduced a new dimension to games such as Ingress.

surroundings of the user with virtual information that is rendered so that it appears to coexist with the real world (Yovcheva *et al.*, 2012). Augmented reality can be experienced through apps that overlay a mobile device's real-world camera view with virtual information. Many of the functions already discussed in this chapter can be delivered through augmented reality. Several travel apps from well-known travel companies like TripAdvisor, Yelp, eTips and Lonely Planet have incorporated augmented reality as a feature. Various destinations have also released augmented reality travel guides, using platforms such as Layar (http://www.layar.com/) and Aurasma (http://www.aurasma.com/). Some of the applications we have already discussed, such as Word Lens, Google's Field Trip and Ingress also provide different applications of

augmented reality. Collaborative applications include Wikitude (http://www.wikitude.org/), which includes different layers superimposed on to the real world.

Key applications for the travel industry include augmented reality for marketing, visitor information, translation, interpretation and gamification. When combined with LBSs and contextual data, augmented reality can display customized, real-time information that changes as a user moves through an environment. For example, a traveler walking down a city street might see vacancies and room rates floating next to the hotels in their field of vision. Menu specials and reviews could be displayed as travelers pass restaurants. Visitors to historic sites could experience historic scenes and characters by applying different virtual layers over the real scene. Good examples of travel apps that provide this functionality include the Street Museum app developed by the Museum of London and the Past View (http://www.past-view.es/) experience developed for the Spanish city of Seville.

All of these applications sound wonderful but in reality travelers are reluctant to walk around in public while viewing through their mobile device. Wearable devices like Google Glass put this information directly in front of a user's eyes. There are many opportunities for tourism organizations – travelers will expect destination guides and visitor information to be delivered through augmented reality as these technologies mature (Linaza *et al.*, 2012).

Reflecting

The final function of mobile devices is to support the reflection and recall of travel experiences. Today's mobile devices make it easy for travelers to capture photos and videos of their travel adventures. As we have seen, mobile devices make it easy for travelers to instantly share photos online using social media platforms such as Instagram, Pinterest and Facebook photo albums (Lo *et al.*, 2011). There are opportunities for travel organizations to engage with this social sharing of experiences to build long-term relationships and encourage repeat visitation.

CHALLENGES AND OPPORTUNITIES

All of the technologies, applications and functions we have reviewed in this chapter

suggest a fantastical future world where many processes are automated by mobile devices and information is conveniently filtered and automatically presented in user-friendly ways. This is a vision of what is possible, based on pockets of innovation already occurring in parts of the world. But in reality, delivering on the hype of these technologies requires further technological advances. There are challenges to overcome in terms of the connectivity, interoperability and cross-platform compatibility of various data sources and systems. Analytic systems designed to harness the potential of big data, contextual data and personal information are still being developed. Travel information is also characterized by product complexity, which makes comparisons challenging for technologies such as recommender systems. There are also legal, security and privacy challenges that need to be resolved. Network providers still charge high global roaming fees, creating a barrier for many international travelers. Finally, it is also important to remember that in spite of the many benefits afforded by mobile technologies there will always be travelers who will choose not to use them (Okazaki and Hirose, 2009; Fuchs *et al.*, 2011).

SUMMARY

In this chapter we have reviewed how mobile technologies can be used by the travel industry to support travelers while they are on the move. We have discussed how the broader impact of these technologies can be understood using a mobilities paradigm. We have reviewed some of the key aspects of the mobile technologies ecosystem, including mobile devices, signals and sensors, and operating systems and apps. The final part of this chapter presents ten functions of mobile devices in tourism. Mobile devices are perfectly suited to the application of travel. Despite all of these developments and applications, mobile devices are still in their infancy. As these technologies mature a range of new applications and possibilities will emerge for travel organizations and destinations.

KEY TERMS

accelerometer, ambient intelligence, app store, apps, augmented reality, Bluetooth Low Energy (BLE), convergence, digital elasticity, fluidity, gamification, geocaching, geofencing, geographic information system (GIS), geotagging, global positioning system (GPS), graphene, gyroscope, hybridization, Internet of Things, liquidity, location-based services (LBS), magnetometer, micro-coordination, mobile recommender system, mobilities, navigation devices, Near Field Communication (NFC), operating systems (OS), optical head-mounted displays (OHMD), organic light-emitting diodes (OLEDs), pull communication, push communication, Quick Response (QR) code, radio-frequency identification (RFID), saturation, semantic search, smart devices, smartphone, spillover, subscriber identification module (SIM) card, tablet, telepresence, TILES model, touchscreen, ubiquity, virtual assistant, wearable smart devices, WiFi

DISCUSSION QUESTIONS

1. In the introduction we suggest that mobile technologies enable the fluidity and liquidity of experiences. Read some of the mobilities literature dealing with technology and write a paragraph to explain what this statement means.

2. In the past a holiday meant being away from home, both physiologically and psychologically. But it seems that mobile devices are making it more difficult to separate our everyday lives from our travel experiences. Do you think this is a problem? What does this suggest about future travel experiences?

3. In previous chapters we have discussed how the Internet has eroded the influence of traditional travel intermediaries. Arguably mobile devices go further by automating many of the functions performed by travel intermediaries by providing a management tool for the entire travel experience. Do you think that mobile devices will mean the end of traditional intermediaries?

4. We have identified that mobile devices can use a range of contextual data to customize and personalize travel experiences. But frameworks like the TILES model require access to a lot of data, some of which may raise privacy concerns. How might app designers overcome these challenges?

5. Many younger generations have grown up in a culture where games and rewards incentivize performance. How do you feel about the idea of gamification in travel? Would you participate in a virtual "Amazing Race" powered by your mobile phone if you could earn virtual or real prizes? Select a city you are familiar with and design a mobile app based on the concept of gamifying the travel experience.

6. This book was written in 2014. What advances have taken place in mobile technologies since this time? How can these technologies be used by travel organizations and destinations? What opportunities are created by advances in wearable and ubiquitous technologies?

USEFUL WEBSITES

QR code	Website	Description
	6th Sense Transport http://www. sixthsensetransport.com/	A major UK project investigating how context aware technology can be used to reduce fossil-fueled trips and improve quality of life.
	TravelByGPS.com http://www.travelbygps. com/	An online community for sharing GPS waypoints.
	GPS.gov http://www.gps.gov/	Official US Government information about the Global Positioning System (GPS).
	Bluetooth http://www.bluetooth.com/	Learn more about Bluetooth technology and its various applications.
	Near Field Communication http://www. nearfieldcommunication. com/	Information about NFC technologies and applications.

QR code	Website	Description
	EpicMix http://www.epicmix.com/	An example of the gamification of a ski resort.
	Ingress http://www.ingress.com/	Details about the augmented reality game Ingress by Google's Niantic Labs.

Case Study: Google Glass

Google Glass is a ubiquitous wearable computer with an optical head-mounted display (OHMD). The product was released with much hype in 2014 and was the first mass market OHMD. OHMDs are not new and are popular in science fiction, but previous efforts were bulky and required input devices and wiring that made them less portable. Like smartphones, the convergence and miniaturization of various technologies have made it possible to produce a standalone unit that is light enough to fit conformably on the face.

Google Glass displays information in a smartphone-like hands-free format and can communicate with the Internet using natural language voice commands. The device can also be controlled with a series of simple swipes using the touchpad located on the side of the device. Basic features include the ability to take photos, record short videos, interact with others on Google+, send emails, get directions, make phone calls and conduct simple searches. The device can be tethered to smartphone to access the Internet and other features.

Google has designed Glass to take advantage of its Android ecosystem, further tying people into various services such as Gmail, Google Calendar, Google+, Google Search, Google Now, Field Trip and a range of other services. This has many benefits for users. Unless you are completely off the grid Google knows a lot about you. In all likelihood Google knows where you live, where you work, what you like, who you know and what you search for. This is a little disconcerting but as we have discussed in this chapter, the benefits for contextualizing and personalizing information are immediately apparent. This ecosystem also supports the installation of third-party apps, resulting in a range of new travel applications, including virtual tour guides, marketing applications, navigation and augmented reality.

(Continued)

Case Study. Continued.

Despite these features, some users have been disappointed by the first generation of Google Glass. Some people viewed it as a replacement for their smartphone or computer. In reality, OHMDs are like tablets. They represent another form factor and product class for interacting with the increasing amounts of iniquitous information around us. As a result, these devices have strengths and weaknesses and people are likely to own multiple mobile devices and computers well into the future. The launch of Google Glass has also spurred the development of other wearable mobile devices with new features and capabilities.

http://glass.google.com/

Wearable devices like Google Glass present many opportunities for the travel industry, and extend and enhance many of the applications we have discussed in this chapter. In an era of ubiquitous technologies many organizations will find applications for devices that allow us to access and interact seamlessly with the digital information that is all around us. To learn more visit: http://glass.google.com/.

Study Questions

1. The use of Google Glass has created a range of privacy concerns and ethical issues. How can travel organizations and technology companies balance the need for contextualized information against basic human rights to privacy?

2. What new travel applications can you envisage for wearable devices like Google Glass?

3. How do content providers balance the presentations of information and push notifications to ensure that users are not overwhelmed?

4. Devices such as Google Glass bring us pretty close to the ability to communicate telepathically with anyone else using similar devices. What are the implications of this?

REFERENCES

Aguiléra, A., Guillot, C. and Rallet, A. (2012) Mobile ICTs and physical mobility: review and research agenda. *Transportation Research Part A: Policy and Practice* 46(4), 664–672. doi: http://dx.doi.org/10.1016/j.tra.2012.01.005

Cao, L., Luo, J., Gallagher, A., Jin, X., Han, J. and Huang, T.S. (2010). A worldwide tourism recommendation system based on geotagged web photos. Paper presented at the 2010 IEEE International Conference on Acoustics, Speech and Signal Processing (ICASSP).

de Souza e Silva, A. (2006) From cyber to hybrid mobile technologies as interfaces of hybrid spaces. *Space and Culture* 9(3), 261–278.

Deterding, S., Dixon, D., Khaled, R. and Nacke, L. (2011) From game design elements to gamefulness: defining gamification. Paper presented at the Proceedings of the 15th International Academic MindTrek Conference: Envisioning Future Media Environments.

Dickinson, J.E., Ghali, K., Cherrett, T., Speed, C., Davies, N. and Norgate, S. (2014) Tourism and the smartphone app: capabilities, emerging practice and scope in the travel domain. *Current Issues in Tourism* 17(1), 84–101.

Frith, J. (2013) Turning life into a game: Foursquare, gamification, and personal mobility. *Mobile Media and Communication* 1(2), 248–262.

Fuchs, M., Hopken, W. and Rasinger, J. (2011) Behavioral intention to use mobile information services in tourism: the case of the tourist guide dolomitisuperski.mobi. *Information Technology and Tourism* 13(4), 285–307. doi: 10.3727/109830512x13364362859858

Green, N. (2002) On the move: technology, mobility, and the mediation of social time and space. *The Information Society* 18(4), 281–292.

Gruber, G. (2011) Designing a successful mobile strategy for travel. *tnooz.com*. Available at: http://www.tnooz.com/article/part-two-of-three-designing-a-successful-mobile-strategy-for-travel/ (accessed 1 January 2014).

Hwang, Y.H. (2010) A theory of unplanned travel decisions: implications for modeling on-the-go travelers. *Information Technology and Tourism* 12(3), 283–296. doi: 10.3727/109830511x12978702284516

Hyun, M.Y., Lee, S. and Hu, C. (2009) Mobile-mediated virtual experience in tourism: concept, typology and applications. *Journal of Vacation Marketing* 15(2), 149–164.

Jansson, A. (2007) A sense of tourism: new media and the dialectic of encapsulation/decapsulation. *Tourist Studies* 7(1), 5–24.

Kang, M. and Gretzel, U. (2012) Perceptions of museum podcast tours: effects of consumer innovativeness, Internet familiarity and podcasting affinity on performance expectancies. *Tourism Management Perspectives* 4, 155–163.

Kaplan, A.M. (2012) If you love something, let it go mobile: mobile marketing and mobile social media 4x4. *Business Horizons* 55(2), 129–139.

Lee, D.H. (2010) Digital cameras, personal photography and the reconfiguration of spatial experiences. *The Information Society* 26(4), 266–275.

Linaza, M.T., Marimon, D., Carrasco, P., Alvarez, R., Montesa, J., Aguilar, S.R. and Diez, G. (2012) Evaluation of mobile augmented reality applications for tourism destinations. *Proceedings of Information and Communication Technologies in Tourism, ENTER 2012*. Springer-Verlag, Vienna, pp. 260–271.

Line, T., Jain, J. and Lyons, G. (2011) The role of ICTs in everyday mobile lives. *Journal of Transport Geography* 19(6), 1490–1499. doi: http://dx.doi.org/10.1016/j.jtrangeo.2010.07.002

Lo, S.T., McKercher, B., Lo, A., Cheung, C. and Law, R. (2011) Tourism and online photography. *Tourism Management* 32(4), 725–731. doi: 10.1016/j.tourman.2010.06.001

MacKay, K. and Vogt, C. (2012) Information technology in everyday and vacation contexts. *Annals of Tourism Research* 39(3), 1380–1401. doi: 10.1016/j.annals.2012.02.001

Manes, G. (2003) The tetherless tourist: ambient intelligence in travel and tourism. *Information Technology and Tourism* 5(4), 211–220. doi: 10.3727/109830503108751144

Mirski, P.J. and Abfalter, D. (2004) Knowledge enhancement on site – guests' attitudes towards m-learning. In: Frew. A.J. (ed.) *Information and Communication Technologies in Tourism 2004*. Proceedings of the International Conference in Cairo, Egypt, 2004, pp. 592–600.

Modsching, M., Kramer, R., Ten Hagen, K. and Gretzel, U. (2007) Effectiveness of mobile recommender systems for tourist destinations: a user evaluation. Paper presented at the Intelligent Data Acquisition and Advanced Computing Systems: Technology and Applications, Dortmund, Germany.

Modsching, M., Kramer, R., Hagen, K. ten and Gretzel, U. (2008) Using location-based tracking data to analyze the movements of city tourists. *Information Technology and Tourism* 10(1), 31–42. doi: 10.3727/109830508785059011

Molz, J.G. (2012) *Travel Connections: Tourism, technology, and togetherness in a mobile world*. Routledge, New York.

Okazaki, S. and Hirose, M. (2009) Does gender affect media choice in travel information search? On the use of mobile Internet. *Tourism Management* 30(6), 794–804. doi: 10.1016/j.tourman.2008.12.012

Paganelli, F. and Giuli, D. (2008) Context-aware information services to support tourist communities. *Information Technology and Tourism* 10(4), 313–327. doi: 10.3727/109830508788403150

Pearce, P.L. (2011) *Tourist Behaviour and the Contemporary World*, Vol. 51. Channel View Publications, Bristol, UK.

Pearce, P.L., Murphy, L. and Brymer, E. (2009) *Evolution of the Backpacker Market and the Potential for Australian Tourism*. CRC for Sustainable Tourism, Gold Coast, Australia.

Pellegrino, G. (2009) Technology and mobilities. *Soziale Technik* 2, 10–12.

Pesonen, J. and Horster, E. (2012) Near field communication technology in tourism. *Tourism Management Perspectives* 4(0), 11–18. doi: http://dx.doi.org/10.1016/j.tmp.2012.04.001

Ricci, F. (2010) Mobile recommender systems. *Information Technology and Tourism* 12(3), 205–231. doi: 10.3727/109830511x12978702284390

Richards, G. and Wilson, J. (2006) Developing creativity in tourist experiences: a solution to the serial reproduction of culture? *Tourism Management* 27(6), 1209–1223. doi: http://dx.doi.org/10.1016/j.tourman.2005.06.002

Riebeck, M., Stark, A., Modsching, M. and Kawalek, J. (2008) Studying the user acceptance of a mobile information system for tourists in the field. *Information Technology and Tourism* 10(3), 189–199. doi: 10.3727/109830508787157308

Rodríguez, B., Molina, J., Pérez, F. and Caballero, R. (2012) Interactive design of personalised tourism routes. *Tourism Management* 33(4), 926–940. doi: http://dx.doi.org/10.1016/j.tourman.2011.09.014

Schlatter, B.E. and Hurd, A.R. (2005) Geocaching: 21st-century hide-and-seek. *Journal of Physical Education, Recreation and Dance* 76(7), 28–32.

Sharma, P. and Nugent, D. (2006) Mobile Technologies and Tourism. In: Unhelkar, B. (ed.) *Handbook of Research in Mobile Business: Technical, Methodological and Social Perspectives*, Vol. 1. Idea Reference Group, Hershey, Pennsylvania.

Sheller, M. (2011) Mobility. *Sociopedia.isa*. Available at: http://www.sagepub.net/isa/resources/pdf/mobility.pdf

Sheller, M. and Urry, J. (2006) The new mobilities paradigm. *Environment and Planning A* 38(2), 207–226.

Shoval, N. and Isaacson, M. (2007) Tracking tourists in the digital age. *Annals of Tourism Research* 34(1), 141–159. doi: 10.1016/j.annals.2006.07.007

Spindler, A. de, Norrie, M.C. and Grossniklaus, M. (2008) Recommendation based on opportunistic information sharing between tourists. *Information Technology and Tourism* 10(4), 297–311. doi: 10.3727/109830508788403178

Sugimoto, K. (2011) Analysis of scenic perception and its spatial tendency: using digital cameras, GPS loggers, and GIS. *Procedia - Social and Behavioral Sciences* 21(0), 43–52. doi: http://dx.doi.org/10.1016/j.sbspro.2011.07.010

Tan, E., Meng-Yoke, F., Schubert, G., Dion, H.L. and Theng, Y.L. (2009) TILES: classifying contextual information for mobile tourism applications. *Aslib Proceedings: New Information Perspectives* 61(6), 565–586.

Tussyadiah, I.P. (2012) Territoriality and consumption behaviour with location-based media. In: Fuchs, M., Ricci, F. and Cantoni, L. (eds) *Information and Communication Technologies in Tourism 2012, Helsingborg, Sweden, January 25-27, 2012*. Springer, Helsingborg, 259 pp.

Tussyadiah, I.P. and Zach, F.J. (2012) The role of geo-based technology in place experiences. *Annals of Tourism Research* 39(2), 780–800. doi: http://dx.doi.org/10.1016/j.annals.2011.10.003

Uriely, N. (2005) The tourist experience: conceptual developments. *Annals of Tourism Research* 32(1), 199–216.

Urry, J. (2002) Mobility and proximity. *Sociology* 36(2), 255–274.

US Government (2013) GPS.gov. Available at: http://www.gps.gov/ (accessed 29 December 2013).

Vela, D. (2012) A quick way to generate new business: think QR Codes. Available at: http://www.eyefortravel.com/mobile-and-technology/quick-way-generate-new-business-think-qr-codes/ (accessed 1 January 2014).

Wang, D. and Xiang, Z. (2012) The new landscape of travel: a comprehensive analysis of smartphone apps. In: Fuchs, M., Ricci, F. and Cantoni, L. (eds) *Information and Communication Technologies in Tourism 2012*. Springer, New York, pp. 308–319.

Wang, D., Park, S. and Fesenmaier, D.R. (2012) The role of smartphones in mediating the touristic experience. *Journal of Travel Research* 51(4), 371–387.

Yovcheva, Z., Buhalis, D. and Gatzidis, C. (2012) Smartphone augmented reality applications for tourism. *e-Review of Tourism Research (eRTR)* 10(2), 63–66.

Zichermann, G. and Cunningham, C. (2011) *Gamification by Design: Implementing game mechanics in web and mobile apps*. O'Reilly Media, Inc., Sebastapol, California.

chapter 7

Aviation and Information Technology

LEARNING OBJECTIVES

After studying this chapter you should be able to:

- analyze the impact of IT on airlines and air travelers;
- explain how airline reservation systems work and how they connect with other information systems;
- understand how information systems support management decision-making in airlines;
- examine how information technologies are used by airports to streamline the passenger experience; and
- evaluate the present and future information technology applications in airport operations.

INTRODUCTION

Travelers in developed countries often take air travel for granted, but the business of putting planes in the sky is a complex human endeavor. This complexity is because airlines and airports operate in environments that are sensitive to geopolitical, economic, technological and environmental change. Aviation also involves many stakeholders – government authorities, international organizations, employees, travelers and residents. The operation of airlines and airports is logistically complex, requiring the expertise of engineers, accountants, IT specialists, managers, meteorologists, environmental scientists and pilots, to name a few.

This complexity creates a heavy reliance on information systems and other technologies, although human interaction is also critical (Oyewole *et al.*, 2008). Flying "heavier than air" machines was accomplished just 120 years ago thanks to the industrial revolution and human ingenuity. Today over 3 billion passengers fly annually and 3.5% of the global economy relies on aviation (International Air Transport Association, 2014). By 2030, it is estimated that 5.9 billion passengers will fly annually and the global airline fleet will be almost double the 24,000 aircraft in service today (Air Transport Action Group, 2014). The modern aviation industry would not be possible without the use of technology to design and build aircraft, sell seats and ensure the safety of travelers. In this chapter we examine how IT is supporting the operations of airlines and airports.

AIRLINES

Airlines are the most intensive users of IT in tourism. The operation of an airline requires many sophisticated systems to deliver a satisfying and safe travel experience while maximizing the airline's profitability. Since the mid-1980s many countries' airline industries have been deregulated and privatized, and ownership of some national airlines has transferred to public or private companies, creating opportunities for new airlines to enter the market. Generally airlines can be divided into the following categories.

1. **National Flag Carriers**: many governments, particularly in the Asia-Pacific, the Middle East, Africa and Latin America, continue to own national airlines, which operate full service scheduled services. Examples include Air India, Air New Zealand and Aerolíneas Argentinas. These airlines provide services for taxpayers' benefit, are often heavily subsidized by governments, serve routes that would otherwise be unprofitable, and use IT less extensively.

2. **Commercial Airlines**: a mix of new airlines and older, established non-government owned airlines or flag carriers that were privatized. Examples include British Airways, Qantas and Lufthansa. Deregulation in developed countries has allowed new carriers to emerge. Examples include Virgin Atlantic, Delta and Eva Air. Many commercial airlines developed the global distributions systems (GDSs) and have benefitted by sharing technological innovations with alliance partners or establishing OTAs such as Orbitz and Zuji.

3. **Low Cost Carriers (LCCs)**: these airlines keep base fares low and charge extra for food, priority boarding, seat allocation and baggage. This is the "user pays" business model and examples include Ryanair, AirAsia X, Spring Airlines, easyJet, Jetstar and Southwest Airlines. LCCs airlines use IT to automate processes, improve efficiency and reduce operating costs.

4. **Charter Airlines**: charter airlines lease aircraft for itineraries such as packaged tours that travelers purchase through a tour operator. Cruise lines, sports teams, governments and the military also use charter airlines. Examples include Thomson Airlines and North American Airlines but scheduled airlines also offer charter services. To be viable, charter flights usually operate at near 100% seat occupancy. IT solutions facilitate the scheduling and booking of entire aircraft or a block of seats.

Airline use of information technology

Airlines use IT for a wide range of applications at all stages of the tourist experience, including marketing, distribution, customer service and operations. In fact, modern airlines would not exist without IT to ensure the efficient distribution and safe operation of flights. Figure 7.1 provides an overview of these key IT solutions.

The **airline reservation system (ARS)** is at the core of most modern airline IT systems. ARSs interface with a range of **decision support systems** and **departure systems** to ensure that reservations and passenger processing are handled efficiently. In Chapters 2

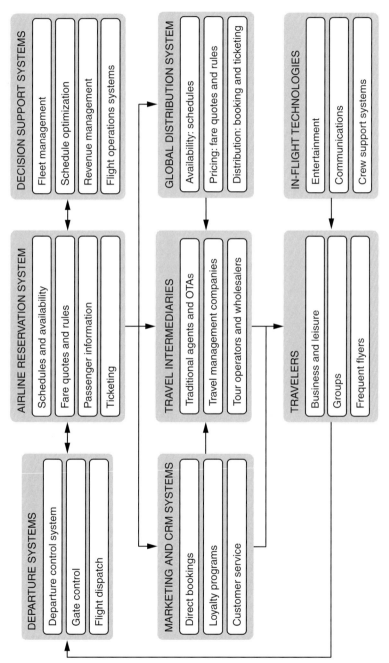

Fig. 7.1. Key information technologies used by airlines.

Industry Insight: Altéa Suite

In addition to providing one of the world's leading GDSs, Amadeus has diversified and provides IT solutions for the travel industry. Its Altéa Suite includes software solutions that automate sales and reservations, inventory management and departure control processes. Altéa allows airlines and airports to outsource their IT operations using an open platform that shares information with both airline partners. The Altéa Suite consists of three components.

1. Altéa Reservation: customer profiles, availability, booking, pricing and ticketing management.
2. Altéa Inventory: schedule and seat capacity management.
3. Altéa Departure Control: a departure control system including check-in and boarding applications, baggage management, aircraft weight and balance, and disruption management.

http://youtu.be/oWX8W7G8m_s

Amadeus also provides an e-commerce suite to support online bookings and distribution. All of these components are based on PNRs, customer profiles, schedules, seat maps and codeshare records. Altéa Airport Link connects the Altéa Suite and airport workstations serviced by an airline. Watch the following video to learn more about how Amadeus supports the aviation industry: http://youtu.be/oWX8W7G8m_s/.

and 3 we explored how travel intermediaries and the GDSs interface with these systems to support the booking of travel products. Most airlines also rely heavily on information systems to support **marketing** and **customer relationship management (CRM)**. These systems are integrated or offered as part of a suite, such as Amadeus' Altéa (see Industry Insight). Once passengers are onboard a range of **in-flight technologies** enhances the travel experience. The following sections discuss each of these applications in more detail.

Airline reservation systems

A passenger reservation system, or **airline reservation system (ARS)**, is the most important application of IT. At its core is a database of flight schedules and seat availability, fares and rules and passenger information. An ARS shows the schedules for a single airline, whereas a GDS shows many carriers' schedules. Furthermore, ARSs are used by airline staff while GDSs are used by travel intermediaries to source and book seats. It is important for an ARS to connect to other systems such as GDSs and Internet booking engines (IBEs). Interoperability is critical between airlines that are part of the same alliance. The ARS typically interfaces with other systems using a standardized message format to book seats in real time. A major goal of IATAs **New Distribution Capability (NDC)** is to facilitate seamless connectivity with a common XML-based data transmission standard for communications between ARSs, GDSs and travel intermediaries.

Some airlines develop their own ARSs but they are functionally complex and expensive to operate and maintain in-house. Consequently, many airlines use a CRS hosted by the GDSs or third-party IT vendors. Although each airline's reservation system may have unique features, most functions are similar and discussed below.

Flight schedules and availability

An important function of an ARS is to display flight schedules and availability in response to the requests of passengers and intermediaries. Therefore an ARS has to interface with all touch points where this information is needed, including the airline's own website, third-party websites, mobile apps, GDSs and traditional travel intermediaries. An airline's **availability display** shows all flights for a particular route (or city-pair) and the available seats in different classes. The availability display usually includes the airline's own flights and those of code-share partners using the airline's flight codes. If direct flights are not available the availability display will show connecting flight options.

Fare quotes and rules

The **Fare Quote System** stores fares and rules for each booking class. **Fare rules** regarding booking and ticketing deadlines, stopovers, maximum or minimum length of stay and blackout dates are stored for each fare. Airlines typically divide seats into **cabin classes** (e.g. first, business or economy class) and **booking codes** that contain different fare quotes and rules. Booking codes are also known as booking classes or fare classes. A single cabin class may contain several booking codes (see Table 7.1), which are shown on the passenger's booking confirmation and

boarding pass. Different frequent flyer points are awarded based on booking codes so this information must be communicated to the airline's frequent flyer system.

The combined set of fare quotes and associated rules is called a **fare basis code (FBC)**. For international itineraries, fares may involve multiple segments, multiple currencies, taxes and sets of regulations. This requires the interchange of fare data between airlines, GDSs and other intermediaries. Most of this fare data is distributed either by the Airline Tariff Publishing Company (ATPCO) or Société Internationale de Télécommunications Aéronautiques (SITA) using a common set of standards.

By combining scheduling and seat availability information with the Fare Quote System an ARS provides the best fare for

Table 7.1. Examples of booking codes used by airlines.

Booking class	Code
First Class	F
First Class Premium	P
First Class Discounted	A
First Class Suites	R
Business Class	C
Business Class Premium	J
Business Class Discounted	D
Economy	Y, Q
Economy Premium	E, S, W
Economy Discounted	B, H, K, L, M, N, T, V, X

every seat. Real-time decision support systems, such as schedule optimization systems and revenue management systems, determine the fares (see below) by monitoring the demand and supply of seats and using algorithms to maximize revenues. Once determined, these fares are fed into the ARS and GDS for display.

Passenger information

The third core function of an ARS is to store passenger information required for reservations, check-in and other operational procedures. Bookings for individual passengers or groups are stored using a **passenger name record (PNR)**. A PNR contains the passenger's name, contact details, payment details, frequent flyer number and a **record locator**. The record locator is a six character alphanumeric code used to access a reservation. The PNR also stores **special service requests (SSRs)** such as seat preferences (e.g. aisle or window), special meals (e.g. vegetarian, kosher, diabetic), wheelchair requests, and assistance for unaccompanied minors. It is therefore important that the passenger information in an ARS can be transmitted to other systems. For example, before a flight departs a **passenger name list (PNL)** is transmitted to departure and gate control systems so that passengers can be checked in and a **flight manifest** can be generated. Special service requests are transferred to flight operations and catering systems while passenger data are transmitted to customer loyalty databases to update frequent flyer accounts. Data from a customer loyalty database may also flow to the PNR to populate fields with existing information and passenger preferences. Data needed for financial systems and reporting are transmitted to back-office systems.

Electronic ticketing

The final key function of an ARS is ticketing. Historically airlines required passengers to travel with paper tickets to validate their reservation. Electronic tickets, or **e-tickets**, were devised in the mid-1990s and became mandatory for all IATA airlines in 2008. Once a reservation is confirmed, passengers are provided with a hard copy or electronic copy of their e-ticket itinerary, which contains a record locator and itinerary details. An e-ticket itinerary also includes the terms and conditions of carriage, fare and tax details (including the fare basis code), fare restrictions and baggage allowances. The e-ticket allows the passenger to check-in online or at the airport to obtain a **boarding pass**. Because of these different check-in procedures an ARS must manage e-tickets at a number of touch points.

Decision support systems

Airline managers make many decisions about an airline's flight activity. Computer systems can analyze such situations and recommend solutions to problems, particularly scheduling and control problems. These systems are based on sophisticated models called **Operations Research (OR)** models, which use "what-if?" and sensitivity analyses to investigate the impact of various factors on operations. Skilled staff with OR training build and use these models. **Decision Support Systems (DSSs)** based on OR models constitute a significant amount of airline computer applications. The following section will discuss the DSSs used for fleet management, flight and crew scheduling, revenue management and flight operations.

Fleet management

The aircraft fleet represents a significant investment and investors expect profits. IT solutions can optimize the use of the fleet as follows:

1. Fleet acquisition: an airline needs data to support decisions about what type, when and how many of each aircraft to acquire (Belobaba *et al.*, 2009). IT systems provide information such as operating costs and profitability of different aircraft types on particular routes. This information is linked to scheduling and revenue management data, although aircraft acquisition may also be based on customer preferences (Bhatia, 1988).

2. Fleet assignment: the assignment of aircraft to routes should maximize profits while ensuring the efficient use of the fleet. Computers model time–space networks to ensure the optimal assignment of an airline's fleet.

3. Fleet maintenance: safety regulations require close monitoring of the maintenance schedule for each aircraft. Computerized systems ensure that all aircraft receive maintenance checks at specified intervals. Databases contain information about each aircraft and the maintenance schedule for individual parts. They generate reports so that checks and servicing are not overlooked.

Fleet management systems are intricately linked with flight scheduling systems, as we will explain below.

Flight scheduling systems

Flight scheduling is a complex task requiring route-planning to maximize an airline's return on investment in aircraft, terminal facilities and people. Route selection considers the most profitable routes and the frequency of service on those routes. We can develop a better understanding of the role IT plays in scheduling by adopting an **input–output** perspective.

The complexity of scheduling is due to the wide range of **inputs** that impact the airline's operation and its passengers, including:

- **Strategic goals**: strategic decisions such as which markets to serve, how to respond to competing schedules and pricing, and access to resources such as suppliers, employees and terminal facilities can impact the long-term viability of routes.
- **Route network**: route networks ensure that aircraft utilization is maximized and connections are convenient for passengers.
- **Passenger demand**: airlines use sophisticated revenue management models to project demand for each route (see below). Scheduling flights on high demand days and times optimizes load factors and profits.
- **Alliances**: an airline must consider not only its own schedules but also those of alliance partners so that connecting flights are convenient.
- **Aircraft type**: operating characteristics such as the capacity, range and fuel efficiency of different aircraft, maintenance schedules and turnaround times all impact scheduling.
- **Human resources**: the availability of flight crew and industrial relations legislation governs the working conditions of flight crew. Maximum shift durations, recuperation and changeover of fresh crews need to be considered (see below).
- **Environmental and safety regulations**: airlines and airports must comply with stringent environmental and safety requirements, including inspections, maintenance schedules and noise restrictions, which affect scheduling.
- **Airport restrictions**: curfews, congestion, air traffic control, landing slots and gate

availability can limit departure and arrival windows for a particular route. Some airports also have physical limitations restricting the type of aircraft that can land.

- **Contingency planning**: exogenous and erratic factors such as weather, air traffic control delays and technical failures must also be considered by scheduling systems.

The **outputs** are flight schedules that maximize **load factors** and **revenue per available seat mile (RASM)** and minimize **costs per available seat mile (CASM)**. These inputs and outputs mean that airlines face a complex set of variables. The input–output approach helps us to understand that the ideal schedule for an airline amounts to the optimization of the entire company, or in the case of alliances, the entire industry. This optimization is difficult to achieve without technology. Flight scheduling systems provide an IT solution to model various scheduling scenarios using these inputs and outputs. A sophisticated flight scheduling system allows decision makers to adjust the inputs to model the effects on load factors, revenue and costs. Flight scheduling is a never-ending task because schedules fluctuate with market and competitive forces and seasons.

Crew scheduling systems

Once the flight schedules have been determined, the pilots and flight attendants must be scheduled. A computer program called a **pairing optimizer** assembles flight schedules for each crewmember. The process of requesting a particular schedule is called **bidding**. Generally each crewmember submits their bids monthly. The monthly work schedule allocated to a crewmember is called a **line**, which consists of a series of **crew pairings**. A crew pairing is a sequence of flights or legs that start and end at the same base destination (i.e. a round trip). Sometimes **deadheading** is necessary, which involves flying crewmembers free of charge on other flights. It is inefficient and is avoided whenever possible. The challenge for an airline is to minimize costs by finding the minimum number of crews to cover all scheduled flights. A pairing optimizer also identifies **reserve** crewmembers in case scheduled crewmembers cannot fulfill their duties.

A pairing optimizer considers various inputs to create the most efficient schedule for the airline. Examples of inputs are crew requests for their preferred routes, crewmember seniority, and their base city. Other constraints are work rules, such as maximum work hours stipulated by industrial relations or unions; minimum rest periods; and cost parameters such as salaries and budgets. IT plays an important role here as computers run the complex algorithms that underpin scheduling solutions. Although computers do much of the work, crucial choices and decisions are still made by managers.

Revenue management

Revenue maximization is a major focus of airline management. Like hotel rooms (see Chapter 9), airline seats can be sold at different prices. Airlines can maximize revenue and load factors by selling the right seats, at the right price, to the right people, at the right time. According to Belobaba *et al.* (2009), there are two components of revenue management. The first is **price differentiation**, whereby seats on the same flight are offered at different prices with different rules and features. The second is the use of **yield management** to determine the number of seats (booking limits) for each fare class at any given time.

Maximizing revenue requires an understanding of the market, historic trends, competitor behavior and pricing. Leisure travelers are more price sensitive and have greater flexibility than business travelers. As a result they are attracted to low-cost seats. In peak times (e.g. Friday afternoons) an airline has to control the seat price so that not too many seats are sold at a low price when passengers are willing to pay more. The main objective is to preserve some seats for later booking by high-yield travelers.

Airlines use **Revenue Management Systems (RMSs)** to calculate the booking limits on each fare class for future flights. These RMSs forecast future demand for different fare classes so they can fill each seat with the highest possible revenue. An RMS typically includes the following capabilities:

1. **Historical data**: capturing and analyzing historical booking data to identify patterns and trends.
2. **Forecasting**: predicting future demand based on historical data and other inputs.
3. **Modeling**: recommendations on booking limits and overbooking levels that optimize expected flight revenues using mathematical models.
4. **Decision support**: interactive decision support allows revenue managers to review, accept or reject booking limits and overbooking levels (Belobaba *et al.*, 2009).

RMSs automatically update booking limits and forecasts at regular intervals leading up to flight departure. Historical data are combined with actual booking information to determine whether demand for different fare categories is consistent with forecasts. Airlines sometimes develop their own RMSs but IT solutions are also provided by software vendors and GDS vendors. A good example of the latter is the revenue management component of the Altéa Suite provided by Amadeus (see Industry Insight).

Flight operations systems

Airlines and aircraft manufacturers employ a range of IT solutions to support the operation of a flight. Feeding passengers is one of the most complex challenges faced by airlines (Jones, 2006). A large airline like Emirates employs over 5400 staff and produces 125 different menus and over 70,000 meals a day. **Flight catering systems** capture special meal requests and manage the ordering, storage, preparation and delivery of meals. A range of systems order and track the ingredients required and monitor the freshness, quality and quantity of ingredients so that orders meet passenger demand. For this reason, the flight catering system interfaces with the ARS. Like restaurants (see Chapter 9), airlines and flight catering companies use recipe-costing systems to track meal costs. Bar codes and **radio frequency identification (RFID)** chips keep track of trolleys, trays, cutlery and crockery to reduce the incidence of lost items.

Airlines also employ IT systems to manage operational safety. Most airlines have developed and implemented integrated **Safety Management Systems (SMSs)** to report, monitor and manage incidents. Examples of such incidents include human error, food safety and accidents in the galley, fluid leaks, mechanical and electrical malfunctions. Systems that capture these incidents provide reports to be analyzed by management to improve operational safety.

Marketing and customer relationship management

In previous chapters we reviewed how the travel industry has adopted the Internet, social media and mobile technologies for marketing and customer service applications. Here we discuss how airlines use these technologies to engage directly with passengers by providing information, bookings and loyalty programs.

Direct bookings

Not surprisingly, the Internet has had a major impact on the marketing and distribution of airline seats. The airlines have a "love–hate" relationship with the GDSs and OTAs. GDSs and OTAs are an indispensable part of their distribution chain, but they also increase the distribution costs per booking (Koo *et al.*, 2011). The Internet provided airlines with new opportunities to sell seats directly to passengers (Klein, 2002). Many LCCs emerged at the same time as the Internet and the dominant business model was based on direct distribution rather than paying commissions and fees to intermediaries. The Internet allowed LCCs to bypass intermediaries by using their own **Internet booking engines (IBEs)** (Harcar and Yucelt, 2012). To further entice passengers concerned about online trust and security, many LCCs offered discounts for direct bookings on their websites. As a result, the direct online booking of airline seats spread and full service airlines replicated this functionality. Today, most full service airlines use a multi-channel model to sell tickets through GDSs and OTAs as well as their own websites, but LCCs have focused only on the latter.

Airline websites provide passengers with greater choice and control over seat purchase. Website features can be grouped into three categories, which influence satisfaction differently:

1. **Basic features** such as flight information, booking and check-in tools are expected and will cause dissatisfaction if they are not present.

2. **Pivotal features** that support trust and interaction between the airline and its passengers will create satisfaction. Features like secure online transactions and frequent flyer management tools enhance the utility of airline websites.

3. **Supplementary features** such as the ability to make special requests, buy upgrades, ancillary products and complementary products can enhance satisfaction but may not cause dissatisfaction if they are not present (Benckendorff, 2006).

Airlines offer a range of supplementary features, such as add-ons, upgrades and ancillary products and services during the booking process. Many airlines use **product bundling** by providing passengers with the opportunity to book complementary products such as accommodation, car rental and other services. Typically these products and services are sourced through white-label **affiliate programs** provided by major OTAs and rebranded by the airline. The **dynamic packaging** of these products often results in a lower price than booking each product individually. Many airlines also provide smartphone apps that allow passengers to find and book flights, manage their booking, check-in and receive notifications and offers.

Loyalty programs

Full-service airlines offer customer loyalty programs known as **frequent flyer programs (FFPs)**. Passengers become members of these programs to receive benefits, and enroll in the program to accumulate points (or miles) corresponding to the distance flown on the airline or its alliance partners. Members can also accumulate points through shopping and co-branded credit and debit cards. Points are redeemed for air travel, upgrades, priority seating, airport lounge access, complementary travel products or other goods and services.

Databases keep track of points and manage the relationship between airlines and FFP members (Yang and Liu, 2003). These databases are a good example of a **Customer Relationship Management (CRM)** system because they enable airlines to store individual information about customers and their preferences to build long-term relationships and encourage repeat business. Ideally, FFPs should connect to the airline and partner ARS so that points can be automatically awarded after a trip. Dedicated websites for frequent flyer programs allow members to manage, claim and redeem points. Since these points are valuable, security is tight to ensure that computer hackers cannot access frequent flyer accounts. All of these functions mean that FFPs are underpinned by sophisticated hardware and software systems.

Airlines can now combine big data and social media profiles with FFP accounts to provide personalized offers. Since FFP points are a liability for most airlines, members are encouraged to redeem their points for products and services that do not impact the airline's profitability. **Predictive analytics** combine big data, statistical analysis and artificial intelligence to make predictions about offers that FFP members are likely to respond to. In this new world of big data, privacy and how personal data is used is important.

Customer service

Airlines were early adopters of the web and email as customer service tools (Dickinger and Bauernfeind, 2009). Airlines now use mobile applications and social media to deliver relevant, time-critical procedural information to passengers such as essential airport and flight information, notifications of gate openings and changes, alternative flights in cases of cancellations or missed flights and providing compensation, and offers and coupons (Amadeus, 2012). Mobile devices also offer airlines an opportunity to sell upgrades, even after the passenger has arrived at the airport. The combination of mobile devices and social media creates a mechanism for the exchange of suggestions, complaints, testimonials and ratings throughout the journey. As we have seen in Chapter 5, KLM Royal Dutch Airlines uses social media to update passengers about delays, cancellations and alternative arrangements. This is a good example of a high-tech solution supporting a high-touch response in an otherwise increasingly automated process. Later in this chapter we will explore how airlines and airports work together to deploy technologies to support the entire passenger journey.

Departure systems
Departure control systems

A **Departure Control System (DCS)** automates the processing of passengers at the airport. This includes managing airport check-in and boarding, checked bags, load control and aircraft checks. DCSs typically have the following functionality:

1. **Check-in**: support for touch points including check-in counters staffed by airline representatives, self-service kiosks, mobile check-in and online check-in.
2. **Boarding passes**: able to issue electronic and hardcopy boarding passes formatted according to IATA standards.

systems and communications tools such as phones, WiFi and the ability to communicate with flight attendants and other passengers. Video screens in the seat back allow passengers to view live satellite television or video on demand (VOD), listen to music, shop for duty-free items, order on demand food, send and receive email, play video games and even gamble. A visual **Geographic Information System (GIS)** display that shows the location of the aircraft and its progress is also provided. Live video footage from external cameras and information on aircraft speed, estimated time of arrival (ETA), distance traveled, times at the origin and destination and outside temperature can be accessed by passengers. Some IFEs also provide services for disabled travelers. For example, closed captioning technology provides hearing-impaired passengers with text streamed along with video and spoken audio. These systems can stream text in different languages. Several airlines from Islamic states also provide Qibla directions to allow Muslims to pray toward Mecca (e.g. Emirates, Etihad, Malaysia Airlines, Qatar Airways and Royal Jordanian).

Hardware manufacturers for IFE systems include Panasonic Avionics Corporation, Thales Group, Row 44 and On Air, but the content is licensed from content service providers. The latest systems communicate wirelessly through an on-board intranet. Video and audio content is stored on the main IFE computer system, allowing for on-demand viewing by individual passengers. Some IFEs are compatible with XM Satellite Radio and iPods, allowing passengers to listen to their own music. Some airlines also provide apps for passengers' own devices to access content streamed wirelessly during the flight. This "bring your own device" approach is more common on LCCs.

On-board connectivity allows passengers to communicate with people on the ground using the Internet. These services are supported by satellite communication, which is not as fast as ground-based Internet access. However, they do allow passengers to browse the web, send emails and text messages and update social media. Passengers can also make bookings at the destination after they have left home. Some airlines provide satellite phones while others provide a mobile phone or WiFi signal so passengers can use their own phones. Some new systems also allow passengers to call passengers in other seats or play in-flight games together (see Industry Insight). These social features will be more common as airlines experiment with new technologies.

Crew support systems

A flight will usually be supported by two crews, the **flight deck crew** including the captain, first officer, flight engineer and the **cabin crew**, consisting of a customer service manager/purser and flight attendants. Both crews use different IT systems to support their functions. Pilots traditionally kept their flight papers and other information in a large briefcase; however, some airlines have replaced these with tablets. Unlike paper-based systems, these tablets are easier to carry on board and the information can be updated as conditions change. Once onboard, the flight deck crew use a variety of IT systems to support navigation, communication and the maintenance of flight logs.

Industry Insight: Virgin America

Virgin America is a relatively new and small player in the US market but since its launch in 2007 has received numerous industry awards. The airline is often acknowledged for its state-of-the-art "Red" in-flight entertainment system. The seatback system offers a simple touchscreen interface with a number of features:

- on-demand video and audio;
- live satellite television (news, sports events);
- an MP3 library with over 3000 songs and the ability to create your own playlist;
- interactive Google Maps;
- games, including multi-player games that allow travelers to compete with other passengers;
- on-demand food and beverage ordering and digital shopping;
- ability to send a drink to another passenger; and
- messaging passengers in other parts of the plane.

The airline also offers in-flight WiFi access and has developed apps for passengers to use their own devices to access in-flight entertainment. Future plans involve additional features that provide more control and personalization. The airline is exploring systems that remember individual passenger favorites for future flights including channel and food preferences. For an overview watch http://youtu.be/io39lxCIIBo/.

The cabin crew provides important services to passengers in the main cabin of the aircraft. One of the most important roles of the flight crew is to ensure that the passenger list (also called the manifest) is correct. Airlines traditionally used paper lists but tablet computers are increasingly being used to store and update these lists. Tablets can also be programed to include other useful information such as timetables, safety information and detailed passenger information such as meal requests, frequent flyer membership and itineraries. They also enable the crew to know which passengers have connecting flights, enabling them to make alternative arrangements should there be any delay. In the future, flight crew may use wearable technologies such as Google Glass to access passenger information from the flight manifest to personalize the experience. During the flight wireless point-of-sale (POS) devices can be used to facilitate the sale of beverages, movie headsets and duty-free products on board. In the case of LCCs, the use of technologies such as these may reduce labor costs if fewer flight attendants are needed. The cabin crew also relies on a range of communication systems to communicate with the flight deck and with passengers.

AIRPORTS

Traditionally airports were managed by governments and were seen as important assets for economic and defense capabilities. However, many governments have privatized their airports by either selling the infrastructure or by offering long-term leases to private airport management companies. The privatization of airports has resulted in a strong commercial focus, which has in turn influenced services at both private and public airports. Modern airports are complex ecosystems of businesses, services and features. The scale and size of some airports makes them similar to small cities. The modern airport terminal houses a range of features such as check-in facilities, security, customs and immigration, ground handling, baggage and cargo handling, and **concessions** such as food, beverage and retail outlets. Terminals are either domestic or international, with international airports requiring more security and services. The terminal can also be divided into the **landside** (i.e. areas before security clearance) and **airside** (i.e. areas beyond security clearance), which are managed differently. Other areas of the airport include **air traffic control (ATC)** and the **runways** and **aprons** used for take-off, landing, taxiing and parking aircraft. Managers of privatized airports have also sought to maximize their return on investment by developing unused airport land for warehousing, conference centers, accommodation, leisure, golf courses, entertainment, shopping, personal services and even residential areas.

These complex airport ecosystems required a range of IT applications to ensure the smooth transit of passengers. Computers, tablets, kiosks and mobile devices are used intensively for passenger processing, baggage and cargo handling and concessions. Similarly, contemporary ATC procedures would not be possible without the navigation and surveillance technologies used to manage air traffic. The sustainable management of airport land also requires the use of technology to monitor noise, air and water quality, and wildlife. The following pages will focus on these technologies and how they are being used to enhance passengers' experiences in increasingly busy and complex airports.

Passenger processing

Airlines use a variety of departure and gate control systems to support passengers as they journey through an airport from check-in to boarding. Airports work together with airlines and IT to provide these systems. The passenger journey can be viewed as a series of touch points consisting of pre-arrival, check-in, security, pre-boarding, boarding, transit and arrival. As Fig. 7.2 indicates, the first five touch points occur at the origin airport while the last two stages occur at transit or destination airports.

Pre-arrival

In the past airports and airlines have focused on managing passengers once they enter the airport. However, more rigorous security measures and rapid growth in air travel have created considerable challenges. Fortunately new technological advances allow airports and airlines to shift processes to the pre-arrival stage. For example, passengers are able to check-in using the Internet or a mobile device before they arrive at the airport, reducing waiting times and congestion.

Airports are also using geofencing, which tracks passengers using an airport or

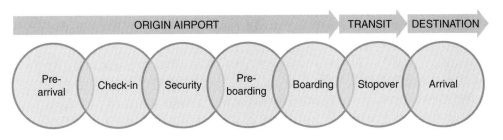

Fig. 7.2. Stages of the passenger journey.

airline app installed on their mobile device (see Chapter 6 for more detail). Virtual geofences are built around an airport at different proximities and triggers are attached to each fence as shown in Fig. 7.3.

When a passenger is en route to the airport the app uses the device's **global positioning system (GPS)** to detect the passenger's location. As they approach the airport different triggers can be activated. For example, a geofence set at 10 kilometers from the airport could determine whether the passenger has enough time to board their flight. If the passenger is late, the system can send an automatic notification offering to rebook them. If the passenger is early the system might notify them about lounge access. As the passenger gets closer to the airport they can be notified about available parking spaces. Similar technology can notify "meeters and greeters" when a flight has landed and when passengers have disembarked and cleared customs so that waiting time is minimized.

These possibilities are possible because of GPS, RFID, NFC and other transmission technologies in mobile devices. While innovations automate and improve the passenger experience, they also offer strategic and operational advantages for airports. Informing passengers about available parking spaces and guiding them to the terminal can alleviate congestion and waiting times. Notifying passengers that they will miss their flight allows airports and airlines to reduce airport crowding caused by delayed passengers.

Check-in

The check-in process is increasingly managed before passengers arrive at the airport, but there has been a major shift away from check-in counters to self-service kiosks. These kiosks are linked with an airline's DCS and passengers can check-in by entering their name and destination, record locator, frequent flyer membership card or passport.

Passengers can also check-in at the airport using their mobile devices (SITA, 2013b). As they enter the terminal a geofence automatically checks the passenger in and issues electronic boarding passes and luggage tags for collection. The passenger can be notified about boarding times and gate information and may also receive special offers such upgrades, priority boarding and lounge access. Passengers with checked bags can leave these at a self-service bag drop. Mobile apps communicate wirelessly with the airline's DCS so that the status and details of passengers are automatically updated when they are checked in. Boarding passes can be stored electronically on the mobile device using an airline's app or apps such as Apple Passbook or Google

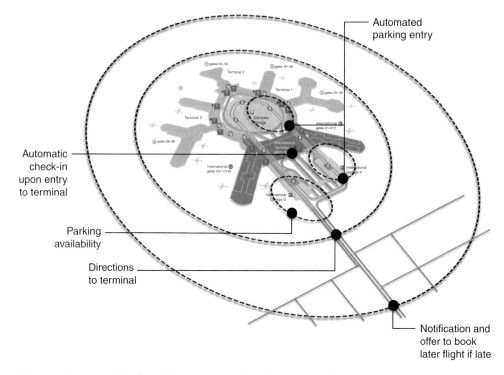

Fig. 7.3. An example of geofencing around an international airport.

Wallet. Additional luggage fees can be paid using these apps. In addition, roving airline or airport representatives use tablets to attend to any check-in issues. In the future self-service check-in kiosks are likely to disappear from airport departure areas (Amadeus, 2012). We may also see virtual service agents guiding passengers through check-in at airports.

Since GPS is not reliable in indoor environments, the functionality described above relies on micro-location technologies such as NFC or Bluetooth Low Energy (BLE). BLE, also known as Smart Bluetooth, is the technology behind Apple's iBeacon. Using BLE, an airport or airline can define more targeted "micro-locations" to trigger an activity. The technology can be used with apps such as Passbook to display passenger itineraries, boarding passes, identification and notifications when passengers cross the geofence threshold of a defined location.

Security and immigration

The protection of passengers, staff and aircraft is one of the most important considerations for an airport. The role of airport security systems is to identify and manage external and internal threats. Internal threats occur when employees inside the terminal pose a risk to passengers or their belongings. Security systems monitor baggage and ground handling facilities to prevent baggage or cargo theft and tampering. External threats arise from passengers and other unauthorized individuals. Both employees and passengers can pose a threat by carrying weapons, explosives or other dangerous items on board.

Threats are managed using equipment to scan people, screen baggage and detect explosives. The perimeter is monitored by electronic alarms and CCTV cameras. CCTV cameras are also used throughout terminal buildings, car parks, runways and apron areas. Staff access to the airside of the airport is controlled by self-locking doors unlocked by PIN codes, ID cards or biometric scanners. At most airports both passengers and staff are required to clear security checkpoints.

Security screening usually involves the following steps.

1. Confirming the identity of travelers. This is done through visual and electronic checks of passports and boarding passes, or biometric systems (see below).

2. X-ray baggage screening. Carry-on luggage and checked bags are screened using X-ray machines monitored by security personnel.

3. Body screening. Passengers are usually screened by walking through a metal detector. Some airports have also installed backscatter X-ray scanners that conduct a non-invasive full body scan.

At international airports passengers can be screened at security and immigration points by using new non-intrusive technologies such as electronic passports, smart ID cards, electronic tags and biometrics. **Biometrics** identify individuals based on physiological traits such as facial structure, iris patterns, fingerprints and voice recognition. Most countries now issue **e-passports** with an integrated RFID chip containing information about the passenger and when coupled with biometric scanning, can be used to verify identity. Examples include Australia's Smartgate system and the Global

Entry system used in the USA. In the future, IT will be able to identify individuals using traits such as their walking gait, body language, heart rhythms or DNA profiles (Amadeus, 2012). Watch the following video from SITA to see an example of biometric technologies: http://youtu.be/xrk7hwqKCZw/.

http://youtu.be/xrk7hwqKCZw/

In the previous section we demonstrated how NFC and BLE technologies can be used to check passengers in and provide them with information. The same technology can also notify passengers about security waiting times so that they can select the fastest lane. These services benefit the airport by streamlining the passenger journey and reducing waiting times.

Pre-boarding

Passengers enter the airside of the terminal after they have cleared security and immigration. When travelers are in unfamiliar airports, they have a critical need for information about airport activities and facilities, preferably in their own language. **Flight Information Display Systems (FIDS)** display flight departure and arrival times, gate numbers and baggage carousel locations on wall-sized displays or individual monitors, which may contain multimedia and graphic displays.

Many airports provide free WiFi and facilities for travelers to recharge their electronic devices. This is done with power cords and adapters, however inductive electrical systems can recharge passengers' devices wirelessly. This technology will be common in airports and other public settings over the next decade (Amadeus, 2012).

Airports have their own apps to assist passengers, and independent apps such as GateGuru cover multiple airports. Airport apps provide maps and navigation tools, information about concessions and amenities and connectivity to the FIDS. They also use location aware services to push offers and coupons from concessions to passengers. Some use augmented reality to assist with navigation, the presentation of information and special offers, often in multiple languages. Airport apps also facilitate social media interactions between passengers. Apart from free WiFi, facilities allowing passengers to download entertainment for in-flight viewing are likely to become more common.

A common thread throughout our discussion has been the use of mobile phones to navigate through key touch points of the passenger journey (SITA, 2013b). These technologies are not just consumer focused; companies such as SITA are developing business intelligence tools that provide real-time performance data such as passenger volumes, queue times and dwell times in different parts of the terminal. Location aware technologies such as GPS, WiFi, NFC and Bluetooth enable airport stakeholders to anticipate and plan for peak events and disruptions. They also enable airlines to see the location of their passengers, allowing staff to take proactive measures for on time departure. This information can be displayed on tablets alongside CCTV footage, allowing airport stakeholders to manage passenger flows and traffic. Tablet devices also update information

displayed on FIDS, such as flight status, gate changes and walking distances to terminal gates. Watch the following video to learn more: http://youtu.be/plfXqnmJdqE/.

http://youtu.be/plfXqnmJdqE/

Modern terminals offer a bewildering array of shopping, dining and entertainment facilities to passengers. **Concessions** are commercial businesses that operate within the terminal. Typically these businesses offer food and beverages, shopping, and leisure and entertainment. Concessions typically pay a proportion of their profits to the airport, which then has a vested interest in maximizing the profitability of each concession. Airports can use business intelligence technologies to monitor how passenger traffic flows impact purchase behavior, allowing the airport to adjust retail elements to maximize non-aeronautical revenues.

Concessions use point-of-sale (POS) systems to record and process transactions. Duty free shopping in particular requires information processing to ensure merchandise is sold only to bona-fide travelers. Computer systems are needed that connect with flight information systems to ensure the right merchandise is delivered to the right flight at the right time. Airports also use technology to entertain passengers while they wait for flights. Examples include the use of technology in 6D cinemas (e.g. Schiphol airport), gaming zones (e.g. Hong Kong International

Airport), electronics zones and science museums (e.g. Changi Airport), interactive walls and tables for games, media and information (e.g. Dubai Airport), and simulated experiences.

There is scope for massive multi-player games (MMPGs) using the airport environment (Amadeus, 2012). This **gamification** of the airport environment could involve geocaching, where passengers use clues to discover different features of the terminal. A good example of how this might work in reality is Ingress, Google's **augmented reality** game in which users join one of two teams to take control of various portals seeded throughout the terminal. Watch the following video to see how augmented reality has been used in a retail environment in Sydney, Australia: http://youtu.be/0AwUK0XuOHQ/.

http://youtu.be/0AwUK0XuOHQ/

Boarding

Boarding commences with a passenger announcement, which in busy airports can create significant background noise. Some airports have a silent policy requiring passengers to use FIDS or mobile passenger devices. Alerts sent to a mobile device can announce the boarding process. Standard IATA Bar Coded Boarding Passes (BCBP) automate the matching of boarding passes with the passenger list. Boarding passes are scanned with an optical scanner that reads the bar code from paper or a mobile screen.

There is scope to use mobile devices to streamline the boarding process even more. New innovations will dynamically update boarding passes. Boarding passes saved to an Apple Passbook coupled with Bluetooth technologies such as iBeacon and biometrics allow passengers to board by passing through an electronic screening point – essentially a geofence. This approach would reduce queues at boarding gates and load the aircraft more quickly.

Stopover

Some itineraries require a stopover to change flights at a transit airport. Transit passengers are likely to use IT facilities discussed at the pre-boarding stage, including free WiFi, airport apps and FIDS. Transit passengers also have special needs to freshen up, get in touch with loved ones, rest and relax. Airports provide free computer terminals where passengers can access the Internet. Digital information indicates where showers and quiet zones are located. Sleep pods are common in airports with large numbers of transit passengers. These pods contain special lighting and audio to lull guests to sleep and alarms to rouse them for their flight. Mobile apps can also support passengers who have missed a connecting flight by booking alternative flights.

Arrival

Airlines and airports have focused heavily on the departure experience. However, there is a need to consider the arrival experience because the destination airport is often the first impression visitors have of the destination. Free WiFi is once again an indispensable tool for arriving passengers. While passengers wait for customs, immigration and baggage claim they can access the Internet to make ground transport or accommodation bookings. NFC and BLE can push visitor information and e-brochures to mobile passenger devices for later reading.

An arduous and time-consuming task in international gateway airports is the processing of passengers' immigration documents. When numerous flights disembark at the same time, delays can be long, and tired passengers become frustrated. The biometric systems we discussed earlier can screen passengers and record their details before they enter a country. In some countries scanners and cameras capture travelers' fingerprints and photographs. In the future airports are likely to move towards intelligent ambient technologies to scan passengers for both security and health risks as they arrive.

Governments have also computerized immigration control by maintaining databases of individuals they do not wish to enter the country, such as the **no-fly list** maintained by the US government. These databases are accessed when travelers show their documentation upon arrival. The digitization of passports and visas also facilitates the processing of passengers. The latest systems use automated intelligent analysis to determine risk profiles based on passenger data.

Once passengers have cleared immigration they go to baggage claim before they can pass through customs to the landside of the airport. IT applications to track and streamline the handling of passenger baggage are discussed in the next section. After moving through customs, passengers can use mobile apps to book taxis and other ground transport and some of these systems are discussed in the next chapter.

Baggage and cargo handling

Airlines and airports must work together to move baggage and cargo from check-in areas to screening points and on to the aircraft. While 99% of checked baggage is delivered on time, lost or mishandled baggage still costs the industry an estimated US$2.6 billion a year or about US$100 per piece of luggage (SITA, 2013a). For this reason airports and airlines invest considerable resources into **baggage handling systems (BHSs)**, which track baggage and prevent lost luggage. Baggage tags with optical bar codes containing the tag number, flight segments and destination of each bag are the most common IT infrastructure used by BHSs. At check-in, the tag information is scanned into a database linked with the airline's reservation and passenger processing systems. This information is also connects to a central baggage tracking system for all carriers such as SITA's Bagtrac.

Computers track the location of individual bags, travel itineraries and flight schedules. Optical scanning technology reads bag tags as they move along conveyor belts connecting check-in counters, baggage check-in points and aircraft at gates. Computers control the conveyor junctions and switches that ensure each bag ends up at the correct destination. A lost bag can be readily tracked with a tag retained by the passenger. The optical bar code on the tag is used to access the database record and determine the bag's location. SITA and IATA provide a service called World Tracer to match found bags with lost bag reports. Self-service kiosks at baggage claim areas allow passengers to scan luggage tags to lodge a lost luggage request.

Watch the following video to see how this works: http://youtu.be/c5ZjnW7wwhc/.

http://youtu.be/c5ZjnW7wwhc/

Many airlines also carry cargo and need IT to handle both reservations and tracking systems separate from the passenger systems. As with passenger baggage, optical bar codes are used to track the cargo's journey.

Recent developments use ambient intelligence in the form of RFID bag tags and RFID chips embedded in luggage. These innovations increase the efficiency of passenger and baggage processing by supporting automated check-in and self-service baggage drops. The technology also sorts and tracks baggage more reliably, leading to faster delivery of luggage to travelers at baggage claim. Passengers on some airlines can track the status and location of checked bags throughout the journey, much like customers follow a package sent by a courier company. Websites and mobile apps allow passengers to monitor their luggage location in real time, including during flight if WiFi is available onboard. Amadeus (2012) predicts that by 2025 all baggage will be self-scanning and that airports will employ robotic end-to-end baggage handling systems.

Air traffic control

Air Traffic Control (ATC) plays a crucial role in the safety and efficiency of aviation operations, by tracking every flight from takeoff to landing. The role of ATC is to ensure the safe and efficient flow of air traffic (Belobaba *et al.*, 2009). This is achieved through the use of four interrelated IT systems:

1. Communications systems: pilots and dispatchers communicate with air traffic controllers using very high frequency (VHF) over short distances, high frequency (HF) shortwave or satellite-based communication (SATCOM) systems for longer distances, and the Aircraft Communications Addressing and Reporting System (ACARS) for data transmission. Recent progress has been made with a new system called the Aeronautical Telecommunication Network (ATN).

2. Navigation systems: pilots and controllers use a number of different navigation systems during takeoff, cruising and landing. Signals generate a visual display of the aircraft's position on a monitor.

3. Surveillance systems: controllers use surveillance systems to monitor the flow and positioning of air traffic. Many rely on **radar** to display the position of each aircraft on a monitor.

4. Flight and weather information systems: decision support systems help controllers optimize the flow of traffic at congested airports. Flight plans are lodged and disseminated by flight data processing systems while weather information systems provide weather observations, forecasts and alerts (Belobaba *et al.*, 2009).

Across all four of these elements IT plays a critical role in providing controllers with the real-time information required to track and manage air space.

Environmental management systems

Airports use IT to manage the environmental impacts of their operations by using environmental management systems (EMS). Aviation impacts the environment at the local, regional and global levels. Examples of these impacts include:

- **Water quality**: the quality of waterways is affected by: runoff from terminal buildings, runways and aprons; deicing operations; fuel leaks and spills and other solid and liquid wastes.
- **Noise pollution**: noise from aircraft causes sleep disturbance and impacts on property values.
- **Air pollution**: pollution from aircraft adversely affects air quality by increasing greenhouse gases such as CO_2 into the atmosphere.
- **Wildlife**: aircraft movements impact wildlife feeding, breeding and migration patterns and are a threat to birdlife around airports.

To manage these impacts governments impose strict environmental regulations on airports (Belobaba *et al.*, 2009). Technologies manage or reduce the impact of aviation operations on the environment, including:

- **Environmental monitoring**: computers and specialized equipment are used to analyze, record and report air and water samples collected by airports as part of the regulatory requirements.
- **Energy use**: IT systems monitor energy use and shut down non-essential services when not in use. Chapter 12 discusses these systems in more detail.
- **Noise reduction**: computers are used to model aircraft and engine designs before prototypes are produced. New technologies supporting a continuous

descent approach also alleviate some noise (see Chapter 12).

- **Carbon emission reduction**: computer design of engines and aircraft has also dramatically improved fuel efficiency. Passengers can purchase carbon offsets when booking flights through the ARS or website. Scientists are also using IT to monitor greenhouse gas emissions and model their impact on climate change.
- **Water quality**: computerized spraying systems apply aircraft deicing fluids to reduce wastage, overspray and runoff into waterways. Ice detection systems that rely on magnetostrictive, electromagnetic and ultrasonic technologies detect the ice (Belobaba *et al.*, 2009).

SUMMARY

In summary, the application of IT in aviation is ubiquitous, comprehensive and dynamic. The aviation industry has used IT intensely and creatively to thrive in a competitive and volatile market. Its need for massive information processing and data communications has created the many systems discussed above. In the process, the airline industry has become a classic example of the successful application of information systems to operations, marketing and management. As demands on airlines and airports increase, airlines must investigate and invest in new technologies to improve the efficiency, comfort and safety of air travel. Throughout this chapter we have suggested how IT can improve the passenger experience and aviation operations. A variety of technologies and innovations are converging to streamline passenger processing. The following video from Amadeus provides an excellent overview of future IT use in airports: http://youtu.be/KwCUwgk1oko/.

http://youtu.be/KwCUwgk1oko/

KEY TERMS

Aeronautical Telecommunication Network (ATN), affiliate programs, air traffic control, Aircraft Communications Addressing and Reporting System (ACARS), airline dispatcher, airline reservation system (ARS), airside, ambient intelligence, apron, augmented reality, baggage handling system (BHS), bid line, biometrics, Bluetooth Low Energy (BLE), booking code, cabin class, cabin crew, costs per available seat mile (CASM), charter airline, commercial airline, concession, crew pairing, customer relationship system (CRS), deadheading, decision support system, Departure Control System (DCS), dynamic packaging, e-passport, e-ticket, fare basis code (FBC), Fare Quote System, fare rules, flag carrier, flight catering system, flight deck crew, flight engineer, Flight Information Display Systems (FIDS), flight manifest, frequent flyer program (FFP), global positioning system (GPS), Geographic Information System (GIS), high frequency (HF), in-flight entertainment (IFE), Inertial Navigation System

(INS), instrument landing system (ILS), Internet booking engine (IBE), landside, load factor, Local Area Augmentation System (LAAS), low cost carrier (LCC), married segment control, near field communication (NFC), New Distribution Capability (NDC), no-fly list, operations research (OR), pairing optimizer, passenger name list (PNL), passenger name record (PNR), Passenger Service System (PSS), predictive analytics, price differentiation, product bundling, radar, radio frequency identification (RFID), revenue per available seat mile (RASM), revenue management system (RMS), safety management system (SMS), scheduled airline, special service request (SSR), terminal, very high frequency (VHF), VHF Omni Directional Radio Range (VOR), workflow technology, yield management

DISCUSSION QUESTIONS

1. How will advances in smartphones and apps impact the marketing, distribution and delivery of aviation products?

2. Throughout this chapter we have identified a number of applications allowing airlines and airports to track passengers by using signaling technologies such as NFC, RFID and BLE embedded in baggage tags and smartphones. What are the pros and cons of these applications? What privacy or ethical issues might arise? How can airlines and airports overcome these issues?

3. Visit the FFP website for an airline you know. Look for information about redeeming and earning FF points (miles). List all the ways in which members can earn and redeem points. How does the technology on the website support the FFP? What improvements would you like to see?

4. By 2020 the global airline fleet is expected to be twice as large as in 2012 and by 2030 passenger numbers are expected to be double. Watch the following video from SITA to learn more about this growth: http://youtu.be/NPi7aeP-LLo/.

http://youtu.be/NPi7aeP-LLo

Supplement the information in this chapter and in the video with your own research and discuss how IT can help airlines and airports cope with the challenges of this expected growth.

5. Visit the website for Changi Airport in Singapore and browse through the pages about terminal facilities and services. Note down examples requiring use of IT. What IT-inspired airport services do you expect to see in 10 years?

6. How might airports and airlines use new technologies such as augmented reality to streamline and improve the passenger experience?

USEFUL WEBSITES

QR code	Website	Description
	SITA http://www.sita.aero/	Visit this website to get a good overview of the range of aviation sector services and IT solutions offered by SITA.
	Amadeus IT Solutions http://www.amadeus.com/airlineit/	This website provides information about the IT solutions offered by Amadeus for airlines and airports. Of particular note is the Amadeus Altéa Suite.
	Virgin America http://www.virginamerica.com/	A world leader in flight entertainment systems.

QR code	Website	Description
	SkyTrax http://www. airlinequality.com/	Rating and reviews for over 681 airlines and 725 airports.
	Boeing http://www.boeing. com/	Boeing is a major manufacturer of commercial aircraft and their website contains details about airline and airport technologies.
	Changi Airport http://www. changiairport.com/	Consistently ranked among the world's top airports, Changi Airport in Singapore offers high-tech solutions for airlines and passengers.
	GateGuru http://www.gateguru. com/	An innovative app that provides a range of features to streamline the passenger journey.
	Future Travel Experience http://www. futuretravelexperience. com/	A useful website focused on the future of the air travel experience, including useful news items, reports and content on a range of aviation technologies.

Case Study: SITA

SITA, originally known as the Société Internationale de Télécommunications Aéronautiques, was formed in 1949 by a consortium of European and British airlines to create cost efficiencies by sharing infrastructure and ICT networks. While ARPANet introduced the first worldwide packet switching network, SITA developed the world's first packet

(Continued)

Case Study. Continued.

switching network dedicated to business. This network, known as the High Level Network (HLN), was implemented in 1969. SITA also introduced the world's first air-ground communications service (VHF AIRCOM) in 1984 followed by a real-time air-to-ground voice communication system called Satellite AIRCOM in 1992. Recently the company has developed Asynchronous Transfer Mode (ATM) technology to support mixed voice and data traffic. In 2005 the company co-developed the OnAir system with Airbus Industries to enable the use of mobile phones and other personal communications devices onboard aircraft.

In the last decade SITA has diversified by developing a range of IT solutions for the aviation industry. Today the company employs over 4500 staff in more than 200 countries. The company manages a portfolio of technology solutions, which include:

- communications and infrastructure: voice, data, messaging, mobility and desktop applications to support aircraft operations, air–ground communications, air traffic control and flight operations;
- airports: passenger processing, baggage management and operations management;
- airlines: passenger management, reservations, e-commerce solutions, fare and ancillary services; and
- government: border management, biometrics, risk assessment and identity verification.

SITA also works proactively with the aviation community to develop systems and standards to simplify communications and processes for air transport. Examples include the WorldTracer baggage tracking system, common use terminal equipment (CUTE) and "Type B" IATA standard messaging.

SITA invests about 5% of its revenues into research and development. This has resulted in: innovative location-aware smartphone and tablet solutions for "always connected" passengers, crew and staff; business intelligence apps that harness real-time information; augmented reality in airports; and a social booking and check-in engine on Facebook. The company is constantly updating its data centers and command centers with the latest hardware and systems. SITA has invested in next generation passenger service systems (PSS) and in 2013 unveiled its Horizon platform. Horizon provides an "end-to-end" passenger system designed to capture information about the passenger from the sales query

http://youtu.be/EkflsB617iQ

through to the flight. It was built from the ground up using an agile service-oriented architecture that is accessible through multiple channels and touch points.

SITA also produces a range of surveys and reports on industry trends and emerging technologies to support industry decision-making. For more information, watch the following video on YouTube: http://youtu.be/EkflsB617iQ/.

(Continued)

Case Study. Continued.

Study Questions

1. Why would airlines and airports outsource IT solutions to a company such as SITA? What are the operational and strategic benefits?

2. Visit the SITA website at http://www.sita.aero/ and watch some of the videos to develop a better understanding of this company. Compare and contrast the products and services of SITA with Amadeus. If you were managing an airline, which of these companies would you work with? Why?

3. SITA provides border control technologies that use biometrics. What are the advantages and disadvantages of these technologies? Do you think that machines will eventually replace immigration officers?

Sources: Vikas (2011); SITA (2014)

REFERENCES

Air Transport Action Group (2014) Aviation: Benefits Without Borders. Available at: http://aviation-benefitsbeyondborders.org/ (accessed 12 December 2013).

Amadeus (2012) *Reinventing the Airport Ecosystem: A New Airline Industry Report*. Amadeus, Germany.

Belobaba, P., Odoni, A.R. and Barnhart, C. (2009), *The Global Airline Industry*. Wiley, Chichester UK.

Benckendorff, P. (2006) An exploratory analysis of traveller preferences for airline website content. *Information Technology and Tourism* 8(3/4),149–159. doi:10.3727/109830506778690867

Bhatia, M.J.S. (1988) An economic analysis of optimal adoption of aircraft technology in the Canadian airline industry: the case of wide-body jet aircraft. *Dissertation Abstracts International, A (Humanities and Social Sciences)* 48(9), 2400.

Dickinger, A. and Bauernfeind, U. (2009) An analysis of corporate e-mail communication as part of airlines' service recovery strategy. *Journal of Travel and Tourism Marketing* 26(2),156–168. doi: 10.1080/10548400902864651

Harcar, T. and Yucelt, U. (2012) American consumer's attitudes towards different airline companies channels: a comparison of transaction methods. *PASOS: Revista de Turismo y Patrimonio Cultural* 10(2), 59–68.

International Air Transport Association (2014) International Air Transport Association. Available at: http://www.iata.org/ (accessed 12 December 2013).

Jones, P. (2006) Flight-Catering. In: Becker, H. and Grothues, U. (eds) *Catering-Management: Portrait einer Wachstumsbranche in Theorie und Praxis*. Behr's Verlag, Hamburg, pp. 39–55.

Klein, S. (2002) Web impact on the distribution structure for flight tickets. In: Wöber, K.W., Frew, A.J. and Hitz, M. (eds) *Information and Communication Technologies in Tourism 2002. Proceedings of the International Conference in Innsbruck, Austria, 2002*. Springer Computer Science, Springer, New York, pp. 219–228.

Koo, B.W., Mantin, B. and O'Connor, P. (2011) Online distribution of airline tickets: should airlines adopt a single or a multi-channel approach? *Tourism Management* 32(1), 69–74. doi: 10.1016/j.tourman.2009.11.008

Oyewole, P., Sankaran, M. and Choudhury, P. (2008) Information communication technology and the marketing of airline services in Malaysia: a survey of market participants in the airline industry. *Services Marketing Quarterly* 29(4), 85–103.

SITA (2013a) *2013 Baggage Report*. SITA, Geneva.

SITA (2013b) *Flying into the Future*. SITA, Geneva.

SITA (2014) About SITA. Available at: http://www.sita.aero/about-sita/ (accessed 2 January 2014).

Vikas, S. (2011) Leveraging technology to provide cost effective communication and IT solutions for the global air transport industry: the case of SITA. *Journal of Hospitality Application and Research* 6(2), 56–72.

Yang, J.Y. and Liu, A. (2003) Frequent Flyer Program: a case study of China airline's marketing initiative - Dynasty Flyer Program. *Tourism Management* 24(5), 587–595. doi:10.1016/s0261-5177(03)00007-4

chapter 8

Surface Transport and Information Technology

LEARNING OBJECTIVES

After studying this chapter you should be able to:

- explain the components of an Intelligent Transportation System and how they are applied to surface transport;
- describe the different applications in road, rail and water transport; and
- evaluate how technology facilitates the connection of systems in intermodal transport.

INTRODUCTION

Getting to and around a destination is critical for a successful trip. In addition to the airlines covered in the previous chapter, there are many surface transport modes that tourists use for mobility. This chapter covers the use of IT in surface transport modes including road (car rental, bus, taxi, bicycle), rail (regular and metro or subway) and water (cruise ships and ferries). These transport modes not only provide the utility of moving from place to place, they can also be at the core of the tourist experience (e.g. cruises, epic rail journeys, cable car gondolas). Surface transport operators vary significantly in size and scope. Some are operated by private companies (tour bus, cruise lines, taxis) and some by public agencies (bus, rail, subway), and increasingly public-private partnerships are teaming up to offer intermodal transport in destinations. Some operators are local to a city or a destination and some have national and international networks and coverage. IT enhances all surface transport by making it faster, safer, more efficient and user-friendly for the tourist.

We start this chapter by introducing the concept of Intelligent Transportation

Systems (ITSs) since they provide a comprehensive framework for the application of IT to increase the efficiency of all land transport systems, and are relevant to tourist usage in a destination. The chapter will then go on to discuss IT developments in automobiles, taxis and car rental organizations. Rail and metro uses of IT will constitute the next section followed by water transport applications.

INTELLIGENT TRANSPORTATION SYSTEMS

The movement of tourists via ground transport systems is becoming more challenging as traffic volumes increase in many destinations. This is particularly true in large cities, on heavily traversed highways and in popular touristic areas where congestion and delays are commonplace. As highways become more congested, they also become more difficult for tourist drivers who are in unfamiliar surroundings. Congested conditions compromise safety, generate more accidents, use more fuel and create more emissions, therefore further compromising the environment. Individual transport operators can make some headway in solving such problems by using vehicles that pollute less. But public transport agencies need to strategically plan to create integrated systems that support safer, cleaner transport. Such systems are called **Intelligent Transportation Systems (ITSs)**.

The definition of an ITS (Intelligent Transportation Society of America, 2014, p. 1) is:

> a broad range of information and communications technologies that improve the safety, efficiency, and performance of the transport system. When integrated into the nation's roadways, vehicles and public transport network, ITS can help reduce congestion, improve mobility, save lives and optimize our existing infrastructure.

ITSs are systems that can connect and manage all land transport modes, although most commonly they are used for road and highway systems. ITSs are being implemented in numerous locations around the world but as yet they are not universal. Significant efforts exist regionally in Europe, America, Australia and Japan. Increases in safety and decreases in congestion are already reported in areas where these technologies have been used. Cooperation and commitment of private transport operators in the implementation of such systems are also needed to maximize their benefits.

According to ERTICO (2014), there are many benefits that an ITS can provide for a destination and its drivers, such as:

- detecting hazards on the road ahead and informing drivers of them even before they are visible;
- keeping vehicles at a safe distance from one another;
- allowing vehicles to communicate directly with the infrastructure around them and with one another;
- enabling drivers to make better decisions about their route and responding to warnings of congestion and accidents;
- keeping drivers informed of the local speed limit;
- monitoring drivers for signs of fatigue and inform them when it is time to take a break;
- giving public transport users real-time service information as well as smart and seamless ticketing solutions;

- integrating public transport into traffic management systems, giving priority to buses and trams;
- improving the efficiency of passenger and goods transport and easing congestion on the network – with obvious benefits for the environment; and
- providing reliable real-time travel and traffic information, anywhere, anytime.

National intelligent transportation systems

A number of destinations are designing and implementing ITSs. In Europe, an ITS initiative called ERTICO based in Brussels, Belgium brings together partners in IT, transport, research and public authorities to infuse intelligence into mobility for people and goods across Europe. The objective is a transport system with zero accidents, zero delays, reduced impact on the environment and fully informed people. View the following video for more details on their initiatives: http://youtu.be/zhDZFSY5e1U/.

http://youtu.be/zhDZFSY5e1U/

In the USA, the National Automated Highway System Consortium was tasked in 1993 to deploy a fully automated national highway system by early 21st century. This would be a fully automated "hands-off, feet-off" highway system, however various institutional and social problems have forestalled the operationalization of this program, and

funding was discontinued in 1997. Information on how the ITSA is currently working on systems for the USA can be found on their website at http://www.itsa.org/. Watch the following video to learn about the ITS aspects that the USA is working on: http://vimeo.com/68062973/.

http://vimeo.com/68062973/

In Australia an integrated intelligent transportation system called STREAMS has been in operation for a number of years. The system uses signal timing based on traffic flows, and also provides automated real-time passenger information. Another component of STREAMS is free-flow tolling, so that vehicles do not have to stop at tollbooths. Video cameras and lasers tag vehicles and payments are automatically linked to credit card payment systems. Other countries are developing national ITS such as Qatar, as described in the Industry Insight Box below.

Components of an intelligent transportation system

To understand the various components of a fully integrated ITS, Fig. 8.1 shows a hypothetical system that integrates multiple transport modes – air, ocean, vehicle and train. It shows the communication technologies needed to transfer information from points to vehicles – these include radio communications, mobile towers, satellite communications and terrestrial

---

Industry Insight: Qatar's Intelligent Transport System

Tourism mega-events can often be the impetus for significant transport systems development. Qatar is re-visioning its nation's future as a trade and transport hub between Africa, Asia and Europe. It also plans to attract and host mega-events such as the 2022 FIFA World Cup, which will bring large numbers of tourists to the country. Qatar realizes that intelligent transportation systems will play an important role in this envisioned future, as well as contributing to a more sustainable outcome. Qatar's ITS project aims to enhance safety, facilitate smoother traffic flows, increase customer satisfaction and reduce environmental impact. The plan also includes a new subway system, the new Doha International Airport and a new port facility (Nazer, 2013).

Over 29 new road projects will be built and ITS solutions will be used for urban and inter-urban networks for the improved mobility of people and goods. This will include tunnel management systems, incident detection, lane and speed control signs, over-height vehicle detection and weather sensors. Connected vehicles and car-sharing systems will be part of the development including dynamic messaging signs on roads. Automated payment mechanisms and intelligent parking management will also be part of the system. In addition to the roadway ITS, a multi-modal traveler information system will be created and the national transport management center will oversee operations.

---

broadcasts. It also includes automated tolls, automated traffic signals, passenger information and trip planning facilities, and safety systems. Many of the systems in the diagram are discussed below. The ITS features most relevant to tourists are route guidance systems and traveler information systems, both of which help drivers to find their way in unfamiliar locations.

There are three different types of technology and information transfer in ITS systems as follows.

1. In-vehicle systems: these technologies are the responsibility of the vehicle manufacturers and tend to focus on safety. One system provides electronic stability control in which electronic sensors detect when the car is in danger of skidding or losing control and applies the brakes automatically. Another system detects lanes on the road and alerts the driver if they are unintentionally outside the lane, or if they change lanes without indication. Adaptive cruise control detects the distance and speed of the vehicle in front and modifies the speed and following distance. Intelligent speed assist alerts the driver when they are exceeding the speed limit by determining the vehicle's location with a GPS system. It then matches this with a digital road map containing speed limit information for each road.

2. Vehicle-to-vehicle systems: these transmit information from one vehicle to another and are again designed to increase safety. The arrival of other vehicles at intersections can be detected and all drivers can be alerted. They also include collision avoidance systems, and emergency notification systems of traffic events, accidents and other incidents.

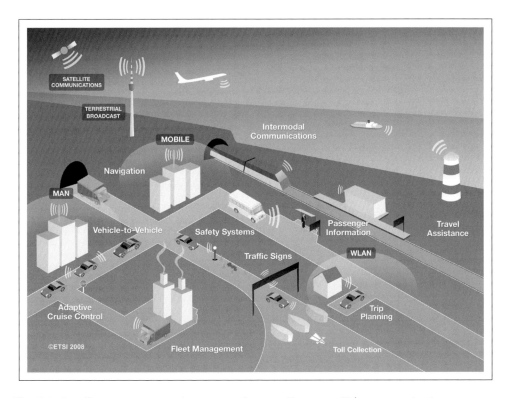

Fig. 8.1. Intelligent transportation system (source: European Telecommunications Standards Institute, 2012).

3. Vehicle-to-infrastructure systems: these represent the largest number of applications of ITS. They provide traveler information services such as real-time navigation, roadside electronic messages advising of delays, congestion, accidents, car parking and fuel availability, traffic signal and variable speed control. These signs receive information through closed circuit TV systems that monitor traffic flows, or from intelligent sensing devices on the roadside. Communication between the vehicle and sensors installed in the road infrastructure is wireless. They facilitate Automated Traffic Management Systems (ATMSs), Traveler Information Systems and Fleet Management Systems as discussed below.

Automated Traffic Management Systems (ATMSs) manage the flow of road traffic using a variety of technologies. Some systems favor public transport vehicles by ensuring automatic green lights when they arrive at an intersection. A device inside the vehicle identifies it as a bus, tram or other public vehicle and communicates with a roadside device via radio waves. The signal automatically changes to green as the vehicle approaches, allowing it through without delays. On-time performance of public transport can be significantly improved in this way, which can cause more people to take public transport instead of driving. Two other technologies are ramp meters, which smooth the flow of traffic on to freeways, and **electronic tollbooths (e-tolls)**, which shorten the time to cross a toll.

A related technology is **Electronic Road Pricing (ERP)**, first introduced in Singapore to manage traffic congestion. It requires drivers to pay different tolls at different times, paying more at peak times, with the intent that drivers will choose other modes of transport or time-shift their travel at peak times. Travelers place cash cards in a slot in their vehicle and as they pass ERP points, the charge is automatically debited from their account with short-wave radio communications. Tourist use of e-tolls and ERP systems can be a problem particularly if they are in a destination for a short time. Arranging for the in-vehicle technology to use the system is either inconvenient or impossible. Some e-toll systems use digital cameras to capture the license plate of every car that passes through the toll. Optical character recognition is used to read the number plates in these photos. Travelers can then pay the toll charge at pay stations located at major airports or by visiting a website and entering the vehicle's license plate number. Some rental car companies also provide plans that cover toll use when travelers rent a vehicle. Unfortunately some travelers who are unfamiliar with fully automated e-tolls do not even realize that they have passed a toll point until they receive a fine many weeks later. In Portugal, drivers must stop at a checkpoint as they cross the border from Spain and insert a credit card into a reader, which is matched with the vehicle's license plate. This allows the automatic payment of tolls even for tourists driving through.

Electronic message signs at the roadside are another component of ATMSs. They inform drivers of delays, congestion, roadwork and accidents, and recommend speed limits depending on road conditions. These signs receive their information through closed circuit TV systems that monitor traffic flows or from intelligent sensing devices on the roadside.

Traveler Information Systems provide online, real-time information on road conditions in the region for drivers. Dynamic details of congested streets, accident locations and parking lot availability are examples of such information. The information is received at a central monitoring location from video cameras and other sensing devices. It is then transmitted to vehicles either with satellite communication or ground communication systems. A system in Japan called **Vehicle Information and Communication System (VICS)** collects real-time information on road conditions from the Japan Road Traffic Information Center and other traffic authorities, edits and processes it and then transmits it to roadside devices. These devices use infrared beacons, radio-wave beacons and FM radio transmission to emit signals to the computer in the vehicle. The government provides the service free to drivers but the receiving device in the vehicle must be purchased by the owner. This system has reduced congestion, accidents and petroleum consumption and has also reduced carbon emissions by 2.14 million tons per year. When combined with route guidance systems, traveler information systems can be used to generate alternative routes to bypass congestion, thereby empowering drivers to avoid long delays and reach their destination easily.

Drivers also need information on the status of their vehicle to drive safely. Certain key pieces of information such as their speed, the status of their turn signal, lights, fuel, water and oil indicators are typically displayed on dials in the dashboard. The lag time that it takes for a driver's eyes to refocus on the road after viewing the dashboard displays can be a safety problem. Avis Car Rental Company has introduced a windshield display of this information so that drivers can see it without looking down and having to refocus their eyes. These systems, called "head-up" displays, were first used in aircraft and later in boats, so pilots could view the information while keeping their eyes on the environment. The digital display appears to float above the car's front bumper, can be adjusted in position and is visible at all times. Studies of drivers who have used head-up displays have shown that 82% of respondents feel safer driving cars with a head-up display.

Another type of in-vehicle technology is a **route guidance system**, which helps a driver navigate the best routes to a given location. The vehicle must be equipped with an on-board computer, which retrieves data from a central database located elsewhere. The database is a **Geographic Information System (GIS)** that stores graphical information and maps of a given region. The information from the database is communicated to the car's computer via a satellite. A monitor on the dashboard displays the information and a touch panel allows the driver to choose options through a menu-driven interface.

Drivers can request directions to a given street address, to a given intersection, or to specific tourist attractions. They can request routes with certain characteristics such as fastest routes, scenic routes, and routes with or without freeways. The response from the GIS includes driving instructions, maps of designated routes with street intersections and landmarks, and the vehicle's location relative to the maps. Voice prompts assist the driver in making turns, and in the event of a wrong turn, the system generates a new route. The memory in the computer can store numerous routes to commonly visited destinations for easy access. Many smartphones now also provide the same functionality. As we have discussed in Chapter 6, drivers and passengers with smartphones or an Internet connection in the car can use mobile apps that provide some of the features of ITS systems. Examples of some popular apps are described in Table 8.1.

For tourists who do not know their way around a city or region, these systems can reduce frustration, delays and accidents that can detract from a good vacation. Many of these systems are installed in some rental cars and their use is expected to grow in the future as more car manufacturers equip cars with on-board computers.

Vehicle technology

As mentioned above, many ITS functions require the vehicles themselves to have certain technologies installed at the point of manufacture. Some vehicles augment the driving experience and some are totally self-driving vehicles. Technology augmented cars, or **smart cars**, have the in-vehicle features described above as well as the ability to self-park, to monitor blind spots, to recognize traffic signs and to notify drivers of possible collisions. Vehicles with sensors not only make driving safer so that cars can drive closer together but also expand highway capacity. **Connected cars** are cars that are connected to the Internet in some

Table 8.1. Examples of mobile apps for route guidance.

Name	Function
Field Trip	Alerts the traveler when they drive past an interesting feature and provides information, e.g. local history, restaurants, attractions.
Real-time Ridesharing	The Avego iPhone app allows drivers to offer vacant seats in their car to other passengers who pay at the end of the journey. The app also allows anyone to locate available rides.
ISpotSwap	Encourages user participation to find parking spots and trade these spots with other ISpotSwap users.
Cheap Gas!	This app has an augmented reality feature showing local features overlaid with the name of the gas station, distance to the gas station and price of the gas.
Sigalert	Provides information on current road conditions, speed information and access to live cameras to aid commuters.
Waze	Relies on user participation for reporting of traffic, car accidents and the presence of speed traps. Once a report is made by one user, other users are able to access that report using the Waze map.
iTraffic	Provides live traffic maps, showing traffic speeds and incidents on major routes for hundreds of cities and suburbs to help you plan your schedule and route.
traffic.com	App gives users information on traffic congestion, incident information, savable routes and real-time traffic maps.

way and provide additional features such as smart navigation, infotainment in the car, and social and service information overlaid over the navigational display. These ambient intelligent features are part of the "Internet of Things" we have discussed in other chapters.

The EO Smart Car project funded by the German Ministry of Transport has electrical cars equipped with sensors and computers to understand and navigate its global environment. It will automatically develop routes and can be connected with other similar vehicles. This kind of car augments the driver's con-

trol, but a driver is still needed. Visit http://tiny.cc/eosmartcar/ for more details.

http://tiny.cc/eosmartcar/

A true ITS will utilize **driverless cars** with no person in control of the car. Driverless cars have been a dream of humanity since General Motors presented the idea in 1939. Google has now created a driverless car, and after a license was given in May 2012, three US states now permit their use: California, Nevada and Florida. Driverless cars can be organized into platoons of 8 to 25 cars which move together. This platooning is not only safer but also reduces fuel consumption. It also expands the capacity of highways by about 30% (Tientra-kool *et al.*, 2011). The following video provides a good introduction to Google's driverless car: http://youtu.be/bp9KBrH8H04/.

http://youtu.be/bp9KBrH8H04/

Fleet management systems

ITSs can also assist tour bus companies and taxi companies in managing their fleets of vehicles. Fleet management systems use **Automated Vehicle Location (AVL)** technology to provide information on the location of each vehicle in the fleet. The vehicle is equipped with a GPS that determines the position of the vehicle. This information can then be superimposed on a street map in a GIS to determine the exact location of the vehicle. AVL systems used by taxi companies can inform fleet operators of the location of each vehicle. Based on this information, the company can give travelers an estimated time of arrival at a given location. AVL systems also have advantages for public transport vehicles. Real-time schedule information on public transport vehicles can be passed on to the

public in two ways. First, information displays on board public vehicles can advise passengers of the expected time of arrival at their destination. Second, information can be displayed at terminals or stops to advise passengers of the exact position of the vehicle along its route and how long they have to wait for the next vehicle.

AVL systems have also been found to increase tourist safety in situations where travelers may be stranded due to vehicle problems, criminal activities or inclement weather. Information on the exact location of the tourist's vehicle can be immediately communicated to the police department or other emergency agency. Knowing their exact location enables the agency to dispatch assistance immediately. For travelers driving in areas of high crime, this can be a very comforting feature. Individual or group tourists in the outdoors with or without vehicles can also benefit from carrying GPS sensors, although smartphones also provide a similar function.

VEHICLE RENTAL COMPANIES AND INFORMATION TECHNOLOGY

This section will examine the use of IT for reservation systems by vehicle rental companies. Because major vehicle rental firms have offices and vehicles in numerous locations they need computer reservation networks to process bookings. Large chain operations use a central computer system with databases on passenger reservations, rental agreements and car inventory, which is also accessible to travel planners and consumers themselves on the web.

Reservation systems

Vehicle rental websites give global access to central reservation systems. On the website, travelers can decide on the type of vehicle, the rates, drop-off and pick-up places, dates and times. Reservation software also manages sales trends, analyzes vehicle utilization and availability, and typically has a yield management feature. There are numerous vendors of such software that provide the service for a monthly fee. Car rental reservations systems sometimes connect with government computers to reject high-risk drivers resulting in between 6 and 10% of renters being rejected.

Frequent renter databases give frequent renters special treatment and express booking procedures. Fast processing upon arrival and at departure are important service elements and IT reduces transaction times in a number of ways. By bypassing counter service, the frequent renter can go immediately to the designated car where the keys are already located. Mobile apps are also being used to move travelers more quickly through the airport-to-car process (e.g. Silvercar). A traveler creates a profile on their mobile app in advance of their travels (including a credit card and insurance details), allowing them go directly to the car and unlock it by scanning a QR code on the windshield. The return process is also faster. Express returns are processed using handheld terminals to record the car mileage and to generate a receipt for the passenger.

Vehicle inventory control

Another database contains information on the vehicles themselves. Details on each individual vehicle, its classification, its features, rates, mileage and maintenance records are stored. It also orders vehicles, depreciates their value over time, and tracks their movement, maintenance and repair. Such systems maximize the utilization of each vehicle and increase company revenues. Inventory control of cars is done either with bar codes on the back window, or the vehicle identification number may be optically read through the front window. This latter choice avoids identifying the car as a rental in areas where theft is likely to occur. A challenge to car rental companies is to match their supply of vehicles with customer demand. This is not easy in a changing touristic environment. The applications discussed above help, but more sophisticated computer applications are needed to make strategic decisions. The use of Operations Research (OR) models have been successfully integrated into their systems to assist with decision-making.

Vehicle sharing

Travelers seeking mobility in a destination may not always want to rent a vehicle or use public transport, but may want the independence of a car but for a short period of time. Also residents in cities may not want to own a car, but have access to one. The increasingly popular concept of **car sharing**, which is also known as **collaborative mobility**, relies on computer technology to operate. The first car sharing system was offered by the city council in Amsterdam, Netherlands in the 1960s, however modern-day systems started in Switzerland in 1987, Germany in 1988 and North America in 1994 (e.g. http://www.carsharing.net/). In 2012, car sharing was operating in 27 countries and five continents.

A car sharing system gives travelers and residents access to a car without the challenges of car ownership. The system has a fleet of cars throughout the destination and users must register and be approved to drive the car online. They can make their reservation and view the location of cars, usually near public transport stations, on their mobile device. This system is preferred to renting a car as there are no limiting hours of operation, and vehicles can be rented by the minute, hour or day. Car-sharing companies usually require drivers to obtain a special RFID card that communicates with the car to unlock it. For safety and security and to reduce abuse of the system, the car cannot be started without the card. When the driver ends the journey, the car is parked in designated lots, locked with the card, and made available for the next user. All information about the trip is stored online and is available for access. Lyft and Zipcar are two examples of on-demand car-sharing services. The following video explains the procedure for one company: http://youtu.be/cX2xJOo5LIs/.

http://youtu.be/cX2xJOo5LIs/

As concern about the environment grows, and transport is blamed for much of the carbon emissions, tourists are re-evaluating their transport modes and often choose the bicycle, which of course does not pollute. **Bicycle sharing programs** started in 1965 in Amsterdam, Netherlands where 50 bicycles

were painted white and made available for anyone to use. Now they are in place in hundreds of locations around the world such as Spain, Italy, Australia and China. There are four different types of systems. One type is unregulated where a city provides bicycles and allows free access to anyone; a second type requires a small deposit to unlock the bike. The third and more sophisticated system requires users to pre-register as members on their smartphones. The bikes are fitted with GPS buttons, and can either be returned to the original location, or left anywhere allowing the next user to locate them on their mobile phone. The fourth type is known as a demand-responsive, multi-modal system, which has the benefit of linking with public transport systems in the destination. A single payment smartcard allows access to all public transport options and bike stations are conveniently located near transit stations (Shaheen and Guzman, 2011). Even though pre-registration in such a system may not be convenient for short-term tourists, longer-stay tourists can make good use of the system. Some systems allow for long-term checkout where the user can keep the bike for a few months. Bike-sharing systems are sometimes run by cities or in partnership with carshare operators or car park operators.

Taxis

Information technology is changing taxi use also, particularly in big cities, and is making the wait for a taxi a thing of the past. Taxi firms are now making it possible for customers to order taxis on their smartphones either in advance or at the time they need them. Examples of such taxi firms are GetTaxi and Uber. Apps identify taxis that are close by, and provide details about the driver, license plate and the distance away. Customers can track the vehicle and also receive a text message when it arrives. Passengers' details and credit card information are stored in the app and when the ride is complete their credit card is billed.

Another way for travelers to access rides is by finding a resident who is willing to drive them to their destination. These are called **ride-share systems** and IT again facilitates this type of travel. Companies such as Sidecar, established in 2012, match drivers with riders, in direct competition to taxis. Computer systems store information about the drivers and allow travelers to connect with the car owner through smartphone apps. Drivers must register and meet rigorous safety standards before they can be listed as a ride-share driver. Once registered and approved, they can give rides anywhere. This is another example of a C2C business model that reduces the cars on the road and gives car owners some additional revenue.

RAIL TRANSPORT AND INFORMATION TECHNOLOGY

Rail travel is an important land transport mode, more in some countries than others. It is becoming more popular than air travel by removing the inconvenience of airports and taking the traveler into the center of the city. Rail travel includes both surface rail systems (e.g. rapid transit, light rail) and subway (e.g. metro or underground) systems. Surface rail travel has more needs for IT application than subway since it is likely to consist of longer journeys, and more planning and reservations by travelers.

Rail companies use web-based computer reservation systems to manage the seat capacity on trains, book seats or berths, and provide timetable information. The rail computer reservation systems (CRSs) respond to passengers' requests for schedules and timetables. Some rail systems have links to the GDS, so that schedules can be viewed and tickets purchased by travel agents for their clients. Travelers' smartphones allow secure ticket purchases, generating a square bar code that can then be checked by personnel or by scanners on trains and at stations.

Electronic ticketing is in use by surface rail and subway operators to monitor entry into stations and vehicles more efficiently. Different types of tickets (season, monthly, weekly, day) can be purchased from automatic ticket machines in stations. By using stored value payment cards for multiple journeys or season tickets, passengers receive discounts and no longer have to carry cash or purchase a ticket for each journey. Some cities allow intermodal public transport tickets that can be used on surface rail, subway, buses, trams and ferries. The Chunnel (tunnel joining the UK to France), which has automated check-in "gates", faced a particular challenge in automating its departure control and ticketing system since it involved integrating multiple systems in multiple countries. A systems integrator was used to accomplish the task more easily.

Cross-border rail ticketing has only recently been possible as nations are linking their rail CRSs together. This is particularly necessary in Europe where there are so many different countries and rail travel is popular. A digital platform to connect European rail CRSs together and make them accessible to travel planners called SilverRail has recently been developed. It is a single place to buy

European rail tickets requiring cross-border ticketing, and in a way is like a mini-GDS for the rail industry. This has required developing standards for fares, rules, schedules, routes, settlement methods, ticketing, journey planning, and commission tracking for travel agent bookings. The SilverRail CRS processes rail reservations made on eBookers.com, Skyscanner.com and Sabre's GetThere (O'Neill, 2013). Quno rail is the B2C version of SilverRail and focuses on direct bookings from travelers.

When traveling inter-city, travelers often consider train and bus options. Information about these modes of transport is not always easy for travelers to find and typically many companies offer these services making it difficult to view comprehensive information in one place. One example of an innovative website where both inter-city bus and inter-city rail services can be searched and booked is called Wanderu.com. A similar site which provides multi-modal (air, bus, rail and car rental) searching and booking for European destinations is http://www.GoEuro.com/. In India, a bus reservation system called Ticket-Goose has partnered with more than 700 bus operators, 6000 agents and serves 3000 destinations in India. TicketGoose has a unique Hipmunk-style user interface designed to appeal visually and keep the text as minimal as possible.

WATER TRANSPORT AND INFORMATION TECHNOLOGY

Water transport operators include passenger and car ferries, and cruise ships on rivers, large lakes and oceans. The IT needs for each are different with ocean-going cruise lines needing more than ferry boats since the passengers are on board longer and the vessels have more facilities. Therefore, most of this section will focus on cruise lines' application of IT.

Both cruise lines and ferries need computerized reservation systems. Roll-on roll-off (RORO) ferries take vehicles as well as foot passengers on board as they often provide transport to small islands. This requires a CRS that can book both people and vehicles. The database needs to store information on the length and type of vehicle so that space can be reserved on the deck. Passenger information is also stored in the database. There are many individual ferry CRSs, but http://www.aferry.com/ has access to about 150 ferry companies around the world and takes international ferry bookings.

Cruises, particularly multi-day ocean cruises, are more complex products than ferries, airlines, rail and car rentals, requiring more complex reservation databases. More information is required in the booking process. Each reservation needs to choose a destination sailing and ship, a rate code, a type of cabin and a PNR. This complexity is one reason for the small percentage of cruises booked electronically compared to those booked through travel agents. Cruise line reservation systems are accessible through online portals such as Travelocity and Expedia, however only 10% of cruise bookings are booked this way. CruiseMatch is a cruise booking system for travel agents, which links them to over 40 cruise companies such as Royal Caribbean Cruise Lines, Azamara Club Cruises and Celebrity Cruises.

Cruise line extranets can help travel agents and tour operators sell cruises, as they provide more information and improve the relationship between the travel agent and the cruise operator (Papathanassis and Brejla, 2011). Online booking systems for large cruise-lines allow pre-paid or pre-deposited customers to access the reservation system to book land excursions, spa treatments and other requests online prior to their cruises. Crystal Cruises' FastTrack Check-In system uses a bar code on cruise tickets and a ticket scanning system in port waiting areas, which eliminates ship check-in procedures completely. They quickly and efficiently transition guests from dock to security.

Technology is used in passenger areas to provide them with more information and in the back office to make cruisers' experience more informative and enjoyable. Royal Caribbean International (RCI) has the Wayfinder system, which helps passengers find their way around the huge 5000 berth ships. WayFinder touchscreen terminals throughout the ship have interactive screens that allow staff and customers find information about the ship. Information includes maps of the ship and customized routing, restaurant locations and reservation availabilities, schedule of onboard activities, real-time updates, and customized directions and routing are at guests' fingertips. RCI has recently placed iPads in staterooms to help guests access similar information (see Industry Insight box below). Norwegian Cruises has a similar system called iConcierge Smart Phone App which connects iPhone, iPad, Android and Windows7 users to Norwegian Epic's onboard guest information and service systems during their cruise.

Other ships provide high-tech entertainment, particularly for younger cruisers with 3D-formatted films with special effects such as squirting water and bubbles, vibrating and shifting seats and wind and scent that entertain viewers. Other ships bring the outside into inside staterooms with a virtual "Magical Porthole" giving guests a real-time view outside the ship via high-definition cameras placed on the ship's exterior. Other cruise lines continue to develop energy-saving technology, such as LED and compact fluorescent lighting installed fleet-wide at a potential saving of approximately US$100,000 annually per ship. Others have developed new reverse osmosis systems for freshwater production that consumes 40% less power (Cruiselines International Association, 2013).

Global navigation systems and GPS technology on the bridge of the vessel use satellite communication to assist in navigation. The **Global Maritime Distress and Safety Systems** (GMDSSs) assist with medical emergencies at sea. Communication between a medical facility on land and the vessel in distress can provide online assistance in a medical emergency. Search and rescue operations at sea are enhanced by GMDSSs, and better treatment is provided for sick or injured passengers. Satellite communication links from ship to shore also facilitate day-to-day business transactions on board ship. Point-of-sale systems are used on board many ships in the shops and bars. As most cruises include all meals in the price of the cruise, the restaurants do not need point-of-sale systems, except for the sale of alcoholic beverages. Computers are also used to monitor and control inventories of merchandise and supplies on board. This is especially important for long journeys between ports, requiring high levels of supply inventory. Ships can use computers to determine purchase requirements at each port, and orders can be electronically communicated to shore before the ship arrives in the port.

Tourists who cruise may arrive at the point of embarkation a few hours or even a day or so before their cruise departs. Information on places to eat, shop, sightsee or stay overnight could make their time more enjoyable. In Florida, a large cruise port, the DMO has cooperated with cruise companies to place QR codes in their brochures so that tourists can access the information with their smartphones. This increases the revenue for the destination and can lead to more satisfied cruisers. IT has also changed the way tourists arrange their onshore excursions. Traditionally they were controlled by the cruise line, which had exclusive contracts with local operators making these excursions a lucrative operation. Local operators had no chance to communicate with tourists before they arrived at the destination. Now, with the Internet and mobile technologies travelers can book their own local, personalized and less expensive independent operators' tours.

Industry Insights: Royal Caribbean International

Royal Caribbean International (RCI), one of the world's largest cruise lines, uses technology for strategic advantage. It is headquartered in Miami, Florida and has over 40 ships that typically carry over 5000 passengers each, covering 260 destinations worldwide. It was founded in 1968 and owns a suite of different brands including Royal Caribbean International, Celebrity Cruises, Azamara Cruises and Pullmantour operating in Europe and the USA.

On board each ship, the IT applications are extensive. They must handle the embarking and disembarking of 5000 passengers within 6 hours each week, to navigate the ship and to improve the guest experience. The company's reservation system called RES receives reservations from guests directly through the Royal Caribbean International website or a call center. Most reservations (85%) come through travel agents using CrusingPower.com or other sites. The on-board hotel computer system processes credit card data, the guest folio, customer preferences, pictures, health records and behavioral data. This can be stored, aggregated and used to predict passenger behavior and optimize the customer experience and guest relations.

Other applications are point-of-sale software in the shops, Internet for guests, email for employees and software to count the number of checked-out towels at the pool to name a few. Many routers on the ship provide fast Internet connectivity for guests and employees. As ships can only connect back to shore via satellite – which is very expensive and slow – all vessels also have fully functioning independent data centers. During sailing there are additional IT requirements such as navigation software and systems for propulsion, fuel monitoring and weather.

The customer experience is greatly enhanced with IT. Every floor on the ship has a 32-inch touchscreen giving interactive directions to guests' staterooms, events, restaurants, or

(Continued)

Continued.

the nearest restroom. iPads in the staterooms help customers make restaurant reservations, select wine and appetizers, schedule excursions and order room service. Since iPads have cameras they pose a privacy risk, so each iPad is wiped clean after each week's use. All wait staff use wireless point-of-sale (POS) devices, allowing guest purchases to be processed anywhere on the ship. These devices are also used to obtain electronic waivers from guests for shipboard activities such as rock climbing or ice skating. They have also enhanced workflow for processes such as food safety inspection, which now typically requires 2 hours instead of 5.

IT systems are also used to enhance guest security. A high-resolution photo is taken of each guest using face-recognition software, which is linked with a passenger's stateroom key. The picture is then placed in the security system and the POS system for later use. Parents can use a child-tracking system by renting a special iPhone with an app that communicates with a child's smart wristband to identify the child's location on the ship. This vastly reduces the number of lost children alerts. Shape-recognition cameras count the number of people seated in and waiting for restaurants. This information is fed to 300 digital signs throughout the ship in the form of red-yellow-green signals, so guests can self-select the least-crowded venues.

http://tint.cc/rcicurisetech

Social media is also part of RCI's strategy; they encourage customers to share videos and photos online. They also pay for banner ads on Facebook and paid search on the search engines. For more information check out the following blog from President and CEO Adam Goldstein: http://tiny.cc/rcicruisetech/.

INTEGRATED PUBLIC TRANSPORT SYSTEMS

Different types of public transport exist in many cities for tourists and residents to move around. Rail, subway, tram, bus or ferries are some of the systems run by public authorities. IT is helping these systems in two ways. First, it helps to integrate the various modes together into an intermodal system, so that passengers can move seamlessly between different modes. It does this by collecting data on each system and sharing that information with the other systems. This also ensures efficient and on-time transport, and keeps passengers informed of where the vehicles are and of any delays. To learn more about urban intermodal transport systems and how IT is making them more efficient view the following video: http://youtu.be/bUyourDcWzw/.

http://youtu.be/bUyourDcWzw/

Second, IT is helping to integrate and simplify the ticketing process so that travelers do not have to buy a ticket each time they board a mode of transport. Instead, a smartcard gives them access to any transport mode in the system, making their journeys smoother. This encourages the use of public transport and reduces traffic congestion. Examples of such systems are the Oyster Card in London, the Go Card in Brisbane and Singapore's EZ-Link Card. Most systems rely on travelers having a smartcard and contactless ticketing that uses RFID or NFC technology to communicate between the card and the validation device. Different types of tickets can be purchased (e.g. single, return, daily, weekly, or monthly pass, or for a certain number of journeys). Fares are automatically calculated for intermodal trips across different zones of the public transport network. Credit is added to smartcards at ticket machines, ATMs, by automatic recharge through a bank account, online or with a mobile phone. Mobile tickets are issued using SMS or mobile bar codes. Each of these systems has a website that provides information such as schedules, ticket types, top-up details and updates of transport delays. Such smartcards can be used for trains, trams, buses, ferries, subways and even bicycle-sharing schemes.

To ride Singapore's MRT, for example, travelers must purchase a stored-value, contactless smartcard, which can then be used for public transport throughout Singapore, to pay ERP tolls, electronic parking system carparks, and at some stores. For tourists, a Singapore Tourist Pass contactless smartcard is available from numerous locations including visitor centers. Some cities' systems also allow tourists to use the cards for entry into museums and leisure attractions, making the visitor experience more convenient. The challenge for cities is to make sure that tourists know about the systems and provide information in multiple languages.

SUMMARY

Information technology is successfully being used to make land and water transport more efficient and smooth for passengers and operators. As travelers increase in number, the need for efficient use of highways and waterways increases. Intelligent Transportation Systems are the framework for these developments. The individual companies in land transport need to be aware of the various technologies discussed above to operate more efficiently. They will all need, over time, to install on-board computer systems as part of a more intelligent transportation system. Intermodal transport is likely to become more prevalent in the future, and will make more demands on computer systems used by transport companies. Intermodal reservations and ticketing will require more connectivity between individual companies' computer systems and standardization of documents and databases. All aspiring tourist destinations need to carefully examine the benefits provided by the systems discussed above. Ignoring these technologies can only produce more chaotic, congested, slow transport systems, which many travelers will no longer tolerate. The success of a tourist destination depends heavily on the quality of its transport system.

KEY TERMS

automated traffic management system (ATMS), automated vehicle location (AVL), automated vehicle locator systems, bike sharing, car inventory control, car sharing, collaborative mobility, connected cars, cross-border rail ticketing, driverless cars, e-toll, electronic road pricing (ERP), fleet management systems, Geographic Information System (GIS), global maritime distress and safety systems, global navigation systems, in-vehicle communication, intelligent transportation system (ITS), multi-modal transport system, ride-share systems, route guidance systems, smart cars, traveler information systems, vehicle information and communication system (VICS), vehicle-to-infrastructure communication, vehicle-to-vehicle communication

DISCUSSION QUESTIONS

1. Which of the transport developments discussed in this chapter are most important for tourists (as opposed to residents)? Why?
2. Explain what is meant by collaborative mobility. Describe different modalities for this type of transport. Are there any disadvantages that would prevent you from using this type of transport as a tourist? What are its benefits?
3. Research the various national rail networks other than those in Europe. What type of IT applications are they using? How easy is it for passengers to make cross-border reservations in that part of the world?
4. Spend some time researching driverless cars more. What do you see as the real advantages? How relevant are these advantages to tourists? Are there some types of tourists for which they would not be relevant?

USEFUL WEBSITES

QR code	Website	Description
	Intelligent Transportation Society of America http://www.itsa.org/	ITS America is the nation's largest organization dedicated to advancing the research, development and deployment of ITSs.
	Intelligent Transportation Systems Society http://www.sites.ieee.org/itss/	The ITS Society advances the theoretical, experimental and operational aspects of electrical engineering and information technologies as applied to ITS.

QR code	Website	Description
	US Department of Transportation Research and Innovative Technology Administration http://www.its.dot.gov/	The US government's ITS program focuses on intelligent vehicles, intelligent infrastructure and the creation of an intelligent transportation system.
	ERTICO http://www.ertico.com/	ERTICO is a network of Intelligent Transport Systems and Services stakeholders in Europe.
	Intelligent Transport Systems Australia http://www.its-australia.com.au	ITS Australia promotes advanced technologies to deliver safer, more efficient and environmentally sustainable transport.
	ABI Research http://www.abiresearch.com/research/service/intelligent-transport-systems/	A research organization that produces many research reports on ITS.
	CruiseMatch http://www.cruisematch.com/	A web portal for multiple cruise lines.
	The World Carshare Consortium http://www.ecoplan.org/carshare/	The World Carshare Consortium is an informal shared public interest knowledge-building network.

Case Study: Zurich's Transport System

Switzerland is a well-known tourist destination. One of its major cities, Zurich has invested heavily in an intelligent transportation system to improve mobility for residents and tourists in the region. Zurich has a population of 1.37 million and 13,000 hotel rooms, making it one of the top tourism destinations in Switzerland. In 2000, 36% of trips were made by scheduled public transport and 19% by bicycle or walking. Public transport is important to allow independent tourists to get around and Switzerland has one of the densest railway networks in the world, which is finely networked with city buses, trams and Postbus. It also has the largest airport in Switzerland with over 22 million passengers per year.

Public transport in Zurich consists of long-distance and regional rail, trams, trolleybuses, urban bus services, outer suburban bus services and on-demand responsive transport. Trams (S-Bahn) create the backbone of Zurich's public transport with buses and trolleybuses playing a complementary role. VBZ, an integrated multi-modal transport provider with a single consolidated ticketing system, is responsible for transport in and around Zurich. VBZ operates a total of 654 vehicles in Zurich (313 trams, 80 trolleybuses and 261 urban buses) and there are 451 stops in the urban area. On average, each day VBZ operates about 90,000 vehicle-kilometers, carries 800,000 passengers and deals with six street blockages and four collisions.

Dispatchers work from a central control center to manage the network with each dispatcher overseeing 10–15 transport lines. There are strict expectations that vehicles should not be more than 30 seconds ahead of their scheduled time and not more than 1 minute late.

To operate at this level of efficiency, VBZ uses the following applications of ITS:

- automated vehicle location;
- operations management including incident management;
- traffic signal priority;
- electronic fare collection;
- real-time passenger information pre-trip, at stations and in vehicles;
- automated passenger counting;
- timetabling; and
- vehicle and driver scheduling.

Each vehicle includes an on-board computer, GPS, radio (voice, data), wireless LAN, driver console, display screens, voice announcer (interior and exterior) and transponder to interface with roadside detectors. Recent developments in 2011 created seamless integrated travel throughout the Canton.

Passengers buy tickets (smartcards) from self-service vending machines on the platform. The machine accepts cards or cash but can be difficult for foreign tourists to

(Continued)

Case Study. Continued.

use if they are not familiar with the system or the language. There is no fare collection on board.

Communication for operations management is by private analog radio and close range communication is by wireless LAN. Data transfer includes uploading of reference data (e.g. routes, stops and schedules), download of transaction data (e.g. date, statistics logs) and upload of software. Passengers are provided with information on how to use the systems, such as journey planners, real-time passenger information, and incident information and alerts. This is provided either at stop displays, in-vehicle displays, or delivered to mobile devices. The information shows the line number, destination and minutes to arrival. In-vehicle displays have a light sensor to change the luminance level depending on ambient light.

Zurich gives a high level of priority to public transport at traffic signals. Traffic signal priority is triggered by detection of public transport vehicles. Zurich has about 400 sets of traffic signals and about 4000 traffic detectors, most of which are induction loops. The induction loop detects the vehicle presence and identifies if it is a public transport vehicle. Early green lights and zero wait time are given, and the total cycle time cannot exceed 72 seconds, and pedestrians cannot wait more than 30 seconds. The Zurich Traffic Control Centre coordinates with VBZ's Control Centre in the event of road closures or disruptions.

Adapted from The World Bank (2013)

Study Questions

1. Identify another tourist city that has a multi-modal intelligent transportation system. Compare and contrast the two systems.
2. How could Zurich develop its transport even more so that it is more user-friendly for tourists?

REFERENCES

Cruiselines International Association (2013) North America Cruise Industry Update. (February). Available at: http://www.cruising.org/sites/default/files/pressroom/CruiseIndustryUpdate2013Final.pdf (accessed 13 June 2014).

ERTICO (2014) ITS can help improve our daily lives. Available at: http://www.ertico.com/about-ertico-its/ (accessed 2 January 2014).

European Telecommunications Standards Institute (2012) Intelligent Transport Systems. Available at: http://www.etsi.org/index.php/technologies-clusters/technologies/intelligent-transport/ (accessed 2 January 2014).

Intelligent Transportation Society of America (2014) Intelligent Transportation Systems. Available at: http://www.itsa.org/ (accessed 2 January 2014).

Nazer, Z. (2013) Qatar invests $70 billion to pave the way to world beating transportation. ITS International. Available at: http://www.itsinternational.com/ (accessed 2 January 2014).

O'Neill, S. (2013) SilverRail's strategy for European rail ticketing. Available at: http://www.tnooz.com/ (accessed 15 August 2013).

Papathanassis, A. and Brejla, P. (2011) Tourism extranet acceptance in the cruise distribution chain: the role of context, usability, and appearance. *Information Technology and Tourism* 13(2), 105–117. doi: 10.3727/109830512x13258778487399

Shaheen, S. and Guzman, S. (2011) Worldwide Bikesharing. *Access* 39(Fall), 6. Available at: http://www.uctc.net/access39_bikesharing.pdf (accessed 13 June 2014).

The World Bank (2013) Case Study: Zurich, Switzerland. Toolkit on Intelligent Transport Systems for Urban Transport. Available at: http://www.robat.scl.net/content/ITS-Toolkit/case-studies/zurich-switzerland.html/ (accessed 21 August 2013).

Tientrakool, P., Ho, Y.C. and Maxemchuk, F. (2011) Highway capacity benefits from using vehicle to vehicle communication and sensors for collision avoidance. Paper presented at the Proceedings of Vehicular Technology Conference CAIEEE conference, San Franscisco, USA.

chapter 9

Hospitality Information Systems

LEARNING OBJECTIVES

After reading this chapter you should be able to:

- understand the nature of the hospitality industry and its unique applications of IT;
- be able to explain how a hotel's property management system works and connects to other systems in the hotel;
- know the ways a hotel can service its guest better with IT applications throughout the hotel;
- know how restaurants can use IT for improved operations; and
- to understand how a hotel or restaurant can use IT for improved management and decision-making.

INTRODUCTION

The places where travelers stay and eat vary immensely and yet almost all of these institutions benefit from IT. The hospitality sector includes lodging operations (hotels, motels, guest houses, bed and breakfasts, self-catering apartments and cottages, caravan parks and campsites) and food and beverage operations (fine dining, fast food, convention and event foodservice). Each of these types of institutions consists of a variety of operations. Some are small and independent, some are large multinational chain operations; some are specialized and attract niche markets, others cater to the mass market.

Hospitality is about maximizing guest satisfaction through excellent experiences and personal service. The use of IT has sometimes been viewed as incompatible with this ethos, causing the hospitality sector to lag behind other sectors in applying IT. Indeed, IT has sometimes been viewed as an impediment to personal service by creating a cold, impersonal atmosphere. A shift in this belief is now happening and IT is becoming more widespread. The ability of IT applications to reduce operational costs has also fueled this change (Buhalis and Law, 2008; Ip *et al.*, 2011). Service quality is especially important in luxury hotels where IT increases customer satisfaction and delight (Chathoth, 2007). It is evident now that IT increases the competitiveness of lodging operations, that "high tech" and "high touch" are not mutually exclusive, and together they can increase efficiency, reduce costs and provide higher levels of personal service. This chapter examines how accommodation firms and foodservice enterprises use IT to meet these goals.

INFORMATION TECHNOLOGY SYSTEMS IN THE ACCOMMODATIONS SECTOR

The hotel industry's first experience with IT was not inspiring. The first hotel computer was installed in 1963 in the New York Hilton (Sayles, 1963). It was an IBM minicomputer programed to automate guest room management. However, at the time the technology was not well suited for the task, requiring front-desk clerks to use punch cards for data entry, which were then batch processed. The resulting time delays caused such long lines at the front desk that the system was removed soon after its installation. Almost a decade passed before more appropriate online systems were successfully installed in large hotels in the USA and then the rest of the world. Typically hotels have used IT first as clerical support, then as administrative support, third as tactical support and lastly in creative and connected ways to help strategy (Murphy, 2004). Although the hotel industry is often criticized for being half a generation behind other industries in its adoption of IT (O'Connor and Murphy, 2008), many IT applications exist including Property Management Systems (PMS), financial and accounting systems, resource planning, yield management, human resource management, electronic customer relationship management,

intranet, email marketing, websites with booking capabilities, e-procurement and online platforms (Fuchs et al., 2009; Leung and Law, 2012).

Large and luxury hotels perceive more benefits from automation and can finance their purchase more easily. Small and medium-sized hotels have experienced more challenges installing IT and Internet applications due to lack of financial resources, lack of IT knowledge and experience, their resistance to change and their location, which is often rural with poor connectivity (Anckar and Walden, 2001). Chain hotels and more complex properties (e.g. convention hotels, resort properties with multiple restaurants, spas, golf, casinos) are heavier users of technology as there is more information to process, transfer and store. IT implementation tends to be lowest for motels, small guest houses and bed-and-breakfasts (Siguaw et al., 2000).

Consideration of how hotel clientele will be affected by technology is necessary to determine the appropriate level of automation in a hotel. Business travelers value efficiency and speed of service, and appreciate more technology. Some leisure guests prefer hotels where technology does not intrude into their vacation experience. In addition, the degree of technology in a hotel is effected by management's conviction that IT can support core business processes, and the expectation of guests and partners such as suppliers and travel agents (Fuchs et al., 2009).

In summary, the most common lodging IT applications are the following:

1. **Front-office applications**: reservation system, check-in/check-out, room status and housekeeping management, in-house guest information functions and guest accounting modules.
2. **Back-office applications**: personnel, purchasing module, accounting modules (account

receivable, account payable and payroll), inventory module, sales and catering, and generating financial reports and updating statistics.

3. Guest-related interface applications: call-accounting system, electronic locking system, energy management systems, guest-operated devices (in-room entertainment, in-room vending and guest information services) and auxiliary guest services (automated wake-up call system and voicemail).

4. Restaurant and banquet management systems: menu management system, recipe management, sales analysis and forecasting, menu-item pricing, beverage-control system, and cost control (pre-costing and post-costing applications) (Ham *et al.*, 2005; Karadag and Dumanoglu, 2009).

These will be discussed in more detail in the sections below.

Property management systems

A **Property Management System (PMS)** handles the core functions of information processing for an accommodation property. This includes reservations, front-office operations, some back-office operations and management reporting, and is the hub for all interconnectivity with other systems in the hotel. PMSs have many levels of operational functionality, some basic and some more specialized. A detailed coverage of PMS capabilities can be found in Kasavana and Cahill (2011). The following sections highlight the major functions and discuss trends and developments in each.

Reservations management

The PMS handles reservations at the property level. Property reservations come to the hotel as phone calls or emails from consumers and travel planners, from the hotel's website or central reservations system, from a GDS, or from an online travel agent (OTA) or accommodation aggregator. The incoming reservation requests are entered into the PMS either manually or through an electronic interface. If the hotel is part of a chain or other central reservation agency (CRS), reservations may be received online directly into the interfaced PMS. The **reservation module** of a PMS records details of the reservation, the preferred room type and special requests, dates of stay, deposit information, details about the booking agent (if any) and generates confirmation notices. Group reservations modules which assist in the handling of tour groups are also needed by many properties. This module is more complex since home rooms, pre-assigned room rates and block bookings must be dealt with.

Data from the reservations module are used to forecast room occupancy and revenue. Hotel PMS can include a **revenue management system (RMS)** to maximize occupancy and revenue, however less than 25% of hotels use revenue management tools. These systems are based on one of three different revenue management strategies: (i) room rates are varied based on market demand; (ii) participation in different Internet channels varies based on market demand; and (iii) rates are differentiated on Internet channels during peak demand (O'Connor and Murphy, 2008).

Hotel chains can integrate their central CRS with each property's PMS, into a system called an **Integrated Property System (IPS)**. In addition to seamless connectivity between the CRS and the PMS, this configuration allows guests in one property to make reservations in others in the chain. The CRSs store and process reservations for all properties and forward each reservation to the specific property either online (in the case of IPS) or offline. The chain CRS contains a proportion of rooms from each property, however local control of some inventory is kept for direct business and walk-in business. The local property updates the CRS online with room availability information. Best Western Hotels, for example, has a communications network that instantly updates rates and room availabilities by the individual properties. This allows faster processing of reservation requests.

In the 1970s a computer **switch** called Ultraswitch was created by THISCO (The Hotel Industry Switching Company), a consortium of major hotel chains who pooled resources to facilitate electronic reservations. Ultraswitch, which later became TravelWeb, formats the requests from GDSs into hotel CRS language and transmits them to the CRS directly. TravelWeb is now the booking engine for many other travel products, including car rental companies and OTAs such as Priceline. com. If the hotel is not affiliated with a chain it can subscribe to a **non-affiliate** CRS to list its rooms online. Independent companies such as Pegasus (formerly UTELL) operate these non-affiliate systems. Some hotel chains such as Best Western Hotels offer space on their CRS to other hotels for fees. Hotel websites are an increasingly important source of reservations, as we will see below.

Guest folio and billing

Guests really value efficient check-in and check-out (Dube *et al.*, 2003). The PMS can manage this process through its **front-office** system. The check-in process brings the guest's reservation file into an active in-house file and a **guest folio** is opened. If there is no reservation upon check-in, then a "walk-in"

file is created. As part of the check-in process, the PMS connects to credit card verification systems to ensure adequate funds for the length of stay. To process credit card payments securely, the system must comply with the **Payment Card Industry Data Security Standard (PCI-DSS)** otherwise hotels risk fines or loss of their merchant account.

In some hotels **self-service check-in kiosks** allow guests to bypass long check-in lines. These terminals connect to the PMS, and are activated by the swipe of a credit card or by motion detectors when guests approach. They greet the guest, guide them through the check-in procedure, assign a room, generate keys and provide directions to the room. They can also activate the energy management system, the phone and voicemail for the room. Some hotels, such as Yotel, have dispensed with check-in staff entirely and rely on automated check-in kiosks. Handheld, remote, wireless check-in terminals can also be used for remote check-in, for example, at the airport or in the taxi driving to the hotel. Mobile check in is also being installed in some hotels (see the Marriott case study for details).

Once the guest folio is initialized at check-in, all guest charges throughout the stay are posted to this folio either manually or electronically. Manual postings done by clerks are prone to time delays and errors. Electronic postings through hardware and software interfaces are completed rapidly and without error. This removes the possibility of bad debts incurred by guests not reporting last minute charges before checkout. The **night audit** function is another major beneficiary of automation. All financial transactions during the previous 24 hours are posted and consolidated into reports in a fraction of the time that a manual night audit would take.

Research Insight: Self-Service IT and Cultural Differences

As self-service check-in and check-out terminals become more common in hotels, the appropriateness of technologies must be considered. In a sense, they go against the traditional concept of hospitality, and make it harder to recover from service failure. They also reduce interpersonal contact and social engagement that some cultures value very much. Technology can also create a sense of anxiety for some cultural groups, age and lifestyle groups.

Fisher and Beatson (2002) argue that cultural differences affect how tourists respond to self-service technologies. They focus on the difference between high power distance cultures and low power distance cultures. A high power distance culture associates service staff with lower social class and expects them to render service to guests. Some Asian cultures fall into this category. Low power distance cultures tend to view service staff more equally. The research proposes that hotel guests from high power distance cultures:

- are less likely to accept self-service technology;
- value "saving face" and are less willing to utilize unfamiliar self-service technology;
- are less likely to report service failures involving self-service technology; and
- are less likely to return to hotels if there is a perception that self-service technology will not meet service delivery expectations.

The research highlights the importance of understanding cross-cultural differences related to technology, and indicates that managers should take care to install appropriate levels of technology for different types of guests.

Source: Fisher and Beatson (2002) The impact of culture on self-service on technology adoption in the hotel industry. *International Journal of Hospitality and Tourism Administration* 3(3), 59–77.

With a PMS, checkout does not require the guest to pay at the front desk. Automated funds transfer provides automated **express checkout**, in which the guest's folio is presented under the guest room door overnight, and if no discrepancies exist the credit card is automatically billed. Alternatively, guests may view the bill on the TV and check out using the remote control if the PMS is interfaced to the in-room entertainments system. PMS software to translate the bill into numerous languages is necessary for hotels with a large international clientele.

Rooms management

The **rooms management module** of the PMS tracks the status of guest rooms and assists the housekeeping department with their duties. The hotel room masterfile contains data on each room such as room number, room type, room features (bed types and amenities), room rates, locations and room status. Typical room statuses in a PMS are "occupied", "vacant", "dirty", "clean", "inspected", "uninspected" or "out of service". After each check-in and checkout, the room status is updated so that rooms can be sold as soon as they are available – an important consideration for hotels running at high occupancy levels. Room status updates are done manually by the housekeeping staff calling the front desk, sending periodic reports, or electronically via PMS terminals in the housekeeping department. Even more rapid updates can be made via the room telephone via the electronic lock network if interfaced with the PMS. Staff productivity and access can be tracked since staff must punch in and out as they begin and end cleaning each guest room.

Hotels are also using technology to count sheets, towels, robes and table linens by stitching in small radio frequency ID tags. These tags transmit radio waves, so that items on a laundry cart are automatically counted by a sensor in the laundry areas. It also reduces theft.

Specialized PMS functions

A PMS can include many other specialized modules depending on the needs of the accommodation unit. Some of these features are travel agent accounting, function room scheduling, golf, tennis, spa and other amenity scheduling, and condominium or time-share management. Each will be discussed briefly below.

- **Travel agent accounting**: for hotels with a large proportion of bookings through travel agents, commission accounts due to each travel agent must be kept, which is tedious to perform manually. The PMS can track commissions by capturing the information at the time of reservation. Payments can then be automatically generated at the end of each month for prompt payment of commissions. A central computerized clearing house called the **Travel Agency Commission**

Settlement (TACS) assists hotels in generating commission checks.

- **Function room scheduling**: hotels with function and banquet rooms for conventions, meetings, seminars and social events can use computer systems to manage function and activity details. Reservations for individual rooms, furniture configurations, equipment and food and beverage needs are stored in these systems. Such software used by hotels is similar to systems used by meeting and convention planners (see Chapter 10).

- **Amenity management**: hotels that provide sports, health and spa facilities and other amenities must keep track of bookings and requests. Golf and tennis courts need to track tee times and court scheduling and transmit fees to the guest folios in the PMS. Spa modules handle the appointments, room usage, scheduling of practitioners and guest payments.

- **Condominium and time-share management**: this type of accommodation units has different owners of units in a building. If PMS are used they must be modified to include details on the separate owners, and to track entitlements and rental payments from guests.

Back-office applications

Back-office IT systems can bring many efficiency benefits in the processing of large volumes of information related to human resource applications, payroll and employee information, accounts payable and receivable, inventory and purchasing, and other data that does not directly relate to the front desk. Many reports used by managers for decision-making are generated by back-office systems. Web-based PMSs typically offer this software functionality while properties with server-based systems may or may not have separate back-office systems. An interface with the PMS is needed so that data can be transferred and shared as necessary.

Hotel websites

Most hotel properties and chains have their own websites through which the consumer can search and book online. They give hotels greater control over their inventory in the midst of many other electronic booking opportunities discussed earlier in this book (OTAs, accommodation aggregators). Reservations from the hotel's own website avoid the commissions required of other distribution channels. Studies show that the higher the star rating the more likely a hotel is to have its own website even though not all have online reservation capability with immediate confirmation (Law and Hsu, 2005; Athey, 2011). Researchers have investigated what makes an attractive and well-designed hotel website (Chan and Law, 2006; Au and Ekiz, 2009). While visual factors such as amount of text, color, use of fonts, placement of images are aesthetically important, Au and Ekiz (2009) suggest that it must consider customers' needs and wants, be interactive, be easily navigable and be linked with existing marketing activities.

Other important functions of a hotel website are online booking capability, a price comparison feature, maps, email, a search engine, and multiple language support (Lexhagen, 2004). Since consumers are three times more likely to book a hotel if the website is in their own language, multilingual capabilities are also important and software can do this automatically (Li and Law, 2007). A study in Portugal showed that hotel websites presented only in the local language did not attract many international travelers (Athey, 2011). Functionality can be improved by adding more links to local points of interest, simplifying the pathways to other products, providing more detailed information on room facilities and pricing, and avoiding third-party reservation systems (Essawy, 2006). Overall, the **quality** of the information on the website is the most significant dimension motivating the intention to purchase (Jeong *et al.*, 2003; Wong and Law, 2005; Essawy, 2006).

Hotels in developing countries have unique challenges to developing websites due to political considerations, lack of infrastructure and government support, lack of support by professional associations, lack of technological knowledge, and general hesitation (Au and Ekiz, 2009). In some developing countries, hotels are choosing not to use websites but leapfrog the technology and use social media and Internet communities to reach their markets (Hashim *et al.*, 2012).

Electronic hotel reservations

About 35% of hotel rooms were booked digitally in the USA in 2010 compared to 8% in 2002 and this number is certain to increase (Carroll and Siguaw, 2003; Green and Lomanno, 2012). Of these digital bookings, 81% of room nights in the USA were made through direct channels and 20% through OTAs and GDSs (Green and Lomanno, 2012). In 2010 hotels paid US$2.7 billion in OTA commissions and US$1.3 billion to travel agents booking through GDSs. See the following video to understand more about this trend: http://youtu.be/3BRue1gdylA/.

http://youtu.be/3BRue1gdylA/

Many types of electronic channels are used to book accommodation as discussed in Chapter 3. OTAs such as Expedia and Travelocity consolidate room inventory from multiple hotels and sell at rates often lower than direct bookings with the hotel. Booking.com, RatesToGo.com, ihotelier by Travelclick and others offer the same functionality as Expedia but specialize in accommodation. Sites such as Wotif.com and lastminute.com are OTAs specializing in distressed hotel inventory. Metasearch engines such as kayak.com are commonly used and TripAdvisor has added a metasearch tool and Google has created Hotel Search with metasearch features. All of these sites not only erode profitability but also cause hotels to lose control of their inventory and pricing. In 2012 six leading hotel companies (Choice, Hilton, Hyatt, IHG, Marriott and Wyndham) fought back by establishing their own metasearch engine called Roomkey, which allows users to book direct with partner hotels. However, loss of inventory control and pricing continues to be a source of tension between hotels and OTAs.

The proliferation of online channels has re-engineered and redefined reservations management for hotels (Sigala, 2001; Sigala *et al.*, 2001), and managing their complexity is an important part of the reservations manager's job. It requires promoting their own website for direct bookings while also offering room inventory on various other electronic platforms. TravelClick's RateView assists hotels in managing the different electronic channels. It provides reports on rates and percentages of bookings on different channels, providing insight into the most productive channels. Strategic management of online reservations are being outsourced to **Channel Managers,** which specialize in managing multiple electronic distribution channels for hotels. The various players in the electronic distribution of hotel rooms are shown in Fig. 9.1.

Managing this complexity of distribution paths also requires understanding the search engines behind the systems. What determines the results of an online hotels search in a search engine such as Google or Bing? Searches often favor the aggregators and OTAs over the hotel itself (Beldona and Cobanoglu, 2007), whereas the hotel prefers direct bookings. As hotel managers struggle with the right balance of distribution channels, chain hotels are advised to build a strong CRS system that can connect with new distribution options as they emerge (O'Connor and Frew, 2002).

Travelers can use mobile devices to book accommodation, making it essential for hotels to design their own mobile apps. For example, InterContinental Hotels Group reported mobile revenues of US$330 million in 2012, accounting for 9.7% of online revenues, while Choice Hotels International stated that mobile bookings accounted for 13% of its online sales (Grant, 2013). Mobile apps by OTAs and metasearch engines are popular, and one in five mobile bookings come from tablets. Hotels such as Shangri-La, Marriott, Hyatt and Intercontinental Hotels have their own integrated platform apps, which travelers can use to search and book hotels, and access their frequent stay accounts. They are increasing call volume at their reservation sites as travelers call in bookings after using the app.

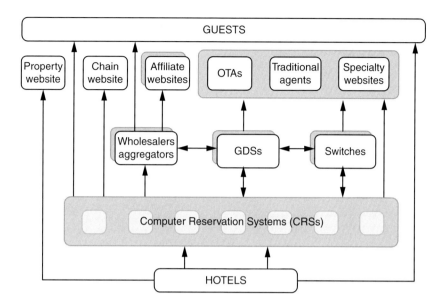

Fig. 9.1. Electronic hotel room distribution (adapted from: Carroll and Siguaw, 2003).

Electronic word-of-mouth (eWOM) and user-generated content (UGC) are strongly influencing online hotel reservations (Hills and Cairncross, 2011). Almost 80% of US customers use UGC websites to inform their accommodation choices (Gretzel, 2006), perhaps because they are more up-to-date than information provided by hotels themselves. The accommodation reviews found on OTAs and user-generated sites also add value. The importance and accuracy of customer reviews suggests that hotels should link their sites to the various review sites.

Hotels using email to communicate with their clients should seek their permission first. This is called **permission based email marketing**, which requires prior guest permission before sending personalized emails about products, special rates and promotional packages (see Chapter 4). The title of the email is important and can influence whether the email is opened. Building loyalty through this type of email can increase repeat guests

(Miller, 2004). Emails can also go in the other direction. Travelers often use email to contact hotels with questions about their stay, however studies have shown that most hotels, whatever the rating, do not respond to email queries, particularly in the busy season (Schegg *et al.*, 2003; Matzler *et al.*, 2005). This is an area for hotel managers to attend to as email is an important way for travelers to communicate with hotels.

Customer relationship management

Details of guests' consumption patterns and preferences are recorded in the **guest history** module. This enhances marketing activities, facilitates future reservations and customizes guests' future visits by informing staff about individual needs and preferences. For example, the housekeeping department can be informed that a guest requires a non-allergenic pillow or that it is her birthday. When guest history databases are used throughout the chain, a guest can be given the same personal service in any property in the chain. Ideally customer relationship management (CRM) occurs before guests arrive, during their stay and after they depart. It helps to focus employees on personalization and customer retention, and generate the right attitudes and commitment. However, care must be taken to ensure that guest information is not misused. Issues of online consumer privacy are important as hotels use IT to connect with their customers (O'Connor, 2007). True CRM in hospitality, however, goes beyond a PMS guest history database and demands a broader knowledge-based approach requiring a hotel culture where every customer interaction is perceived as a learning experience and each customer contact as a knowledge-building opportunity (Sigala, 2005).

Guest room amenities

The comfort, enjoyment and security of the guest room can be significantly enhanced by IT. In fact IT amenities can effect overall guest satisfaction and the likelihood of repeat visits (Cobanoglu *et al.*, 2011). Guest room amenities include electronic locking systems, guest entertainment and information systems, and guest service technology such as electronic refrigerators, in-room safes and guest room offices. Applications in each of these categories are discussed below.

Safety and security

Electronic locking systems (ELS) increase the safety and security of guests, by removing illegal entry into the guest room and illegal duplication of keys. Indeed, many meeting planners, government travelers and corporations require hotels to be equipped with electronic locks before they consider booking with the

hotel. Hotels pay significantly lower insurance premiums when electronic locks are installed, since fewer claims are expected.

ELS can have different designs and configurations. In each case they consist of a central computer console, a key-making device, and keys that are encoded for each new guest. The central computer stores codes, which are placed together with pertinent guest information on to the electronic key. The most common encoding methods include the use of punched cards, magnetic strips, radio-frequency identification (RFID) chips or smartcards. When the key is inserted in the door lock, if it matches the door code, the door is unlocked. Inside the door, a solenoid for the magnetic keys, and light beams for the punched keys, check the accuracy of the code. The computer also monitors all entries and exits into each room (both guest rooms and other spaces) so that security breaches can be tracked.

ELS can be either micro-fitted or hard-wired, each using a different technique to match the lock and key codes before the door is opened. **Micro-fitted** systems require a microprocessor in the door lock to store a sequence of entry codes. **Hard-wired systems** require cabling or radio transmission between the door lock and the computer so that the code can be transmitted to the door via Group Controller Units (GCUs) from the key-making device at the front desk. Electronic locks may control access to common areas for guest use only such as the spa or health facility. Cleaners and other service people have keys permitting them access to the rooms their job requires. Figure 9.2 shows a diagram of a hard-wired electronic locking system.

Numerous other benefits come from ELS. They can be used as point-of-sale verification in hotel restaurants, by ensuring that guests are actually in-house before meals are billed to their room. Hard-wired systems can also be used to update room status. After the staff have cleaned the room, the key in the door lock transmits the room status change to the PMS. Electronic locking systems can also work in conjunction with an energy management system (EMS).

New methods of ensuring security are being tested. The use of the guest's credit card for door entry is one method. The code is taken from the credit card and put into the computer and the door lock. Systems, however, must account for multiple occupancies, and this may be a problem with credit cards as keys. Smartphones can also be used for secure access to guest rooms. For example, Samsung's Galaxy S3 has been tested in a Holiday Inn in the UK to unlock doors, control lighting and act as an in-room phone extension.

Biometric methods of identifying guests and providing access to guest rooms and other spaces are also being tested. Examples of these technologies are: finger-printing, eye retina, face recognition, hand geometry and palm print scanning, voice recognition and signature recognition. These biometric methods easily identify a guest without them carrying any card or key with them. They are used to open guest room doors and to enhance security in general. Finger-printing is the most common with hand geometry the next most common, but cost issues keep many hotels from investing in biometric systems (Bilgihan *et al.*, 2013). Research shows that some hotel guests react favorably to biometric systems (Morosan, 2012) although some may find it unacceptable to give their unique fingerprint or voiceprint etc. to a hotel. The systems can also be used to track employees in their work and to reduce their need to remember passwords and codes to access parts of the hotel. Safety for guests' property is provided by electronic safes in the guest room.

Guest information and entertainment devices

Business travelers expect to remain electronically connected in a hotel and the three most

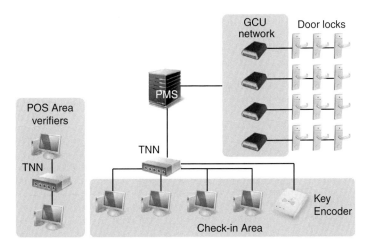

Fig. 9.2. Hardware configuration for an electronic locking system. TNN, terminal node network; GCU, group controller unit; POS, point of sale; PMS, property management system.

important in-room IT devices for them are: enough conveniently located jacks and plugs to charge their portable devices; satellite/cable television; and WiFi or high-speed Internet access (Chan, 2004). Even though most hotels provide Internet access for guests, charges are applied for different guest categories, although it is likely that soon it will be free (Beldona and Cobanoglu, 2007). Strong WiFi signals for hotel guests and the hotel's operation are as critical as electricity in the room. Guests carrying three or four mobile devices expect fast WiFi connectivity often for multiple devices at the same time. Hotels can provide good WiFi capability by including WiFi routers in every room or add it as a feature to the TV box. Sometimes guests bring their own router with them. The Aloft Hotel in Bangkok gives guests a smartphone on check-in, which can connect them in the hotel and around town at no extra cost.

A range of entertainment and information services such as satellite programing, on-demand videos and movies, and video games are provided through high-definition TVs in the room. A central computer system monitors the usage of these services and automatically bills guests through a PMS interface. The TV can also act as a computer monitor allowing guests to retrieve information such as their bill. Guests can then check themselves out with the TV remote control. They can also complete customer satisfaction surveys, order room service or bellman service, and view voicemail messages on screen through the TV set. The guest room TV is a central information and entertainment device, but the merging of TV, computer and smartphone technology is also occurring. There are numerous interactive possibilities between guests' personal devices, such as TV controls, the locking system and in-room controls.

Hotels are also placing iPads in hotel rooms to provide guests with information. This removes the need for the traditional leather binder and the US$300–500 printing cost. For example, the Four Seasons Hotel in Beverly Hills, Los Angeles has installed iPads in all guest rooms, which are used to order in-room dining, request housekeeping, check the bill, book spa services and sometimes even control the room lights. The cost of installation is balanced by increases in room service and other sales. Also the iPads are secured in the room and if found missing US$800 is charged to the guest's bill. The concierge helps hotel guests with local information, but this function is also being replaced with IT. Tablets can be loaded with local information and given to guests to search for themselves.

Guest services technology

Enhancement of the guest experience is the overriding concern when deciding which technologies to install. However, benefits from guest services technologies also include increased efficiency, ease of guest room maintenance and reduction of labor costs.

Two examples of **guest services technology** are the provision of food and drink in the hotel refrigerator, and room service. IT brings efficiency in the form of in-room electronic refreshment centers. Electronic refrigerators monitor daily consumption and send charges directly to the guest folio. These refrigerators contain an electronic sensor below each item, a microprocessor to store price and inventory data, and a connection to a central computer. When the item is removed, the sensor notifies the microprocessor of the items consumed and their prices. This information is then transmitted either via radio waves or cable to the central computer, which in turn communicates it to the guest folio in the PMS. The sales data for all guest room usage can predict future demand for the various products. The system also tracks the inventory of items in the refrigerators so that replenishment can be done efficiently, and ordering is facilitated.

Room service can also be improved in two ways with technology. First, guests can order room service on their mobile devices or the room TV, a special benefit for guests who do not speak the local language well. Also **smart room service carts** containing a microchip can minimize the sight of unappetizing trays of food in corridors, and guest disturbance by housekeeping to collect the tray. When the used food tray is placed outside the room, the microchip alerts housekeepers to collect it immediately.

Hotel communications

Telecommunication needs in the accommodation sector include the transmission of voice, data and images both within the hotel and with the outside world. Specialized equipment, broadband networks, WiFi and fiber optic cabling are necessary to ensure that multimedia communication services such as videoconferencing can be offered to guests. Computerized telephone switches, multiple function phones (including cellular phones), cabling that can accommodate voice, data and image transmission are needed. This section discusses the computer systems that facilitate voice and data communications in a hotel, called **private branch exchanges (PBX)** and **call accounting systems (CAS)**.

Private branch exchange (PBX)

Call switching between hotel guests, hotel employees and the outside world used to be done mechanically with a device referred to as a "spaghetti board". The operator inserted a plug into the socket connecting the caller to the party being called. For an outside line the connection was made to the telephone company operator. "Spaghetti boards" were soon replaced by private branch exchanges (PBXs), which control the connections of hotel telephone calls to the outside world for guests and employees (see Fig. 9.3).

There are two types of PBXs: the electromechanical (analog) PBX and the electronic (digital) PBX. Digital PBXs are now in common use and provide additional features over analog PBXs such as voicemail, automatic wakeup calls, room status updates through the phone, and guest name recognition. Voicemail provides a more efficient way for callers to leave messages, and is a particular benefit for hotels with international or conference clientele. Messages can be

Fig. 9.3. Analog telephone switch PBX (source: Seattle Municipal Archives, 2008).

picked up in the caller's language and fewer telephone operators are needed. Automatic wake-up calls can be handled by a digital PBX. The guest's wake-up call details are entered through the telephone by the guest, and are stored in the PBX until the time of the call. Both of these features reduce labor costs. An example of a hotel digital PBX system is shown in Fig. 9.4.

Some digital PBXs also provide a guest name recognition feature. This displays the name of the guest who is calling the telephone operator or hotel staff and, due to an interface with the PMS, permits the hotel staff to address the guest by name. Automated room status updates by housekeepers from the guest room phone to the PMS are also possible when a digital PBX is interfaced with the PMS. A digital PBX can be used for data communication between the PMS terminals and PCs. Guest mobile phones have reduced the volume of calls going through a PBX, and Voice over Internet (VoIP) is now an option for hotels to route their calls in a less expensive manner.

Call accounting system (CAS)

Tracking guest calls and billing them to the guest folio is an important task. Call Accounting Systems (CASs) allow the hotel to route and track calls without using the local telephone company. Using a CAS, hotels can substantially increase their revenues, since they need no longer pay the telephone company for their charge tracking services. Toll-free, credit card and collect calls are also a revenue source for the hotel. CASs track call activity with a feature known as **Station Message Detail Recording (SMDR)**. This feature records the duration of the call, the number called, the extension dialed from and the cost of the call. It does this in one of two ways. Either the "time-out" method, in which the number is dialed and a certain time elapses (30–90 seconds) before the CAS commences billing (whether or not the connection is made) or the "answer detection" method, which ensures that only answered calls are recorded. Another feature of a CAS is Least Cost Routing (LCR), which chooses the lowest cost carrier for all hotel phone calls.

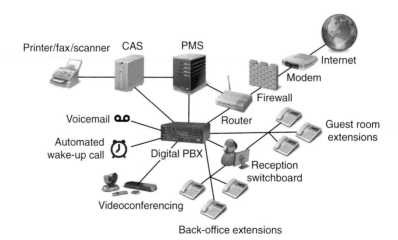

Fig. 9.4. Example of a digital PBX system.

Energy management systems

Technology to reduce energy consumption is readily embraced by most hotel managers as energy costs are a significant cost item and are increasing (typically US$2000 per room per year). Some energy management systems (EMSs) reduce hotel energy costs by up to 65% (Kapiki, 2010) and also help the environment. Some 87% of hotel managers agree that efficient energy management increases hotel profits, and 53% agree that tourists select their accommodation based on the hotel's environmental image (Zografakis *et al.*, 2011). Websites such as bookdifferent.com show consumers the hotels' green awards representing their energy efficiency. Also Travelocity has its Green Hotel Directory.

Energy is consumed in hotels through heating, air-conditioning, hot water heating, lighting, elevators and cooking. Intelligent EMSs monitor, control and optimize energy consumption in the hotel. For example, an EMS can connect to the ELS to determine when the room is occupied, thereby automatically adjusting air conditioning, lighting and heating. Intelligent thermostats connected to the room occupancy sensor adjust the temperature of the room to either "occupied" or "unoccupied". When the guest leaves the room, all power is cut off or reduced to a background level. When they return, insertion of their card key into a slot in the room activates the electrical power. Infra-red body scanners connected to the electronic doorbell which silently scan the space to detect body heat are another energy-saving technology. In some hotels, guests can use their mobile devices to choose in-room temperatures. Other integrated guest room management systems provide electronic bedside control panels for lights, TV, air conditioning, "do not disturb" signs, heating and the movement of the drapes.

Interfaces between property management systems and other systems

Many specialized computer systems enhance hotel information processing by connecting with the PMS. Information transferred rapidly to the PMS from the interfaced system without manual input reduces labor costs, increases accuracy and timeliness of the data transferred, and minimizes unpaid guest bills due to slow information transfer prior to checkout. For example, the restaurant point-of-sale system can be interfaced with the PMS to instantly post restaurant charges to guest folios. The ELS is efficient if interfaced to the PMS. Interfaces with guest room electronic devices, hotel telephone systems, energy management systems and credit card verification systems are other examples of valuable PMS interfaces.

Interfaces bring technical complexity to the hotel. Compatible hardware, software and communications protocols must be installed to establish connections. Also a higher skill level is required of the IT staff to manage day-to-day running of these interfaces. Smooth operations require cooperation between the PMS vendors and the vendors of the system to be interfaced, particularly in the event of data transfer problems. Figure 9.5 shows the variety of systems that can be interfaced to a PMS.

A PMS can run on different hardware platforms and software environments depending

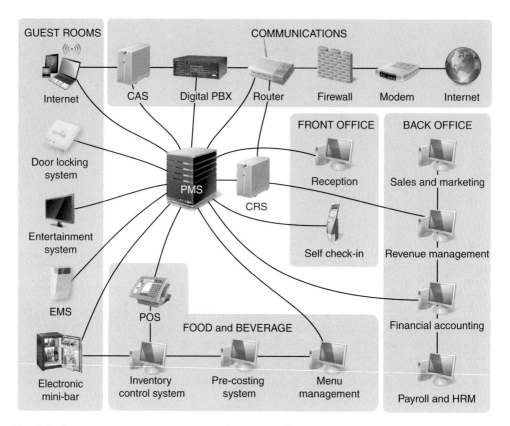

Fig. 9.5. Property management system (PMS) interfaces.

on the size and type of accommodation and the requirements of the installation. Traditionally PMS hardware was installed at the property, and owned and maintained by the accommodation provider or a computer provider. More recent PMSs are hosted online, requiring no installation of server hardware or software at the property. The next section discusses the strengths and weaknesses of each type of installation.

Server-based or web-based PMS

The **server-based PMS** requires a financial investment upfront and IT staff to support the system. If this option is chosen, it is usually a **turnkey system** (a package of hardware, software, training support and maintenance) sold by an **application service provider (ASP)**. The large number of vendors of turnkey systems makes the task of choosing a system difficult. Some of these vendors are international and provide their software in multiple languages. Others are country specific, particularly in Asia where the character sets are different. To identify the best vendor for a particular hotel, careful research must be done or a specialized consultant can assist with this choice. In very unique cases the PMS may be designed in-house. This only occurs for either very specialized or very large companies.

Web-based PMSs offer the same functionality as in-house systems but are housed on the web and require fast Internet connections. Upfront costs are lower as there is no purchase or installation cost, but there are monthly costs for accessing the system. Web-based systems require less IT staff than server-based options, and are also accessible to staff in case of emergencies out of hours or when off-property. Another advantage is that the vendor is responsible for data backup and software upgrades. In server-based systems this is usually the responsibility of the hotel and the PMS vendor.

Kasavana and Cahill (2011) provide a thorough description of issues involved in system choice and subsequent agreements with vendors. They suggest an evaluation method to choose between vendors and systems. This matrix method weights the desired functions and gives scores to each vendor's product. If a server-based system is chosen, it can be either purchased or leased. Purchasing is more common, but leasing removes concern about the technology becoming outdated. Installation is the vendor's responsibility in cooperation with the hotel's management, and requires the initialization of many parameters, such as room types, rates and other codes before it can become operational. Ongoing training ensures maximum effectiveness and job satisfaction for employees. When the new installation replaces a manual system or an old computer system, a transitional phase is needed. **Parallel conversion** in which the old and new systems run together for a few weeks is recommended over the more risky **direct cut-over conversion** in which the old system is turned off when the new one is turned on.

The failure of a hotel's server-based computer system can create havoc. Therefore, having **redundant PMS hardware** in which two identical machines run side by side can help mitigate such problems. One runs the PMS while the other performs less critical tasks such as back-office applications. If the first computer fails, the other automatically switches over to run the PMS. Critical data and programs should be stored off-site so that they are recoverable in the event of a hotel fire, flood or other disaster.

In the case of web-based PMSs, the concerns mentioned above are not the responsibility of the hotel and this reduces the risk involved. Table 9.1 summarizes the differences between the server-based and web-based PMS.

In summary, there are many IT systems that allow accommodation providers to do a better job of satisfying guests and lowering costs. Even though the section has focused heavily on hotels, other accommodation facilities such as motels, campsites, hostels and bed-and-breakfasts typically use similar functions but a smaller subset of the functionality.

IT APPLICATIONS IN THE FOOD SERVICE SECTOR

Foodservice operations, whether they are part of a hotel or independent, quick service or table service, commercial or institutional, have specific IT needs. This section describes the applications common to most foodservice establishments. Point-of-sale (POS) systems are the most popular applications and increase the efficiency of food delivery and track and analyze sales. Restaurant management systems and back-office systems which control, monitor and analyze food production and menus are also common. Some restaurants and cafes also use customers' mobile devices to transmit data and influence buying behavior.

Table 9.1. Comparison of server-based and web-based PMS (source: http://www.webrezpro.com/).

	Server-based PMS	Web-based PMS
Hardware requirements	Workstation/s (PC), data server, additional back-up servers, operating systems, back-up hard drives.	Workstation/s (PC) and Internet connection.
System deployment and user access	PMS software and data reside in the hotel's computer. The program is installed on each PC from which the PMS will be accessed.	PMS software and data reside on shared servers at the vendor's data center. Users access the system through a web browser, anywhere, anytime.
System and data security and maintenance	Responsibility of the property management.	Responsibility of the PMS vendor, including data back-up. On-property staff are responsible for the Internet connection and PCs.
On-site IT expertise required?	Yes.	No.
Budget/pricing structure	Upfront licensing fee and annual fee for the software. Hardware and IT infrastructure costs also. Capital expenditure.	Subscription charges – usually monthly. Operating expenditure.
Remote access and central reservations functionality	Possible but requires additional hardware and network set-up, or system compatibility.	Yes.
Software upgrades	Additional expenses.	Free.

Point-of-sale systems

A **point-of-sale (POS)** system improves the efficiency of food delivery from kitchen to table and assists in analyzing sales of menu items (Kasavana and Cahill, 2011). POS hardware includes a network of order-entry terminals, cashier stations, manager workstations and printers. There may also be connections for credit card authorization, and uploading of sales data to a central location. An example POS configuration is shown in Fig. 9.6. For many years POS hardware were proprietary and uniquely designed for the foodservice environment, but now POS systems run on PC-based hardware with open operating systems, increasing their ease of use.

Order-entry terminals can be either micro-motion keyboards, touchscreen terminals, handheld terminals or tablets. Handheld devices connect to the processing unit using WiFi and are particularly useful where order entry terminals cannot be connected such as poolside or patio dining. To improve the food delivery system, remote printers or video displays installed in food preparation areas deliver orders electronically to the kitchen without delay, in readable form, and without staff entering the kitchen. Printers print guest bills and reports

for management. Digital menus displayed on tablets tableside allow guests to input their own food order.

POS software analyzes sales, forecasts demand and also performs **pre-costing**. Pre-costing is the determination of the cost of a menu based on food and labor costs, and is particularly useful for banquets and other large functions. **Menu engineering** is an example of software that analyses the sales data in the POS system for decision-making purposes. This menu analysis helps a restaurant to determine whether a particular item should remain on the menu, and the optimum price for each item based on an analysis of sales and food cost. Frequent diner tracking is another module of the POS software. For hotel restaurants, a PMS interface provides the immediate posting of a guest's restaurant charges to their folio. It also allows the hotel restaurant to check that the guest is a resident

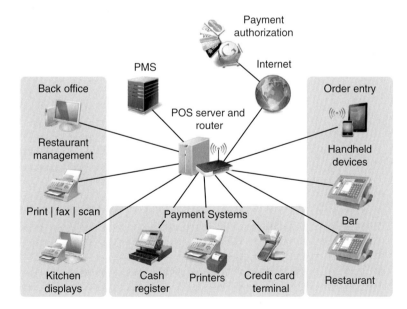

Fig. 9.6. Foodservice IT applications.

(by using the electronic key) before billing the meal to their room.

Restaurant management systems

There are many other functions to be automated in the operation and management of a foodservice establishment. These include the purchasing and inventory control of food items, menu and recipe control, and food costing. Purchasing and inventory control systems track the items on order, details of suppliers, inventory on-hand, and minimum par level so that ordering can be automated. **e-Procurement systems**, which electronically assist the restaurant in procuring its supplies, are common today (Sigala, 2006). Online connections to suppliers transmit standard orders electronically. Menu and recipe management software, which creates files for each recipe and menu item, permit an analysis of the impacts of changes of ingredient costs, ingredient quantities and price changes. Food cost percentages can be calculated with these systems, which then form the basis for the pre-costing of menus and events.

Separate systems called **restaurant management systems (RMS)** handle these functions. They are usually PC-based systems interfaced with the POS for maximum benefit. Such an interface allows **perpetual inventory** of food ingredients to be maintained. When the POS system registers the sale of an item, its component ingredients are calculated and transmitted to the RMS where the food inventory amount is subtracted from the quantity on hand. Automated beverage control systems which control the dispensing of beverages and the analysis of sales are another use of IT in the bar environment.

Marketing and customer relations

Consumers increasingly use online reviews when choosing restaurants. A study conducted by the National Restaurant Association found that almost half of young adults between the ages of 18 and 34 use the Internet to search for new restaurants whereas only one-third of older adults (between 45 and 64) did so (Ong, 2012). There are many mobile apps to assist consumers in finding restaurants in their locale. Examples include UrbanSpoon, Where to Eat, Restaurant Finder, Fast Food, Nearby Food and Yelp. These are important for tourists unfamiliar with local restaurants. The volume of online consumer reviews is positively associated with the online popularity of restaurants, whereas editor reviews have a negative relationship with consumers' intention to visit a restaurant's webpage (Zhang *et al.*, 2010). Managers can learn a great deal by strategically using these sites to understand how the dining experience can be improved.

Cafes and coffee shops are capitalizing on IT and social media to increase their revenues. In addition to POS systems and supply chain management systems, bar codes are used on wrapped food-to-go items, making the sales transaction faster. Starbucks is a heavy user of IT and gives laptops to store managers to access cloud-based collaboration tools. In 2011 it developed a CRM system, and has developed a mobile app called Starbucks Card Mobile Application, which allows customers to make payments on their smartphones, check the balance on their loyalty card and reload the card using their credit card. Many cafes also offer free WiFi to their customers.

STRATEGIC MANAGEMENT OF INFORMATION TECHNOLOGY SYSTEMS IN HOSPITALITY

The strategic management of hospitality enterprises using IT has been limited and deserves more attention (Cobanoglu *et al.*, 2006). Hotel managers tend to spend time on tactical and operational issues and not enough on strategic decision-making and visionary tasks (Pilepic and Simunic, 2009). While the PMS and POS databases provide a wealth of real-time information to better understand their operations, hotel managers may feel hindered to use IT due to the fear of fast-changing technology (Chan, 2004). An ongoing challenge for executives is to glean the critical information for effective strategic decision-making (Law and Giri, 2005).

Hospitality managers are encouraged to understand and use knowledge management to improve performance and service. Knowledge management systems such as **Expert Information Systems (EISs)** and **Decision Support Systems (DSSs)** bring higher levels of intelligence to IT systems and can help managers use technology more strategically. An example of a DSS is a revenue management system that determines the best rates, when to overbook and which rates will maximize yield or revenue. Forecasting modules that are critical to revenue management systems use historical data from the PMS and analyze demand, examine market conditions and generate forecasting modules. Predicted demand is then compared with inventory and availability (either actual or projected) and room rates are generated.

IT can stimulate innovation in the hospitality industry, which will be necessary for hotels to compete in the future. Innovation can come through service innovation, servicescape innovation, technological innovation and others. Technological innovation is seen as one of the strongest paths for innovation for hotels (Jacob and Groizard, 2007; Hertog *et al.*, 2011).

The human resource aspect is strategically important for hotels, as the fast turnover of employees can be a problem for innovation and developing strategic knowledge management. Finding staff with sufficient knowledge of key technologies is a challenge. Ideally IT can help to transform service workers into knowledge workers (Hallin and Marnburg, 2008). Knowledge executives, team circles and knowledge information systems are all needed in a successful hospitality enterprise. Enhancing the individual technological knowledge of hotel employees can be done either on-site or with virtual learning (Bray, 2002).

The application of robotics to hospitality can replace tedious repetitive tasks leaving employees freer to provide guest service. The Industry Insight box below describes a luggage robotic application. This post-Internet age requires managers to understand the relevance of education, experience, globalization capabilities, networking and creativity to be competitive. Hospitality enterprises are encouraged to have a bigger vision of the future and a sense that they can mold the future (Garrigos-Simon *et al.*, 2008).

Industry Insight: Baggage Handling Robots

As the hospitality industry increasingly faces labor shortages, computer technology can sometimes provide a substitute. Robotic technology is being tested for various hotel functions. Robots are devices with intelligence, mobility and manipulation abilities. Some examples of their use in hospitality enterprises are: changing sheets on beds, dishwashing and other cleaning functions, food preparation and luggage handling.

An interesting application of a robot to handle luggage is being used at the Yotel Hotel in New York City, USA. Yobot (Fig. 9.7) is a 15-foot tall automated luggage handling robot, which automatically stores bags for guests and retrieves them when ready. Guests place their belongings to be stored in front of Yobot, who then puts them in one of the 150 available bins pictured above. The guest enters a PIN number and their last name, and Yobot stores their bags safely. Yobot will print a receipt, which is needed for guests to recover their belongings. When the guest is ready to collect their baggage, Yobot scans the bar code on the guest receipt, using the PIN number and last name. It then automatically locates the baggage, picks it up and delivers it to the guest. This robot saves human labor on a repetitive, mundane and potentially dangerous task – the kind that robots fit into well.

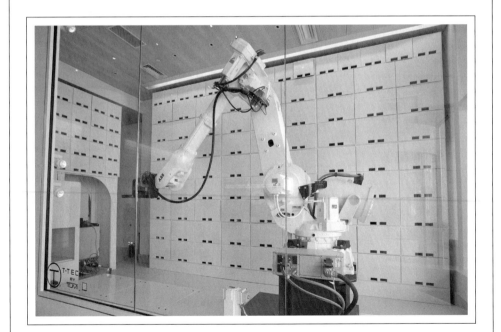

Fig. 9.7 Yobot the Robot.

Source: Jacoby (2012)

SUMMARY

This chapter has examined the use of IT in the hospitality sector. Its initial lag in IT use behind other travel sectors is starting to be overcome. But hospitality remains essentially a "high touch" service-based industry requiring the judicious use of technology. Experience has shown, however, that the appropriate use of technology can increase efficiency, so that more human and financial resources can be funneled into personal service and more satisfied guests. The Internet, social media and mobile technology are providing new opportunities for hotels to connect with customers. Faced with human resource challenges, hospitality must redefine its use of technology to substitute for labor but also raise hospitality jobs to higher levels, and turn hospitality employees into knowledge workers. To gain a competitive edge, hospitality managers must creatively apply the technology and the knowledge it provides. If they can turn data into real knowledge to improve decision-making and customer satisfaction, they are likely to succeed in the future.

KEY TERMS

application service provider (ASP), back-office, call accounting system (CAS), channel manager, decision support system (DSS), direct cut-over conversion, e-procurement systems, electronic locking systems, energy management system (EMS), expert information system (EIS), front-office, guest folio, guest history module, guest service technology, hard-wired, integrated property system (IPS), menu management, micro-fitted, night audit, order-entry terminals, parallel conversion, Payment Card Industry Data Security Standard (PCI-DSS), point-of-sale (POS), pre-costing, private branch exchange (PBX), property management systems (PMS), reservations module, restaurant management systems, revenue management system (RMS), rooms management module, self-service check-in, server-based PMS, Station Message Detail Recording (SMDR), switch, Travel Agency Commission Settlement (TACS), web-based PMS

DISCUSSION QUESTIONS

1. If you were the manager of a campsite in a national park with 30 cabins of different sizes and one restaurant, what functionality would you want from a PMS? Describe the kinds of technology that would be appropriate for this kind of lodging. Which channels would you use to sell your cabins? Why?

2. Explore the website of an international chain hotel and one of an independently owned and operated hotel. Compare and contrast the two sites.

3. Describe all the ways that a restaurant or cafe could use mobile apps and technology to relate to its customers.

4. Visit a local restaurant and find out all you can about their POS and other technical applications.

5. Identify as many hotel booking websites as you can. Choose one hotel that you would like to visit and investigate how it is presented on all the various sites. Visit TripAdvisor and read some of the reviews for the hotel. What conclusions can you draw from this investigation?

6. OTAs have caused many hotels to lose control of their inventory and pricing, and this has eroded not only profitability but also brand equity. Unlike hotels, airlines have not suffered from the same problems. Why are the airlines in a different position? If you were a hotelier, what strategies would you use to overcome this problem?

USEFUL WEBSITES

QR code	Website	Description
	Hospitality Information Technology Association (HITA) http://www.hospitalitynet.org/ organization/17001886.html	HITA advances interactions between IT educators, IT vendors and IT users.
	Hotel Electronic Distribution Network Association (HEDNA) http://www.hedna.org/	HEDNA's goal is to advance hospitality distribution through collaboration and knowledge sharing.
	Pegasus Solutions http://www.pegs.com/	The website of Pegasus, the largest processor of electronic hotel transactions and distribution.
	Booking.com http://www.booking.com/ organization/17001886.html	An online hotel booking site.
	WebRezPro http://www.webrezpro.com/	An example of a cloud PMS system.

QR code	Website	Description
	Silverbyte Systems http://www.silverbyte.com/	An example of a vendor of computer systems for all types of lodging including youth hostels, hotels and cruise-ships.

Case Study: Marriott Hotels

Marriott International, Inc. is a leading lodging company headquartered in Maryland, USA, with over 3800 properties in 72 countries with 325,000 employees. The company operates and franchises hotels, and licenses vacation ownership resorts under 18 brands, including Marriott Hotels, The Ritz-Carlton, JW Marriott, Bulgari, EDITION, Renaissance, Gaylord Hotels, Autograph Collection, AC Hotels by Marriott, Courtyard, Fairfield Inn and Suites, SpringHill Suites, Residence Inn, TownePlace Suites, Marriott Executive Apartments, Marriott Vacation Club, Grand Residences by Marriott and The Ritz-Carlton Destination Club. Marriott is an innovator in applying IT to hotel operations.

Marriott International's Vice President of Global PMS oversees all the PMS operations worldwide. Standardization is important for the chain and one system is used in all properties – the Micros Opera PMS. Each hotel can choose features that uniquely match its requirements. With its geographically diverse operations, its website needed to operate in many languages to facilitate usage by travelers and employees. Therefore their strategic IT plan included local-language content in a cost-effective manner for each website. To do this they used a third-party translation management system which translates 1.4 million words into multiple languages.

Marriott has added mobile check-in for members of its Rewards program. Guests can check-in with their mobile device up to 2 hours before arrival, receive automatic notifications when the room is ready and experience enhanced service at the Mobile Check-in desk where the room key is waiting.

It also required internationalizing the Marriott.com web application and back-end Marriott systems (Accenture, 2013). Marriott was one of the first to establish a website in the lodging industry, and between 2003 and 2006 it rapidly expanded its web presence.

With so many brands and hotels, Marriott changed its corporate marketing practices to support individual brands and hotels' marketing. To do this an online portal was created in 2007 to manage the marketing collateral, and to support the company's new brand standards. The portal is called BrandWorks and allows individual properties and brands

(Continued)

Case Study. Continued.

to create customized marketing materials using the brand guidelines, templates and stock photographs on the portal. Also, much content is available in multiple languages. BrandWorks has been successful in diversifying marketing programs across the chain and content on the site is growing. It is also effective at tailoring marketing and special offers to Marriott Rewards members, which represent 60% of their revenue (Excella Consulting, 2013).

Marriott is acutely aware of the impact of social media on lodging options, uses Facebook and Twitter extensively while also developing new social media strategies for its brands. Bill Marriott himself has had his own blog since 2007. Marriott has its own YouTube page and a special social media community for its Marriott Awards insiders. In 2011 they released a My Marriott Hotel social game, where users can manage different parts of a Marriott hotel. It was designed to excite the Millennial age group about a career in hospitality.

Marriott recently studied the ways in which video is changing the lives of travelers and reported that hotels must embrace customers and employees as co-creators of content. It also found that great advertising is experiential not transactional, and that hotel marketers should design for serendipitous discovery.

In summary, Marriott International is using many IT applications to manage a huge hotel chain efficiently, and satisfy customers at its unique brands and locations.

Study Questions

1. Explore Marriott's social media presence. Compare and contrast it to a similar international hotel chain such as Hyatt or Accor or Starwood.

2. Research the various computer systems (discussed in this chapter) that are used in the Ritz-Carlton brand and the Fairfield Inn and Suites brand. Which systems are integrated? What do you notice about the difference in the IT usage? Can you explain this difference?

REFERENCES

Accenture (2013) Marriott International: Web Content Optimization. Available at: http://www.accenture.com/us-en/Pages/success-marriott-international-web-services-platform-full.aspx/ (accessed 15 November 2013).

Anckar, B. and Walden, P. (2001) Self-booking of high- and low-complexity travel products: exploratory findings. *Information Technology and Tourism* 4(3/4), 151–165.

Athey, S. (2011) Use of the world wide web by the Portuguese accommodation industry. *Information Technology and Tourism* 13(3), 191–204. doi: 10.3727/109830512x13283928066832

Au, N. and Ekiz, E.H. (2009) Issues and opportunities of Internet hotel marketing in developing countries. *Journal of Travel and Tourism Marketing* 26(3), 225–243. doi: 10.1080/10548400902925106

Beldona, S. and Cobanoglu, C. (2007) Importance-performance analysis of guest technologies in the lodging industry. *Cornell Hotel and Restaurant Administration Quarterly* 48(3), 299–312. doi: 10.1177/0010880407304023

Bilgihan, A., Karadag, E., Cobanoglu, C. and Okumus, F. (2013) Biometric technology applications and trends in hotels. *Hospitality Review* 31(2), 1–24.

Bray, J. (2002) Virtual tutoring in hospitality - a "learnt system" of professional practice. *International Journal of Contemporary Hospitality Management* 14(1), 21–27. doi: 10.1108/09596110210415088

Buhalis, D. and Law, R. (2008) Progress in information technology and tourism management: 20 years on and 10 years after the Internet - the state of eTourism research. *Tourism Management* 29(4), 609–623.

Carroll, B. and Siguaw, J. (2003) The evolution of electronic distribution: effects on hotels and intermediaries. *Cornell Hotel and Restaurant Administration Quarterly* 44(4), 38–50. doi: 10.1016/s0010-8804(03)90257-6

Chan, E. (2004) An analysis of the gap in the perceptions of hotel marketing managers and business travelers regarding information technology facilities in hotel guestrooms in Hong Kong. *Tourism Review International* 8(1), 17–31. doi: 10.3727/154427204774809538

Chan, S. and Law, R. (2006) Automatic website evaluations: the case of hotels in Hong Kong. *Information Technology and Tourism* 8(3/4), 255–269. doi: 10.3727/109830506778690858

Chathoth, P.K. (2007) The impact of information technology on hotel operations, service management and transaction costs: a conceptual framework for full-service hotel firms. *International Journal of Hospitality Management* 26(2), 395–408. doi: 10.1016/j.ijhm.2006.03.004

Cobanoglu, C., Dede, P. and Poorani, A. (2006) An analysis of skills and competencies of full service hotel technology managers. *Journal of Teaching in Travel and Tourism* 6(4), 19–35.

Cobanoglu, C., Berezina, K., Kasavana, M.L. and Erdem, M. (2011) The impact of technology amenities on hotel guest overall satisfaction. *Journal of Quality Assurance in Hospitality and Tourism* 12(4), 272–288. doi: 10.1080/1528008x.2011.541842

Dube, L., Bel, J. le and Sears, D. (2003) From customer value to engineering pleasurable experiences in real life and online. *Cornell Hotel and Restaurant Administration Quarterly* 44(5/6), 124–130. doi: 10.1016/s0010-8804(03)90116-9

Essawy, M. (2006) Testing the usability of hotel websites: the springboard for customer relationship building. *Information Technology and Tourism* 8(1), 47–70. doi: 10.3727/109830506778193878

Excella Consulting, Inc. (2013) Case Study: Marriott International Brandworks - An Online Marketing Portal. Available at: http://www.excella.com/case-studies/marriott-international.aspx/ (accessed 13 December 2013).

Fisher, G. and Beatson, A. (2002) The impact of culture on self-service on technology adoption in the hotel industry. *International Journal of Hospitality and Tourism Administration* 3(3), 59–77. doi: 10.1300/J149v03n03_06

Fuchs, M., Scholochov, C. and Hopken, W. (2009) E-business adoption, use, and value creation: an Austrian hotel study. *Information Technology and Tourism* 11(4), 267–284.

Garrigos-Simon, F.J., Palacios-Marques, D. and Narangajavana, Y. (2008) Improving the perceptions of hotel managers. *Annals of Tourism Research* 35(2), 359–380. doi: 10.1016/j.annals.2007.08.002

Grant, M. (2013) Mobile, tablet apps could change industry. Available at: http://HotelNewsNow.com/Article/11006/Mobile-tablet-apps-could-change-industry (accessed 13 August 2013).

Green, C. and Lomanno, M. (2012) Distribution Channel Analysis: A Guide for Hotels. The American Hotel & Lodging Association (AH&LA) and STR special report. HSMAI Foundation, McLean, Virginia.

Gretzel, U. (2006) Consumer generated content - trends and implications for branding. *e-Review of Tourism Research* 4(3), 9–11.

Hallin, C.A. and Marnburg, E. (2008) Knowledge management in the hospitality industry: a review of empirical research. *Tourism Management* 29(2), 366–381. doi: 10.1016/j.tourman.2007.02.019

Ham, S., Kim, W.G. and Jeong, S.W. (2005) Effect of information technology on performance in upscale hotels. *International Journal of Hospitality Management* 24(2), 281–294. doi: 10.1016/j.ijhm.2004.06.010

Hashim, N.H., Scaglione, M. and Murphy, J. (2012) Modelling and comparing Malaysian hotel website diffusion. In: Fuchs, M., Ricci, F. and Cantoni, L (eds) *Information and Communication Technologies in Tourism 2012*. Proceedings of the International Conference in Helsingborg, Sweden, January 25–27, 2012.

Hertog, P. den, Gallouj, F. and Segers, J. (2011) Measuring innovation in a 'low-tech' service industry: the case of the Dutch hospitality industry. *Service Industries Journal* 31(9/10), 1429–1449. doi: 10.1080/02642060903576084

Hills, J.R. and Cairncross, G. (2011) Small accommodation providers and UGC web sites: perceptions and practices. *International Journal of Contemporary Hospitality Management* 23(1), 26–43. doi: 10.1108/09596111111101652

Ip, C., Leung, R. and Law, R. (2011) Progress and development of information and communication technologies in hospitality. *International Journal of Contemporary Hospitality Management* 23(4), 533–551. doi: 10.1108/09596111111130029

Jacob, M. and Groizard, J.L. (2007) Technology transfer and multinationals: the case of Balearic hotel chains' investments in two developing economies. *Tourism Management* 28(4), 976–992. doi: 10.1016/j.tourman.2006.08.013

Jacoby, R. (2012) Hotels of the future: a dozen high-tech options business travelers should love. Available at: http://www.bizjournals.com/bizjournals/blog/travel/2012/08/a-dozen-high-tech-hotel-options-we-love.html/ (accessed 2 January 2014).

Jeong, M., Oh, H. and Gregoire, M. (2003) Conceptualizing web site quality and its consequences in the lodging industry. *International Journal of Hospitality Management* 22(2), 161–175. doi: 10.1016/s0278-4319(03)00016-1

Kapiki, S. (2010) Energy management in hospitality: a study of Theesaloniki hotels. *Economics and Organization of Future Enterprises* 1, 78–97.

Karadag, E. and Dumanoglu, S. (2009) The productivity and competency of information technology in upscale hotels: the perception of hotel managers in Turkey. *International Journal of Contemporary Hospitality Management* 21(4), 479–490. doi: 10.1108/09596110910955712

Kasavana, M.L. and Cahill, J.J. (2011) *Managing Computers in the Hospitality Industry*, 6th edn. Educational Institute of the American Hotel and Lodging Association, Michigan.

Law, R. and Giri, J. (2005) A study of hotel information technology applications. *International Journal of Contemporary Hospitality Management* 17(2), 170–180. doi: 10.1108/09596110510582369

Law, R. and Hsu, C.H.C. (2005) Customers' perceptions on the importance of hotel web site dimensions and attributes. *International Journal of Contemporary Hospitality Management* 17(6), 493–503. doi: 10.1108/09596110510612130

Leung, R. and Law, R. (2012) *Hotel information exposure in cyberspace: the case of Hong Kong*. In: Fuchs, M., Ricci, F. and Cantoni, L (eds) *Information and Communication Technologies in Tourism 2012*. Proceedings of the International Conference in Helsingborg, Sweden, January 25–27, 2012. Springer, Vienna, pp. 132–142.

Lexhagen, M. (2004) The importance of value-added services to support the customer search and purchase process on travel websites. *Information Technology and Tourism* 7(2), 119–135.

Li, K.W. and Law, R. (2007) A novel English/Chinese information retrieval approach in hotel website searching. *Tourism Management* 28(3), 777–787. doi: 10.1016/j.tourman.2006.05.017

Matzler, K., Pechlaner, H., Abfalter, D. and Wolf, M. (2005) Determinants of response to customer e-mail enquiries to hotels: evidence from Austria. *Tourism Management* 26(2), 249–259. doi: 10.1016/j.tourman.2003.10.001

Miller, B. (2004) Building e-loyalty of lodging brands: avoiding brand erosion. *Journal of Travel and Tourism Marketing* 17(2/3), 133–142. doi: 10.1300/J073v17n02_11

Morosan, C. (2012) Theoretical and empirical considerations of guests' perceptions of biometric systems in hotels: extending the technology acceptance model. *Journal of Hospitality and Tourism Research* 36(1), 52–84. doi: 10.1177/1096348010380601

Murphy, H.C. (2004) The diversity of diffusion of information and communication technologies in the hospitality sector - building a contemporaneous model. *Information and Communication Technologies in Tourism* 11, 513–524.

O'Connor, P. (2007) Online consumer privacy: an analysis of hotel company behavior. *Cornell Hotel and Restaurant Administration Quarterly* 48(2), 183–200. doi: 10.1177/0010880407299541

O'Connor, P. and Frew, A.J. (2002) The future of hotel electronic distribution: expert and industry perspectives. *Cornell Hotel and Restaurant Administration Quarterly* 43(3), 33–45. doi: 10.1016/s0010-8804(02)80016-7

O'Connor, P. and Murphy, J. (2008) Hotel yield management practices across multiple electronic distribution channels. *Information Technology and Tourism* 10(2), 161–172. doi: 10.3727/109830508784913103

Ong, B.S. (2012) The perceived influence of user reviews in the hospitality industry. *Journal of Hospitality Marketing and Management* 21(5), 463–485. doi: 10.1080/19368623.2012.626743

Pilepic, L. and Simunic, M. (2009) Applying information technology to business decision-making in the hotel enterprises. *Economska Misao i Praksa* 18(2), 411–428.

Sayles, C.I. (1963). New York Hilton's data-processing system. *Cornell Hotel and Restaurant Quarterly*, 8(3), 41.

Schegg, R., Murphy, J. and Leuenberger, R. (2003) Five-star treatment? E-mail customer service by international luxury hotels. *Information Technology and Tourism* 6(2), 99–112. doi: 10.3727/109830503773048219

Seattle Municipal Archives (2008) Telephone operators, 1952. Available at: http://en.wikipedia.org/wiki/File:Telephone_operators,_1952.jpg/ (accessed on 5 January 2014).

Sigala, M. (2001) Modelling e-marketing strategies: Internet presence and exploitation of Greek hotels. *Journal of Travel and Tourism Marketing* 11(2/3), 83–103. doi: 10.1300/J073v11n02_05

Sigala, M. (2005) Integrating customer relationship management in hotel operations: managerial and operational implications. *International Journal of Hospitality Management* 24(3), 391–413.

Sigala, M. (2006) E-procurement diffusion in the supply chain of foodservice operators: an exploratory study in Greece. *Information Technology and Tourism* 8(2), 79–90. doi: 10.3727/109830506778001438

Sigala, M., Lockwood, A. and Jones, P. (2001) Strategic implementation and IT: gaining competitive advantage from the hotel reservations process. *International Journal of Contemporary Hospitality Management* 13(7), 364–371. doi: 10.1108/09596110110403956

Siguaw, J.A., Enz, C.A. and Namasivayam, K. (2000) Adoption of information technology in U.S. hotels: strategically driven objectives. *Journal of Travel Research* 39(2), 192–201.

Wong, J. and Law, R. (2005) Analysing the intention to purchase on hotel websites: a study of travellers to Hong Kong. *International Journal of Hospitality Management* 24(3), 311–329. doi: 10.1016/j.ijhm.2004.08.002

Zhang, Z.Q., Ye, Q., Law, R. and Li, Y.J. (2010) The impact of e-word-of-mouth on the online popularity of restaurants: a comparison of consumer reviews and editor reviews. *International Journal of Hospitality Management* 29(4), 694–700. doi: 10.1016/j.ijhm.2010.02.002

Zografakis, N., Gillas, K., Pollaki, A., Profylienou, M., Bounialetou, F. and Tsagarakis, K.P. (2011) Assessment of practices and technologies of energy saving and renewable energy sources in hotels in Crete. *Renewable Energy* 36(5), 1323–1328. doi: 10.1016/j.renene.2010.10.015

chapter 10

Tourist Experiences and Information Technology

LEARNING OBJECTIVES

After studying this chapter you should be able to:

- explain the role that IT plays in attracting visitors to attractions and events;
- analyze the different roles of IT in the staging of memorable attraction and event experiences;
- understand how IT can disrupt or moderate some visitor experiences; and
- apply various IT solutions to the management of visitors in attraction and event settings.

INTRODUCTION

Attractions play a critical role in the tourism system because they are the *raison d'être* for travel. They provide the on-site experiences and activities needed to satisfy visitor motives. The attractions sector is one of the most diverse and fragmented parts of the tourism industry. Attractions are usually categorized into natural and cultural attractions (Benckendorff, 2006).

Natural attractions include permanent flora and fauna, terrestrial and marine parks and reserves, landscapes, geological features and temporary events such as volcanic eruptions, astronomical events, wildlife migrations, even coral spawning. **Cultural attractions** include built attractions such as theme parks, art galleries, museums, historic buildings, architectural wonders, zoos, aquaria, sports and entertainment facilities, shopping malls and tourist precincts. Events such as sports games, festivals, concerts, performances, conferences and meetings are also important cultural attractions.

Some of the corporations that operate attractions are large, such as theme parks, stadiums, ski resorts and gaming operations, and have high needs for IT to control their operations. Smaller attractions such as wildlife parks, historic sites and cultural events may also use IT but to a lesser degree. Some renowned attractions such as New York's Statue of Liberty, Sydney's Opera House and the Sistine Chapel are administered by public organizations such as government authorities, heritage trusts or religious groups who may not have many resources to invest in IT.

The application of IT in the attraction and events sectors falls into three categories. First, IT is used to attract visitors by providing various electronic channels for information, sales and distribution. Second, IT is used in the staging of memorable visitor experiences. As tourists have come to expect interactive, multimedia entertainment, the attractions industry has responded with a similar level of technological sophistication, particularly in the area of themed entertainment. Third, IT is used to manage visitors by improving admission, orientation, purchasing, crowding and queue management, business intelligence, and safety and security. This chapter will address these main areas of usage by providing examples from a wide range of different attraction and event settings.

ATTRACTING VISITORS

Visitor information

Attractions and events have increasingly turned to the Internet to market and sell experiences. Many attractions and events maintain their own websites and use social media to build a relationship with past and future visitors. Pre-trip information can help travelers plan details such as transport, parking and activities so their experience is more enjoyable. Some attractions also provide virtual tours of key sights to immerse visitors in a digital experience before they visit. These virtual tours make use of panoramic views, animations and interactive photos, and are particularly effective for cultural attractions (Wan *et al.*, 2007). Apps such as TourWrist allow anyone to create 360° virtual panoramas with little technical training. Alternatively, attractions such as Disneyland have established a presence in virtual worlds such as SecondLife.

Larger attractions also provide interactive online maps so that visitors can explore activities and plan their day. Outdoor attractions such as surf beaches and ski resorts provide live video feeds so that travelers can check the conditions before they travel to the site.

Visitor Information Centers (VICs), called Welcome Centers in the USA, are a special category of attractions designed to inform and help visitors with the trip planning process. Traditionally these centers are found at destinations, national parks, heritage sites and other significant locations. Pearce (2004) suggests that VICs serve the following multiple overlapping functions:

1. **Promotion**: stimulate visitor demand by promoting local attractions and businesses.
2. **Enhancement**: provide displays, information and interpretation to inform visitors about the history and features of the region, and to promote responsible behavior.
3. **Control and filtering**: control visitor flows and access so that resources and settings come under less pressure.
4. **Substitution**: offer a substitute attraction for sites that are inaccessible, dangerous, fragile, or scattered.

They can also provide a site for local events and community meetings and for presenting locally produced goods (arts and craft; cheese and wine). However, many VICs are under threat as the growing use of digital information duplicates many of their roles. In response, some have embedded technology at the heart of their operations (see the Industry Insight below). This innovative use of IT illustrates that visitor information not only creates a virtual presence on the Internet, but also brings digital content into real settings to enhance visitor experiences.

Industry Insight: Manchester Visitor Information Centre

When the City of Manchester in the UK relocated its main VIC, authorities incorporated as much technology as possible to improve the visitor experience. The city spent over £800,000 to redevelop its VIC into a facility that resembles an Apple retail store, with features such as:

- a mediawall – the entire length of one end of the facility, which is used to showcase events and products in the city;
- Twitter feeds are streamed into the center on wall-mounted screens, displaying messages from the VisitManchester website, local tourism businesses, residents and visitors;
- desktop computers positioned throughout the store allow visitors to search and book accommodation, transport and events; and
- large Microsoft surface tablets allow groups of visitors to interact with maps and content in a social and tactile way.

http://youtu.be/gb6srekjix4

Watch the following video to see the center in action: http://youtu.be/gb6srekjix4/.

Source: May (2012)

Sales and distribution

Technologies that scan and verify tickets have created opportunities to distribute tickets in different modes (English, 2010). Many attractions and events use their websites not only to inform but also to sell admission tickets that can be printed at home or delivered to mobile devices. The digital distribution of attraction tickets has several benefits: (i) tickets can be sold prior to arrival, reducing waiting times and congestion at entrances; (ii) admission can be easily packaged with ancillary services such as VIP experiences, parking, transfers, food and beverage deals, season passes, accommodation and admission to other attractions; and (iii) online systems automate the allocation of tickets for attractions with limited capacity at particular times. Online tickets are sometimes sold at a discount to encourage purchases prior to arriving on-site.

STAGING EXPERIENCES

The creation of memorable experiences has received much attention in the tourism and leisure literature over the past 40 years. Theoretical developments in service management and marketing have provided new perspectives for understanding the visitor experience. In particular, Pine and Gilmore (1999) argued that global competition has commoditized services and that competitive advantage can only be achieved by offering experiences that are difficult to replicate. They propose that this **experience economy** consists of four realms: entertainment, escape, aesthetics and education. While the amount of emphasis on each realm varies from one experience to another, most successful experiences include a mix of these. More recent attention has focused on **co-creation**, in which individuals co-construct and personalize their experiences through interactions with the setting, other travelers and suppliers (Prahalad and Ramaswamy, 2004; Neuhofer *et al.*, 2012).

The use of IT adds a new dimension to the co-creation of experiences (Neuhofer *et al.*, 2012). In this context, technology becomes more than just a tool for the tourism industry. Stipanuk (1993) suggests seven major roles for the use of technology in tourism experiences. In Table 10.1 we add three more roles to this framework to explain how technology can contribute to the co-creation of tourism experiences. Some of these roles are visible to travelers while others operate behind the scenes. These roles are also not mutually exclusive, as a particular technology may serve several roles. We will take a closer look at these roles in the following discussion.

Technology as an enabler

As we have discussed in Chapter 2, economic growth is closely linked to technological innovation. Although the enabling role of technology is expansive and the links to travel experiences are sometimes tenuous, technology stimulates the broader socio-economic conditions for travel. New technologies increase productivity and relieve workers from menial and mundane tasks. In the tourism industry, technological innovation in the transport sector has stimulated the movement of billions of international travelers each year by making travel affordable and convenient. In developed economies technologies are used extensively in the production and delivery of goods and services, thereby raising living standards and disposable income. Technological

advances in the media and communications industries have also provided easy access to travel information, generating more interest in travel.

Technology as a creator

Perhaps the most obvious role of technology in tourism is its use to create the infrastructure that underpins tourism experiences. Engineers, architects and other professionals use computer-aided design (CAD) software to plan built tourism and leisure settings such as theme parks, zoos, aquaria and visitor precincts. For a good example of how this technology is applied in the field, take a look at the following video from Disney: http://youtu.be/nE8PvsRqjkg/.

http://youtu.be/nE8PvsRqjkg

Hardware such as 3D printers creates scale models of facilities so adjustments can be made before they are constructed. These technological infrastructures and machines create new opportunities for tourist experiences, such as jet boating, jet skiing and Segway tours, and high-rise observatories. Technology also contributes more directly to the delivery of hospitality and tourism experiences, as we have seen throughout this book. For example simulators, roller coasters and 3D movies require the intensive use of IT in the creation and staging of the experience.

Table 10.1. Technology and the co-creation of tourist experiences (adapted from Stipanuk, 1993).

Role	Description	Examples
Enabler	Technological innovations stimulate travel demand by providing the inspiration, time and economic means for people to travel	Transport technologies, mass media, Internet, social media, mobile devices
Creator	Technology is used in the creation of tourism experiences and settings	Computer-aided design (CAD), simulations, roller coasters, indoor ski slopes, ski lifts
Attractor	Technology can be the focal point for travel experiences	Science museums, theme park rides
Enhancer	Technology can enhance the experience by supporting comfort, orientation, interpretation and translation	Climate control systems, GPS, mobile devices
Protector	Technology can be used to protect travelers and the resources that attract them	Security systems, environmental management systems
Educator	Technology can reveal meanings and understandings of objects, artifacts, landscapes and sites through interpretation	Virtual guides, mobile devices, special effects, virtual reality, holograms, robotics
Substitute	Technology can provide visitors with substitute experiences in instances where the resource is threatened, congested or not accessible	Virtual reality, augmented reality, simulations, cinematics
Facilitator	Technology is a tool for the tourism industry	Back-office systems, Internet, social media
Reminder	Technology can be used to support the recording, reflection and sharing of experiences	Mobile devices, digital cameras, social media
Destroyer	Technology can also destroy the experience by impacting the social, environmental and economic well-being of travelers or employees	Technology failure, visual intrusion, noise or other externalities

Ski resorts also rely heavily on IT to improve the visitor experience, by monitoring and controlling the quality of the snow, and to design and plan their resorts. To improve the snow conditions, snow grooming machines called "snow cats" travel the slopes nightly to detect the condition of the snow and to groom each slope to the quality that skiers prefer. Drivers of the snow cats input data into an on-board computer system to record which trails have been groomed. Artificial snow production can also occur if snowfalls are inadequate. Computerized sprinkler systems throughout the slopes generate a mist that results in high quality snow. In addition to improving the skiing experience, these technologies also extend the skiing season and maximize the revenue of the resorts by making the slopes skiable for more days during the year.

Technology as an attractor

Many sites use technology as the focus of the experience. These include science and technology museums, industrial sites and working farms. Examples include the EPCOT theme park, the Dole Pineapple Plantation in Hawaii, the Guinness Brewery and the House of Waterford Crystal in Ireland, and the Cadbury chocolate factories around the world. Events such as technology expos and motor shows also showcase the latest technologies.

Many theme parks also use technology as a core part of the experience. Theme parks create enjoyable, thrilling and magical experiences using mechanics and electronics. Examples of mechanical technologies include theme park rides and roller coasters. Electronically created experiences are popular because

they can be changed more easily and cheaply than mechanical rides. This is an important consideration since theme parks with new attractions tend to attract more repeat visitors. Audio-visual experiences can be created by employing sophisticated sound, visual and lighting effects. Examples include large screen IMAX formats, 360° OMNIMAX theaters and 3D or 4D movie experiences, which are combined with mechanical rides to create the illusion of movement or flight. A good example is the Soarin' over California simulators at Disney's California Adventures and EPCOT theme parks. Digital surround sound and computer-generated acoustics, together with images create an immersive visitor experience. Computer-generated motion **simulators** give the audience the feeling of moving in a different reality and are part of many different rides. Many water theme parks use computer technology to generate ocean-like waves for surfing and to provide appropriate environments for other water sports.

Virtual reality, wherein the visitor is immersed completely in a computer-simulated interactive environment has been available in attractions for decades (Schwartzman, 1995). Most virtual reality environments are visual experiences displayed through special stereoscopic headsets, but some systems include additional sensory information, such as sound and tactile sensations. Some systems immerse users in a virtual reality "pod" consisting of stereoscopic goggles, surround sound, sensory inputs through body suits to stimulate the skin, motion simulators and other electronic devices. While older systems were bulky and cumbersome recent wireless devices are more user-friendly. **Augmented reality** superimposed on the real world will draw future visitors as wearable technologies such as Google Glass mature. There is scope for the **gamification** of attraction experiences by blending virtual storylines, activities and quests with real-world features. Technology companies have created a lifelike interactive **holodeck** as depicted in science fiction films such as *Star Trek*.

Technology as an enhancer

Often technology is not the focal point of an experience but enhances the comfort and enjoyment of visitors. Applications include visitor orientation, translation, communication and scheduling. Mobile devices are increasingly important in visitor orientation. There are also mobile apps that help users translate written text and verbal communication, and the benefits for travelers are obvious. Some mobile apps can help visitors plan their stay by creating a schedule of activities. They are useful for large attractions with multiple attractions and events (e.g. parades, movies, animal talks, feeding times and so forth). Similar technologies can also benefit conference delegates by building personalized schedules of presentations and exhibits. Virtual queuing systems are used at some attractions to reduce waiting times. Some of these applications are discussed in more detail in other parts of this chapter.

Technology as a protector

In many tourism settings technology protects both tourists and tourism resources from harm. In other chapters we have discussed how IT supports electronic locking systems in hotels and ensures the safety and security of air passengers. Mobile devices can warn travelers of risks such as storms and other natural or man-made incidents. An additional (although less visible) application involves the use of water treatment and refrigeration technologies in food safety.

Technology also creates a protected environment in which tourism experiences can take place. Technology applications to protect destination resources from degradation are particularly evident in heritage and natural settings. Climate control systems provide heating, cooling and air purification. For example, the Sistine Chapel receives over 5.5 million visitors a year, and the dust, humidity and carbon dioxide (from breathing) created by this activity is managed using air filtration systems to dehumidify and purify the air. Technology also pulses visitors through the attraction, to ensure a more sustainable flow of visitors. In museums and art galleries IT also plays an important role behind the scenes to document, record and archive collections (Bennett, 1999). The digitization of fragile ancient texts and artworks makes them accessible by a wider audience.

In natural settings the use of IT to track wildlife can monitor and manage impacts. Tracking technologies in mobile devices can also monitor tourist movements and manage adverse impacts associated with overcrowding. IT plays an important role in the production of renewable energy. Furthermore, Environmental Management Systems (EMS) are used by a range of tourism organizations to monitor and manage energy use and waste. The use of technology for sustainable goals is discussed in Chapter 12.

Technology as an educator

One of the most common applications of IT in visitor attractions involves the use of various **interpretation** techniques to support visitor learning. The goal of interpretation is to reveal meanings and understanding through involvement with objects, artifacts, landscapes and sites. This is important for attractions concerned with preservation or conservation, such as heritage sites, museums, art galleries, zoos and national parks. Visitor interpretation has benefitted from a shift from static educational displays to immersive **edutainment** experiences combining elements of education and entertainment (Reino *et al.*, 2007). Science and technology centers were the first museums to use technology to bring concepts to life. To give the visitor an experience of a "concept", electronic and interactive exhibits have been used extensively. Themed "walk-throughs" of exhibits enlivened by movies, sound and direct interactive experience are common in all types of museum exhibits. Below we briefly review the most commonly used and most promising applications of IT in visitor interpretation.

Virtual guides

Many attractions provide visitors with handheld devices called **audio guides** that provide commentary, narration and stories in different languages. These devices require visitors to enter a number associated with a room, exhibit or item to hear the audio. Some attractions make these audio recordings available as downloadable **podcasts**, which can be played on the visitor's own mobile device (Kang and Gretzel, 2012a,b).

Mobile devices

Newer virtual guides use geofencing to trigger audio-visual content based on the user's location. While Near Field Communication (NFC) and Bluetooth are used indoors, GPS technologies create opportunities to use geofencing to trigger interpretation in outdoor settings such as national parks, botanic gardens and zoos

(Armstrong *et al.*, 2008). **Quick Response (QR)** codes such as those found in this book are used in a range of indoor and outdoor settings. QR codes can be read by any mobile device with a camera and a suitable app. Future applications will involve wearable technologies such as Google Glass to provide virtual tours and contextual information.

Special effects

Attractions are increasingly using cinematic techniques to entertain and educate visitors (Alfaro *et al.*, 2004). Concerts and music festivals use computerized systems to enhance the acoustic quality of performances. Eliminating echoes and reverberations in large settings can be challenging and computers can help by calculating the positioning of speakers and other sound equipment. Some attractions have also installed computerized sound, light and pyrotechnic systems to create perfectly synchronized special effects. A good example is the *Blood on the Southern Cross* sound and light show, which tells the story of the dramatic 1854 Eureka rebellion of gold miners in Ballarat, Australia (see Industry Insight). Other examples include the *Symphony of Lights* show in Hong Kong and the choreographed *Fountains of Bellagio* in Las Vegas.

Virtual and augmented reality

We have already discussed how virtual reality (VR) can immerse visitors, but the same technology can transport visitors to other times and places. One of the earliest applications of VR in heritage settings was a 3D reconstruction of Dudley Castle, England as it was in 1550 (Boland and Johnson, 1996). Augmented reality is also an interpretive technique to provide on-site

---

Industry Insight: Blood On The Southern Cross

Sovereign Hill is an outdoor museum based in the city of Ballarat, Australia. The attraction uses many techniques normally found in theme parks to re-enact life in an 1860s Australian gold rush town. The 25 hectare site comprises over 60 historically recreated buildings, with costumed staff and volunteers who re-enact village life. The recreation is completed with antiques, artwork, books and papers, machinery, livestock, horses and carriages. Villagers work in the stores to produce traditional products such as candles, clothing, furniture, brassware, food and drink. The village also includes a tent city with a creek where visitors can pan for gold. The village is open to visitors during the day but the site takes on an entirely different character at night.

The story of the Eureka Stockade, the dramatic 1854 battle between gold miners and Government forces at Ballarat, is recreated nightly by a sound and light spectacular called "Blood on the Southern Cross". The 90-minute production involves no actors – just voices, sound-and-

http://youtu.be/5z6i-KpOZzw

light effects and an open-air set. More than 70 miles (110 kilometers) of fiber optic cable were buried during construction and eight computers and seven video projectors present the production. Several 10-meter tall lighting towers house state-of-the-art "intelligent" lights that turn night into day. Special effects include holograms, explosions, rain and burning buildings. Watch a short introduction here: http://youtu.be/5z6i-KpOZzw/.

---

reconstructions of archaeological sites or artifacts. Imagine walking through Temple Bar in Dublin and viewing the streetscape as it was in 1600 superimposed on the modern streetscape.

Holographic projection

Holograms are three-dimensional projections of images that change relative to the position and orientation of the viewer, making the projection more realistic. Holograms are used in a range of attractions but particularly in heritage settings where they replace actors to narrate a story or bring history to life.

3D printing

Three-dimensional printing has been possible since the 1980s, however affordable commercial models only became available after 2010. The travel industry has not yet embraced this technology but there are opportunities to precisely recreate sculptures and historic artifacts for display or visitor use. The technology can also be used to restore artifacts and relics. Another application involves the creation of personalized "3D photographs" and souvenirs in the image of the tourist.

Robotics

Theme parks and heritage sites often use **animatronics** and **mechatronics** to create animated creatures or people. Robots used to represent humans are known as **androids**. These techniques are particularly useful for creating creatures that do not exist (e.g. dinosaurs, mythical creatures) and historical or fictional characters. Examples include the Tyrannosaurus Rex at the Natural History Museum in London and many of the characters found in Disney theme park attractions. Recent advances have resulted in interactive animatronics, which use various sensors and artificial intelligence to respond to people.

Interactive surfaces

While touchscreen kiosks are ubiquitous in tourism, advances in electronics have created a wide variety of interactive surfaces, including interactive tables, walls, mirrors and glass. A major benefit of this technology is the ability to update digital content, including streaming live text, video and audio. The mediawall in the Manchester Visitor Centre (see Industry Insight above) is a good example of an innovative application of this technology. In the future, interactive walls will be linked to sensors and cameras that will detect visitor characteristics so that the content can be tailored to the audience.

The use of IT in interpretation offers both opportunities and challenges, and some of these are summarized in Table 10.2. However, technology also can extend the experience to before and after travel (Bennett, 1999; Neuhofer *et al.*, 2012, 2013). This is possible with websites and social media that build and maintain a relationship with visitors before they arrive and after they leave. For example, imagine zoo visitors using a website to plan their day. Once on-site they can use their mobile device to "friend" a panda on Facebook. Updates about the panda's adventures can then be followed through social media, providing an incentive for repeat visits and opportunities to raise funds for conservation.

Technology as a substitute

Often visitors cannot visit or access the sites or objects that are the focus of the tourist gaze. For example, seasonal changes may mean that experiencing plant or wildlife attractions would disrupt feeding or reproduction. Some places of interest may no longer exist, be too dangerous, too fragile or too expensive to access. Examples include volcanoes, underwater sites, or even attractions in space. The use of IT to provide substitute experiences broadens access to people not able to visit the site, such as the elderly or disabled or families with strollers (Bennett, 1999). In all of these cases technology can re-enact or recreate environments, activities or events. Technologies commonly used include virtual or augmented reality, simulators, animatronics, holograms, 3D films and live camera feeds.

Technology as a facilitator

As we have seen throughout this book, technology is a tool for travel organizations and destinations to improve productivity, efficiency and quality. Table 10.3 summarizes some of the applications of technology as a facilitator. Some of these applications are explored in more detail in other sections of this chapter.

Technology as a reminder

IT can facilitate travelers' desire to document their experiences by capturing memories. The recent integration of cameras in mobile devices has facilitated image and video sharing on social media sites such as Flickr, YouTube and Facebook (Green, 2002; Tussyadiah and Fesenmaier, 2009). Likewise, product review sites like TripAdvisor allow travelers to post their experiences, recommendations and

Table 10.2. Opportunities and challenges of using IT for interpretation.

Opportunities	Challenges
Updating content is relatively easy and cost effective	Maintenance and upgrades can be costly
Customization and personalization for different audiences (e.g. languages, age groups, personal interests, disabilities)	Many technologies not designed for exposed environments
Some interpretive technologies are portable	Care needs to be taken to ensure the technology does not interrupt the experience or detract from the ambience of the setting
Visual richness, multimedia and multisensory	Some visitors may not understand how to use the technology
Can link pre-trip, on-site and post-trip experiences together	Lack of cross-platform compatibility
Can be used to collect visitor metrics and market intelligence	Risk of distraction and injury if visitors are not paying attention to other cues and warnings
Can be used to build personal relationships through links with CRM systems, social media etc.	Impact on the experience of other visitors

suggestions (Yoo and Gretzel, 2008). GPS can now tag images with geographic information, allowing travelers to map images to particular locations using software, social media and mobile apps. The Internet has also made it easy for travelers to create travel blogs.

Tourist attractions also use technology to capture visitor experiences. For example, theme parks have installed cameras to photograph guests at various attractions and rides. Guests receive a card with a bar code to retrieve the images at the end of the day. Guests can elect to purchase printed photos at the venue, have their photos emailed to them, or sent to their mobile phone. Often photos can be ordered online for a limited period of time following the visit. While cynical observers might see only the profit motive behind these applications, they also provide an opportunity for visitors to reflect on and share their experiences.

Technology as a destroyer

So far we have discussed the positive roles of IT. However, technology can also bite back, resulting in negative experiences, inconvenience or more serious consequences (Tenner, 1997). This is most evident when technology fails. If tourist attractions and events are too reliant on technology to create, protect or enhance the experience then technology failure

Table 10.3. The role of technology as a facilitator.

Applications	Technology Examples
Marketing and distribution	Websites, online bookings, apps, on-site purchases
Visitor management	Managing access, managing queues and crowding
Business intelligence	Tracking visitor patterns and behavior
Facility management	Property management systems, safety and security
Back-office systems	Revenue management, accounting, payroll systems
Personnel	Employee access systems, laundry and costuming services in theme parks
Automation	Cleaning, order taking, self-service kiosks, robotics

can destroy the experience. This is seen in the failure of booking systems, luggage systems, power outages and even breakdowns of heating or cooling equipment. The failure of safety systems, such as smoke alarms, air traffic control, aircraft technologies, warning systems and safety mechanisms built into theme park rides can have more serious repercussions. Aside from outright failure, technology interference in the form of noise or visual pollution can impact the quality of the experience. A mobile device ringing during a concert or guided tour is an example of this kind of interference. At a global level, technologies using fossil fuels can contribute to resource destruction and climate change. Ultimately these changes impact fragile ecosystems and tourist activities in places like Venice, the Alps, the Great Barrier Reef, and low lying Pacific and Caribbean islands.

The roles identified by Stipanuk (1993) provide a useful framework for understanding the myriad of ways in which technology can impact tourist experiences. While some of these examples relate to airlines, hotels and destinations, the focus is primarily on the role

of technology in attractions and events. With this in mind, we now turn our attention to specific visitor management applications of technology in attractions and events.

MANAGING VISITORS

Admission

Most paid attractions and entertainment facilities can benefit from automated ticketing, admission and systems that monitor usage. IT solutions such as mobile devices, smartcards or bar-coded tickets can be used to gain admission to attractions. These are linked to **electronic ticketing systems** that store individual and group reservations and information about admission dates, times and prices. These databases must handle multiple types of tickets because many attractions and events offer season tickets as well as individual tickets for different categories of visitors (e.g. children, adults, families, concessions). Electronic ticketing systems must also issue tickets on-site for "walk in" visitors. Some systems verify visitors' identity using biometrics and can detect counterfeit or invalid tickets (see Disney Case Study at the end of this chapter). Ticketing systems for theaters, concert halls, stadiums and other attractions with numbered, designated seating need more detailed reservation systems. Seating plans showing occupied and unoccupied seats need to be viewable on screen, and tickets must, of course, show the seat numbers. Bar-coded cards are read by optical scanners connected to turnstiles at sites like theme parks, stadiums and ski lifts. Some smartcards and wristbands embedded with RFID chips are read by scanners as visitors approach entrances and turnstiles, making entry more convenient and facilitating the flow of visitors. Mobile devices also facilitate ticket purchasing and validation, allowing visitors to book tickets on the move (see Accesso Industry Insight below).

Attractions such as museums, zoos and theme parks require only one general admission fee. Others may require payment for individual rides, events or experiences creating a need for more complex systems. Smartcards, wristbands with RFID chips and bar-coded passes can be used to monitor access to these "pay as you go" attractions. They remove the need for payment at each point and the inconvenience created for visitors. Information from the ticket can be sent to a computer system running ticket collection software. This software automatically cancels used tickets, identifies counterfeit tickets, prevents admission fraud by employees and provides other revenue control functions.

Orientation

Paying attention to orientation needs is one of the most critical aspects of managing visitors in larger attraction and event spaces (Moscardo, 1999). Traditionally these orientation and navigation needs were addressed by signage, fixed maps and handheld maps. However, attractions now use IT to help visitors find their way around. Indoor attractions use IT for signage to guide visitors around the attraction for the best experience and to provide information on exhibits. The signage is usually in the form of audio-visual electronic media displayed on LCD screens and can be easily changed. Touchscreen kiosks, interactive surfaces and mediawalls also help guide visitors around larger attractions.

Attractions have also designed apps to be downloaded on to mobile devices to assist with navigation. In indoor environments these apps support NFC or Bluetooth signals, while in larger outdoor spaces such as national parks GPS can assist with navigation. Their main benefit is their ability to locate the user on a digital map and provide visual or verbal directions. Wearable mobile devices extend this capability by using augmented reality to superimpose directions over real environments. The combination of technologies such as Google Glass and Google Now allows visitors to see information such as popular photo spots and nearby attractions.

Ancillary purchases

Attractions and events use cashless payment systems to support ancillary purchases such as parking, accommodation, food and beverages, photos and merchandize. Smartcards, wristbands or bar-coded tickets used for entry can also be preloaded with funds to purchase ancillary products. Many water parks and ski resorts provide smartcards or waterproof wristbands embedded with an RFID chip or a bar code to purchase ancillary products (Pechlaner and Abfalter, 2005). Similar IT solutions are also used at special events to provide access to authorized areas and amenities. In the case of theme parks ancillary purchases can contribute significantly to revenues (Milman and Kaak, 2013). Ancillary revenues at some Disney theme parks make up almost 50% of total revenue (Sorensen, 2012). For an additional fee, visitors can also enjoy extra experiences such as behind the scenes tours or early admission to the park. Guests can also receive post-trip emails offering souvenirs they missed during their visit. This is possible if entry cards, tickets or wristbands are linked to a CRM containing visitor contact details.

Ancillary revenue can also be generated through the use of mobile devices. Apps installed on mobile devices can notify visitors about special offers, promotions and products. In previous chapters we have explored how **geofencing** can trigger activities such as notifications. The same technology can also be used in attraction and event settings to trigger information about offers, special events, show times and other activities. Wearable devices such as Google Glass extend these applications by using augmented reality to overlay real settings with real-time, interactive and context-specific digital information. In the future it is likely that mobile apps will interface with social media and other sources of big data such as previous online search and purchase behaviors to personalize offers and information (Prabu, 2013).

Crowding and queue management

Technology plays a role in **pulsing** visitors through heritage sites with limited capacity to protect the resource and prevent it from becoming too crowded. Some ticketing systems, such as that used at Schönbrunn Palace in Vienna, indicate an entry time on the ticket. The turnstiles at the entrance will only allow access if visitors scan their ticket within the specified time. In larger attractions visitor movements and crowding can be monitored and managed remotely using a range of IT systems. For example, Disneyworld in Orlando monitors crowding from an underground bunker called the Disney Operational Control Center. This state-of-the-art facility uses video cameras, computer programs, digital park maps and other real-time IT tools to identify congestion and deploy countermeasures. Technicians watch flat-screen televisions depicting various areas using different colors to represent wait times. Counter measures can include opening additional cash registers, deploying cast members to queues to entertain guests or launching mini-parades to draw crowds away from busy areas. The company also uses computer systems to forecast visitor demand for any given day by analyzing hotel reservations, flight bookings, historic attendance data and weather information gathered from satellites (Barnes, 2010). Mobile devices can also be used to draw visitors away from congested areas. The tracking of visitors through mobile apps can provide business intelligence that can then be used to push notifications and special offers for underutilized attractions (Brown *et al.*, 2013).

While visitors rarely regard queues positively IT can ease the inconvenience of waiting. Many theme parks have implemented **virtual queuing systems** allowing visitors to use their waiting time to enjoy other rides or attractions. Disney's Fastpass is perhaps the most well known of these systems. A computerized system allows park visitors to secure their place in a virtual queue by issuing a

Fastpass ticket that specifies a time window during which visitors must return to the attraction to take their place at the front of the queue. The ticket must be scanned to gain access to the Fastpass queue. Other virtual queuing systems use mobile phone apps and portable devices such as the Qbot and Qband (see Accesso Industry Insight).

Virtual queuing systems reduce *actual* waiting time, but technology can also reduce *perceived* waiting time. Boredom or a lack of information about queue lengths can make waiting times feel longer, while immersive or enjoyable activities tend to "make time fly" (Pearce, 1989). In these situations IT can provide visitors with estimates of waiting times or entertain visitors. This is done by integrating ride themes into the queue and by providing entertainment using a combination of motion sensors, video displays, computer games, holograms, robotics and other technologies.

Business intelligence and relationship management

In previous chapters we have explored how IT can be used strategically by travel organizations for business intelligence. Like other sectors of the travel industry, attractions

---

Industry Insight: Accesso

Accesso is a provider of ticketing, point of sale and virtual queuing systems for the attractions sector. The company's Passport ticketing suite supports the purchasing and validation of tickets online, on-site and by mobile. The system also allows attractions to manage group bookings, season passes, marketing offers and multiple forms of payment. Attractions configure automatic prompts to encourage cashiers to up-sell products. During busy periods attractions deploy additional staff with mobile devices to process ticket purchases. The suite includes a number of back-office analytics and reporting tools.

Accesso has also developed the LoQueue virtual queuing system, which is available in three formats:

- Qbot: a handheld queuing device allowing guests to reserve rides on-site from anywhere in the attraction. Guests are provided with real-time information about waiting times and reservations are validated using wireless, handheld checkpoints;
- Qband: designed for waterparks, this waterproof RFID wristband allows visitors to reserve rides by scanning the device at touchscreen kiosks located throughout the attraction. The Qband display features a countdown ride timer and the ability to integrate with locker access and cashless payment systems; and

http://youtu.be/VnEkYzkXMuE

- Qsmart: an app allowing guests to set up reservations and manage rides using their own smartphones.

Watch the following video to see how the Qbot system has been implemented at the Six Flags theme parks in the USA: http://youtu.be/VnEkYzkXMuE/.

---

and events can also benefit from the strategic listening opportunities afforded by social media such as product review sites and blogs. Attractions, events and sports facilities can build sustainable long-term relationships with visitors and fans using social media and mobile apps (O'Shea and Alonso, 2011).

The smartcard admission and purchasing systems discussed earlier can provide business intelligence to optimize operational efficiency (Bennett, 1999). In some destinations attractions have collaborated to create destination cards discounting entry to multiple attractions. Examples include the Go City cards by Smart Destinations in the USA and the iVenture card for cities in other parts of the world (see Fig. 10.1).

Destination cards are priced for particular lengths of stay (e.g. 1 day, 3 days, 7 days). Cardholders can access participating attractions by swiping or touching the card to a touch point at the entrance. Some attractions also offer additional benefits to cardholders, such as free public transport, express queues, upgrades and special offers. The cards are sold through various outlets, including visitor information centers, airports and travel intermediaries (who usually earn a commission). Data are collected whenever a visitor swipes the card, allowing attractions to access valuable market intelligence about visitor patterns and preferences. For example, information about the other attractions visitors choose to visit on the same day may highlight further opportunities for partnerships and packaging. Smartcards used in the ski industry to access ski lifts and make purchases also provide similar functionality by allowing resort operators to monitor visitor behavior, use of amenities and purchases (Pechlaner and Abfalter, 2005).

Mobile technologies can also collect business intelligence. Attraction apps installed on mobile devices access location information to monitor the spatial behavior of travelers, allowing attractions to monitor congestion and the time tourists allocate to various activities. Network analysis can identify key pathways and hubs of activity (Modsching *et al.*, 2008). This information is invaluable in helping larger attractions manage the visitor experience.

Disney's MyMagic+ is one of the most sophisticated business intelligence and relationship management systems in the attractions sector (see Case Study). The MagicBands at the heart of the system are linked to a CRM database that allows Disney to personalize the experience. When a MagicBand is scanned, cast members can greet visitors individually from details that are displayed on a small monitor. Cast members can also scan MagicBands with tablets or smartphones. The RFID chips in each MagicBand can be read from up to 30 feet away, allowing Disney to link photographs, including those taken on rides, to individual Photopass

Fig. 10.1. Example of an iVenture destination card (source: iVenture).

accounts. In the future this can combine with wearable mobile devices such as earpieces, smartwatches or Google Glass, so that cast members can see the name of guests. Alternatively, animatronic characters can sense MagicBands, allowing them to personalize messages. The MagicBand comes in a variety of colors and designs and Disney also allows visitors to customize the device with their name and personalized accessories.

The MyMagic+ system is also a valuable business intelligence tool. By touching on or off throughout the park, Disney can track and monitor visitor purchases, patterns and behavior. This information can determine when, where and for how long various market segments use particular attractions and amenities. These technologies can also identify areas of crowding and congestion and to implement strategies to address these issues (Brown *et al.*, 2013).

Safety and security

The safety and security of visitors is paramount in attraction and event settings. We have already seen how Disney uses various systems to monitor visitors at Disneyworld. The following applications provide further examples of IT to ensure the safety of staff, visitors and their belongings.

1. **CCTV systems**: attraction and event areas are monitored using a system of cameras, alarms and sensors to detect suspicious behavior. Security personnel monitor live camera feeds of areas at risk, such as entrances and exits, cash registers, car parks and locker bays.

2. **Secure entry**: attractions and events often have backstage areas restricted to authorized personnel. Access to these areas is managed using electronic locking systems that verify the individual's identity using PIN codes, smartcards or biometric systems.

3. **Electronic lockers**: larger attractions provide lockers where guests store their belongings during the day. These lockers are often a source of ancillary revenue and access is managed using central touchscreen service points. Guests can gain access to their lockers by entering a PIN code or by scanning an RFID smartcard or wristband.

4. **Safety systems**: technology is used extensively in the safety measures required of theme parks and amusement parks. Computers measure and determine the weight, speed and strength of the rides. Radio frequency technology is used in ride and parade control float systems at Walt Disney World Resort. In zoos and aquaria sensors monitor wildlife to reduce the risk of breaches to enclosures and tanks.

Casinos and gaming

Gaming is a large sector of the attractions and entertainment industry. As governments continue to legalize gaming activities, more establishments serve those wishing to gamble. These establishments may be part of hotels and cruise ships, or standalone casinos. Gambling is an established attraction in Europe (e.g. Monaco and Nice, France), in Asia (Macau), in all but two states in the USA, in the Caribbean and Rio de Janeiro (Brazil). Gambling on the Internet, available through home and hotel room computer systems, is a gaming environment requiring IT (Au and Hobson, 1997). It poses legal problems, since anyone with a credit card can play, whatever their age. Gaming on board ships to avoid legislation on land is also occurring in many locations – some on riverboats, some on cruise ships. Onboard gambling requires data networks for ship-to-shore communication with on-shore banks.

Casinos of all types use IT to efficiently manage and control the facilities and to maximize revenue. The functions of these systems include slot machine maintenance and accounting, table games, player tracking and marketing, cage management and staff systems. The mathematical calculations to determine payouts, the probabilities and the models of gaming are all generated by computer systems. Once the probabilities are calculated using payout algorithms and random number generators (RNGs), and they meet minimum government payout standards, they are implemented into the casino hardware.

Automated casinos track players' activities as they move throughout the casino playing different games. This computerized rating system gives management a clear picture of the player's true worth and identify frequent players and high rollers. This tracking is done in numerous ways. First, by giving each player an identifying customer number and/or card to use when playing games. Slot machines, for example, have a reader in which the card is inserted, and the time played, the money spent and the payouts given are all tracked. The systems track information not only on each play but also on multiple visits to the casino.

The resulting database rates the player's value to the casino and based on the rating, the player is given incentives. These incentives include complimentary meals, hotel rooms or entertainment such as shows. The higher the rating the more incentives the player receives. Interfaces from the central database to the point-of-sale systems in the restaurants and to the hotel property management systems are important so that information on complimentary items can be transferred to the restaurant

or hotel front desk. Direct mail campaigns to the high spenders, which include incentives to encourage more play, are also generated from this frequent player database. Similarly in the racing industry, decision support systems are used by both bookmakers and punters (McGrath and Kuzic, 2009).

SUMMARY

The attractions and entertainment industry is changing rapidly to provide visitors with ever more enjoyable, thrilling, educational and diverse experiences. Whilst technology is not leading the way, it is providing more options for the development of entertainment and educational experiences. Virtual and augmented reality technologies are likely to increase and become more refined so that visitors can experience changes in time and place at will. Operators are using IT to efficiently track their operations and to control access to their facilities. They can also use IT to market their activities and to personalize guest experiences. Larger theme parks like Disney are likely to lead the sector in IT use but innovative solutions using visitors' own mobile devices are also being implemented creating opportunities for smaller attractions that cannot afford expensive IT systems.

KEY TERMS

ancillary purchase, android, animatronics, audio guide, augmented reality, climate control system, co-creation, cultural attractions, edutainment, electronic ticketing system, experience economy, gamification, geofencing, holodeck, holographic projection, interpretation, mechatronics, mediawall, natural attractions, orientation, podcast, pulsing, quick response (QR) code, robotics, simulator, virtual guide, virtual queuing system, virtual reality, visitor information centers (VICs)

DISCUSSION QUESTIONS

1. What technologies do you use when you are traveling? How can technology be used in the co-creation of visitor experiences?

2. Some commentators have predicted that virtual reality will eventually eliminate the need to travel. Do you think this is a valid prediction? Discuss your reasoning.

3. Think about places you have visited on your travels. Have you experienced any examples of technology in interpretive experiences? Were these technologies effective in supporting your learning or were they just a gimmick?

4. In this chapter we explored some of the challenges and opportunities of using IT for interpretation. What are some of the operational advantages and disadvantages of using technology in the creation of experiences?

5. Does the use of technology in attractions erode or enhance opportunities for high touch experiences? Discuss your reasoning and compare your points with other students.

USEFUL WEBSITES

QR code	Website	Description
	International Association of Amusement Parks and Attractions http://www.iaapa.org/	IAAPA is the peak international trade association representing attractions, theme parks and amusement parks.
	International Council of Museums http://icom.museum/	ICOM represents museums worldwide and provides resources about the use of technology in museum exhibits.
	iVenture Card http://www.iventurecard.com/	An example of a destination smartcard.

QR code	Website	Description
	PDC http://www.pdcsolutions.com/	A leading supplier of RFID wristbands for attractions and events.
	Accesso http://accesso.com/	A provider of ticketing and virtual queuing systems for the attractions sector.
	Walt Disney Company http://thewaltdisneycompany.com/	The Walt Disney Company is one of the leading users of IT in the attractions sector.

Case Study: Using IT To Create the Magic at Disney

Famous science fiction writer and visionary Arthur C. Clarke once said that any sufficiently advanced technology is indistinguishable from magic. This seems to be a view that is shared by the Walt Disney Company. The Walt Disney Company is a leading international family entertainment and media conglomerate. The company operates a diverse range of businesses organized into five segments: media networks, parks and resorts, studio entertainment, consumer products and interactive media. This diversified portfolio has allowed the company to apply many media and entertainment technologies to its parks and resorts. Disneyland is perhaps the most famous of these theme parks. When founder Walt Disney opened Disneyland in 1955 he created a unique destination built around storytelling and immersive experiences. Today, Walt Disney Parks and Resorts is one of the world's leading providers of family travel and leisure experiences.

Walt Disney Parks and Resorts include six destinations with 13 theme parks and 46 resorts in North America, Europe and Asia. The company also operates the Disney Cruise Line, the Disney Vacation Club and Adventures by Disney. Walt Disney was an early pioneer in the adoption of new technologies to create entertaining experiences. His fascination with the future led him to use animation, live action films, nature documentaries, special exhibits,

(Continued)

Case Study. Continued.

theme park rides and city planning. Disney's "imagineers" have continued this legacy with new technologies in rides and attractions as well as the management of visitors.

One of the most innovative applications of IT is the use of mobile apps to guide visitors to particular rides, attractions and characters. Disney has also developed a state-of-the art system called MyMagic+ to offer new levels of trip planning and interactivity for its visitors. The system combines the My Disney Experience website and mobile app with an RFID wristband called the MagicBand, which is an alternative to Disney's Key to the World smartcard. The MagicBand allows theme park visitors to use a single device for entry tickets and purchases, and eliminates the need for Photopass and Fastpass tickets. When guests arrive at a Disney resort the MagicBand can be used to check in to their room. The device also acts as a guestroom key. To enter a Disney theme park guests need to touch their MagicBand to a kiosk before placing their index finger on a biometric scanner. The MagicBand can also be used to activate various interactive experiences in Disney's parks. For example, the MagicBand allows visitors to play "A Pirate's Adventure" and "Sorcerers of the Magic" at Magic Kingdom. The device can also activate and personalize various experiences to entertain guests while they are waiting in queues.

The service is supported by a CRM database requiring guests to register their details through the My Disney Experience website or app to link resort reservations and tickets to their MagicBand. Guests can also use the website or app to make dinner reservations and book

http://tiny.cc/MagicBand

Fastpass+ selections. The My Disney Experience mobile app also allows guests to plan a schedule for their visit. Kiosks throughout Disney's parks also allow guests to adjust settings and preferences. To ensure guest privacy, the MagicBand contains a randomly assigned code that securely links to an encrypted CRM database. The following video provides an overview of the Disney MagicBand: http://tiny.cc/MagicBand/.

Disney has developed many of the technologies used in other theme parks and attractions. But Disney also keeps many of its behind-the-scenes IT systems secret to ensure that things appear to happen as if by magic. This approach exemplifies the clever use of technology to create magical experiences.

Study Questions

1. Visit the website for Disneyworld in Orlando and browse the various rides and attractions. Make a list of the different technologies used in these experiences and group them into categories. Share your typology with other students.

2. What benefits do technologies such as the MagicBand offer attractions? Do you think this technology might pose challenges for managers and guests?

3. Do you have any privacy concerns about the use of technologies such as the MagicBand? Conduct an online search to learn how Disney manages these concerns with its guests.

4. How might smaller attractions with fewer resources implement some of the technologies used by Disney?

REFERENCES

Alfaro, I., Nardon, M., Pianesi, F., Stock, O. and Zancanaro, M. (2004) Using cinematic techniques on mobile devices for cultural tourism. *Information Technology and Tourism* 7(2), 61–71.

Armstrong, L., Holme, C., Kasinath, G., Sehovic, A., Vadera, Y., LeCoultre, G. and John, B. (2008) *An Investigation into the Incorporation of Leading Edge Mobile Technologies in the Recreational and Adventure Tourism Industries*. CRC for Sustainable Tourism, Gold Coast, Australia.

Au, N. and Hobson, J.S.P. (1997) Gambling on the Internet: a threat to tourism? *Journal of Travel Research* 35(4), 77–81.

Barnes, B. (2010) Disney Tackles Major Theme Park Problem: Lines, *New York Times*, 27 December. Available at: http://www.nytimes.com/2010/12/28/business/media/28disney.html?_r=0/ (accessed 27 December 2013).

Benckendorff, P. (2006) *Attractions Megatrends*. Butterworth Heinemann, Oxford, UK.

Bennett, M. (1999) The role of technology. In: Leask, A. and Yeoman, I. (eds) *Heritage Visitor Attractions: an operations management perspective*. Cassell, London.

Boland, P. and Johnson, C. (1996) Archaeology as computer visualization: virtual tours of Dudley Castle c. 1550. *British Museum Occasional Papers* 114, 227–233.

Brown, A., Kappes, J. and Marks, J. (2013) Mitigating theme park crowding with incentives and information on mobile devices. *Journal of Travel Research* 52(4), 426–436.

English, I. (2010) Making an entry. *Australasian Leisure Management* (78), 36, 38–39.

Green, N. (2002) On the move: technology, mobility, and the mediation of social time and space. *The Information Society* 18(4), 281–292.

Kang, M. and Gretzel, U. (2012a) Effects of podcast tours on tourist experiences in a national park. *Tourism Management* 33(2), 440–455.

Kang, M. and Gretzel, U. (2012b) Perceptions of museum podcast tours: effects of consumer innovativeness, Internet familiarity and podcasting affinity on performance expectancies. *Tourism Management Perspectives* 4, 155–163.

May, K. (2012) How a tourism board made its visitor centre look and feel like an Apple Store. *tnooz.com*. Available at: http://www.tnooz.com/article/how-a-tourism-board-made-its-visitor-centre-look-and-feel-like-an-apple-store/ (accessed 24 December 2013).

McGrath, G.M. and Kuzic, J. (2009) Enhancing the Australian regional racing experience for tourists: a betting aid for novice punters. *Information Technology and Tourism* 11(4), 303–318.

Milman, A. and Kaak, K. (2013) Theme parks revenue management. In: Legohérel, P., Poutier, E. and Fyall, A. (eds) *Revenue Management for Hospitality and Tourism*. Goodfellow, Oxford, UK, pp. 143–156.

Modsching, M., Kramer, R., Hagen, K.ten and Gretzel, U. (2008) Using location-based tracking data to analyze the movements of city tourists. *Information Technology and Tourism* 10(1), 31–42. doi: 10.3727/109830508785059011

Moscardo, G. (1999) *Making Visitors Mindful: Principles for Creating Quality Sustainable Visitor Experiences Through Effective Communication*. Sagamore Publishing, Champaign, Illinois.

Neuhofer, B., Buhalis, D. and Ladkin, A. (2012) Conceptualising technology enhanced destination experiences. *Journal of Destination Marketing and Management* 1, 36–46. doi: http://dx.doi.org/10.1016/j.jdmm.2012.08.001

Neuhofer, B., Buhalis, D. and Ladkin, A. (2013) A Typology of Technology-Enhanced Tourism Experiences. *International Journal of Tourism Research*, unpaginated. doi: 10.1002/jtr.1958

O'Shea, M. and Alonso, A.D. (2011) Opportunity or obstacle? A preliminary study of professional sport organisations in the age of social media. *International Journal of Sport Management and Marketing* 10(3/4), 196–212. doi: 10.1504/ijsmm.2011.044790

Pearce, P.L. (1989) Towards the better management of tourist queues. *Tourism Management* 10(4), 279–284.

Pearce, P.L. (2004) The functions and planning of visitor centres in regional tourism. *The Journal of Tourism Studies* 15(1), 8–16.

Pechlaner, H. and Abfalter, D. (2005) Cultural tourism packages: the role of smart cards in the Alps. In: Marianna, S. and David, L. (eds) *International Cultural Tourism*. Butterworth-Heinemann, Oxford, UK, pp. 40–50.

Pine, B.J. and Gilmore, J.H. (1999) *The Experience Economy: work is theatre and every business a stage*. Harvard Business School Press, Boston.

Prabu, K. (2013) Google Glass – the Next Big Thing in the travel industry? *tnooz.com*. Available at: http://www.tnooz.com/Google-glass-The-next-big-thing-in-travel-industry/ (accessed 26 December 2013).

Prahalad, C.K. and Ramaswamy, V. (2004) Co-creation experiences: the next practice in value creation. *Journal of Interactive Marketing* 18(3), 5–14.

Reino, S., Mitsche, N. and Frew, A.J. (2007) The contribution of technology-based heritage interpretation to the visitor satisfaction in museums. In: Sigala, M., Mich, L. and Murphy, J. (eds) *Information and Communication Technologies in Tourism 2007*. Springer, Vienna, pp. 341–352.

Schwartzman, E. (1995) Digital worlds. *Leisure Management* 15(6), 43–47.

Sorensen, J. (2012) *Profit From Innovation: Benefits of Ancillary Revenue Reach All Over the World*. Ideaworks, Shorewood, Wisconsin.

Stipanuk, D.M. (1993) Tourism and technology: interactions and implications. *Tourism Management* 14(4), 267–278. doi: http://dx.doi.org/10.1016/0261-5177(93)90061-O

Tenner, E. (1997) *Why Things Bite Back: Technology and the Revenge of Unintended Consequences*. Vintage Books, New York.

Tussyadiah, I.P. and Fesenmaier, D.R. (2009) Mediating tourist experiences. Access to places via shared videos. *Annals of Tourism Research* 36(1), 24–40.

Wan, C.S., Tsaur, S.H., Chiu, Y.L. and Chiou, W.B. (2007) Is the advertising effect of virtual experience always better or contingent on different travel destinations? *Information Technology and Tourism* 9(1), 45–54. doi: 10.3727/109830507779637611

Yoo, K.H. and Gretzel, U. (2008) What motivates consumers to write online travel reviews? *Information Technology and Tourism* 10(4), 283–295. doi: 10.3727/109830508788403114

chapter 11

Destination Management and Information Technology

LEARNING OBJECTIVES

After studying this chapter you should be able to:

- explain a Destination Management System (DMS) and the features that it provides;
- describe how a DMS can improve the management of tourism in a destination;
- evaluate the different ways that tourists access destination information electronically;
- explain how Destination Management Organizations (DMOs) use IT to help with management issues such as crisis and risk management, and stakeholder management; and
- understand the concept of a learning destination.

INTRODUCTION

It is increasingly challenging for destinations to attract visitors given that almost every location on the planet seeks to do the same. Gaining a competitive advantage requires the development of a brand image and engagement with effective distribution channels to influence travelers' choice of destination. Promoting and managing a destination is a different endeavor to promoting and managing a private sector firm, requiring coordination with different stakeholders and the management of public sector tourism resources. This task is the responsibility of the **Destination Management Organization (DMO)** also sometimes called a **Regional Tourism Organization (RTO)**, which is typically funded by government or a combination of government and private-sector funds. A DMO may also operate a network of **Visitor Information Centers (VICs)** throughout the country and marketing offices in the country's major markets. IT is critical to a DMOs success as the central agency for destination strategy, marketing and information provision.

Some of the most important tasks of a DMO are:

- information provision to potential travelers and travel intermediaries;
- promotion and marketing activities; and
- collection and analysis of tourism statistics (Pearce, 1992).

As we will see in this chapter, all of these functions are made more efficient with IT. This chapter will first re-visit digital tourism ecosystems (from Chapter 2) in the destination context, moving on to explain the development of **Destination Management Systems (DMSs)**, their functionality, information content and organizational structure. The chapter will then discuss how destinations utilize websites and social media, and position themselves in the online search market. It will then go on to explain how market intelligence, statistics and visitor tracking can be facilitated with IT systems. The chapter will end with key management issues such as crisis and risk management and stakeholder management, and the concept of learning destinations.

DESTINATIONS AND THE DIGITAL TOURISM ECOSYSTEM

As discussed in Chapter 2, a digital tourism ecosystem is composed of the processes and interactions between living entities such as travelers, suppliers, intermediaries, governments and communities, and the nonliving technological environment made up of devices, connections, content and touch points. It is the responsibility of the DMO to ensure that the destination has a strong and healthy digital ecosystem and to play the role of the catalyst in the ecosystem. This requires the DMO to coordinate with other government agencies and organizations to ensure interoperability between agents in the ecosystem, and to develop open systems and standards so that information moves easily within the destination. Coordination with telecommunications vendors, location-based service providers, wireless and mobile enterprises, and standards agencies is an important function of a DMO to ensure the digital ecosystem functions well. In particular the digital ecosystem should support the needs of travelers. It should deliver the necessary multimedia messages to inspire tourists to visit, support transactions with the traveler and intermediaries, use technology to enhance the experience, and provide platforms where visitors can reflect on their experiences with others. Much of the above can be accomplished with a DMS as we will discuss in detail in the next section.

DESTINATION MANAGEMENT SYSTEMS

When first designed and implemented in the 1980s, a DMS was a computer database of the destination's facilities that augmented the traditional methods of information provision such as brochures and VICs. Historically, a DMS filled a gap left by the GDSs in the electronic distribution of destination information. GDSs tended to favor large, chain companies with high price products. Many smaller, independent travel suppliers of travel products were not listed on GDSs because of the costs of establishing connectivity and interoperability. A travel agent wishing to book a vacation in youth hostels or small inns, and with outdoor activities, would find this difficult to do on a GDS. However, a DMS includes all types of travel products. It also includes public sector facilities such as museums, parks and beaches, and charges little or nothing for the enterprise to be listed. Studies have shown that the use of a DMS can significantly improve the competitiveness of a destination, in particular its small and medium-sized enterprises (SMEs) by giving them more market access (Buhalis, 1993; Sheldon, 1993; Yuan *et al.*, 2006).

Subsequently, the Internet and the web have made a huge difference to the dissemination of destination information (D'Ambra and Mistilis, 2004; Douglas and Mills, 2004). Destination information can be found on the websites of online travel agents (OTAs) and online travel magazines, and guides and online travel blogs (Choi *et al.*, 2007). In Taiwan, for example, there are over a hundred websites that provide tourism information by local and regional DMOs (Davidson and Yu, 2004). Since DMOs compete with many other websites as the source for destination information, research has demonstrated that a higher proportion of tourists who visit a DMO website actually visit the destination and have a higher intention to return (So and Morrison, 2003). Since the mid-2000s, DMSs have evolved into highly complex, web-based platforms that support broader functionality and communication through a number of online channels.

One definition of a DMS is a comprehensive electronic database of a destination's facilities and customer information that can be accessed by travel counselors and/or travelers themselves, either in the destination or in the origin region. It can also contain market intelligence information for its suppliers, a photo/video library of the destination, and access to third-party systems for information on transportation schedules, weather information etc.

Another definition that incorporates the web-based nature of most DMSs is provided by Estevao *et al.* (2011):

> A DMS can be defined as a dynamic web-based platform that integrates a wide range of information about a destination's tourism products. It also provides an infrastructure to support different types of e-commerce (e.g., B2B, C2B, and G2B) in the destination. Additionally, it allows interaction with different stakeholders (e.g., suppliers, visitors), data collection and information visualization.

In a study of DMSs in the USA, Zach *et al.* (2007) examined various e-commerce and website features. They identified the following three functions of web-based marketing for DMOs:

1. **Web content**: information provisions such as search functions and listings of tourism facilities, attractions and services.
2. **Web promotion**: techniques to attract visitors from other channels such as search engine optimization and advertisements in other websites.
3. **Web eCommerce**: transaction-related features targeting behavioral outcomes of visitors.

Their research also showed that DMSs tend to focus mostly on information provision and marketing and less on building interactive functions of a DMS website. They advise how DMOs' strategic development of their sites requires a continuous process (Zach *et al.*, 2007). This is important advice as US travelers tend to begin their travel planning using search engines and only visit a DMO website later in the process.

Many issues must be considered by DMOs as they strategically design their DMS. Most important are its economic structure, the typologies of information included, the technology used, its interfaces with other systems and its organizational structure. These factors are affected by issues such as: the geography of the destination; the nature of tourism to that area (independent or group); the preferred mode(s) of travel (air, public transportation or private automobile); the political environment of the DMO; the various sources of funding; and the existence of other travel information and reservation systems in the country or region. The next section will describe the main dimensions that need to be considered when designing a DMS.

Destination management system dimensions

There are five operational dimensions to be considered when a DMS is designed. They are the information dimension, the communication dimension, the transaction dimension, the relationship dimension and the technical merit dimension (Li and Wang, 2010).

The success of a DMS is highly dependent on the **information dimension**, which includes detailed, accurate, comprehensive and current information. This is challenging, since rates, schedules, timetables, events and opening hours change with the days, weeks, months and seasons. Also, many tourism products require detailed descriptions and multimedia to portray each product. Design of this information dimension therefore must consider this time sensitivity and product complexity. Timely information collection is delegated to the local tourist offices, which know and communicate more often with different suppliers. Product information is obtained from suppliers by regular questionnaires sent by the DMO, with more frequent updates coming by phone or online.

Quality control of the DMS information is extremely important. If the data are false or misleading, the entire DMS could lose its credibility. An evaluation or classification system ensures quality control of product information. In some destinations, the chamber of commerce, the hotel association or the automobile club have a classification system that can be used in the DMS. The DMO may check the accuracy of the information to be entered into the DMS or it may trust each supplier's information. The types of information typically included in a DMO are listed in the first column of Table 11.1.

The **communication dimension** refers to the interactive connection between the customer and the DMO and is displayed in the second column. Since search-engines and web portals are entry points for tourism information it is important for DMOs to develop search strategies for their own site and to be included on multiple web portals and predominant in search engine results. Other communication features can be an online forum, online surveys, FAQ's, a place for customers to leave comments, and perhaps an email newsletter.

The **transaction dimension**, which is not part of all DMSs, includes the features listed in the third column. Connection with other travel industry computers allows bookings of many types of suppliers to be made on the DMS website and requires the secure transactions capability. Typical DMS interfaces are with national weather systems, traffic systems, attractions, car rental and hotel databases. A DMS can also connect SMEs together in the destination to make them

Table 11.1. Dimensions of a DMS (adapted from Li and Wang, 2010).

Information dimension	Communication dimension	Transaction dimension	Relationship dimension	Technical merit dimension
Attraction and activities	Search function	Online reservations	Privacy policy	Link workability
Maps and directions	Interactive communication tools	Secure transactions	Deals and discounts	Load time
Destination background information	Online forum	Attraction tickets	Personalization	Search engine recognition
Themed products	Comment box	Events tickets	Cross-selling opport-	Visual appearance
Transportation	Online survey	Shopping carts	unities	Navigation
Events calendar	Frequently asked		Incentive programs	Webpage design
Restaurants	questions (FAQs)		Customer loyalty	Site map
Travel guides	Email newsletter		programs	
Travel agents			Web seal certification	
Accommodation				
Travel packages				
Entertainment				
Local weather				
Shopping tips				
Trip/vacation planner				
Links to regional, city				
or area pages				

Second, it gives all VICs and foreign market offices access to the central DMS database. Third, it facilitates the interface with other travel industry systems such as GDSs or other CRSs. Disadvantages of the centralized system are that data communication costs can make this configuration more costly and prone to technical problems, and updating a centralized database of the entire country's tourism facilities can be a challenge. Some larger suppliers are online and can make their own updates, otherwise it is difficult to keep the database current. A centralized national DMS can also contain a market database of the major tourism-generating countries, information on economics, distribution channels and other tourism trends.

An alternative to the national DMS is a **centralized regional DMS** covering only the state, city or local destination. This is a preferred style in large countries such as the USA, where the central collection of data at the national level can be overwhelming. This design is also more likely when the initiative, development and financing come from the local level, and where the regional and local tourist offices are autonomous. It is particularly appropriate when each region's tourism resources are significantly different from others (city, country, ocean, mountain) since each may require a different database design. Updating regional databases is easier because local staff have more contact with and knowledge of the local industry.

Whether a DMS is national or regional, touchscreen visitor kiosks located outside VICs and in other public places are useful when the office is closed or when staff are busy. With mobile access to DMS databases such terminals are becoming less necessary. In fact the changing roles of VICs with Internet access to DMS has been studied by D'Ambra

and Mistilis (2004). They found that visitors tend to use VICs for goal-directed and experiential information rather than accommodation and logistical information (D'Ambra and Mistilis, 2010).

Destination management system management

Changes in the consumer market and growing competition are causing DMO managers to look to IT as a strategic management tool. When integrated into the organizational fabric of the DMO, a DMS can support the brand image and strategic plan of the destination. This requires a commitment from top management and high levels of technological knowledge of DMO staff. It can be difficult for DMOs to keep pace with new technologies and to ensure that staff are trained in the latest technologies, making the implementation of innovative marketing strategies difficult (Gretzel *et al.*, 2000). Another real challenge for DMOs is to have a consistent message, and synergy between all online and offline strategies. DMO strategy is better if it focuses on cultural identity, heritage and other public goods rather than a product-oriented approach typically used by private sector organizations (Govers and Go, 2004). Other significant challenges that DMOs face are the need to understand that Internet technology does more than replace old ways of marketing, and the need to design websites that cater to customers' unique needs (Gretzel *et al.*, 2006).

Destination managers are advised to ensure that the proper cultural, organizational and technological conditions are in place before they implement the DMS. This involves establishing the social climate, the level of collaboration between firms in the destination, the technological infrastructure and the way firms coordinate (Ndou and Petti, 2007). Taking all of these into consideration will result in a better DMS.

Long-term **strategic planning** for the purchase, implementation, staffing and maintenance of the IT applications is necessary. An appropriate budget is needed not just for the initial purchase but for maintenance, future upgrades, and the hiring and training of human resources to operate the systems. DMOs may choose to outsource IT applications particularly in the design and programing of a DMS if the expertise is not available within the DMO. It is also common to use consulting firms for data collection and analysis. e-Business applications in resource planning and logistics can also be effective in improving DMOs' efficiency levels (Fuchs *et al.*, 2010). Even when outsourcing occurs, there are numerous in-house IT applications that require DMO staff to have skills and qualifications to implement the new Web 2.0 technologies. This is often a problem due to lack of funds for training, lack of time to learn new technologies and the attitude that IT professionals should be hired for that purpose.

Financial considerations of a DMS include the development, implementation and operational costs, and any revenues generated by the system. System development funds usually come from the DMO's budget. In some cases, funds may also be generated from private industry if perceived benefits from the system are well communicated. Once the DMS has been developed and implemented, operational costs include the maintenance and updating of the system. Updating is labor intensive but essential to the quality of the DMS. Few immediate revenues are expected from the DMS. Most DMSs list suppliers at no cost and finance all operating costs as a service to the suppliers and the destination, knowing that increased tourism will ensue. In some cases, suppliers are charged a nominal annual fee to be listed. If suppliers are required to pay, then willingness-to-pay favors larger, more financially secure companies rather than the SMEs and entrepreneurs. If payment is not required or is minimal, all suppliers in the region have the opportunity to be listed, including public facilities such as parks and museums, and environmental conditions such as traffic and weather. A fully comprehensive system can only occur if no payment is required. If the DMS includes the reservation function, suppliers may be charged a commission per booking received through the DMS, making a contribution to operating costs. Transaction costs incurred in processing the reservation must also be offset.

DESTINATIONS, INFORMATION TECHNOLOGY AND CHANGE

Implementation of a DMS implies change wherein the focus of the organization becomes oriented towards partners and building the capacity to support these relationships (Gretzel and Fesenmaier, 2001). However, as discussed below, learning and change is difficult for most organizations and as such there are important barriers limiting the nature and degree of change. Many of these barriers relate to the nature of the organization and include the environment in which the DMO exists (the nature of competition, sophistication), the size and financial capacity of the organization and the nature of the staff (education level, skills). Also, studies have shown that the values of the leader of the organization are essential in successfully implementing new technology. The third important barrier to integrating new technology such as DMS within an organization relates to the cost and extent of change (Yuan *et al.*, 2006). That is, if the system changes are small, then the adoption of new technology is simple and straightforward; however, if DMS implementation implies a large change within the organization (i.e. the creation of new positions and new ways of doing things), then there are many hurdles to be addressed.

As Fig. 11.2 shows, the process of DMS integration is an evolutionary process that includes both "successes" and "failures". In this case, "success" might mean that the system is available to all appropriate staff or that decisions are data driven rather than based upon prior experience; "failures" which represent "set backs" include the loss of a staff member knowledgeable in the use of the DMS or failure to develop new metrics that can be used to evaluate the impact of the system.

Most meaningful change caused by the DMS implies a "new way of doing business" and as such, emphasizes that the staff within the DMO must change. Indeed, in the initial stages of change, DMS implementation focuses largely on organizing existing capacities; that is, doing current activities such as marketing more efficiently. However, as the DMS becomes fully integrated within the departments or functions within the DMO, the focus changes to enabling new activities

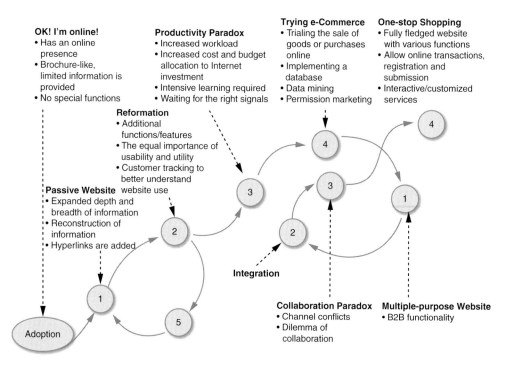

Fig. 11.2. An example of the evolutionary path of DMS implementation (source: Yuan *et al.*, 2006).

and capacities while requiring the organization to develop new metrics (Yuan *et al.*, 2006). Therefore, many costs related to DMS implementation relate to staff training rather than the purchase of computers or DMS systems.

DESTINATIONS, WEB 2.0 AND SOCIAL MEDIA

In the more sophisticated and interactive world of Web 2.0, DMOs must compete with social media by developing their own competitive strategies. A big challenge is that content on social media is mostly user-generated and is therefore almost difficult to control. Consumers can create online communities in the form of blogs, wikis and chat rooms where they write reviews and discuss destinations and other travel products. It is difficult for destinations to influence or inform these media by integrating "official" destination information with user generated content (UGC).

Travelers' online dialogs are affecting the image and reputation of destinations, and the purchasing patterns of tourists (Inversini *et al.*, 2009; Dickinger and Koltringer, 2011; García *et al.*, 2012). DMOs need to respond in some way to regain some control over the destination's online image. Smaller DMOs in particular, who encounter complex barriers when trying to establish online advertising strategies, may need strategic advice when dealing with the complexities of social media (Gretzel *et al.*, 2000).

TripAdvisor features a massive amount of consumer-generated information and evaluations of travel destinations (Gretzel *et al.*, 2006). Another social media site (http://www.virtualtourist.com/) has thousands of

members sharing destination reviews, trip journals and photos. In fact, the online reputation of destinations is strongly influenced by travelers' comments in blogs (Marchiori and Cantoni, 2011). DMOs therefore need to provide more relevant, engaging website experiences with Web 2.0 and social media features to promote their brands to technology-savvy digital customers. Web 2.0 features provide DMOs with the ability to enliven their sites and engage with online customers. Encouraging social engagement between DMOs and travelers, and among travelers is an important part of a DMO website. However, out of 40 DMOs around the world, only 22 made use of any of these tools, and only 15 made use of more than one of the tools (García *et al.*, 2012). Blogs, wikis and chats were the least utilized of all the listed features.

A DMO can use three strategies to respond to the social media challenge and opportunity (Munar, 2011). Munar analyzes the strategies used by a few Scandinavian DMOs in dealing with the social media challenge. She identifies three possible strategies: (i) the **mimetic strategy** where the DMO mimics or copies the style and e-culture of the social network sites; (ii) the **advertising strategy** where banner ads and other advertising are purchased by the DMO on social media sites; and (iii) the **analytic strategy**, where the DMO analyzes the UGC already on the various websites and finds the sites where the information was posted and uses it to analyze and create new strategy. This third strategy is also advised by Inversini and Eynard (2011), who suggest that DMO managers should reverse engineer their online reputations by identifying the sites that are feeding certain images to the consumer and correct them in some way.

Training for DMO staff on Web 2.0 technologies is critical for this to happen. Unfortunately DMO staff are often not well-trained in social media. An interesting study examined the impact of training in various new DMS-related Web 2.0 technologies. The technologies were: social networking; podcasts; MyMaps; Google Street View; Google Earth; mashups; Youtube; virtual tour; Second Life; Rich Sites Summary (RSS) feeds; compact video cameras; tracking devices; portable navigation devices; and multi-functional mobile phones. The results showed that after training, DMO professionals were more willing to use YouTube, map-related technologies, social networks and RSS feeds in their work than the other technologies. Using RSS feeds allowed them to keep up-to-date with travel-related information (Lee and Wicks, 2010).

Travel podcasts are also providing destination information to travelers. Thousands of travel podcasts can be downloaded and listened to or viewed. Some are produced by individual travelers and others by major travel guides, some are audio only and some include video. Table 11.2 shows a few of the travel podcasts that are available.

DMOs can also use podcasts to inform visitors about their destination, however very few do so. A study of city DMOs in the USA found that the minority used podcasts in this way, and so they can be utilized more in the future (Xie and Lew, 2008).

DESTINATION RESEARCH

Research is an important function for DMOs. This involves the collection and analysis of statistics such as economic data on the

Table 11.2. Examples of travel podcasts (http://www.openculture.com/).

Name of podcast	Content
Beautiful Places	Video podcast focusing on the outdoors
Finding America	Travel every road in the USA
Frommer's Podcast	Travel Information from editors of Frommer's
Italy from Inside	Native Italian gives travel advice
Lonely Planet Travelcasts	Very international in scope – audio only
Travel in 10	Ten-minute tours of destinations
Travel with Rick Steves	Many individual country guides
The Travel Destination Podcast	Travel information and guidance on many destinations
Walks of a Lifetime	National Geographic: selection of world's greatest walking tours

number of arrivals, party size, length of stay, mode of transport, daily expenditure and traveler demographics. Social impact data are more qualitative and include resident attitudes and visitor satisfaction surveys. Increasingly data on environmental impacts of tourism are also sought including water purity, noise levels and CO_2 emissions. The following section examines how IT is applied to these otherwise labor-intensive functions.

Tourist statistical data collection and analysis

Data collection for tourism statistics is most commonly done using surveys. Surveys may be administered at entry points into the destination such as airports and seaports, or for land travel at border control points. Surveys may request tourists to fill out the survey themselves or, more commonly, research staff interview the tourists and record the responses. Most on-site data collection is now done with handheld electronic tablets such as iPads, although some is still collected in paper form. Stand-alone kiosks located in airports, VICs or other locations are also used for direct survey responses. It is important, however, that there is some incentive and that the kiosks are placed in locations where tourists have time to respond. One example is at conferences and conventions where responses can be spread out over a few days, and the sample is a "captive audience". Kiosks are not suitable for long surveys or for surveys where the sample of respondents must be carefully controlled.

When surveys involve multiple researchers in the field, rapid consolidation of results is important. Special online software packages can help with this. Software can also be programed to automatically skip questions that respondents do not need to answer. In addition, the software can perform data verification checks to minimize data entry errors. Such systems have been used for example by Disneyland at entry and exit gates to analyze visitor traffic.

Email surveys or web-based surveys using software such as Survey Monkey are appropriate for surveying tourists after they return home or before they leave on their trip. It is easier to control the sample with email and web-based surveys. Surveys that assess tourists' satisfaction with a destination and those which determine travelers' future plans lend themselves well to these electronic surveys. They also tend to be cheaper than traditional survey methods. Internet surveys have also been used by destinations to gather input from residents to ensure socially sustainable tourism development (Bond *et al.*, 1996).

Once the data have been collected, they must be analyzed into meaningful statistics and reports. Statistical software programs such as Statistical Package for the Social Sciences (SPSS) or Statistical Analysis System (SAS) are two comprehensive and commonly used packages in DMOs. They generate tables, frequencies and histograms of the responses, and perform hypothesis testing so that researchers can investigate the responses more thoroughly. Multivariate analyses such as perceptual mapping and factor analysis can give deeper interpretation of the data. Trend analysis of tourist arrivals and forecasts can be performed. When the analysis is complete, desktop publishing software helps DMOs to produce their own reports and place them online for stakeholders to view. Some destinations protect the reports with a password and charge some stakeholders for the reports, giving a new revenue source.

DMOs need to understand tourism trends in their tourist-generating regions. Information on economic trends, outbound travel behaviors and patterns, spending patterns, media information, types of travel intermediaries and distribution channels are all needed for strategic decision-making. This information can be collected by the DMO and included in the DMS. Suppliers can then use this information to help them plan their marketing and promotion strategies. As an example of a higher level application of data analysis software, the Austrian Tourist Office in conjunction with the Vienna University of Economics and Business has created a decision support system called **TourMIS**. This system incorporates statistical analysis and other decision-making tools with key European market data. The system has a user interface so that DMO managers can perform their own analyses of data (Wöber, 1994). See the explanation of TourMIS in the Industry Insight box below.

Industry Insight: TourMIS

IT provides a platform for multiple destinations to share their information with each other, thereby increasing their joint competitiveness. European Cities Tourism (ECT) is an example of destinations sharing tourism information for mutual benefit. The organization was founded in 1991 with the overall aim to strengthen city tourism in Europe. The purpose of ECT is to build opportunities for joint marketing activities, and to represent city tourism industry interests at the European Union. It does this by sharing information and knowledge among its members. It also strives to improve the compatibility and integration of statistics between European cities by working on the harmonization of definitions and compiling methods, and supports interested ECT members in adapting their own data systems.

The knowledge base that drives the ECT platform is called TourMIS (Tourism Management Information System) and was designed by Professor Karl Wöber, President of MODUL University, Vienna, Austria. TourMIS is a comprehensive and accurate source of European tourism statistics including overnight stays, tourist arrivals and accommodation capacities. Data collection in TourMIS is quite unique in that it relies on DMO managers in more than 150 European tourist offices to enter it online themselves. The quality of the data therefore depends solely on the participation of DMO managers. It is the most commonly used marketing decision-support system in tourism that also encourages the harmonization of tourism statistics. It provides a unique platform for tourism associations to exchange data, information and knowledge (Wöber, 2003)

Access to TourMIS is free, guaranteeing broad utilization among the many cities, and widespread discussion about the trends based on the data. In doing so TourMIS meets user and DMO managers' needs. Great importance is attached to the reliability of information and its competent analysis for effective planning, monitoring and management of tourism. In 2012 TourMIS won the UNWTO award for innovative technology in tourism.

Sources: Regional Tourism Destination Knowledge Sharing: TourMIS (http://www.tourmis.info/) and European Cities Marketing (http://www.europeancitiesmarketing.com/).

Another application of IT for destinations to use to study tourist behavior is spatial tracking technology based on GPS systems. This provides an understanding of how tourists move throughout a destination and is useful for the design of infrastructures and transportation systems. The Research Insight box below gives examples of how destinations are using this technology.

Research Insight: Spatial Visitor Tracking

Numerous studies around the world have used GPS systems to investigate socio-spatial movement of tourists in cities. Examples of such cities are: Sydney and Melbourne in Australia; Hong Kong; Norwich, UK; Rouen, France; and Koblenz, Germany (van der Speck, 2008; McKercher et al., 2012; Edwards and Griffin, 2013). "GPS tracking offers a precise means of determining how tourists move around a city, the routes they select, the places they spend time, modes of transport used" (Edwards and Griffin, 2013, p. 581). It is easier to track tourist behavior in urban rather than rural destinations where tourists stay within a smaller radius and are not so visibly different from residents.

In an Australian study, researchers identified a group of tourists who were willing to join the study. They first identified places where tourists could be recruited such as hotel lobbies, attractions, transportation stations, etc. They met to describe the study and offer an incentive (shopping coupon) and give the tourists the GPS tracking device to wear. They then advised them to go about their day as normal forgetting about the device. Two different GPS tracking devices were used (Garmin Forerunner 305 and Holux Loggers), and each recorded the time, speed, distance, position, altitude and direction of the tourists. The tracking software (called SportTracks) registered and analyzed the movement data. It was then overlayed on to Google Earth giving clarity to the paths taken and speed traveled. The researchers met with the tourists at the end of the day to retrieve the GPS, download the data, and to confirm the data results with the tourists.

Their results showed the different transportation routes used, the landmarks visited and for how long, and other details of the tourists' day. This study's results point to intense use of some areas whereas other areas of potential interest were under-utilized. It also identified the main landmark attractions that tourists visited as they walked about 10–35 kilometers a day in the city. In a similar study in Hong Kong, researchers found that first-time visitors have different patterns of movement than repeat visitors. Repeat visitors do not wander around the city so much but focus more on dining and shopping locations.

The technology has implications for a destination's development of transport facilities and other infrastructures such as signage, landmarks, placement of VICs and

(Continued)

Continued.

the development of tourist routes around the city. It can also measure the impact of certain targeted marketing campaigns highlighting specific city attractions by identifying whether tourists are visiting the attraction more than before the campaign. This technique gives a better understanding of the socio-spatial behavior of tourists and can be a critical component of tourism planning for the city.

Edwards, D. and Griffin, T. (2013) Understanding tourists' spatial behaviour: GPS tracking as an aid to sustainable destination management. *Journal of Sustainable Tourism* 21(4), 580–595.

CRISIS AND RISK MANAGEMENT

Tourism is an information-intensive industry and when in chaos its information needs are exacerbated. The severity and frequency of tourism crises and disasters are increasing dramatically and destinations need ways to mitigate the impact of these crises or avoid them altogether. Knowledge and information technology are powerful resources to help governments, private firms and the communities prevent, plan for, and recover from various types of disasters and crises. Given the many crises (both natural and man-made) that have affected destinations in the last two decades, a response by DMOs is needed. A crisis often stimulates the transition for a destination to value knowledge more acutely, and take the initiative to gather it. The DMO often needs to be the hub of information transfer during the crisis and must call on as many types of IT as possible to save lives and recover. This is best done by using knowledge management, IT and a multi-stakeholder approach (Blackman *et al.*, 2011). Crisis management requires flexibility, evaluation and potential modification to strategy along the way depending on the nature of the disaster and the stakeholder response.

A shared knowledge system involving all stakeholders in the destination is needed to address crises and disasters. Destinations need knowledge in three stages of disaster management identified by numerous authors as: **pre-crisis, crisis and post-crisis** phases. Ritchie (2004) calls these three stages:

1. **Prevention and planning**: includes proactive planning and strategy formulation before the crisis. IT systems can store policies and databases of relevant information.
2. **Strategic implementation**: involves strategic evaluation and strategic control, crisis communication and control, resource management, and collaborating with stakeholders. IT and data networks are critical at this stage.
3. **Evaluation and feedback**: involves crisis resolution and a return to normality. Again IT can provide communication facilities, websites and mobile sites for the feedback.

These three stages have their own respective knowledge bases that constitute a knowledge framework (see Table 11.3). Of course all are interconnected and part of one system, so the content of each knowledge base is centrally accessed and not duplicated (Mistilis and Sheldon, 2006).

Table 11.3. Knowledge management for destination crises and disasters.

Pre-crisis	Strategic implementation	Post-crisis
Prevention and planning	**Activation of plan**	**Evaluation and recovery**

Create databases of:
    Possible disasters with probabilities
    Cases of previous disasters
    Best practices from other destinations
    Experts
    Insurance firms
    Environmental and social scanning technologies
Assign Tourism Central Command Center
Design monitoring and warning systems
Design policy and procedure manuals
	Activate Tourism Central Command Center (in DMO)
	Enact disaster policies and procedures
	Initiate media communication
	Oversee monitoring and warning systems
	Communicate with other general disaster centers in the destination
		Ongoing situational awareness
		Stakeholder consultation
		Communication with tourists and travel suppliers and intermediaries
		Feed back any best practices and lessons learned into database
		Design of tourism recovery plan when disaster is over

In the first step, information and knowledge are retrieved and stored. This includes databases of possible disasters and their probabilities, best practices, environmental monitoring and scanning systems. It would also include the policies and procedures, manuals, and the design of the tourism command and control center within the DMO. This knowledge base is ready for preventative planning in the pre-crisis stage. The second stage is the activation of the plan and the enacting of the policies during the crisis, overseeing the monitoring systems and communicating with the media. Informing tourists' friends and family of their well-being, and encouraging the hospitality industry to tend to homeless or injured tourists and residents are two important tasks for which communication technologies are needed. After the crisis is over, the third stage requires ongoing situational awareness, consulting and communicating with all stakeholders, feeding back to the knowledge base any lessons learned, and designing a tourism recovery plan for the destination.

In all of these stages, IT is crucial to create the knowledge bases and to the communication networks that are critical to meet the disaster. The destination website can be a platform for information in the three stages of the crisis, however few destinations are using it for that purpose (Volo, 2007). Social media such as Facebook and Twitter are well documented to be of enormous help in disaster situations by rapidly transmitting information to those that need it.

STAKEHOLDER MANAGEMENT AND LEARNING DESTINATIONS

Tourism destinations can benefit from urban planning researchers to understand how cities and towns become intelligent and "learn". While not all tourism destinations are towns or cities, an understanding of the key ideas from this literature can benefit what might be called **knowledge-based destinations**. Some of the features of a knowledge-based destination are as follows.

1. Ubiquitous access of new IT technology for all stakeholders (including local residents, businesses, visitors).
2. Instruments to make knowledge and information accessible to stakeholders in a systematic and efficient manner.
3. A culture that encourages development of innovative goods and services for the stakeholders.
4. Mechanisms to ensure that every stakeholder group is given an opportunity to participate in the innovation process (Racherla *et al.*, 2008, p. 412).

Campbell (2009) suggests that cities need to create a **soft infrastructure** to become **learning destinations**. This includes local knowledge, learning and creativity, trust, networks, conversion of tacit to explicit knowledge, and collaboration and cooperation. A good IT infrastructure is necessary for these features. A soft infrastructure includes keeping track of events, documenting findings, building databases and tracking performance indicators. It also can involve using the knowledge economy provided by **non-governmental organizations (NGOs)** as foundations for their knowledge acquisition.

A crucial component of a learning destination is a network of stakeholders, formal or informal, engaged in a collective endeavor. The task of the DMO is to work with all stakeholders in the destination to communicate and have a common vision. Stakeholder groups include private industry, SMEs, government offices, local residents, NGOs, tourism associations and tourists themselves. It is the job of the DMO to foster communication and cooperation between all stakeholders creating networks based on trust, identity and allegiance within and between networks in the destination. The use of knowledge management in DMOs is important as destinations become more complex and the need to compete increases. The Research Insight box below describes how the state of Illinois in the USA created a knowledge-based network for the destination.

Research Insight: Developing the Illinois Travel Network

Business-to-business (B2B) communities provide tourism organizations such as DMOs with substantial opportunities to create competitive advantage through information exchange, partnering and value chain integration. The power of these B2B value networks or digital ecosystems lies in the integration of an essential front-end understanding of customer needs with the back-end structure that is crucial for delivering holistic and coherent customer experiences. Importantly, designing a knowledge-based B2B community for the tourism industry requires an understanding of the nature of knowledge and knowledge creation processes in the organization. Nonaka

(Continued)

Continued.

and Takeuchi (1995), two leading scholars in knowledge management, stress the importance of two different forms of knowledge: tacit versus explicit and individual versus organizational/ industry knowledge. They indicate that a knowledge-based B2B network needs to foster the dynamic transformation of knowledge so that it can facilitate organizational learning and change. Fesenmaier *et al.* (1999) translate this theory of knowledge creation and transformation into four basic system elements/functions for tourism management information systems: marketing intelligence system, marketing research system, analytical marketing system and internal reporting system. They define marketing intelligence as a set of sources and procedures to obtain secondary information from outside the system. Marketing research refers to efforts of gathering primary data relevant to the knowledge-based community. The analytical marketing function deals with the analysis and interpretation of data. Last, the internal reporting system incorporates elements related to the collection, storage, retrieval and dissemination of knowledge.

The Illinois Tourism Network (ITN) was developed for the Illinois Bureau of Tourism and fosters value creation through inter-organizational relationships, sharing and trust in virtual communities that empowers organizations and their ability to learn (Gretzel and Fesenmaier, 2004). We learn in this article that the successful implementation of knowledge-based systems such as ITN use bulletin boards, FAQs, newsletters and more sophisticated functions such as IKNOW Illinois Tourism provide important communication features and sharing opportunities. These system elements are actively promoted through announcements, incentives and workshops and are moderated so that information sharing and community participation can be encouraged. Ongoing development and evaluation encourages further learning and consequently are seen as critical to the growth of tourism enterprises.

Gretzel, U. and Fesenmaier, D.R. (2004) Implementing a knowledge-based tourism marketing information system: the Illinois Tourism Network. *Information Technology and Tourism* 6(4), 245–255.

IT has many tools to assist in bringing together stakeholders to discuss and decide on mutually acceptable policies. The DMO can help the private sector by offering advice, formal education, or simply serving as a role model. For example, the Canadian Tourism Office makes research on IT and travel marketing available to its suppliers. It also offers seminars for travel suppliers to learn about electronic marketing. A DMO can also share their hardware and software such as a web server with suppliers. DMO management may also become involved in national and international telecommunica-

tion regulatory policy as interconnectivity issues are addressed in the destination.

Table 11.4 categorizes ways that destinations can create networks or collaborative partners to share knowledge and learn more. There are four categories of learning destination groups. First, proactive destinations which strive to gain knowledge, put resources toward it and integrate results into policy. An example is the sustainable tourism optimization management model (TOMM) in Kangaroo Island, Australia. Second, where similar type destinations form clusters to create and

Table 11.4. Classifications of learning destinations (adapted from Campbell, 2009).

Type of grouping	Characteristics of learning	Examples
Proactive Destinations	Take initiative and commit resources to outward search for knowledge. Incorporates knowledge into policy.	Kangaroo Island, Australia http://www.tourkangarooisland.com.au/
Destination Clusters	Some networking with similar types of destinations.	TourMIS; UNESCO World Heritage Cities http://whc.unesco.org/
Destinations One-To-One	Agreements between destinations for exchange purposes .	Sister Cities International http://www.sister-cities.org/ Destination pairs in proximity e.g. Spain/Portugal; Australia/New Zealand
Destination Networks	Membership organizations with convening power.	European Cities Network http://www.eukn.org/ The European Network of Cities for Sustainable Tourism http://www.europeancitiesmarketing.org/

share knowledge bases together. An example is UNESCO World Heritage Cities and TourMIS discussed earlier. Third is a one-on-one collaboration between destinations. Examples of this type of collaboration are Sister Cities International, and also destination pairs that do joint marketing. Finally, some destinations create network organizations to achieve some learning goals.

The European Network of Cities for Sustainable Tourism is an example of a knowledge network of tourism destinations. It was founded in 2001 and consists of cities throughout Italy, Spain, Turkey, Greece and Israel, coordinated by the International Council for Local Environment Initiatives (ICLEI). Some of the objectives of the network are:

- to develop and implement joint projects to pursue sustainability in the tourism sector;
- to exchange information and experiences (also organizing study visits and exchanges);
- to develop common training and distance-training projects for local authority officials; and
- to develop common strategies to new potential markets by taking into account the sustainability targets.

Another network is the European Cities Marketing. This network links City Tourist Offices and Convention Bureaus to share their expertise and work together on business opportunities. More than 134 major cities from 32 countries belong to this network (http://www.europeancitiesmarketing.org/).

IT and its application are the keys to supporting destinations in becoming learning destinations. In fact the three drivers that move a destination to become a knowledge-based destination are innovation, community participation and IT technologies (Racherla *et al.*, 2008). They cannot do it without a ubiquitous IT infrastructure throughout the destination to bring together all stakeholders for input to policy making. Some destinations are becoming completely connected, where residents and tourists can be electronically connected at any time. Destinations that are leading in this endeavor are: South Korea, which provides government-sponsored Internet access on a free network country-wide; Taiwan, which allows tourists to register on arrival for free WiFi; and a public WiFi network in the UK called "Cloud", which benefits tourists and residents alike. More destinations will need to consider the benefits of becoming a connected learning destination.

SUMMARY

This chapter examined the role of IT in destinations. It describes the importance of a DMS in destination management organization and the various dimensions that need to be considered in its design. It analyses how the web has changed the way tourists search for destination information using search engines and recommender systems and an array of Web 2.0 travel sites. The impact of social media both within the DMS and in other travel firms is explained, and the challenges that DMOs have in attracting visitors to their sites is explained. The need to train staff in new technologies and incorporate social media into their strategies is stressed. The chapter then explained how IT could be used for market research and data collection to assist the DMO in its market intelligence. Two very important responsibilities of DMOs in today's world are managing risk and crisis, and becoming learning destinations with all stakeholders connected. The chapter ends by explaining how IT can assist with both.

KEY TERMS

algorithms, analytic strategy, centralized regional DMS, collaborative filtering, communication dimension, content filtering, destination integrated computerized reservation management system (DICRMS), destination management organization (DMO), destination management system (DMS), destination search, global positioning system (GPS), information dimension, knowledge-based destination, learning destination, mimetic strategy, regional tourism organization (RTO), non-government organization (NGO), online survey software, podcast, recommender systems, relationship dimension, soft infrastructure, spatial tracking systems, technical merit dimension, TourMIS, transaction dimension, visitor information centers (VICs)

DISCUSSION QUESTIONS

1. Choose a destination not mentioned in this chapter and describe and analyze its DMS and information infrastructure. What recommendations do you have for the destination to become more of a knowledge-based destination?
2. Compare and contrast the social media strategies of two destinations in promoting their destination. What recommendations can you give them to improve?
3. With a destination of your choice, analyze its visibility on various search engines. Suggest how the DMO could improve its visibility.
4. Choose two of the websites below and describe each of their strengths and weaknesses.

USEFUL WEBSITES

QR code	Website	Description
	Destination Marketing Association International (DMAI) http://www. destinationmarketing.org/	An international organization representing destination marketing organizations.
	iTourist http://www.iTourist.com/	A travel-based social networking community and guide.
	Tiscover http://www.tiscover.com/	A well-designed website for the Austrian Alps.
	Travelers For Travelers http://www. travelersfortravelers.com/	A travel community where travelers can meet destination locals and other travelers.
	National Geographic http://www. nationalgeographic.com/	A website with information on geo-destinations.

QR code	Website	Description
	MySwitzerland.com http://www.myswitzerland.com/	Switzerland's DMS website.
	Virtual Tourist http://www.virtualtourist.com/	Information on destinations around the world; answers your individual questions.

Case Study: Australian Tourism Data Warehouse (ATDW)

The Australian Tourism Data Warehouse (ATDW) is the national platform for digital tourism information on Australia. It was founded in 2001 jointly by Tourism Australia (the national DMO) and all of the Australian state and territory government tourism organizations. The ATDW system is a central storage and distribution facility for tourism industry product and destination information from all Australian States and Territories. It focuses on travel suppliers and intermediaries, and less on providing access to the tourist directly. In addition to providing comprehensive information on the country's tourism facilities, it includes an online bookings feature and industry education.

The content of the data warehouse, which is currently over 35,000 tourism product listings, is compiled in a nationally agreed format and electronically accessible by tourism business owners, wholesalers, retailers and distributors for use in their websites and booking systems. It is updated daily by the state government tourism offices and provides multi-channel distribution for the travel industry. The following categories show the diversity of information that is available:

- **Accommodation:** accommodation establishments allowing short-term stay. Property styles can range from apartments, backpacker and hotels, bed-and-breakfasts, caravan and camping, farm stays, holiday houses, motels, hotels and resorts;
- **Attractions:** places of interest open to visitors;
- **Destination information:** destination information about the town, suburb, city, area, state or region;
- **Events:** includes activities which are scheduled events, may be once only, annual,

(Continued)

Case Study. Continued.

biennial, biannual, weekly, fortnightly, etc. Events can be local, minor, or major events.

- **Hire:** hire services including vehicle, boat, equipment and houseboat hire, and yacht and boat charters;
- **Information services:** information on visitor services including airports, cruise terminals, national operators and visitor information centers;
- **Journeys:** suggested journeys, which can include a series of routes and waypoints. May include walking trails, scenic drives and suggested itineraries;
- **Restaurants:** restaurants, which are of high quality or particular interest to visitors;
- **Tours:** organized excursions usually with a guide and commentary. May vary in duration from less than a day, to one day to extended touring; and
- **Transport:** transfer services and air, coach, ferry and rail point-to-point services.

ATDW, in collaboration with a technical partner, assists SMEs to enter the online market by providing booking widgets. These are programed functions such as availability, payment solutions or customer support services, can be added to a supplier's website. It also offers a "white label site", which is a pre-built, hosted, flexible and fully customizable website for travel suppliers and distributors to use to create their own site. A geospatial interface called ATLAS (Australian Tourism Location Aware Search) is also offered to facilitate the search for Australian tourism products. There are costs for these various services and packages.

ATDW also is an accreditation agency for tourism products. By becoming a member of ATDW enterprises can place the quality logo (T-QUAL) on their sites, along with other ecotourism certifications such as Earthcheck. Guidelines for the use of these logos are available on the website.

The data warehouse is supported by an online tourism e-kit (http://www.atdw.com.au/) with online training sessions, and a team of trainers who assist tourism enterprises to get online.

Study Questions

1. Based on reading this chapter, what are the strengths of ATDW as a DMS? What features could be added to make it even more multi-functional?

2. Could any destination follow this model of a DMS? Explain why or why not?

REFERENCES

Blackman, D., Kennedy, M. and Ritchie, B. (2011) Knowledge management: the missing link in DMO crisis management? *Current Issues in Tourism* 14(4), 337–354. doi: 10.1080/13683500.2010.489637

Bond, S.C., Brothers, G.L. and Casey, J.F. (1996) Application of the Internet as a tool for enhancing resident involvement for sustainable rural tourism development. In: *Proceedings of Travel and Tourism Research Association 27th Annual Conference*, Travel and Tourism Research Association, Kentucky.

Braun, P. (2004) Regional tourism networks: the nexus between ICT diffusion and change in Australia. *Information Technology and Tourism* 6(4), 231–243.

Buhalis, D. (1993) RICIRMS as a strategic tool for small and medium tourism enterprises. *Tourism Management* 14(5), 366–378. doi: 10.1016/0261-5177(93)90005-6

Buhalis, D. (2003) *eTourism: Information Technology for Strategic Tourism Management*, 1st edn. Prentice Hall, Essex, UK.

Campbell, T. (2009) Learning Cities: knowledge, capacity and competitiveness. *Habitat International* 33(2), 195–201.

Choi, S.J., Lehto, X.Y. and Morrison, A.M. (2007) Destination image representation on the web: content analysis of Macau travel related websites. *Tourism Management* 28(1), 118–129. doi: 10.1016/j. tourman.2006.03.002

D'Ambra, J. and Mistilis, N. (2004) Information resource use and uncertainty reduction at visitor information centres. In: Frew, A. (ed.) *Information and Communication Technologies in Tourism 2004*, Proceedings of the International Conference in Cairo, Egypt, 2004. Springer-Verlag, Vienna.

D'Ambra, J. and Mistilis, N. (2010) Assessing the e-capability of visitor information centers. *Journal of Travel Research* 49(2), 206–215.

Davidson, A.P. and Yu, Y.M. (2004) The Internet and the occidental tourist: an analysis of Taiwan's tourism websites from the perspective of Western tourists. *Information Technology and Tourism* 7(2), 91–102.

Dickinger, A. and Koltringer, C. (2011) Extracting destination representation and competitiveness from online content. *Information Technology and Tourism* 13(4), 327–339. doi: 10.3727/109830512x 13364362859939

Douglas, A. and Mills, J.E. (2004) Staying afloat in the tropics: applying a structural equation model approach to evaluating national tourism organization websites in the Caribbean. *Journal of Travel and Tourism Marketing* 17(2/3), 269–293. doi: 10.1300/J073v17n02_20

Edwards, D. and Griffin, T. (2013) Understanding tourists' spatial behaviour: GPS tracking as an aid to sustainable destination management. *Journal of Sustainable Tourism* 21(4), 580–595.

Estevao, J.V., Carneiro, M.J. and Teixeira, L. (2011) The role of DMS in reshaping tourism destinations: an analysis of the Portuguese case. *Information Technology and Tourism* 13(3), 161–176. doi: 10.3727/ 109830512x13283928066751

Fesenmaier, D.R., Leppers, A.W. and O'Leary, J.T. (1999) Developing a knowledge-based tourism marketing information system. *Information Technology and Tourism* 2(1), 31–44.

Fuchs, M., Hopken, W., Foger, A. and Kunz, M. (2010) E-business readiness, intensity, and impact: an Austrian destination management organization study. *Journal of Travel Research* 49(2), 165–178.

García, B.B., Carreras, A.O. and Royo, E.R. (2012) User generated content in destination marketing organisations' websites. *International Journal of Web Based Communities* 8(1), 103–119.

Gertner, R.K., Berger, K. and Gertner, D. (2006) Country-dot-com: marketing and branding destinations online. *Journal of Travel and Tourism Marketing* 21(2/3), 105–116.

Govers, R. and Go, F.M. (2004) Projected destination image online: website content analysis of pictures and text. *Information Technology and Tourism* 7(2), 73–89.

Gretzel, U. and Fesenmaier, D.R. (2001) Measuring effective IT use among American convention and visitors bureaus. In: Sheldon, P.J., Wöber, K.W. and Fesenmaier, D.R. (eds) *Information and Communication Technologies in Tourism 2001. Proceedings of the International Conference in Montreal, Canada, 2001*. Springer-Verlag, Vienna, pp. 52–61.

Gretzel, U. and Fesenmaier, D.R. (2004) Implementing a knowledge-based tourism marketing information system: the Illinois Tourism Network. *Information Technology and Tourism* 6(4), 245–255.

Gretzel, U., Yuan, Y.L. and Fesenmaier, D.R. (2000) Preparing for the new economy: advertising strategies and change in destination marketing organizations. *Journal of Travel Research* 39(2), 146–156.

Gretzel, U., Fesenmaier, D.R., Formica, S. and O'Leary, J.T. (2006) Searching for the future: challenges faced by destination marketing organizations. *Journal of Travel Research* 45(2), 116–126.

Inversini, A. and Eynard, D. (2011) Harvesting user-generated picture metadata to understand destination similarity. *Information Technology and Tourism* 13(4), 341–351. doi: 10.3727/109830512x 13364362859948

Inversini, A., Cantoni, L. and Buhalis, D. (2009) Destinations' information competition and Web reputation. *Information Technology and Tourism* 11(3), 221–234.

Kim, H.J. and Fesenmaier, D.R. (2008) Persuasive design of destination web sites: an analysis of first impression. *Journal of Travel Research* 47(1), 3–13. doi: 10.1177/0047287507312405

Lee, B.C. and Wicks, B. (2010) Tourism technology training for destination marketing organisations (DMOs): need-based content development. *Journal of Hospitality, Leisure, Sport and Tourism Education* 9(1), 39–52.

Lee, W.J. and Gretzel, U. (2012) Designing persuasive destination websites: a mental imagery processing perspective. *Tourism Management* 33(5), 1270–1280. doi: 10.1016/j.tourman.2011.10.012

Li, X. and Wang, Y.C. (2010) Evaluating the effectiveness of destination marketing organisations' websites: evidence from China. *International Journal of Tourism Research* 12(5), 536–549.

Li, X. and Wang, Y. (2011) Measuring the effectiveness of us official state tourism websites. *Journal of Vacation Marketing* 17(4), 287–302.

Marchiori, E. and Cantoni, L. (2011) The online reputation construct: does it matter for the tourism domain? A literature review on destinations' online reputation. *Information Technology and Tourism* 13(3), 139–159. doi: 10.3727/109830512x13283928066715

McKercher, B., Shoval, N., Ng, E. and Birenboim, A. (2012) First and repeat visitor behavior: GPS tracking and GIS analysis in Hong Kong. *Tourism Geographies: An international Journal of Tourism Space, Place and Environment* 14(1), 147–161.

Mistilis, N. and Sheldon, P. (2006) Knowledge management for tourism crises and disasters. *Tourism Review International* 10(1), 39–46.

Munar, A.M. (2011) Tourist-created content: rethinking destination branding. *International Journal of Culture, Tourism and Hospitality Research* 5(3), 291–305. doi: 10.1108/17506181111156989

Ndou, V. and Petti, C. (2007) DMS business models design and destination configurations: choice and implementation issues. *Information Technology and Tourism* 9(1), 3–14. doi: 10.3727/109830507779637602

Nonaka, I. and Takeuchi, H. (1995) *The Knowledge Creating Company*. Oxford University Press, New York.

Park, Y.A. and Gretzel, U. (2007) Success factors for destination marketing web sites: a qualitative meta-analysis. *Journal of Travel Research* 46(1), 46–63. doi: 10.1177/0047287507302381

Pearce, D. (1992) *Tourist Organizations*. Addison-Wesley Longman, Harlow, UK.

Racherla, P., Hu, C. and Hyun, Y.H. (2008) Exploring the role of innovative technologies in building a knowledge-based destination. *Current Issues in Tourism* 11(5), 407–428. doi: 10.1080/ 13683500802316022

Ritchie, B.W. (2004) Chaos, crises and disasters: a strategic approach to crisis management in the tourism industry. *Tourism Management* 25(6), 669–683.

Sheldon, P. (1993) Destination information systems. *Annals of Tourism Research* 20(4), 633–649.

So, S.I. and Morrison, A.M. (2003) Destination marketing organizations' web site users and nonusers: a comparison of actual visits and revisit intentions. *Information Technology and Tourism* 6(2), 129–139. doi: 10.3727/109830503773048237

van der Speck, S. (2008) Spatial metro: tracking pedestrians in historic city centers. In: Shaick, J. and van der Speck, S. (eds) *Urbanism on Track: Application of Tracking Technologies in Urbanism*. IOS Press, Delft University, Amsterdam.

Volo, S. (2007) Communicating tourism crises through destination websites. *Journal of Travel and Tourism Marketing* 23(2/4), 83–93.

Wöber, K.W. (1994) Strategic planning tools inside the marketing-information-system in use by the Austrian National Tourist Office. In: Schertler, W., Schmid, B., Tjoa, A.M. and Werthner, H. (eds) *Information and Communications Technologies in Tourism*. Proceedings of the International Conference in Innsbruck, Austria, 1994. Springer, Vienna, pp. 201–208.

Wöber, K.W. (2003) Information supply in tourism management by marketing decision support systems. *Tourism Management* 24(3), 241–255. doi: http://dx.doi.org/10.1016/S0261-5177(02)00071-7

Xie, F.F.P. and Lew, A.A. (2008) Podcasting and tourism: an exploratory study of types, approaches, and content. *Information Technology and Tourism* 10(2), 173–180.

Yuan, Y.L., Gretzel, U. and Fesenmaier, D.R. (2006) The role of information technology use in American convention and visitors bureaus. *Tourism Management* 27(2), 326–341. doi: 10.1016/j.tourman.2004.12.001

Zach, F., Xiang, Z. and Fesenmaier, D. (2007) An assessment of innovation in web marketing: investigating American convention and visitors bureaux. *ENTER* 16(1), 365–376.

chapter 12

Sustainable Tourism and Information Technology

LEARNING OBJECTIVES

After studying this chapter you should be able to:

- analyze how IT can improve the environmental, social and economic sustainability of tourism organizations, communities and destinations;
- explain how IT systems can be used to ensure environmental preservation, purity and physical integrity;
- describe the role of IT systems in promoting social equity and community well-being, local empowerment and the preservation of cultural diversity;
- understand how IT systems can ensure economic viability and local prosperity; and
- explain how IT systems can facilitate tourists to behave more sustainably in tourist settings.

INTRODUCTION

So far we have examined how IT has reshaped tourism organizations, tourists and destinations by increasing productivity, creating new markets, and connecting tourists with each other and with tourism enterprises in new and exciting ways. We have also discussed how social media is influencing the industry and travelers and have considered the impact of technology on tourist experiences. However, one crucial area not yet fully explored is the impact of IT on the sustainability of tourism destinations and the potential that IT has to assist tourism in transforming the world for the better.

Sustainable development has as its focus futurity, equity and holism and has become an important global paradigm in recent decades (Sharpley, 2000). International concern over the planet's sustainability (environmentally, socio-culturally and economically) was first expressed at the United Nations World Commission on Environment and Development (WCED) in 1983. That commission produced *Our Common Future*, also known as the Brundtland Report, laying out details to encourage countries to pursue sustainable development together. It defined sustainable development as: "development that meets the needs of the present without compromising the ability of future generations to meet their own needs" (WCED, 1987, p. 39). IT is an important tool in making headway toward sustainable development, by infusing society with knowledge, wisdom and responsible management practices.

Tourism is central to the sustainability debate because it is a large, global industry that has the potential to impact both positively and negatively environments, economies and societies. Tourism's history has many examples of unsustainable, unplanned developments that degrade the socio-economic and environmental fabric of the destination. This history and the pressing global issues of climate change, human rights, wealth inequalities and environmental pollution, demand that sustainable principles be front and center in tourism policy to avoid the destruction of the resources upon which tourism is built.

Sustainable tourism is defined by the United Nations as "tourism that takes full account of its current and future economic, social and environmental impacts, addressing the needs of visitors, the industry, the environment and host communities" (Geels, 2002). This style of management is needed at three levels: the private enterprise, the destination and the tourists. This chapter will discuss how IT can enhance all these areas to become more sustainable. Certification programs, and mandatory and voluntary compliance systems, help tourism organizations operate more sustainably. Tourists make more sustainable choices as a result of schemes and websites. Sustainable tourism indicators and monitoring systems use IT to create measurement tools to shift destinations towards more sustainable management (Miller and Twining-Ward, 2005).

The body of knowledge on IT to address sustainable tourism is limited. Most IT developments in tourism have focused on improved marketing, distribution and profitability rather than investigating ways in which IT can facilitate responsible tourism. Its potential to do so, however, is large. The growth of green technology, the depletion of natural resources, and the institutionalization of environmentalism and the Internet are driving forces that demand more investigation (Weaver, 2012). As academic knowledge in sustainable tourism is developed, there are gaps in its transfer to public sector practice, and a knowledge management approach using technology is needed to fill those gaps (Ruhanen, 2008).

The annual ENTER Conference (http://www.ifitt.org/) and its related *Journal of Information Technology and Tourism* focus on knowledge creation in tourism and IT. The conference and the journal have a sprinkling of papers addressing sustainability, but a critical mass of research on the topic has not yet emerged. A landmark publication *Information and Communication Technologies for Sustainable Tourism* (Ali and Frew, 2012) has added a comprehensive analysis of the topic. The authors describe many computer technologies and their relevance to sustainable tourism. Table 12.1 lists these technologies and provides some examples of how they can be used in a sustainable tourism context.

IT can be harnessed in many ways to shift tourism to be more sustainable. This chapter is organized to focus on the goals and aims of sustainable tourism – environmentally, socioculturally and economically – and the technologies that can achieve those goals. The framework designed by the United Nations Environmental Program (UNEP; Nielsen, 2000)

Table 12.1. Applications of IT in sustainable tourism (Adapted from Ali and Frew, 2012, by permission of the copyright owner, Taylor & Francis).

IT application	Uses for sustainable tourism
Carbon calculator	Measures and monitors carbon emissions relative to behavior. Helps environmentally conscious travelers and organizations make choices that are less polluting.
Community informatics	Computer applications (e.g. networks, email bulletin boards) to enhance community participation. Develops social capital by empowering individuals and strengthening community identity.
Computer simulations	Use of IT to simulate real-world settings. Can help people visualize alternative policy scenarios in destinations and participate in the decision-making process.
Destination management systems (DMSs)	Manage fragile resources in a destination, promote economic sustainability by giving SMEs visibility, and provide tourists with information to make wiser choices.
Economic impact analysis	Software used to track data on tourist spending and linkages between different sectors. Calculation of tourism's impact on the destination's economy with computer models.
Environmental management systems (EMSs)	Computer systems that collect, analyze and report information relative to waste tracking and emissions, allowing organizations to improve their environmental performance.
Gamification	Use of computer game software in non-game situations. Can help to connect tourists with the local community or encourage sustainable behaviors.
Geographic information systems (GISs)	Systems that store, analyze and display geographic information in three dimensions. Valuable for sustainably monitoring natural resources.
Global positioning systems (GPSs)	Systems that through satellite communication identify the position of tourists and locations. Can track or direct tourist movements in more sustainable ways.
Intelligent transportation systems (ITSs)	Integrated central and vehicular computer systems to reduce congestion, guide traffic, inform travelers of public transport and improve safety.

(Continued)

Table 12.1. Continued.

IT application	Uses for sustainable tourism
Location-based services (LBSs)	Computer systems that communicate with mobile devices and provide location-relevant information. Can create awareness of local attractions and provide maps and guidance.
Virtual tourism	Sophisticated multi-sensory systems that allow the tourist to experience the destination and its attractions without being there. Has zero impact on the actual destination, thereby contributing to its sustainability.
Weather and climate change systems	Used to monitor weather and climate change. Can prepare destinations for upcoming hazards and weather risks.

identifies 12 aims to increase sustainability in destinations. This framework will be used to organize this chapter, and IT applications that progress each of the goals will be discussed. The UNEP/UNWTO framework is shown in Fig. 12.1 below.

This framework builds on the current thinking of sustainable tourism and focuses the reader on the impacts of the technologies rather than the technologies themselves, which are well described earlier in this book and in the book by Ali and Frew (2012).

In the area of **environmental sustainability** in tourism, the aims of resource efficiency, environmental purity, biological diversity and physical integrity are paramount. In the area of **socio-cultural sustainability** in tourism, social equity, local control, community well-being and cultural richness are the primary aims. Under the umbrella of **economic sustainability** in tourism, economic viability, local prosperity, employment quality and visitor fulfillment are the most important. Each of these categories will be discussed below.

ENVIRONMENTAL SUSTAINABILITY AND INFORMATION TECHNOLOGY

This section focuses on the use of IT to improve environmental resource efficiency, and to educate travelers to travel more responsibly. Related issues of climate change and carbon offset programs are included in this section. This section will also examine how computers can contribute to environmental purity and physical integrity in nature-based and cultural tourism destinations. It will discuss technology's contribution to biodiversity in the context of tourism, and the opportunities to reduce environmental impacts to zero by replacing travel entirely with virtual experiences.

Resource efficiency

Resource efficiency minimizes the use of scarce and non-renewable resources in the development and operation of tourism facilities and services (Nielsen, 2000). The two

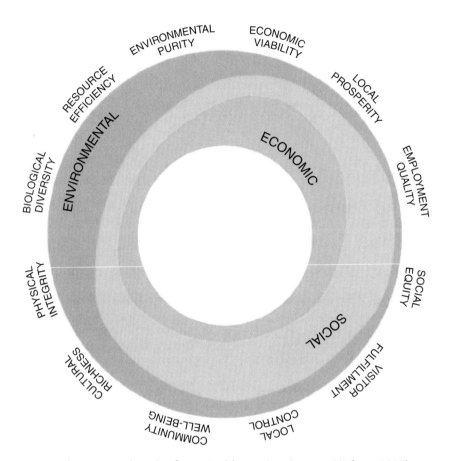

Fig. 12.1. Twelve aims and goals of sustainable tourism (source: Nielsen, 2000).

non-renewable resources most heavily debated in tourism are fossil fuels and water. Intelligent computer systems can monitor and curb their usage in travel firms, and inform tourists about modifying their activities to conserve the resources. Different types of tourism use these resources at different levels with mass tourism and luxury tourism being the heaviest users. In order to be more sustainable, careful management to conserve these resources and curb activities that deplete them are needed. The debate over fossil fuel usage in tourism tends to focus on the transportation sector, in particular the airline industry, which is a heavy user. Other sectors such as land transport and luxury accommodation are also significant users of fossil fuels. However, the airline industry is the most highly consumptive, and fuel is often one of the largest expenses for an airline. The search for alternative fuel sources increases as fossil fuels become depleted. Airlines are increasingly using computer technology to help minimize fuel usage and as a result reduce carbon emissions. In the USA 2% of greenhouse gas emissions are from commercial aviation (Negroni, 2009).

Current applications of IT to reduce fuel usage fall into three categories.

1. Computer systems that automatically select flight routes to minimize fuel consumption are common. They select the shortest routes, and the ones with the least weather disturbances.

2. The elimination of aircraft circling at high-traffic airports caused by gates not being ready to receive aircraft is managed by computer systems (see Chapter 7). They ensure that flights depart from the origin gate when traffic at the destination airport will not delay arrival.

3. The preferred use of continuous descent paths as the aircraft comes to land, which uses less fuel during landing (Negroni 2009).

In addition, computer design technology is making aircraft lighter using new materials and thereby minimizing fuel usage (Boeing, 2013). A good example of the outcome of these technologies is the Boeing 787 Dreamliner.

Industry Insight: Boeing 787 Dreamliner

In 2011 Boeing delivered its first 787 Dreamliner to All Nippon Airways (ANA). The Boeing 787 Dreamliner is the world's first major airliner to use composite materials in the construction of its airframe. The environmental credentials of this aircraft are most impressive and pave the way for a more sustainable aviation industry in the future. The aircraft is Boeing's most fuel-efficient airliner, thanks to the use of lighter composite materials, advanced engines and wing design. A number of IT innovations have made the Dreamliner more environmentally sustainable:

- Design: Computer Aided Design (CAD) and other IT tools have been instrumental in modeling and testing wing, fuselage and engine designs that reduce fuel consumption, carbon emissions and noise.
- Manufacturing: all Boeing manufacturing sites are ISO14001 certified and the company has worked hard to reduce its use of energy, water and hazardous materials. For example, technicians and engineers now use mobile devices instead of paper. IT systems have supported the testing and fabrication of components to precise specifications and reduced the need for many small parts.
- Flight deck: new technologies on the flight deck, together with better air–ground integration and new air traffic control (ATC) procedures are improving flight routing and arrivals. Reducing every flight by just 1 minute can reduce carbon dioxide emissions by 4.8 million tons per year.
- Recycling: Boeing aims to recycle 90–95% of a retired aircraft by 2016 and IT systems play an important role in improving recycling processes and helping the company track components and materials.

(Continued)

Continued.

http://youtu.be/7CkAND4v8o

In addition to these achievements, Boeing is working with researchers to advance the use of sustainable aviation biofuel. Many new environmentally friendly concepts are being tested as part of Boeing's ecoDemonstrator flight test program. For an overview take a look at the following videos: http://bcove.me/04n62ia2/ and http://youtu.be/7C_kAND4v8o/.

National and international agencies are also contributing to minimizing fossil fuel usage in air travel. For example, the "Greener Skies Initiative 2", a research project funded by the US Federal Aviation Administration, was launched in 2011 (Federal Aviation Administration, 2013). Greener Skies uses on-board computers to evaluate navigation procedures and improve air traffic management efficiency. The advanced navigation is supported by GPS-based technology that allows aircraft to land at busy airports where the runways are very close together. As a result, departures and landings are more efficient, use less fuel, and reduce emissions and noise. Intelligent transportation systems as discussed in Chapter 8 can also minimize fossil fuel usage by guiding vehicles through the least fuel consumptive routes.

The accommodation sector also is a heavy consumer of energy and water resources. Chapter 9 describes the type of computer systems that are commonly used to reduce energy usage in hotels. Water is an essential resource likely to become scarcer in the future as climate change impacts weather and rain patterns. Monitoring and controlling its careful use is critical for sustainable destinations. The consumption of water by tourists in hotels is a concern in some destinations, particularly where residents compete with tourists for water. Water consumption by the average guest in a luxury property in particular is much higher than resident consumption. Other tourist attractions such as golf courses, zoos, parks and restaurants also use high levels of water. Computer systems that monitor and track water usage and assist in its conservation must be used. Sustainable certifications for tourist facilities often audit their water usage and conservation policies.

Environmental purity and physical integrity

Much tourism depends on the pristine quality of environments: water resources (lakes, oceans and rivers), air and land resources (forests, parks, animal habitats, beaches, wilderness areas). **Environmental purity** is particularly important to ecotourism, nature-based tourism, wellness tourism and adventure tourism. Therefore the minimization of air, water and land pollution and the reduction of waste must be addressed. Physical integrity is a related concept referring to the physical and visual quality of urban and rural landscapes. This section will examine how IT can help keep environments pure and enhance touristic landscapes.

Destination management systems (DMSs) that include data on environmentally sensitive tourism resources can help to manage their use electronically. By requiring environmentally sensitive resources to be reserved online through the DMS (hiking trails, campsites, beaches and waterways) their usage can be controlled. This control at predetermined carrying capacity levels reduces the damage caused by large volumes of tourists. GIS applications that are part of a DMS can assist in natural resource management, land use and rural tourism economic development (Savitsky *et al.*, 1999). In a study of e-tourism experts, 35% of the respondents saw in-trip use of these technologies as important to the sustainability of the destination (Scott and Frew, 2013). Visitor management technologies also improve the sustainability of tourist attractions by reducing crowding and congestion and ensuring that tourists do not damage cultural and environmental resources (see Chapter 10).

Educating tourists to act in ways that do not damage the environment is made easier with IT. Location-based services can connect travelers' smartphones and tablets to information databases about sensitive resources. Interpretative information about the resource and advice on appropriate behavior can be given to tourists to protect the resource. Mobile apps access vast amounts of information on touristic environmental issues, and when connected to location-based services, GIS systems and GPS technology can guide tourists through an attraction. For example in a national park, a tourist could be warned to stay away from wildlife feeding and breeding sites, or alternatively be encouraged to visit an area where a rare plant is in bloom. Some systems are less destination-specific and more global in nature and include knowledge of such things as weather and climate change, carbon offset schemes and global biodiversity.

Table 12.2 describes some of the apps that tourists could use to help keep the environment pure.

These technologies are helpful for environmentally aware tourists in their selection of a destination and their trip-planning. They can also be used in-trip to decide on routes, attractions and events that cause less environment pollution. In-trip apps include maps, driving directions, information on events, attractions, restaurants, weather and travel advisory information technologies to influence the sustainability of the destination (Scott and Frew, 2013). More research on these apps is needed to investigate how they change travelers' behavior to be more sustainable (Miller *et al.*, 2010).

Environmental purity also includes recycling, waste management systems and the reduction of many types of pollution. Tourism can produce noise pollution, air pollution, water pollution and land-based pollution. These pollutants not only impact the long-term sustainability of natural resources, they also affect the short-term visual, aural and olfactory amenity of tourist sites. IT systems can monitor air and water quality and noise levels, and also remove pollutants before treated waste is returned to the environment. The Great Barrier Reef (GBR) in Australia provides a good example of how IT is used to preserve the purity of marine environments. Resorts operating on islands within the GBR Marine Park are legally required to treat wastewater and sewage before the water is returned to the marine environment. This requires high-tech monitoring systems as well as IT systems to manage treatment plants. Water quality is monitored by taking samples at regular intervals and analyzing and documenting pollutants using specialized laboratory equipment. These systems

Table 12.2. Mobile apps for environmental awareness.

Name	Designer	Purpose
Carbon Emissions Calculator	ICAO approved by UN environment management group	Calculates CO_2 emissions from air travel
Climate Change DataFinder	World Bank	Provides global information on climate change indicators
Climate Counts	www.climatecounts.org	To educate corporations about climate change issues. Calculates climate change responsibility of different sectors including airlines, hotels and foodservice
Climate Mobile	Geo-Optics Inc.	Provides latest worldwide climate change data from international satellites and land instruments
Earth Now	NASA	Data from satellites displayed in colored maps of sea level rises, water, temperatures etc.
Fragile Earth	Harper Collins Publishers	Unique views of how places on earth are transforming with extreme weather events and climate change
Drive Alternatives	Drive Alternatives	Provides information about alternative fuel stations, e.g. ethanol, biodiesel, CNG, electric

are also used to report water quality measures to the GBR Marine Park Authority and other stakeholders. Similar systems are also used in the cruise-shipping industry to manage the pollution of marine environments.

Physical integrity is related to a sense of place in the destination. Destinations ideally are vibrant with unique cultural, historic and natural resources that permeate all aspects of the destination, creating strong sense of place. For example, buildings made of local natural materials create more of a sense of place than those made of concrete. The US National Park Service recognizes seven aspects that constitute the integrity of tourism places and facilities. They are location, design, setting, materials, workmanship, feeling and association (National Park Service, 2013). Ideally all of these are infused with a sense of place. **Computer-aided design (CAD)** systems can help to assure that buildings have some of these qualities. A CAD system is a combination of hardware and software that assist engineers and architects in designing buildings, railway stations, airports or any physical structure. They can view their design from any angle on a computer screen and see the effects of changes to one aspect or the whole design. As new destination facilities are designed, CAD systems can encourage innovative designs reflective of the destination's sense of place.

In order to monitor and manage their environmental footprint, tourism organizations use Environmental Management Systems (EMSs) that are supported by IT. Green tourists increasingly expect tourism facilities to practice environmental management. This pressure, along with the desire to be eco-certified, is giving rise to more computer-driven EMSs in tourism enterprises. An EMS is "a set of procedures and practices that enable an organization to reduce its environmental impacts and increase its operating efficiency" (United Nations World Tourism Organization, 2013). The International Standards Organization (ISO) has a special classification for environmental management systems for organizations known as ISO14001. Certification systems are often based on these standards. QFinance (2013), however, observe that most hotels do not implement EMSs due to lack of resources and knowledge, and suggest creative financing tools to overcome the finance barrier. Computer technology monitors and manages efficient use of resources including water (low-flush toilets, low-flow showerheads) and energy (solar power generators, energy-saving light-bulbs etc.), pollution of all kinds (noise, air and visual pollution), recycling and waste management.

Biological diversity

Areas with great **biodiversity** naturally attract tourists. People enjoy traveling to view special animals, birds and plants in their habitats. Severe damage to plant and animal species can occur if tourism is not managed adequately and tourists do not behave appropriately. This section will examine how information technology can assist in tourism making a positive contribution to the biodiversity of destinations.

Tourists who travel with handheld devices and are interested in species and environments can improve a destination's biodiversity. They can become **citizen scientists** and monitor animal and bird species and other environmental phenomenon on their digital devices as they travel. Working under the guidance of scientists, they become important data gatherers for biodiversity, while also increasing the enjoyment of their vacation. The data collected become part of a large database that tracks aggregate data about the biological diversity in a destination in real time. This is an example of the use of big data in a sustainability context.

Combining tourism, research, conservation and computers can be called "tourist science". It requires careful planning by environmental experts in the tourism destination and the training of the tourists. The Earth-Watch Institute is an example of a **tourist scientist** initiative. It is a non-profit organization that engages people worldwide in scientific research and education to promote the understanding and action necessary for a sustainable environment (EarthWatch, 2013). EarthWatch recruits volunteers (tourists) to assist scientists in identifying plants and animal species. Volunteer tracking of species is not new, however only recently has this process been digitized with smartphone apps and free open-sourced software. An example of such an app is Cyber Tracker, designed to track animal species in their habitats. Cyber Tracker, a non-profit organization, monitors the environment to anticipate and prevent negative impacts on animal species due to pollution, climate change, habitat destruction and loss of biodiversity. **Cyber tracking** connects the user and the main computers via satellite links. Smartphone users upload their findings to the Cloud after which the aggregate data are analyzed to help visualize changes in the global ecosystem in real time (Silvertown, 2009). To understand how cyber tracking is being used on safaris in Africa, view the video at http://youtu.be/sG9rnLPbEqs/. It also shows how cyber tracking can keep the ancient skills of animal tracking alive.

Fig. 12.2. An indigenous person using the handheld cyber tracker (Photo Credit: Rolex/Eric Vandeville).

http://youtu.be/sG9rnLPbEqs

Cyber Trackers can be used in many types of locations. The photograph in Fig. 12.2 taken in 2008 shows a community member working with a device during a research project run by Conservation International in the Western Kgalagadi Conservation Corridor in the Kalahari Desert in Southern Africa.

Applications of citizen/tourist science projects in tourism exist, but not yet on a wide scale. The Galapagos Islands in Ecuador are using tourists to monitor environments, birds and animals, and enhance environmental stewardship, in this resource-rich destination (Galapagos Conservancy, 2013). The Caribbean uses tourist scientists to monitor the status of the coral reefs and has helped to generate policy development for coral reefs in Jamaica. Self-selected SCUBA divers were the EarthWatch volunteers who collected the data (Crabbe, 2012).

Voluntourists are a natural market segment to engage in these projects by making meaningful contributions to the communities and wildlife in destinations. Research shows that volunteers received "more intense experiences" than average tourists through their wildlife interactions (Weiler and Richins, 1995). A study of volunteer tourists monitoring parrots and macaws in southeastern Peru makes the case that volunteer tourism, conservation biology, technology and ecotourism make an excellent combination with mutual benefit to each (Brightsmith *et al.*, 2008). Such projects can be a source of repeat visitation for destinations as tourists return to see the results of their efforts.

Virtual substitute travel experiences

Tourists can experience some benefits of travel by staying home and using technology to virtually experience the destination, removing any environmental damage to the destination. Virtual trips can replace – or partially replace – actual trips in a number of ways. The simplest is to use the Internet's audio-visual resources to view destinations and 360-degree videos of landmarks, heritage sites and hotels.

There are numerous examples of these sites. "The World in Virtual Reality" has a website (http://www.virtual-travels.com/), which contains high quality photographs of destinations all over the world. These high-resolution virtual reality photos provide 360-degree views of features. A similar site called "360 cities" (360cities, 2013) contains panoramic photos and videos of many of the world's most interesting cities, their museums and attractions. Google Earth also has a platform for experiencing destinations virtually. It has teamed with the National Trust in the UK and UNESCO Heritage Sites in Europe to allow the user to virtually view castles, country houses and other heritage attractions. Google Russia and Russian Railways have produced a virtual experience of the Trans-Siberian Railway complemented by city tours along the way, balalaika music and readings of Leo Tolstoy's *War and Peace*. Travel intermediaries such as Virtual Travel Events now offer business travelers a virtual alternative to meetings, conferences and seminars using videoconferencing. Even visiting friends and relatives travel can sometimes be replaced by technology links such as Skype.

Simply seeing a destination online as discussed above is rarely enough to replace the trip. **Virtual reality** (VR) (Fig. 12.3), the ultimate in multimedia, goes further and allows the user to experience sound, motion, even smells related to a touristic experience and presents possibilities to enhance and replace touristic experiences (Cheong, 1995). VR creates computer-generated worlds in which people can experience other realities and interact with them (Virtual Reality, 2013). This capacity has implications for sustainable tourism as the virtual reality world mimics real world destination experiences.

VR can also give travelers a "taste" of a tourism experience, by surrounding them in multiple sensory inputs of a different reality. As such it is the ultimate travel brochure. Travel retailers willing to invest in the technology can allow their clients to "try on" a vacation experience such as white-water rafting, walking through the colorful markets of Indonesia or other rich virtual worlds. Tourists can experience this taste before purchasing an expensive vacation that they may not enjoy.

It is difficult to say how much tourism will be replaced by VR in the future, but as the earth's resources are depleted, travel becomes

Fig. 12.3. Virtual reality equipment (source: Strickland, 2007).

increasingly expensive, safety and security concerns continue, it offers a feasible alternative. It also removes the need for long air flights, the inconvenience of currency exchange and foreign languages, and exposure to strange and potentially dangerous environments. Its contribution to sustainability is its reduction of carbon emissions and damage to natural environments. VR may never simulate the experience completely, but a small selection of trips may lend themselves to substitution in the future. Its use in theme parks for short-lived entertainment experiences, trips with a single purpose, for example to visit a particular museum or to see a particular monument, are more feasible than complex trips. **Augmented reality (AR)** has been described in earlier chapters. Its relevance to sustainability is less than VR, however the interpretative and information provision features of AR can affect tourists' behavior and choices in a way that are more sustainable.

SOCIO-CULTURAL SUSTAINABILITY AND INFORMATION TECHNOLOGY

The socio-cultural applications of IT include applications that help to provide social equity and community wellness in destinations, facilitate local control of the tourism sector, and those that enhance the cultural richness of the destination society.

Social equity and community well-being

How can IT increase **social equity** and **community well-being** in a tourism destination? A major contribution of IT is that it democratizes and equalizes the community by giving all residents and enterprises equal access to technology and therefore the world. Formerly these benefits were only available to large international firms and the wealthiest and most powerful residents allowing them to influence tourism development more. IT networks create the ability for people to connect to knowledge, education, tourist markets and destination management systems. Remote destinations have often been left out of this connectivity, but now telecommunications providers can install networks to reach the smallest and most distant rural communities. This is known as **last-mile connectivity** and is critical for the residents to experience the equity that technology can provide. The constantly decreasing price of handheld devices also gives access to technology for more of the population.

Disadvantaged resident groups can suffer from **information asymmetry**, which perpetuates the cycles that often prevent participation in the benefits of tourism. Access to IT and the training to use the technologies can break these cycles. For example, Digital Divide Data is a social enterprise providing digital data services to organizations worldwide while making a social impact at the same time (Digital Divide Data, 2013). It does this by training young people in emerging economies in IT skills such as data entry, and newspaper and archive digitization. By recruiting and training these young people, a positive social impact is made. This is relevant to the tourism sector where tourism small and medium-sized enterprises (SMEs) could benefit from employees with these skills. The Research Insight box below discusses how IT can help pro-poor tourism development.

IT can also contribute to social equity by attracting the right kind of tourists. Those who want to enhance the residents' well-being,

---

Research Insight: Pro-Poor Tourism and IT Systems

Nadkani, S. (2008) Knowledge Creation, Retention, Exchange, Devolution, Interpretation and Treatment (K-CREDIT) as an economic growth driver in pro-poor tourism. *Current Issues in Tourism* 11(5), 456–472.

A concern of enlightened tourism policy makers is how to ensure that the benefits and advantages of IT systems reach poor communities in tourism destinations. This is often referred to as pro-poor tourism or poverty alleviation for tourism. In this article Nadkani explains how the information asymmetry between the rich and the poor can create a downward spiral of poverty. Access to IT systems and therefore to knowledge can turn this vicious cycle around for poor communities.

He states that "pro-poor tourism value chains can serve as eco-friendly and economical instruments in poverty alleviation efforts". In particular those at the end of the tourism value-chain, or the "last mile" as it is often called, need an information infrastructure to benefit from tourism. He uses the term K-CREDIT, which stands for knowledge creation, retention, exchange, devolution, interpretation and treatment rather than the more common term Knowledge Management (KM) to refer to the use of IT to transfer knowledge to the poorer communities. Last mile connectivity (bringing IT infrastructure to the most isolated and rural locations) and capacity building in poor areas both require intervention at the grassroots level. The involvement of benign intermediaries such as NGOs and local administration, donors and investors, Destination Management Organizations (DMOs) and international agencies to bring IT to the local level is important. The author also calls for a much-needed research agenda to deal with IT intervention for pro-poor tourism development (Nadkarni, 2008).

---

particularly those that are poor, disadvantaged, disabled, or socially or geographically marginalized can make a difference. When tourists engage with the local community, stay in local accommodations and buy locally made souvenirs, there is a stronger chance to improve social equity and community well-being. This includes volunteer tourism, community-based local tourism and **pro-poor tourism** development, all of which can be enhanced with IT.

A new wave of enterprises called **social enterprises** is building sustainable communities and addressing the UN Millennium Development Goals (UNMDG). In tourism they are bringing more equity and well-being to communities, and numerous IT platforms support this type of tourism. Social entrepreneurs are passionate people who want to change the world. They tend to display similar characteristics as business entrepreneurs: passion, risk-taking etc. When their creative ideas to improve the social good are matched with funding agencies much work can be accomplished. An example of IT support for social enterprises is a website (http://www.socialfirmsinfomine.org.uk/) which provides numerous tools and knowledge for social enterprises to start and grow (Social Firms UK, 2013). An online forum called Hospitality and Tourism Social Entrepreneurs provides a platform where hospitality and tourism social entrepreneurs can learn about best practices, network and share ideas.

One of the largest social entrepreneurship organizations is Ashoka, which uses IT effectively to accomplish its mission of changing the world. Its website provides information on its many projects and over 100 of these relate somehow to tourism. It also communicates through blogs and an e-magazine. Ashoka Hub is an IT platform connecting social entrepreneurs to resources, people in the community and clusters of other social entrepreneurs working in their areas. Social entrepreneurs use crowdsourcing and crowd-funding to pursue their goals. Ashoka has also designed a skill-sharing platform called @Skillshare to help people find others with certain skill sets so they can work together (Ashoka, 2013).

Another aspect of social equity is providing adequate information and accessibility to handicapped travelers as they make travel choices. It is important for travel providers to consider how information about their facilities is displayed on websites. Darcy (2011) found that handicapped travelers often do not have adequate access to information about tourism facilities. In particular they valued textual material, floor plans and digital photos of the facility. Visually impaired travelers in particular experience difficulty when researching and booking travel online. Han and Mills (2007) give suggestions on how travel sites can be more usable for visually impaired travelers. An innovative online tool that assists tourism managers in determining the accessibility of their facilities for disabled tourists has been developed at the Biomechanical Institute of

Valencia, Spain (Biomechancial Institute of Valencia, 2013). Another development to improve accessibility in tourism facilities in Italy is called Village for All. This uses iPad technology to generate multimedia data (photos, movies, vector drawings etc.) about a particular tourism facility, which is then stored in the Cloud. This is then analyzed with reference to accessibility standards and generates a report on how the facility can be improved for physically and mentally disabled travelers, as well as blind, deaf and dumb travelers (Village for All, 2013).

Technology can also assist in reporting and recording human rights abuses. If tourists are traveling and see violations in the facilities or attractions they visit, they are able to act. The advancement of audio and video recording from large video cameras, to camcorders and now small smartphones, and the ability to rapidly send pictures and videos over the web allows tourists to become on-site reporters. An organization called Witness (http://www.witness.org/) uses videos made by citizens or tourists to bring to light human rights violations. For example, if tourists witness child labor in a destination, they could take a video with their smartphone and upload it to the Witness website. Once on the website, investigations into the situation can begin. Another interactive website with the goal of reporting human rights abuses relative to tourism was used in Nepal to raise awareness of sex crimes; the website encourages victims to make online contact and thereby bring the crime to light (Brown, 1999).

Tourism Concern, a non-profit organization supporting ethical tourism, uses its website to promote various campaigns to bring more equity in tourism. Examples of such campaigns are water equity in tourism, and the displacement of local people for tourism development. Their website shows how to take action to make a difference on such issues (Tourism Concern, 2013). Equitable access to funding in tourism is also an important part of community well-being. IT can assist aspiring small businesses by providing information on how to access micro-finance loans, and how to use **crowd funding** on the web. Also tour operators are now offering micro-finance tours, providing the opportunity for visitors to see how small amounts of funding can help reduce poverty.

Local control

To be sustainable, tourism development needs to be controlled by local interests. This requires engaging and empowering local communities in the planning and decision-making and future development of tourism in conjunction with other stakeholders. **Stakeholder engagement** is considered to be crucial in sustainable tourism planning (Murphy, 1988; Goeldner and Ritchie, 2006). This must involve all who are affected by tourism development including the community and its residents, local governments, activist organizations, hotels, transportation, NGOs, and the tourists themselves. Applications of IT to these issues are what Gurstein (2000) refers to as **community informatics**.

Stakeholder engagement in tourism planning and decision making is not easy due to place and time constraints. Many destinations have sparsely populated areas where physical attendance at planning meetings is not possible. In other cases key stakeholders may not be in the destination as the planning is taking place. Here IT can help with solutions. Remote input to town meetings through the Internet or Skype can facilitate input for those unable to attend meetings. Electronic polling software such as Turning Point (http://www.turningtechnologies.com/) operating on small computers and handheld terminals can provide virtual stakeholder input and opinions.

Technology can also break down barriers to collaboration among tourism stakeholders. For example, **scenario-based design (SBD)**, which engages stakeholders in envisioning innovative, technology-based tourism services in a destination, can generate innovative ideas for destination development (McCabe *et al.*, 2012). Bringing stakeholders together to envision new electronic services for the city of Leipzig, Germany highlights the need for collaboration for a sustainable urban destination (Paskaleva and Megliola, 2010). It shows how collaboratively developed electronic platforms with all stakeholders involved can increase access to local heritage, improve the tourist experience and boost sustainable urban tourism.

The Industry Insight box below describes the need to view tourism as an ecosystem built up of IT networks. It is written by the founder of a unique sustainable tourism education platform called Conscious Travel and synthesizes some of the ideas in this section relevant to the sustainability of destinations.

Cultural richness of host communities

Tourists often travel to experience the unique culture and heritage of destinations. It is therefore important to build the respect for and enhancement of historic heritage, authentic culture, traditions and the distinctiveness

Industry Insight: Conscious Travel

Conscious Travel: An Approach to Using IT in a Networked Age, Anna Pollock

Many IT applications in tourism are developed individually in response to the specific needs and opportunities associated with rigid and self-contained sectors (e.g. accommodation, transport, activities, attractions, food and beverage outlets) and functions (marketing, operations, customer service, research and planning). Competition, rather than collaboration, has been the primary mode of behavior. As a consequence, the means to act collectively in response to external or internal change is limited and rapid diffusion of innovation is impeded.

The founder of Conscious Travel, Anna Pollock, suggests that a speedier, more widespread deployment of IT to the development of sustainable tourism will occur once we change our understanding of how tourism "works". Pollock suggests that it would be more helpful to perceive tourism as a business ecosystem, organic network or complex adaptive system made up of many self-organizing and interdependent agents (e.g. guests, hosts, intermediaries and host communities) that are embedded in and supported by the biosphere. The hardware and software associated with various information technologies constitute the nervous system or neural network of such a system. Living systems operate in a constant state of flux and change and their members – self-organizing agents (humans, animals, plants) – respond to the behavior of each other and the larger systems (environmental, economic, social and political) of which they are a part. They emerge in response to a set of enabling conditions and their goal is to evolve into higher states of order while maintaining an internal balance (between member agents) and an external balance with the larger systems in which they are embedded. Information exchange is vital to any living system and an intelligent system uses information exchange to better anticipate change, become more resilient to shocks and create value.

At least seven factors have combined to make it technically possible to create an intelligent destination: unimaginable improvements in processing power; miniaturization and the "Internet of Things"; ability to connect agents on the move (mobility); the ubiquity of technology; the ability for systems to talk with one another (open systems); cloud storage and "always on" computing and consumers' desire to create as well as receive content. The challenge is no longer the technology – it is the mindset of tourism hosts that needs to change. They need to understand that their success depends on collectively evolving a neural network that will enable information to be collected and shared. Conscious Travel is designed to create multiple, small and highly collaborative learning communities of hosts who together, consciously, join up to create a highly dynamic, intelligent whole. Each community will identify its own issues, challenges and opportunities, and set action priorities appropriate for its time, place, culture and circumstance. Hosts can use a collaborative software platform and data management protocols to enable them to collect and share information about customers, impacts (waste generation, resource use), costs, market opportunities, trends, congested areas, cross selling opportunities and destination well-being.

of host communities. IT can connect, inform and interpret cultural attractions for tourists in many ways (Pechlaner and Osti, 2001).

In particular, (Buhalis, 2002) suggests that IT can assist in these aims by:

- disseminating better understanding of customs and traditions to the benefit of tourists and host communities;
- promoting the visibility of cultural resources – especially new or small ones;
- monitoring tourism impacts on cultural resources and visitor flow management strategies; and
- building partnerships between cultural and tourism operators to strengthen their market position.

Cultural products and services can be made more visible by including them in the DMS. Many destinations do this; for example, in the Tyrol, Austria, a part of the DMS website includes cultural and lifestyle information. Hawaii's website includes many cultural and community events. To do this successfully requires close and careful cooperation between cultural and heritage tourism operators and the DMS (Pechlaner and Osti, 2001).

The Croatian World Heritage Sites website is an example of how a country can build its heritage tourism sector with the help of IT. The Croatian destination website provides interactive demonstrations of cultural attractions and amenities. It also is a platform that links stakeholders together so they can work together to provide sustained growth in heritage tourism. Another option for heritage destinations is to collaborate with UNESCO World Heritage Sites to create clusters with other attractions and use the Internet to brand and inform visitors about their sites (Hawkins, 2004).

Advanced information technology can protect cultural and heritage tourist resources from environmental dangers such as fires. A system using a ubiquitous sensor network has been successfully tested at a temple in South Korea (Joo *et al.*, 2009).

Tour guiding is another important part of cultural tourism. Multimedia, context-aware digital tour guiding systems that tourists access with handheld devices are increasingly common as a replacement for human guides. When connected to GIS systems they can access location-based information at hotspots throughout the cultural or heritage attraction. The quality and capacity of handheld devices determine the effectiveness of such guides (O'Grady and O'Hare, 2002).

It is particularly important for indigenous communities to preserve their culture because they often have the richest culture and the least ability to access IT. A study of online technologies in Australian indigenous communities noted that limited skills, high costs and physical access barriers have made it difficult for indigenous communities to effectively use online technologies (Pramod and Carson, 2002). In 12 Aboriginal tourism websites they identified "content" issues and "delivery" issues as continuing problems. Content issues refer to the accuracy and authenticity of the online content, and delivery issues refer to the available infrastructure and the available online platforms for them to work with. Cultural artifacts and handicrafts are often a critical part of indigenous communities. The Internet can provide access to more markets and better revenue to the artists. In fact, indigenous people can benefit more from tourism if they are electronically connected and trained to use the technology (Harris *et al.*, 2007).

Digitization of cultural and historic information in destinations is increasingly common. Computer technology in museums can bring to life cultural, heritage and historic information about communities. Cultural and heritage digital interpretation is a growing field that utilizes many types of information systems such as the recording of multimedia local histories, stories and genealogical records in rural, minority and indigenous populations (Rahaman and Tan, 2009). Whilst some welcome the advent of cyber-technology, others fear that it may eventually destroy the very mechanisms by which individuals in community derive social capital (Ross, 2005).

ECONOMIC SUSTAINABILITY AND INFORMATION TECHNOLOGY

The economic goals of sustainable tourism are economic viability, local prosperity, employment quality and visitor fulfillment (United Nations Environment Programme and World Tourism Organization, 2005). This section will address how IT can affect all of these to make a destination more economically sustainable. IT's influence on visitor fulfillment has been covered earlier in the book and so will not be covered in this chapter.

IT can improve the economic success of tourism enterprises by facilitating innovation and providing access to new markets. However, larger tourism firms with more capital, expertise and a broader geographic distribution of products tend to implement more IT systems than smaller firms (Buhalis, 2003, p.140). SMEs often constitute a large proportion of tourism firms. They are usually locally owned and can contribute more to the

sustainability of a destination. This section examines how IT can help bring prosperity to tourism SMEs.

Economic viability and local prosperity

A destination that has more locally owned businesses is likely to be more sustainable because economic leakages are minimized and economic linkages are strengthened. The majority of tourism firms worldwide are locally owned, **small and medium enterprises (SME)** with less than 250 employees. Those with less than ten employees are known as micro-enterprises, those with 11–50 employees are classified as small enterprises and those with 51–250 employees are known as medium enterprises (Buhalis, 2003). Many restaurants, small hotels and guest houses, ground transportation services, attractions and entertainment operators fit into the SME category. IT can help to strengthen the economic viability of the destination by supporting tourism SMEs.

IT can impact the livelihood of small-scale enterprises and local entrepreneurs by building:

- **Financial capital**: by providing online communication with lending organizations, for example micro-credit banks and organizations;
- **Human capital**: by providing increased knowledge of new skills through distance learning and processes required for certification;
- **Natural capital**: by providing opportunities to access national government policies online;
- **Social capital**: by cultivating contacts beyond the immediate community; and

- **Physical capital**: by lobbying for the provision of basic infrastructure including data and telecommunications infrastructure (Nadkani, 2008).

These five types of capital help to build the level of e-readiness of small, locally owned tourism enterprises through electronic networks making more inter-firm linkages at the local level possible. This will support their efforts in B2B commerce, B2C commerce, and collective marketing initiatives. Also it will tend to reduce the amount of imports needed and create import substitution thereby increasing the economic multiplier. E-commerce can drive income closer to the actual providers of tourism experiences by deconstructing the tourism value chain. It will also strengthen communities, locally owned firms and indigenous populations.

Many challenges exist for SMEs to digitize their enterprises. First, it may be difficult for SMEs to find the level of investment necessary to computerize their operations. Second, learning how to use the technologies can also be a challenge due to perceived lack of time, and unskilled personnel. Research indicates that improving SME managers' knowledge of and proficiency in web technology is particularly important. Third, tourism SMEs in rural and remote locations may lack both financial and technological infrastructures, making it difficult to process online payments, particularly from international customers. Fourth, language creates a problem in technological adoption for many tourism SMEs in non-English-speaking countries. Often computer software is not written in local languages and English may not be spoken by the hosts. There are technical solutions to this multilingual problem so that

non-English-speaking SMEs can access the internet (Ho, 2002).

Many factors affect the use of IT in SMEs. They can be categorized into push and pull factors as described in Fig. 12.4 (Buhalis, 2003).

Pull factors relate to the opportunities that SMEs can enjoy as they embrace the new technologies. These include the extra demand from tourists, the opportunities for increased connectivity with intranets and extranet systems, the ability to connect with other industry members via consortia or marketing alliance, the benefits that certification provides, and finally the opportunities from adopting certain accounting standards. In contrast, **push factors** are related to the threats of not using the technologies. Some of these are new demands from digitally savvy tourists, from new government policies affecting the SME's operation, developments in technology that the IT vendors propose to them, competition in the global marketplace, the influence of their strategic partners use of IT, or from the new levels of education and training of tourism employees.

One notable initiative on IT for sustainable tourism at the global level is by United Nations Conference on Trade and Development (UNCTAD). This initiative called E-Tourism assists tourism enterprises in developing countries to access tourism markets through the use of IT (http://www.unctad.org/). The demand-driven initiative focuses on developing and implementing IT-based tools to help communities tap the international market by strengthening and including local institutional and human capacities in the global market, and promoting local involvement and ownership.

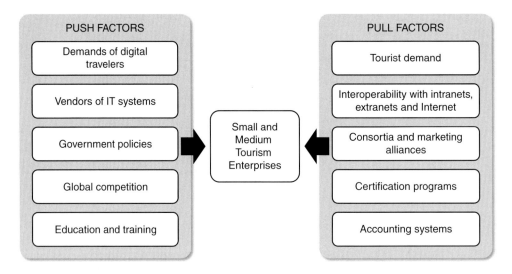

Fig. 12.4. Push and pull factors determining the use of IT by SMEs (Adapted from Buhalis, 2003, p. 143, by permission of the copyright owner, Pearson Education. Further reproduction or publication without the express permission of Pearson Education is prohibited).

The **digital divide**, which describes the difference in technological infrastructures between developed and developing countries and small island states, can be equalized with tourism. The need to connect with the international visitor is a strong incentive to bring more technology to a region. As developing countries gain more technological sophistication, sometimes they **"leapfrog"** technological adoption. Leapfrogging occurs when developing countries "leapfrog" over the legacy computer systems, and adopt more modern technologies (Hashim *et al.*, 2014).

The creation of e-marketplaces for regions or destinations can give more visibility to SMEs. Destinet (http://destinet.eu/market-place/) is an initiative of the European Environment Agency and is the single European gateway for sustainable tourism information (ECOTRANS, 2013). It provides information and knowledge resources on sustainable and responsible tourism products and a communications platform for

SMEs. The information on the site is quality assessed, carefully selected and includes an atlas, news bulletins and links to relevant topics, information on certification programs, attractions and tour operators.

The supply chains used by tourism organizations also impact the sustainability of the destination and must be managed carefully (Ali and Frew, 2012). There are numerous stages in sustainable supply chain management that must be attended to. Some of them are: the design of a sustainable product or service; the sustainable procurement from suppliers who adhere to sustainable practices; sustainable production; and sustainable distribution of the product or service (Sigala, 2008).

Ensuring that supply chain members are practicing environmental and social sustainability spreads the positive impact. For example, a green hotel may only wish to trade with supply firms (food providers, laundries, furniture manufacturers) that are certified as sustainable. Another example is the Tour

Operators Initiative (TOI), a consortium of tour operators who ensure that their suppliers use sustainable management practices (Tour Operators Initiative, 2013). Their website provides information on best practices for sustainable supply-chain management and advice on how to integrate sustainability criteria into suppliers' contracts. Tour operators are advised to apply sustainable principles into their accounting procedures, to plan tours that minimize the environmental and cultural impacts, to select suppliers that integrate sustainable practices into their operations, and to use local tour guides.

Employment quality and capacity building

A sustainable destination needs quality employees with good levels of pay, job satisfaction, training, working conditions and opportunities for advancement. Tourism employment also must be nondiscriminatory in terms of age, gender, race and other ways. The IT sector has much to offer to improve employment, education and training of the workforce, and capacity building in general. Attracting the brightest and best students into tourism studies is an important way to improve the quality of tourism. These students tend to be tech-savvy and want to work in firms that further develop their IT skills.

Online learning programs can improve the quality and satisfaction of employees in tourism. Managers and employees alike can learn from online courses offered by many schools, colleges and universities. The development of **Massive Open Online Courses (MOOCS)** provide opportunities for education from anywhere with an Internet connection. The courses are free and open to anyone who

wishes to learn irrespective of their educational level. View the video "What is a MOOC?" on YouTube: http://youtu.be/eW3gMGqcZQc/. At this time, very few of these courses are tourism-related but many relate to topics in business, IT and sustainable development. There is enormous potential to use these technologies to build community and employee capacity for sustainable tourism in developing economies.

http://youtu.be/eW3gMGqcZQc

Many other sustainable tourism organizations provide online learning. Three are highlighted below. First is the network called Building Excellence in Sustainable Tourism Education Network (BEST Education Network). Modules related to various aspects of sustainable tourism are designed by groups of international tourism educators. These course modules are then either posted online or published in books and journals (http://www.besteducationnetwork.org/). The second organization that provides online learning opportunities in sustainable tourism is The International Ecotourism Society (TIES). TIES offers on its website a professional learning series called Tourism and Community Development. Webinars focus on topics such as building strong partnerships, vibrant supply chains and developing local well-being. It also offers face-to-face workshops and a certificate in sustainable tourism management (The International Ecotourism Society, 2013). The third organization that provides online training opportunities is Rainforest

Alliance (Rainforest Alliance, 2013). Their courses focus mostly on tourism professionals. Special courses and certification programs for tour operators, hotels, restaurants and transportation operators are available.

SUMMARY

The process for tourism destinations and travel enterprises to become more sustainable requires constant education, monitoring and collaboration. This chapter has identified some of the technologies for environmental, cultural and economic sustainability, and the issues surrounding their implementation in the quest for sustainability. The advancement of networks for collaboration, to build social capital and environmental integrity are necessary for a destination to move more towards sustainability. Many applications of technology including the Internet, handheld devices, GPS, GIS, location-based services and environmental management systems, and how they can be harnessed to enhance destination sustainability, are described in this chapter. Technologies that educate tourists and assist them in making more sustainable and responsible choices are also important to reduce the negative impacts of tourism. More creative ways to use IT for sustainability goals in the future will undoubtedly emerge as systems become more intelligent and affordable.

KEY TERMS

augmented reality, biodiversity, carbon calculator, citizen scientists, community informatics, community well-being, computer aided design (CAD), computer simulation, crowd funding, culture and heritage, cyber tracking, destination management system (DMS), digital divide, economic impact analysis software, economic sustainability, environmental management system (EMS), environmental purity, environmental sustainability, gamification, geographic information system (GIS), global positioning system (GPS), human rights, indigenous communities, information asymmetry, intelligent transport system (ITS), last-mile connectivity, leapfrog technology, local empowerment, location-based service (LBS), Massive Open Online Course (MOOC), physical integrity, pro-poor tourism, pull factors, push factors, resource efficiency, scenario-based design, small and medium enterprise (SME), social capital, social entrepreneurs, social equity, social sustainability, stakeholder engagement, sustainable development, sustainable supply chain management, sustainable tourism, tourism scientists, virtual reality, voluntourist, weather and climate change system

DISCUSSION QUESTIONS

1. What kind of digital infrastructure is needed for tourists to become citizen scientists in destinations?
2. What are the special needs and challenges faced by SMEs regarding the sustainable use of technologies in the digital age?
3. How can indigenous communities in tourism destinations be empowered with IT? Find examples of how technology has been used to improve the well-being of indigenous communities.
4. Identify a specific tourism destination or protected area that uses location-based services. How are these services likely to improve the destination's sustainability?

5. Find a Destination Management System with features focusing on the environmental integrity of the destination. Describe these features and their likely impact.

6. Study the UNCTAD e-tourism platform in more detail (http://www.unctad.org/). Explain how joining this initiative could help the poor in a destination to benefit from tourism.

USEFUL WEBSITES

QR code	Website	Description
	Global Sustainable Tourism Council http://www. gstcouncil.org/	An international body promoting the widespread adoption of global sustainable tourism standards to ensure the tourism industry continues to drive conservation and poverty alleviation.
	Sustainable Tourism Online http://www. sustainabletourism online.com/	An online information resource of research, data and tools within the three areas of "Destinations and Communities", "Business Operations" and "Parks and Culture". Developed by Australia's STCRC.
	National Geographic Center for Sustainable Destinations http://travel. nationalgeographic. com/travel/ sustainable	Promotes wisely managed tourism and enlightened destination stewardship and provides a rich multimedia site which includes destination scorecards.
	European Commission's Directorate General for Enterprise and Industry http://ec.europa. eu/enterprise/ index_en.htm/	Focuses on promoting smart and sustainable growth in Europe, with a special focus on sustainable tourism.

QR code	Website	Description
	UNESCO Sustainable Tourism http://www.unesco.org/education/tlsf/mods/theme_c/mod16.html/	UNESCO site developed for teaching and learning about sustainable tourism.
	The International Ecotourism Society (TIES) http://www.ecotourism.org/	Works to unite conservation, communities and sustainable travel. Has developed an online university consortium certificate for sustainable tourism. Travel choice.
	Rainforest Alliance http://www.rainforest-alliance.org/	Offers training to tourism businesses to run more sustainably. It also provides travelers, tour operators and travel agents with listings of destinations that benefit communities, flora and fauna.
	Conservation International http://www.conservation.org/	Works to ensure a stable climate, clean air, fresh water, abundant food and biodiversity. Projects are all over the globe.

Case Study: US National Park Service

National parks have been established in many countries to both preserve and provide access to unique natural landscapes and places of natural beauty. The US National Park Service (NPS), which is part of the Department of the Interior, has about 400 national parks with many archaeological sites, hundreds of species of animals and plants, hiking trails and museums. The NPS celebrates its 100th anniversary in 2016 after being founded by Woodrow Wilson in 1916. IT is now being used in a number of ways to assist parks in accomplishing their dual missions of protection and access.

Taking inventory of and monitoring the parks' natural resources is important to protect species and natural resources. Data and information management based on

continued

Case Study: Continued

state-of-the-art standards and practices is part of the NPS program. Twelve different resources in the NPS are monitored on a regular basis. Some of the 12 are water quality, air quality, species, geological resources, vegetation, soil and climate. Scientists and citizen scientists capture data on the 12 datasets. For example, in one park, more than 170 citizen scientists documented almost 3800 specimens of butterfly. These data are entered and reported into the North American Butterfly Association national database.

GIS systems such as ArcGIS are used to store data coming from the monitoring activities. The GISs have multiple layers of data entered into the system from electronic observations in the field. Soil quality, vegetation, stream flow and bird habitats are all different layers in the GIS that are monitored and analyzed.

As data are collected in different locations, climate-related trends and patterns can be revealed. Eighteen of the parks have digital web cameras providing data every 15 minutes on air quality including ozone, particulate matter, visual range and weather conditions.

Community and public engagement is a strong ethos of NPS, and IT helps to accomplish this goal. NPS has a web-based Planning, Environment and Public Comment (PEPC) system used for NPS National Environmental Policy Act (NEPA) planning and project tracking. PEPC engages the public in the planning process by allowing them to access, review and comment on NPS NEPA planning and compliance documents on the website. Since its launch in 2005, over 500,000 comment submissions have been received through the system. For more information see: http://www.nps.gov/gis/.

Study Questions

1. Identify another country's national park service or natural tourist resource and investigate how it uses IT to support its activities.

2. Visit the US NPS site (http://www.nps.gov/) and identify one resource (e.g. soil, water, animal species) and describe in more detail how data on that resource are gathered, stored and analyzed.

REFERENCES

360cities (2013) Available at: http://www.360cities.net/ (accessed 12 November 2013).

Ali, A. and Frew, A.J. (2012) *Information and Communication Technologies for Sustainable Tourism.* Routledge, London.

Ashoka (2013) Available at: http://www.ashoka.org/ (accessed 11 October 2013).

Biomechancial Institute of Valencia (2013) Available at: http://www.turacces.ibv.org/ (accessed 7 September 2013).

Boeing (2013) Available at: http://www.boeing.com/aboutus/environment/ (accessed 12 November 2013).

Brightsmith, D., Stronza, J.A. and Holle, K. (2008) Ecotourism, conservation biology and volunteer tourism: a mutually beneficial triumvirate. *Biological Conservation* 141(11), 2832–2842.

Brown, H. (1999) Sex crimes and tourism in Nepal. *International Journal of Contemporary Hospitality Management* 11(2/3), 107–110. doi: 10.1108/09596119910250986

Buhalis, D. (2002) Introduction. Special issue on Information Communication Technologies: Tourism Culture and Art. *Journal of Information Technology and Tourism* 4(2), 75–76.

Buhalis, D. (2003) *eTourism: Information Technology for Strategic Tourism Management*, 1st edn. Prentice Hall, Essex, UK.

Cheong, R. (1995) The virtual threat to travel and tourism. *Tourism Management* 16(6), 417–422.

Crabbe, J. (2012) From citizen science to policy development on the coral reefs of Jamaica. *International Journal of Zoology* 2012, 102350, 6 pp.

Darcy, S. (2011) Developing sustainable approaches to accessible accommodation information provision: a foundation for strategic knowledge management. *Tourism Recreation Research* 36(2), 141–157.

Digital Divide Data (2013) Available at: http://www.digitaldividedata.org/ (accessed 12 November 2013).

EarthWatch (2013) Available at: http://www.earthwatch.org/ (accessed 12 November 2013).

ECOTRANS (2013) Available at: http://destinet.eu/market-place/ (accessed 12 November 2013).

Federal Aviation Administration (2013) Greener Skies over Seattle = Greener Skies over the USA. *NextGen Performance Snapshots*. Available at: http://www.faa.gov/nextgen/snapshots/stories/?slide=6.

Galapagos Conservancy (2013) Available at: http://www.galapagos.org/conservation/citizen-science/ (accessed 12 November 2013).

Geels, F.W. (2002) Technological transitions as evolutionary reconfiguration processes: a multi-level perspective and a case-study. *Research Policy* 31(8), 1257–1274.

Goeldner, C.R. and Ritchie, J.R.B. (2006) *Tourism: Principles, Practices, Philosophies*. Wiley, Hoboken, New Jersey.

Gurstein, M. (2000) *Community Informatics: Enabling Communities with Information and Communications Technologies*. Idea Group, Hershey, Pennsylvania.

Han, J.H. and Mills, J.E. (2007) Are travel websites meeting the needs of the visually impaired? *Information Technology and Tourism* 9(2), 99–113. doi: 10.3727/109830507781367401

Harris, R.W., Vogel, D. and Bestle, L.H. (2007) E-Community-based tourism for Asia's indigenous people. In: Dysin, H.A.G. (ed.) *Information Technology and Indigenous People*. Idea Group, Hershey, Pennsylvania.

Hashim, N.H., Murphy, J., Doina, O. and O'Connor, P. (2014) Bandwagon and leapfrog effects in Internet implementation. *International Journal of Hospitality Management* 37, 91–98.

Hawkins, D.E. (2004) Sustainable tourism competitiveness clusters: application to World Heritage Sites network development in Indonesia. *Asia Pacific Journal of Tourism Research* 9, 293–307.

Ho, J.K. (2002) Multilingual e-business in a global economy: case of SMEs in the lodging industry. *Information Technology and Tourism* 5(1), 3–11.

Joo, J., Yim, J. and Lee, C. (2009) Protecting cultural heritage tourism sites with the ubiquitous sensor network. *Journal of Sustainable Tourism* 17(3), 397–406.

McCabe, S., Sharples, M. and Foster, C. (2012) Stakeholder engagement in the design of scenarios of technology-enhanced tourism services. *Tourism Management Perspectives* 4(0), 36–44. doi: http://dx.doi.org/10.1016/j.tmp.2012.04.007

Miller, G. and Twining-Ward, L. (2005) *Monitoring for a Sustainable Tourism Transition: the Challenge of Developing and Using Indicators*. CAB International, Wallingford, UK.

Miller, G., Rathouse, K., Scarles, C., Holmes, K. and Tribe, J. (2010) Public understanding of sustainable tourism. *Annals of Tourism Research* 37(3), 627–645.

Murphy, P. (1988) *Tourism: A Community Approach*. Methuen, New York.

Nadkani, S. (2008) Defining the ICT4D Plus Pro-poor tourism convergence: synergies for natural allies in the global war on poverty. *Electronic Journal of Information Systems in Developing Countries* 33(5), 1–17.

Nadkarni, S. (2008) Knowledge Creation, Retention, Exchange, Devolution, Interpretation and Treatment (K-CREDIT) as an economic growth driver in pro-poor tourism. *Current Issues in Tourism* 11(5), 456–472. doi: 10.1080/13683500802316048

National Park Service (2013) Available at: http://www.nps.gov/ (accessed 12 November 2013).

Negroni, C. (2009) Altering planes, and the way they fly, to save fuel. *New York Times* 29 April, 2009.

Nielsen, J. (2000) *Designing Web Usability: The Practice of Simplicity*. New Riders Publishing, Indianapolis.

O'Grady, M.J. and O'Hare, G.M.P. (2002) Accessing cultural tourist information via a context-sensitive tourist guide. *Information Technology and Tourism* 5(1), 35–47.

Paskaleva, K. and Megliola, M. (2010) Innovative technologies for advanced urban tourism e-services. *Information Technology and Tourism* 12(3), 269–282. doi: 10.3727/109830511x12978702284471

Pechlaner, H. and Osti, L. (2001) Reengineering the role of culture in tourism's value chain and the challenges for destination management systems - the case of Tyrol. In: *Information and Communication Technologies in Tourism 2001: Proceedings of the International Conference in Montreal, Canada, 2001*, pp. 294–302.

Pramod, S. and Carson, D. (2002) Online opportunities and challenges for indigenous cultural tourism in Australia. *Information Technology and Tourism* 4(2), 77–90.

QFinance (2013) Information Technology Industry. Available at: http://www.qfinance.com/sector-profiles/information-technology/ (accessed 15 November 2013).

Rahaman, H. and Tan, B. (2009) Interpreting digital heritage: a conceptual model with end-user's perspective. *International Journal of Architectural Computing* 1(9), 99–113.

Rainforest Alliance (2013) Available at: http://www.rainforest-alliance.org/tourism/training/ (accessed 8 September 2013).

Ross, G.F. (2005) Cyber-tourism and social capital: ethics, trust and sociability. *Tourism Recreation Research* 30(3), 87–95.

Ruhanen, L. (2008) Progressing the sustainability debate: a knowledge management approach to sustainable tourism planning. *Current Issues in Tourism* 11(5), 429–455. doi: 10.1080/13683500802316030

Savitsky, B., Allen, J. and Backman, K.F. (1999) The role of geographic information systems (GIS) in tourism planning and rural economic development. *Tourism Analysis* 4(3/4), 187–199.

Scott, M.M. and Frew, A.J. (2013) Exploring the role of in-trip applications for sustainable tourism: expert perspectives. In Cantoni and Zheng (eds.) *Information and Communication Technologies in Tourism: Proceedings of the International Conference in Innsbruck, Austria, January 22-25, 2013*. Springer, Heidelberg, Germany, pp. 36–46.

Sharpley, R. (2000) Tourism and sustainable development: exploring the theoretical divide. *Journal of Sustainable Tourism* 8(1), 1–19.

Sigala, M. (2008) A supply chain management approach for investigating the role of tour operators on sustainable tourism: the case of TUI. *Journal of Cleaner Production* 16(15), 1589–1599.

Silvertown, J. (2009) A new dawn for citizen science. *Trends in Ecology and Evolution* 24(9).

Social Firms UK (2013) Available at: http:www.socialfirmsinfomine.org.uk/ (accessed 8 November 2013).

Strickland, J. (2007) How Virtual Reality Gear Works. *Howstuffworks.com*. Available at: http://electronics.howstuffworks.com/gadgets/other-gadgets/VR-gear.htm/.

The International Ecotourism Society (2013) Available at: http://www.ecotourism.org/ (accessed 13 August 2013).

Tour Operators Initiative (2013) Available at: http://www.toinitiative.org/ (accessed 6 August 2013).

Tourism Concern (2013) Available at: http://www.tourismconcern.org.uk/ (accessed 13 November 2013).

United Nations Environment Programme and World Tourism Organization (2005) *Making Tourism More Sustainable: A Guide for Policy Makers*. Paris, France.

United Nations World Tourism Organization (2013) Why Tourism? Available at: http://www2.unwto.org/en/content/why-tourism/ (accessed 15 November 2013).

Village for All (2013) Available at: http://www.v4ainside.com/ (accessed 13 November 2013).

Virtual Reality (2013) Available at: http://www.vrs.org.uk/ (accessed 12 November 2013).

WCED (1987) *Our Common Future*. Oxford University Press, Oxford, UK.

Weaver, D.B. (2012) Organic, incremental and induced paths to sustainable mass tourism convergence. *Tourism Management* 33(5), 1030–1037. doi: 10.1016/j.tourman.2011.08.011

Weiler, B. and Richins, H. (1995) Extreme, extravagant and elite: a profile of ecotourists on EarthWatch expeditions. *Tourism Recreation Research* 20(1).

chapter 13

The Future of Information Technology and Tourism

LEARNING OBJECTIVES

After studying the chapter you should be able to:

- identify the technological developments that will affect the future of the travel industry;
- understand the relationships between the development of various information technologies, the traveler and the tourism industry; and
- apply this understanding to anticipate the strategic, operational and structural changes that will impact on tourism.

INTRODUCTION

The nature of society and the tourism industry have changed in many ways since the Internet was commercialized more than 20 years ago. As discussed in earlier chapters, there are important interactions within and between socio-technical systems whereby the actors in these systems influence each other and lead to changes in the structure of the system itself. And as we learned, there has been much research seeking to understand IT in travel and tourism. With technology continuing to advance, we conclude this book by discussing the factors affecting travelers' use of the information technology in the future, and how they shape the development of new technology and the industry.

The world has experienced significant social, economic and environmental traumas, many of which have transformed tourism. These events are not discussed in detail in this chapter, but rather briefly acknowledged in their vital role in shaping the foundational systems for the travel industry. Arguably, the most important was the emergence of China as a leader in the world's economic and political systems; in particular the growth of the middle class, its dominance within the region and its growing competition for global leadership. Along with the growth in China, Russia, India and Brazil (BRICs), South Korea, Indonesia and Venezuela have also reshaped the geography of world travel.

While these seismic population and economic shifts were taking place, the world was also buffeted by the war on terrorism. The worldwide response to terrorism was radical with many governments passing new laws to combat it. In particular, Germany enacted two laws to limit the ability of organizations to fund terrorist organizations while another law enabled intelligence to be gathered. In the USA, the Department of Homeland Security was created and the US Patriot Act provided additional powers to fight terrorism. Worldwide, the response to this "new" threat was immediate and as a result, most countries created new barriers to the "open skies" sought by the travel industry. These developments also had repercussions for the safety and security systems used by travel organizations.

The changes in social, economic and political structures were recognized along geographic borders and also related to generations. The baby-boomer generation has begun to retire while younger generations have watched as markets have adjusted. Huge cruise ships have been built and retirement communities developed for the boomers. However, with the changing economic reality, many of the older generation have not retired and many members of younger generations do not want a world dominated by work. Research suggests that Generation Y travelers have distinctly different values, attitudes and behaviors from previous generations as a response to the technological and economic implications of computer technology (Benckendorff *et al.*, 2010). The nature of travel differs substantially between generations as the younger generation is more interested in more personalized and authentic experiences.

The European Union and its common currency is an important development; the Great Recession and the financial restructuring of many countries is another. A more

important and lasting force of change is environmental change. Although some have expressed doubt about the reality of human-induced climate change, many tourism organizations recognize the need to follow basic principles of sustainable tourism. These important social, political and environmental events have had an enduring impact on the world, and in turn, shape the nature of tourism and its relationship with IT.

THE VIRTUOUS CYCLE OF TECHNOLOGICAL DEVELOPMENT

A **virtuous cycle of technology use** can describe the process of technology development and redevelopment (Fig. 13.1). This framework is based upon a number of conceptual underpinnings including systems theory and structuration theory whereby the traveler population is an open system interacting with technological systems and the industry, resulting in continual evolution (Giddens, 1976). Another conceptual underpinning of this process is the diffusion of innovations theory discussed in Chapter 1, which explains how and why new ideas and technology spread

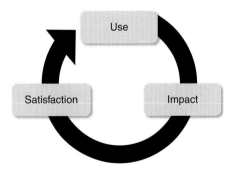

Fig. 13.1. Virtuous cycle of technology use in travel.

through societies (Rogers, 1962). Four main elements influence the spread of a new technology: innovation, communication, time and social systems. Once the innovation is widely adopted and reaches a critical mass, it will become self-sustainable. Adopters can be described using five categories including innovators, early adopters, early majority, late majority and laggards.

Diffusion of innovations manifests itself in different ways in various cultures and fields, and is highly subjective to the type of adopters and innovation-decision process. Thus, the virtuous cycle consists of three sets of "actors", which form a feedback loop in the development of technology for everyday experiences. This use "spills over" to travel planning, enabling travelers to take advantage of the new channels, and in turn, leads to their evaluation of the experience. The outcome of this evaluation process, then, either acts to reinforce or diminish the use of this technology in future travel.

As illustrated in Fig. 13.1, there are three important drivers that directly impact the nature of this evolutionary cycle of travel planning behavior. Most important, the Internet is now comprised of a huge amount of information, which serves as a type of external memory for many people. Tools such as Google and other search engines provide instant access to this galaxy of information, and as a result, individuals are increasingly reliant upon it for everyday life. In travel and tourism, this unimaginable amount of information has been made available through destination portals and online distribution channels for promotional and transaction-related purposes. The huge growth of social media in recent years has changed the dynamics of online communications and the composition of the tourism domain (Gretzel and Yoo,

2008; Xiang and Gretzel, 2010). Indeed, as discussed in previous chapters, travel-related social media has influenced travel information search and sharing behavior and, consequentially, mediates the way travelers perceive and interact with travel products and tourism destinations (Tussyadiah and Fesenmaier, 2009; Sigala *et al.*, 2012). Last, recent developments in mobile computing, particularly with the emergence of smartphones and their travel apps, address travelers' situational needs for information and communication, and are becoming increasingly prominent and more effective in guiding travel decisions in-trip (Wang *et al.*, 2012).

TRENDS IN TOURISM INFORMATION TECHNOLOGIES

The forces of change (technological, social, economic and environmental) have fundamentally altered how travelers experience travel, how destinations market themselves, which in turn, influences how the tourism industry develops and measures its success. Evidence of this restructuring is demonstrated in many ways, none more so than in an article by Gretzel (2010), which uses the concept of networks as a metaphor to describe the various systems that have fundamentally changed the travel experience. MacKay and Vogt (2012) suggest that there is a huge **spillover effect** which links our daily lives, both in terms of how we behave and our use of technology, and the way we experience travel. These two articles are essential reading in that they clearly explain the formation of new models of travel behavior, new models for product design and new models for research and evaluation, which in turn establishes a new paradigm of tourism experiences.

Travel today differs substantially from travel in the mid-1960s, when mass tourism began in earnest. Indeed, it appears that changes in travel reflect the "stages of change" model proposed by Gretzel *et al.* (2000). In particular, the first two stages of technology use create an expansion in activity, but not necessarily a change in behavior. It is only in the third stage that we see real structural changes in travel behavior. A recent book by Turkle (2011) is mirrored by Gretzel (2010) and MacKay and Vogt (2012), who suggest that there are now important structural changes in travel behavior whereby travelers tend to extend daily life into travel; become more involved in co-creating and controlling the tourism experience and sharing it with others; and are more engaged and creative as they seek authentic experiences. Today's travelers also appear to adapt better to local settings by using mobile technology to support their understanding of places, people and processes.

These new notions indicate a number of conditions that shape tourism. First, instead of simply seeing travelers as users of technology, today's travelers are active partners in **technology-supported networks**, which consist of the numerous information spaces discussed throughout the book that support the information activities of the traveler. Thus, the Internet is no longer a monolithic eCommerce platform; instead, it offers countless networks and platforms vying for the traveler's attention and spending power.

Second, technology-supported networks are social and community-based. Indeed, tourism information has been such from the very moment when the Internet became a public and commercial infrastructure; virtual places travelers congregate to share their experiences. The explosive growth of Web 2.0 with tools and platforms that support consumer-generated content has further provided networks for social interactions relevant to tourism wherein word-of-mouth is created, distributed and shared among peer travelers and consumers. As a result, tourism marketing has shifted to participating in, and being part of, the online conversations.

Third, for many people, a mobile phone is far more than a communication tool or an accessory of daily lives; it has become an inseparable part of life or even the body. As such, these devices intensify and encourage participation in mobile social networking. As a result, the uses of social networks and messengers have become one of major components in terms of mobile Internet traffic.

The following ten trends provide some insights into the future of IT in travel and tourism. The first trend focuses on the development of artificial intelligence and the continuing importance of innovation in computer design; the following four trends focus on the traveler response to various developments; while the last five trends relates to broader technological developments in analytics, mechatronics, material technologies, connectivity and convergence.

Trend 1: Ubiquitous artificial intelligence

Many futurists have concluded that there is much to be accomplished before information technologies can truly enable society to benefit from their power. In *The Unfinished Revolution*, Dertouzos (2001, p. 6) concluded that "the real utility of computers, and the true value of the Information Revolution, still lies ahead". He further wrote that over the past 20 years society has evolved to fit around computers and that the productivity gains have been more hype than reality. He argued that the real benefits will be realized only when computer technology becomes more human-centered; that is, when technology adapts to the needs and lifestyles of human beings. They argue that information appliances – computer systems that focus on specific tasks and are connected through the Internet or wireless technology – are the basis of ubiquitous human-centric artificial intelligence.

It appears that emerging technologies are becoming powerful enough to empower the individual within the framework of the human experience rather than defining human behavior around the needs of computer designers. Examples of tourism technologies that are becoming mainstream include websites and apps that provide travel recommendation systems, virtual reality, travel guidance systems such as Google Maps and Google Street View as well as wearable computers such as Samsung Galaxy Gear, Google Glass, Nike Fuelband and Oakley Ski Goggles. Advances in voice recognition and semantic search capabilities also allow humans to interact with machines in more natural ways.

A number of basic recommendation systems are available in a variety of travel-related websites including Ski-europe.com, Travelocity.com and TIScover.com. These systems are designed not only to help the traveler, but also to engage travelers and guide them into visiting new and different places. As already discussed in this book, virtual reality and augmented reality enable travelers to sample experiences prior to the trip. This technology is merging with tour guides within museums and attractions to provide a much richer experience. Essentially, these aids interpret anything – from a museum or art gallery to a city or region. In addition, GPS-supported travel guidance systems are more fully integrated into automobiles as discussed in Chapter 8, and more notably, wearable computers such as exercise equipment and goggles aid skiers and snowboarders to navigate the slopes. With these new systems in mind, it is easy to imagine new context-aware systems that actively interact with others in sharing and creating virtual and real experiences.

Looking further into the future, many futurologists have speculated about an event known as **the singularity**. In Chapter 1 we introduced Moore's Law – the prediction that the number of transistors and integrated circuits in computers double roughly every 2 years. So far this has been the case and although this growth in computer power may now be slowing, computers continue to become faster and more powerful. The technological singularity is the point at which artificial intelligence transcends human intelligence (Kurzweil, 2005). An extrapolation of Moore's Law suggests that the singularity has an 80% probability of occurring between 2017 and 2112 (Armstrong, 2012). What will happen when humans are no longer the most intelligent entities on the planet? Various scholars from fields as diverse as IT, philosophy, psychology and sociology have pondered the implications of the singularity but it is unclear whether such a change would be beneficial or harmful to humans. One view is that humans will use these technologies as tools to improve their own capabilities and that there will eventually be no distinction between humans and machines (Kurzweil, 2005). While this is a hypothetical scenario, the **hybridization** of human and artificial intelligence is already occurring through the use of mobile technologies and augmented reality. There is no doubt that as the power and intelligence of computers continues to increase, it will become more important to contemplate what this means for the travel experience.

Trend 2: Fragmentation of information

There is a growing fragmentation in how travelers use the Internet resulting in further competition in the areas traditionally occupied by primary travel products. This trend suggests that the growth of secondary products such as dining, shopping and ticketing services offers opportunities for businesses to develop novel combinations of products to gain market share. This trend impacts particularly on destinations. There is a risk that the importance of Destination Management Organizations (DMOs) will continue to decrease as destination websites decrease and, once a destination has been chosen, the likelihood for the traveler to look further for information about the particular destination will decrease (see Research Insight). This is caused by the fragmentation of the travel distribution system and the

growth of other channels (e.g. online travel agents and social media) and mobile Internet access. Destinations are losing their ability to communicate effectively with travelers as a result of the following developments:

- a variety of online systems (e.g. GDSs and CRSs), which exert control over a huge portion of the hotel, airline, cruise ship and events markets;
- search engines such as Google and Kayak have increased their impact within the online search market; and
- travel community websites and other forms of user-generated content such as TripAdvisor and Facebook have become more popular as travelers can overcome the control that marketers seek to effect over traveler decisions.

Organizations such as DMOs must re-establish their online identity by offering more relevant and competitive services or shifting their focus to supporting other organizations that directly connect to the visitor. The fragmentation of information also creates opportunities for other organizations to create solutions to help travelers find more relevant information.

Research Insight: The Future of Destination Marketing

In April 2002, a workshop at the University of Illinois asked representatives of leading American destination marketing organizations a question: What is the future of destination marketing in the United States? Over the past decade, American destination marketing organizations have made substantial changes in the way they market to the traveler. Two of the most important are briefly described below.

Service Design and Personalization

There was a sea change within tourism marketing led by the publication of *The Experience Economy* (Pine and Gilmore, 1999). The emergence of the Internet enabled DMOs to

(Continued)

Continued.

realize the catchphrase "markets of one". Parallel to this evolution in destination marketing, our understanding of services emerged from the general marketing literature. Vargo and Lusch (2004, 2008) compellingly argued that services are essentially different than goods and therefore the economic models of exchange and marketing should differ. This is based on **service-dominant logic** whereby service businesses including tourism marketing organizations can (and should) use a variety of business models in order to create value, communicate with, and ultimately realize revenue from the visitor. Further, this new paradigm has led to a new area called **service (or experience) design**, which now unifies some of the basic concepts proposed by Gunn (1988). Examples of the emergence of service-dominant logic within the tourism and hospitality setting include:

- the initial success of themed restaurants such as the Rainforest Café and the Hard Rock Café;
- the growth of boutique, and niche hotels and resorts;
- the dominance of social media like TripAdvisor.com, whereby the experiences of the travelers provide the core product; and
- the success of Disney in that they have designed "mass market products", which are now highly personalized.

Based upon the success of these organizations, DMOs have shifted their focus from a traditional "marketing" and "advertising" approach to new techniques such as permission marketing and customer relationship management (CRM). This shift toward "markets of one" has been exemplified by the sophistication in the second and third generation design of destination websites, the use of search engine optimization strategies and destination recommendation systems, and the realization that success is led by the innovativeness of their partnerships and their efforts in "long tail" marketing. Importantly, the foundations created by investing heavily in adapting to the new "experience marketing" paradigm have enabled DMOs to respond to the challenges of social media.

Market Control and Branding

Destination branding has become the logic *de jour* as destination marketing organizations tried to model the success of consumer products such as Nike and Coca Cola, hotels such as Hilton, Marriott, and Holiday Inn and the Ritz-Carlton, and cities such as Las Vegas, New York and Paris. Initiated by Aaker (1991, 1995), marketing managers argued that a destination should promote its "brand" in order to define itself with respect to its competitors and to break through the overwhelming clutter of information available through many channels. Essentially, the goal of branding was to exert some kind of control over the marketplace. Importantly, a new form of branding was achieved when tourism organizations began defining a vital organizational structure within the destination as well as a "place" within the minds of existing and potential visitors. Unfortunately, it seems that

(Continued)

Continued.

many destination branding efforts stopped short as they focused more on the slogan that could be used to best represent the essential place (e.g. "I love New York", "Incredible India", "Italy Much More", "I feel sLOVEnia") and less on creating the internal architecture needed to support the branded destination.

Many destination marketing organizations have adjusted their focus to include managing their online reputations based upon the assumption that brands can be hurt or even destroyed by the complaints of a small number of visitors and "Black Swan" events such as floods, hurricanes, wars and atomic plant explosions. For example, The Greek National Tourism Organization (GNTO) recently introduced "True Greece", an Internet-based reputation management initiative, which aims to clarify any existing "inaccuracies or speculations" regarding Greek tourism destinations (Modiano, 2012). It is argued that destination reputations should be a central focus as they are more dynamic and therefore more easily managed across the various online platforms.

Trend 3: Digital elasticity

As we have already discussed, an important growing trend is the shift from a static and rigid notion of trip planning to one that is dynamic and evolving. That is, the traditional perspective assumes that information search will identify the optimal solution to the problem, which is constrained by factors including travel party, time and financial constraints. However, trip planning is becoming more open, fluid and fragmented due to the ubiquity of the mobile technologies and access to the social world. This **digital elasticity** dissolves the boundaries between work and play and means travelers remain electronically linked with everyday life as they explore different places (Pearce, 2011). Mobile technologies enable organizations to blend together publishing, real-time communication, broadcast and narrowcast.

The Internet is special in that both consumers and firms can interact with the medium, provide content to the medium, communicate one to one or one to many,

and have more direct control over the way they communicate than other media. Using these capabilities will lead to deeper relationships with customers and greater personalization of goods and services. Also, it is interesting to note that online videos are increasingly significant in trip planning and indicate that travelers seek product advice from these offline channels, which potentially create a "boutique" shopping experience.

Trend 4: Storytelling

Travelers will increasingly evaluate products more on their experiential aspects than on objective features such as price and availability. Tourism organizations should focus on the experiential aspects that make the consumption of the product most compelling – that is, the five senses (Schmitt, 1999). Effective experiential marketing is sensory and affective. It approaches consumption as a holistic experience and acknowledges that consumers can be either rational or emotional or both at the same time. Whereas traditional marketing is based on consumer behavior, product features and benefits, experiential marketing is driven by an understanding of consumer experiences, the need for personalization and the ability to inspire creative experiences.

Travelers will expect advertising and experiences that are entertaining, stimulating, and at the same time informative. Importantly, brands are no longer seen as mere identifiers but become themselves sources of experiences by evoking sensory, affective, creative and lifestyle-related associations. Thus, the central focus on storytelling blurs the borders between the destination, advertising, purchase and use (the activities at the destination) as they merge the destination and the travel experience. Indeed, following from the previous trends, the traveler will soon be able to create seamless "stories" wherein they interpret and experience places as if they are located within a museum or art gallery.

Trend 5: The empowered digital traveler

IT empowers travelers by enabling them to control the process of co-creating and shaping brands. Empowered travelers are independent in making consumption decisions and like to share stories about their travel experiences with members of different communities. Importantly, the increasing scarcity of time and trust will mean that digital travelers will rely more heavily on electronic word-of-mouth and the expert opinions of like-minded others.

Digital travel communities are brand communities or communities of interest and are imagined, involve limited liability, and focus on a specific consumption practice. Digital travelers try to cope with this problem by scanning information depending on personal relevance and ignore irrelevant advertising. They therefore pay more attention to organizations that have asked for permission and established a long-term relationship with the consumer. In return for this valuable attention, the empowered traveler expects highly personalized services. Attention peaks when these travelers reach a psychologically balanced state of mind and the focus shifts to the holistic travel experience.

Trend 6: Big data and analytics

The new economic and political environment has forced tourism organizations to examine their core functions and to consider alternative strategies for allocating budgets according to new measures of performance. The old strategies based upon "intuition" have given way to a variety of new paradigms based upon measurement and benchmarking. The importance of evaluation in destination competitiveness, organization structure and service quality through benchmarking has always been important.

Leading tourism organizations such as Destination Marketing Association International (DMAI), Tourism Canada (now called The Canadian Tourism Commission), Tourism Australia, the European Travel Commission and European Cites Marketing (ECM), are developing guidelines and tools needed to support destination evaluation. For example, DMAI has developed a series of measures to assess (and benchmark) performance across a range of activities within the organization.

Tourism Canada offers the Canadian tourism industry cutting-edge tools to support knowledge creation including an online library, interactive tools to access online marketing data, and to facilitate connections between and among travel firms/organizations located throughout the country; similarly, Tourism Australia has developed a toolbox enabling destinations to conduct research and to evaluate their marketing strategy.

Various systems are now collecting data such as how travelers perceive their hotel stay, the restaurants where they eat and places they visit; indeed, leading European cities such as Amsterdam and Barcelona are now part of IBM's efforts to create smart cities wherein they actively market to and manage travelers to their cities. Travel creates a huge amount of data through the multitude of "touch points" in the trip where travelers leave "traces" based upon product searches, reviews and purchases, and the sharing of experiences with family and friends. The networks surrounding travelers encompass systems that capture and generate enormous amount of consumer data.

These new capabilities to collect and analyze vast amounts of **big data** are leading the way toward the development of very sophisticated marketing and management systems. For example, destinations and tourism organizations are now engaged in brand and reputation management by tracking and monitoring consumer sentiments about their products and brands in social media and search queries. Clickstream data can be used to make inferences about the visitor volume to a destination and even hotel revenues; tweets by travelers are collected, analyzed and interpreted; and geo-location data is collected to identify movement patterns, preferences, and levels of loyalty within a destination. Thus, the new systems supporting a variety of metrics (typified by Google Analytics) will enable tourism organizations to better understand where and how visitors live, the nature of information used to plan a trip, and with whom travelers share their experiences before, during and after the trip.

These business analytic applications support this new paradigm by offering enhanced customer intelligence, improving business processes and, ultimately, enabling the development of new strategies for navigating an increasingly competitive environment. As such, one of the most important trends as we look into the future is that the travel industry will use these data to design extremely personalized experiences. Further, it will begin to develop much more traveler-centric CRM programs, which essentially realize the vision that the Internet and related IT enable travelers to realize their dreams.

Trend 7: Smart machines

The increasing trend toward ambient and artificial intelligence is connected with parallel hardware developments in mechanics and electrical engineering. In this book we have presented several applications of robotics in the travel industry, from animatronics and driverless cars to Yobot, the baggage-handling robot. An extension of robotics is the use of **mechatronics** to create hybrid systems that combine mechanics, electronics and computing. Many tasks required to create memorable tourist experiences can be automated. While travel will always be a people-focused industry, further developments in artificial intelligence and mechatronics will result in new back-stage and front-stage applications in hotels, attractions, airports and other travel settings. We are already starting to see the use of biometric technologies in airports, hotels and attractions. Imagine a hotel where intelligent machines check guests in and do a majority of the cleaning and baggage handling. This vision is not that far removed from the experience of staying at one of Yotel's properties.

Trend 8: Material technologies

Technologies are also creating new materials that have applications in the travel industry. In particular, advances in the field of **nanotechnology** will result in new materials that are stronger and lighter and have a vast range of applications. New materials such as **graphene** are lightweight, flexible and durable and can be used in the development of mobile display screens, electric circuits, solar cells, energy storage, aircraft bodies and surface transport applications. These materials further support the miniaturization of mobile devices, allowing for improved portability, or alternatively more space to incorporate new features. They will also enable the more efficient capture and storage of energy, creating potential for more sustainable tourism futures. Another application is the possibility of smart surfaces that change color to match customer preferences. It may be possible in the future to change the color of walls and furnishings in hotel rooms to personalize the experience for guests. Some nanotechnologies are so small that they can be used to coat various objects and surfaces to enable them to interact with smart devices – further

enabling the ubiquity of technology and the "Internet of Things".

Trend 9: Open systems

One of the major limitations to smart systems is that the various technologies and systems created by different organizations in the travel industry cannot "talk" to each other. Different systems are incompatible because they use different languages or architectures. However, there is a trend towards **open systems** that enable interoperability, portability and open software standards. Open systems and standards are the key to unlocking the enormous potential of big data and streamlining many of the information-intensive processes used in the travel industry. This trend can be seen in efforts such as IATA's New Distribution Capability (NDC). The trend toward open systems will facilitate cross-platform compatibility, open-source access and interoperability between various IT systems that currently do not interact with each other. Travelers will come to expect that these systems will automatically exchange data without the need for human intervention.

Trend 10: Convergence

We have seen how technology **convergence** has resulted in devices such as smartphones, which pack a lot of punch into tiny handheld computers. The convergence trend is linked with many of the other trends in this chapter, including artificial intelligence, smart machines, open systems and materials technologies. New technological advances are continually being embedded into devices to increase their ubiquity, functionality and sensory abilities. While it is likely that travelers will continue to use a range of technologies, they will increasingly expect interoperability to enable any of these devices to be used for a range of tasks. The convergence of technologies will support a growing range of functions including communication, information access, purchasing, ticketing, admission and physical access, navigation, identity verification, and safety and security.

SUMMARY

The tourism industry has responded to the various forces of change by adopting a new paradigm embracing innovation led by travelers' co-creation activities. Once thought of as a "problem" which could not be controlled, leaders within the industry now recognize the "brilliance" of this strategy through the extensive use of CRM programs, the use of social media/user-generated media, videos, blogs and tweets, and customer-driven innovation (CDI) to create new travel products. Advances in technology are creating new materials and enabling machines and everyday objects to become "smart". A move toward open systems will allow all of these technologies to interact with each other, resulting in new opportunities to stream travel processes. All of these developments are converging to create a bold new world that may be even more disruptive than the development of the Internet and social media. The revolution over the past two decades appears to have taken hold, and now offers the means for both the traveler and the industry to realize a future just imagined a few years ago.

KEY TERMS

big data, co-creation, convergence, digital elasticity, experience design, graphene, hybridization, mechatronics, nanotechnology, open systems, sensory marketing, spillover effect, storytelling, technology-supported networks, the networked society, the singularity, travel-activated networks, virtuous cycle of technology use

DISCUSSION QUESTIONS

1. What are the key forces of change in society as we face the next decade? How do they relate to the travel industry and its use of IT?
2. What is in a virtuous cycle? What are the "actors" that comprise the virtuous cycle and how do they relate to each other in shaping travelers' use of the Internet? How do the actions differ between each of the actors? How does this relate to use of Internet by the travel industry? Last, how do these two actors influence the products developed by technology firms?
3. Ten trends were identified that will shape the future of the travel industry. Are these short-term or long-term trends? Which are more important? Discuss in detail how these trends affect travelers and the travel industry.
4. What role will IT play in shaping how travelers use the Internet in the future? How do tourism organizations adjust to these changes?
5. We have briefly discussed the concept of a technological singularity. Conduct your own research to learn more about this idea. What are the implications for travel, and indeed for humankind?

USEFUL WEBSITES

QR code	Website	Description
	Google Glass http://glass.google.com/	Emerging head-mounted display technology for augmenting reality.
	Tripit.com http://www.tripit.com/	A cross-platform itinerary planning tool for travelers.
	Tourism Futures http://www.tourism-futures. org/	A community website about tourism futures.
	Tourism Canada http://en-corporate.canada. travel/ resources-industry/ tools	Examples of well-designed brochures focusing on experience marketing.
	Tourism Australia http://www.tourism. australia.com/industry-advice.aspx	A comprehensive toolkit for marketing destinations.
	SMART Tourism http://www.smarttourism. org/	An organization in Scotland that uses IT to support innovation in tourism.

QR code	Website	Description
	Smarter Planet http://www.ibm.com/ smarterplanet/	IBM's Smarter Planet initiative, which includes useful information about big data and smarter cities.

REFERENCES

Aaker, D.A. (1991) *Managing Brand Equity*. The Free Press, New York.

Aaker, D.A. (1995) *Building Strong Brands*. The Free Press, New York.

Armstrong, S. (2012) How We're Predicting AI. Available at: http://fora.tv/2012/10/14/Stuart_Armstrong_How_Were_Predicting_AI/ (accessed 5 January 2014).

Benckendorff, P.J., Moscardo, G. and Pendergast, D. (2010) *Tourism and Generation Y*. CAB International Wallingford, UK.

Dertouzos, M.L. (2001) *The Unfinished Revolution*. Harper Collins Publishers, New York.

Giddens, A. (1976) *New Rules of Sociological Method: A Positive Critique of Interpretive Sociologies*. Hutchinson, London.

Gretzel, U. (2010) Travel in the Network: redirected gazes, ubiquitous connections and new frontiers. In: Levina, M. and Kien, G. (eds) *Post-global Network and Everyday Life*. Peter Lang, New York, 41–58.

Gretzel, U. and Yoo, K.H. (2008) Use and impact of online travel reviews. *Information and Communication Technologies in Tourism* 2008(1), 35–46.

Gretzel, U., Yuan, Y.L. Fesenmaier, D.R. (2000) Preparing for the new economy: advertising strategies and change in destination marketing organizations. *Journal of Travel Research* 39(2), 146–156.

Gunn, C. (1988) *Vacationscape: designing tourist regions*. Van Nostrand Reinhold, New York.

Kurzweil, R. (2005) *The Singularity is Near: When Humans Transcend Biology*. Penguin.com, New York.

MacKay, K. and Vogt, C. (2012) Information technology in everyday and vacation contexts. *Annals of Tourism Research* 39(3), 1380–1401. doi: 10.1016/j.annals.2012.02.001

Modiano, D. (2012) Greece: Online Reputation Management and Destination Marketing. Available at: http://www.aboutourism.com/online-reputation-management-destination-marketing-the-case-of-greece/ (accessed 5 January 2014).

Pearce, P.L. (2011) *Tourist Behaviour and the Contemporary World*, Aspects of Tourism Vol. 51. Channel View Publications, Bristol, UK.

Pine, B.J. and Gilmore, J.H. (1999) *The Experience Economy: Work is Theatre and Every Business a Stage*. Harvard Business School Press, Boston, Massachusetts.

Rogers, E.M. (1962) *Diffusion of Innovations*. Free Press of Glencoe, New York.

Schmitt, H.B. (1999) *Experiential Marketing*. The Free Press, New York.

Sigala, M., Christou, E. and Gretzel, U. (2012) *Social Media in Travel, Tourism and Hospitality: Theory, Practice and Cases*. Ashgate Publishing, Farnham, UK.

Turkle, S. (2011) *Alone Together: Why We Expect More From Technology and Less From Each Other*. Basic Books, New York.

Tussyadiah, I.P. and Fesenmaier, D.R. (2009) Mediating tourist experiences. Access to places via shared videos. *Annals of Tourism Research* 36(1), 24–40.

Vargo, S. and Lusch, R. (2004) Evolving to a new dominant logic for marketing. *Journal of Marketing* 68(1), 1–17.

Vargo, S. and Lusch, R. (2008) Why service? *Journal of the Academy of Marketing Science* 36(1), 25–38.

Wang, D., Park, S. Fesenmaier, D.R. (2012) The role of smartphones in mediating the touristic experience. *Journal of Travel Research* 51(4), 371–387.

Xiang, Z. and Gretzel, U. (2010) Role of social media in online travel information search. *Tourism Management* 31(2), 179–188. doi: 10.1016/j.tourman.2009.02.016

Index

Page numbers in **bold** refer to illustrations and tables